SECOND EDITION

Mainstreaming Handicapped Students
A GUIDE FOR CLASSROOM TEACHERS

Jane B. Schulz
WESTERN CAROLINA UNIVERSITY

Ann P. Turnbull
THE UNIVERSITY OF KANSAS

Allyn and Bacon, Inc.
BOSTON • LONDON • SYDNEY • TORONTO

*To our families,
who taught us the meaning and value
of the individual and the group.*

 Copyright © 1984, 1979 by Allyn and Bacon, Inc., 7 Wells Avenue, Newton, Massachusetts 02159. All rights reserved. No part of the material protected by this copyright notice may be reproduced or utilized in any form or by any means, electronic or mechanical, including photocopying, recording, or by any information storage and retrieval system, without written permission from the copyright owner.

Library of Congress Cataloging in Publication Data

Schulz, Jane B., date.
   Mainstreaming handicapped students.

   Rev. ed. of: Mainstreaming handicapped students /
Ann P. Turnbull, Jane B. Schulz.
   Bibliography: p.
   Includes index.
   1. Handicapped children—Education—United States.
2. Mainstreaming in education—United States.
I. Turnbull, Ann P., date. Mainstreaming
handicapped students. II. Title.
LC4031.T86 1983   371.9′046   83–11811
ISBN 0-205-08043-X

Photo Credits:
Photo on page 12 by William Lupardo; photos on pages 31, 47, 303 © Media Vision; photo on page 367 by Anthony Taro. All other photos by Jos de Wit.

Illustrations by Mary de Wit

Printed in the United States of America
10 9 8 7 6 5 4 3 2   87 86 85

Contents

Preface   *vii*

 1 *Educational Characteristics of Handicapped Students*   1
  Mental Retardation   *3*
  Orthopedic Impairments   *8*
  Health Impairments   *13*
  Learning Disabilities   *17*
  Speech Impairments   *22*
  Visual Handicaps   *27*
  Hearing Impairments   *32*
  Serious Emotional Disturbance   *38*
  Summary   *43*
  References   *44*

2 *Principles of Mainstreaming*   47
  What Mainstreaming Is Not   *48*
  What Mainstreaming Is   *49*
  Background of Mainstreaming   *56*
  Legislative Principles and Requirements   *59*
  Shared Responsibility   *68*
  References   *73*

iii

3 Developing Individualized Education Programs 77
Referral 78
Evaluation 81
Individualized Education Programs 85
References 95

4 Implementing Individualized Education Programs 97
Adaptations in Curriculum Content 98
Adaptations in Instructional Strategies 104
Coordinating Instruction Between the Classroom and Special Education Services 124
Evaluation Procedures and Grading 126
References 133

5 Teaching Language Arts: Listening, Speaking, Writing 137
Life Experiences 138
Listening 139
Speaking 147
Reading 157
Writing 157
References 181

6 Teaching Language Arts: Reading 185
Assessment 186
Goals and Objectives 193
Instructional Approaches 196
Materials and Techniques 219
References 227

7 Teaching Mathematics 231
Assessment 232
Goals and Objectives 240
Instructional Approaches 242
Instructional Materials 265
References 269

8 Teaching Social Studies and Science   271
Social Studies   *272*
Science   *285*
Social Studies and Science   *295*
References   *300*

9 Teaching Physical Education, Music, and Art   303
Physical Education   *307*
Music   *317*
Art   *324*
Summary   *334*
References   *334*

10 Managing Classroom Behavior   337
Defining Teacher Expectations   *339*
Defining Student Behavior   *340*
General Management Strategies   *341*
Behavior Management Principles and Strategies   *348*
Basic Procedures   *353*
References   *365*

11 Enhancing Social Integration   367
Need for Social Integration Intervention   *369*
Teacher Variables   *371*
Student Variables   *375*
Resource Materials   *391*
References   *393*

Appendix A   Professional and Consumer Organizations   395

Appendix B   Addresses of Publishers   397

Index   401

Preface

Legislative, philosophical, and educational influences have contributed to the implementation of the mainstreaming concept. The major question teachers are posing has changed from Why should we integrate handicapped students into our classes? to How can we do a better job integrating handicapped students?

In the attempt to help teachers answer this question, we have addressed three issues in the second edition of *Mainstreaming Handicapped Students*. One issue lies in the earlier emphasis on strategies to be used for teaching young children. In this edition, we have approached each curriculum area from the secondary, as well as the elementary, viewpoint.

A second issue is the plight suggested by many subject area teachers. Social studies teachers, for example, may not have backgrounds in teaching reading and yet find themselves teaching students who do not read well. We have addressed each curriculum area and have identified problems and strategies for teaching handicapped students.

The third issue is the need for practical strategies and materials that can be used in any classroom. The inclusion of activities and techniques at every level form a major portion of the book. We feel that the addition of many illustrations and examples adds to the clarity of the suggestions.

We believe in mainstreaming; we believe that classroom teachers have the qualities and skills necessary to implement it. We are advocates of *all* students and believe that mainstreaming can provide positive instructional and school experiences for them. *Mainstreaming Handicapped Students,* second edition, is written for classroom teachers. We believe it will help you to understand, teach, and enjoy handicapped students.

We wish to acknowledge our deep appreciation to the classroom teachers, special educators, handicapped children and adults, and parents of handicapped people who have shared their thoughts and experiences with us. Particular gratitude is expressed to teachers from Shawnee Mission, Kansas, Kansas City, Kansas, Jackson County, North Carolina, and the Cherokee Reservation who shared their creative teaching strategies. These teachers have inspired and taught us.

Mary and Jos de Wit, through their illustrations and photographs, have added a visual dimension to our ideas. We gratefully acknowledge their contributions. Manuscript preparation was made possible through the efforts of Sally Parsons, Mary Beth Johnston, Lori Llewellyn, Jean Roberts, Thelma Dillon, and Marilyn Fischer. We appreciate their skills, encouragement, and concern. We are also grateful to Susanne Canavan, Developmental Editor, Allyn and Bacon, and to Grace Sheldrick, Managing Editor, Wordsworth Associates, for their efforts in the smooth and efficient production of the second edition.

This book has been more than a joint project. It has evolved from experiences shared with our families and the unfailing support provided by them.

Finally, each of us would like to acknowledge the other. Our longstanding friendship has been strengthened through the privilege of collaboration. Although separated by miles, responsibilities, and time constraints, we have been bound through shared efforts, concerns, and joys. Honesty and humor have saved us.

J.B.S.
A.P.T.

1

Educational Characteristics of Handicapped Students

Diversity characterizes regular classrooms—students are different. They possess unique characteristics along the dimensions of achievement levels, language acquisition, social interaction, physical size, motor development, general health, vision, hearing acuity, and other personal attributes. The students in each regular classroom have a unique mixture of abilities/disabilities, strengths/weaknesses, likes/dislikes, and successes/failures.

Individual differences of children and youth in regular classrooms fall along a continuum. The differences of the great majority are not extreme and can be accommodated within the usual routine of the regular class program. Other students deviate significantly from the expected norm at a given grade level along varying dimensions. This deviation may single them out as being handicapped in learning capability, communication, motor development, sensation, and/or emotional adjustment.

What does it mean to be handicapped? Webster's *New Collegiate Dictionary* defines handicap as "a disadvantage that makes achievement unusually difficult." The disadvantages experienced by handicapped students in regular classes can be minimized as teachers recognize the students' mixture of assets and liabilities and tailor the curriculum to their special needs. Before teachers can make necessary curriculum adaptations, however, they must become familiar with the population of students who are operating at a disadvantage in terms of school success—the 10 to 12 percent of school-age persons who are considered handicapped.

Handicapping conditions have been defined in many different ways. The definitions to be discussed in this chapter are based on those included in P.L. 94–142, The Education for All Handicapped Children Act. P.L. 94–142 is the federal legislation that sets forth the requirements and procedures for educating handicapped students. This legislation will be discussed in detail in chapter 2. The important point for the current discussion is that the P.L. 94–142 regulations define handicapped children and youth as:

> Those children evaluated as being mentally retarded, hard of hearing, deaf, speech impaired, visually handicapped, seriously emotionally disturbed, orthopedically impaired, other health impaired, deaf-blind, multi-handicapped, or as having specific learning disabilities, who because of those impairments need special education and related services. (*Federal Register,* 1977, pp. 42478–42479).

Each of these handicapping conditions (excluding deaf-blind and multi-handicapped) is discussed in this chapter. Attention is directed to general characteristics and the educational implications of these characteristics in each area. The information in this chapter should help teachers identify the types of educational handicaps that occur in regular classes. Awareness of these factors is the first step in planning successful instructional strategies.

This chapter also serves as an overview to the rest of the book. The reader will be directed to particular chapters for "how-to" suggestions related to specific student characteristics and educational implications.

MENTAL RETARDATION

Mental retardation is related to delayed intellectual development in areas considered important for school success. Students classified as mentally retarded in most cases achieve below grade level in academic subjects and usually experience difficulty throughout their school career.

P.L. 94–142 defines mentally retarded as:

> . . . significantly subaverage general intellectual functioning existing concurrently with deficits in adaptive behavior and manifested during the developmental period, which adversely affects a child's educational performance. (*Federal Register,* 1977, p. 42478)

It is important to understand the meaning of the major terms in this definition. *Subaverage general intellectual functioning* typically means a score of less than 68 to 70 on an intelligence test such as the Stanford-Binet or the Wechsler Intelligence Scale for Children (WISC). *Adaptive behavior* refers to an individual's general effectiveness in meeting expectations for independence and social responsibility set for his or her age group (Grossman, 1973). The following are examples of adaptive behavior areas.

During infancy and early childhood in:
1. Sensory-motor skills development and
2. Communication skills (including speech and language) and
3. Self-help skills and
4. Socialization (development of ability to interact with others) and

During childhood and early adolescence in:
5. Application of basic academic skills in daily life activities and
6. Application of appropriate reasoning and judgment in mastery of the environment and
7. Social skills (participation in group activities and interpersonal relationships) and

During late adolescence and adult life in:
8. Vocational and social responsibilities and performances (Grossman, 1973, pp. 11–12).

The final major term in this definition, *developmental period*, refers to the fact that the child's mental impairment must be manifested by the chronological age of eighteen years (Grossman, 1973).

One of the most important aspects of this definition from an educational perspective is that an individual must have impairments in both intellectual functioning and adaptive behavior to be classified as mentally retarded.

Rebecca was classified as mentally retarded when she was in the second grade. Her IQ was assessed to be 66 and she had substantial difficulty in all academic subjects throughout her elementary and secondary years. Rebecca took a babysitting and a first-aid course from the local YMCA and developed knowledge and skill in the care and nurturing of young children. Although her baby-sitting started with one or two families, she was soon in high demand because of her competence and enthusiasm. For two summers, she served as a counselor-in-training at the YMCA summer camp. During her senior year, Rebecca has worked as a teacher aide in a daycare center from 3:00 to 5:30 P.M. She has received excellent evaluations from the teacher and generous praise from the parents. Rebecca will graduate from high school this year and has been accepted in a child care assistant program at a community college.

During her school career, Rebecca had impairments in adaptive behavior as reflected in her academic work. As a young adult, she is able to meet societal expectations for vocational and social responsibility. Thus, Rebecca's classification must change. In her case, it is clear that a retarded child grew up to be a nonretarded adult.

The important consideration is that mental retardation is diagnosed on one's *current* level of functioning. Thus, the possibility exists for persons to be considered mentally retarded at one point in their lives and not at other points (MacMillan, 1982).

Mental retardation falls along a continuum. Educational classifications for this continuum vary somewhat from state to state but typically are referred to as educable mentally retarded (EMR), trainable mentally retarded (TMR), and severely mentally handicapped (SMH). The approximate IQ ranges of these groups are:

- EMR—50 or 55 to 70
- TMR—30 or 35 to 50 or 55
- SMH—below 30 or 35.

The majority of mentally retarded children who attend regular classes are classified as EMR. Additionally, some TMR students have been successfully integrated into regular classes, but such placement has been more the exception than the rule for these students. As will be discussed in the next chapter, students whose achievement substantially deviates from that of nonhandicapped students are usually educated in specialized programs, such as full-time special classes. The majority of TMR students and the SMH population as a whole fall into this group. In many states, the classification of educable mentally retarded is referred to as educable mentally handicapped (EMH), and trainable mentally retarded is referred to as trainable mentally handicapped (TMH). Both terms are used interchangeably throughout this book.

The concept of individual differences applies to students with mental retardation as well as to all other students. No two mentally retarded students have identical problems. Certain characteristics of this student group do exist, but they do not apply to every student in equal proportions. However, teachers of regular classes should be aware of the types of disadvantages that are often associated with mental retardation. Some of these disadvantages are discussed here with particular focus on resulting classroom implications.

Educational Implications

Intellectual Functioning. The aspects of intellectual functioning related to mental retardation considered in this section include attention span, memory, generalization, and conceptualization. With respect to *attention span*, students may be able to work for relatively short periods before they need a change of pace. Every teacher is familiar with the student who almost never stays on task for more than five minutes. A student with this type of problem not only is at a personal disadvantage, but also often disrupts the concentration of others. One response considers the student "troublesome" and punishes the inappropriate behavior, usually with minimal success. As teachers recognize that in many cases attention problems are cognitively based rather than deviously contrived by students, teachers can learn systematic instructional procedures and management techniques to teach students to increase their attention span.

Another deficit associated with students with mental handicaps is memory. Teachers may find that although they repeat directions over and over, the students still forget. These situations can be frustrating for everyone, and often an automatic response is to assume students are not listening. Research has clearly indicated that many of these students are at a distinct disadvantage in recalling information immediately after they have received it (Belmont & Butterfield, 1969; Ellis, 1970). They do not automatically use active strategies to remember, as most students do who are not mentally retarded; therefore, these students forget much important classroom information. The most encouraging aspect of memory research with mentally retarded students is that they can successfully be taught memory skills, significantly improving their performance in this area (Butterfield, Wambold, & Belmont, 1973; Turnbull, 1974).

Other disadvantages associated with mental retardation may be in the areas of *generalization* and *conceptualization*. In respect to generalization, a third-grade student may learn the essential elements for living things in science yet not realize that the shaded backyard garden at home is dying for lack of sunlight. Teachers who help mentally retarded students form linkages between academic content and application to everyday living assist them in learning to make generalizations. Students who have difficulty conceptualizing may be referred to as "concrete thinkers." Difficulty with the abstract principles of a mathematical problem, inferring the meaning of a poem, or formulating the hypothesis of a scientific experiment are examples of problems with conceptualization.

Learning Rate. Considering the characteristics of intellectual functioning associated with students who are mentally handicapped, it automatically follows that their learning rate in most instances is slower than their classmates' rate.

There are several significant curriculum implications of a decelerated learning rate. First, many students enter kindergarten and first grade lacking academic readiness. When their peers are ready, for example, to move ahead in an academic area such as reading, mentally retarded students might need more priority placed on such important readiness areas as language development, visual and auditory skills, and increasing attention span. These students, from the first day of school, are at a disadvantage compared to their peers. Many compensatory education programs have been quite successful in giving students inclined to start school at a disadvantage a "head start" for school success (Tjossem, 1976; Zigler & Valentine, 1979). Regardless of the quality of many of these programs, learning rate will continue to impede many students from their initial entry into school throughout their school careers.

A second curriculum implication is that new concepts and/or skills presented will require more practice for the student to reach mastery. For example, the concept of regrouping in subtraction will require much more practice for these students; therefore, when other classmates are ready to move on to higher-order mathematical skills, mentally retarded students probably will not be ready to move with them. If they are required to leave the concept of regrouping before they have mastered it, they will be penalized for their lack of understanding from that point on, and failure on subtraction problems will be inevitable. Systematic instruction and student success depend on a solid foundation of step-by-step mastered skills and concepts. The additional time required to build this solid foundation has a snowballing effect on learning rate. In a standard curriculum devised for nonhandicapped students, mentally retarded students typically fall farther and farther behind their classmates in academic achievement.

It is necessary for teachers to make adjustments in goals and objectives for students with slower learning rates. Mentally handicapped students will probably learn less than other students. Quantity adjustments have to be carefully focused on the most relevant and functional information, omitting content less applicable to everyday living. For example, it is more important for students to learn about their city and county in an adapted social studies curriculum than about customs associated with foreign countries. To minimize the effects of delayed achievement, the teacher must continually ask, What essential information must students know to get along in everyday living?

Environmental Factors. It has been estimated that approximately 80 to 90 percent of the students identified as mentally retarded have no evidence of organic brain damage. Their retardation is attributed to lack of early educational stimulation, malnutrition, poor health, parental deprivation, and other related factors. They may be recognized by the teacher as those who come to school hungry or sleep through class because they were up late the night before. They may have chronic respiratory problems attributable to lack of medication, inadequate clothing, or a host of other reasons. Students coping with a variety of environmental problems have delayed achievement when they enter school and often are unable to concentrate fully on academic subjects. Teachers can help minimize the disadvantages imposed on these students by being sensitive to their environmental needs. Taking the time to get a carton of milk and crackers from the school cafeteria for a hungry student will greatly increase the likelihood that the student will concentrate on the reading lesson.

A barrier in school for many students from minority backgrounds is language. Consider students whose major language is Spanish and who attend school where they hear only English. These students are automatically at a significant disadvantage. One strategy many school systems have used successfully is to hire bilingual teacher aides. Many schools also teach courses in English as a second language.

Students whose environmental backgrounds have contributed to their mental retardation have, in the past, been prime targets for placement in special classes. Various combinations of factors, such as impoverished backgrounds, language barriers, different sociocultural mores, impaired intellectual functioning, and a general lowered learning rate, have resulted in categorizing a group of students as mentally retarded. The label *mentally retarded* does not mean that students cannot make academic progress; it does not mean that students are socially deviant; it does not mean that students belong in a special class; it does not mean that students are failures in all they attempt. It basically means that they scored below 70 on an IQ test and that they have problems in the area of adaptive behavior. It also most likely means that these students are at a disadvantage in terms of school achievement. The opportunity exists for the teacher to minimize the disadvantages associated with mental retardation through specially designed instruction.

CASE STUDY

Mental Retardation

Larry is in my sixth-grade class and teaching him is not always easy. His cumulative records state that he has been classified as EMH, which stands for educable mentally handicapped. Do not misunderstand or underestimate him. Although he does have learning and behavior problems, Larry is capable of far more than most people realize. His life history is a story of moving from one place to another. He has been in four different schools in six years and has moved away from his parents to live with his aunt.

From the time Larry entered first grade, he has been behind academically. He must have lacked the readiness that the teacher expected from the first day he set foot in the school door. Because his learning rate is slower, he has increasingly fallen behind over the years. Now in the sixth grade, he reads on a fourth-grade level and is learning to multiply in math. He has real problems with spelling but has nice handwriting and excels in physical education. Sometimes I am unsure if I am doing the right thing with him, but I have had some success hitting on some strategies that seem to work. First, he works with the special education resource teacher for one hour per day in reading. With this kind of intensive help, he seems to be making progress. I plan special work for him to do in math, since his achievement is below all the other students'. Recently he has been working with cuisenaire rods, which seem to help him understand abstract concepts. In social studies, we are studying Europe. I found a fourth-grade textbook on Europe that Larry uses in place of the regular sixth-grade text. He really likes having a book he can read. Filmstrips and visual aids are his favorites. He seems to learn more effectively when we use them.

The biggest concerns I have about Larry are his short attention span and low frustration level. On most days he will work for a short while and then just give up. I try to accommodate this by giving him short tasks that can be completed before he runs out of steam. After he works, he sometimes will play a game like Easy or Monopoly, or read library books about sports. I let him do this because I think he is learning from these games and books.

Larry loves to help out with classroom tasks like giving out books or setting the room up for a special activity. He would work all day long to help me. He loves to do things and move about.

There is no doubt that Larry does have some strengths. I think he benefits from being around his classmates. I know he is making some progress, but sometimes I wonder if he is working up to his potential.

Ms. Julia Tyson, Glenwood Elementary School

ORTHOPEDIC IMPAIRMENTS

Orthopedic impairments result in disadvantages associated with the motor development and functioning of students. This category is defined by P.L. 94–142 as:

> . . . a severe orthopedic impairment which adversely affects a child's educational performance. The term includes impairments cause by congenital anomaly (e.g.,

clubfoot, absence of some member, etc.), impairments caused by disease (e.g., poliomyelitis, bone tuberculosis, etc.), and impairments from other causes (e.g., cerebral palsy, amputations, and fractures or burns which cause contractures). (*Federal Register,* 1977, p. 42478)

It is obvious from this definition that orthopedic handicaps can be congenital—present from birth—or acquired during childhood or adult years, sometimes resulting from accidents. Like all other handicapping conditions, orthopedic handicaps vary greatly depending on the age of onset, the level of severity, the extent of involvement, and the treatment provided by special therapists, the family, and teachers. Sometimes students with such handicaps also have secondary problems in the areas of speech, vision, or mental retardation. In other cases, students may have the singular disadvantage of an orthopedic handicap, such as dwarfism, but have gifted intelligence and accelerated academic achievement.

It is also important to realize that orthopedic impairments may be educationally and socially debilitating to one student but not to another. Different persons have differing coping abilities in minimizing handicaps. Consider the student with paralyzed legs who has satisfactory or above-average academic achievement. He adapts such games as basketball, tennis, and softball to be played from his wheelchair and participates in peer and family activities. Another student with an identical physical impairment may be academically deficient, physically inactive, and socially excluded. What is the difference? It is the individual flair that characterizes all students coupled with the support the student has received from parents, teachers, other helping professionals, and peers. Orthopedic handicaps can only be evaluated in relation to the relevant behavior of each person affected. This chapter, rather than focusing on the etiology of particular conditions from a medical perspective, highlights educationally relevant behaviors that are often associated with orthopedically handicapping conditions.

Educational Implications

Mobility.   Mobility basically refers to one's capacity to move about, stand, or to use the hands in manipulating environmental objects. Students with limited mobility may need to develop compensatory ways of moving around the classroom, entering and leaving the school building, going to the school cafeteria, participating in playground activities, or learning to write. In educational implications, mobility must be considered in light of three factors: the locus of involvement, the nature of the handicap, and the rate and stability of motion.

The locus of involvement can occur in various parts of the body and in various combinations of body parts. For example, a student in a regular class may have mobility problems in any of the following aspects: one limb, all four limbs, only the legs, only the arms and hands, the right side of the body, the left side of the body, and speech mechanisms (larynx, oral cavity, diaphragm, lungs). The educational implications and the resulting adaptations planned by the physical therapist, occupational therapist, and teacher depend on the student's particular locus of involvement.

Disadvantages of mobility differ, depending on the *nature of a student's handicap*. One way to view the nature of these disadvantages is from the perspective of paralysis, problems with coordination, and loss of limbs. Paralysis results in the limitation of moving parts of the body, ranging from mild limitations to total incapacity. Students whose legs are paralyzed gain mobility through the use of a wheelchair, braces, and crutches. The elimination of architectural barriers in schools is necessary for these students to gain access to educational services and opportunities. Minimizing the disadvantages of these students means creating accessibility through ramps, aisles, and doorways, adjusting desks to the comfort of the students, and accommodating toilet facilities and water fountains. Plans for fire drills and other emergency procedures sometimes have to be adapted according to the particular needs of orthopedically handicapped students and the physical plant of the school.

Students with handicaps related to coordination may have too much movement as opposed to the limited movement resulting from paralysis. Coordination problems might also be characterized by tenseness, jerkiness, or difficulty in directing one's movements in desired patterns. Helping these students to position themselves while sitting, standing, or moving about can contribute significantly to their adaptability to coordination handicaps. Correct positioning is an individual matter based on the particular needs of each orthopedically handicapped student. Teachers should discuss positioning with the student's parents, physical therapist, or occupational therapist for specific classroom guidelines. Academically, impairment in coordination of the arms and hands is usually reflected in a student's writing. Remedial techniques and compensating strategies discussed in chapter 5 can help the teacher minimize this type of handicap.

Finally, some students have lost limbs either through congenital malformations, accidents, or diseases. In almost every case, students are fitted with a prosthesis—an artifical arm or leg. Prosthetic devices, in most cases, drastically minimize the educational disadvantages of these students.

Mobility rate is an important factor in classroom success. Some students with no major, overt orthopedic impairment may generally have slow mobility. They are the students who are chosen last on the playing field, because they can never make it to first base before the ball gets there; or, they rarely have time to complete classwork or tests because of the snail's pace at which they write. These students are at a definite disadvantage in attaining school success. The characteristics of mobility problems discussed in the previous two sections also frequently result in lowered rates of motion.

Curriculum accommodations, as discussed in chapter 4, can be fairly simple. If a student requires significantly more time to complete a written assignment, the teacher might reduce the length of the assignment so that it is not physically overwhelming. All classroom tasks can be reduced in length if necessary. This practice often allows the student with a low mobility rate to complete tasks and to achieve success. The behavior management principles discussed in chapter 10 can be very helpful in working with students capable of increasing mobility rates.

As to the *stability of motion*, some students with orthopedic handicaps fatigue more quickly than others. Teachers should be alert to this factor and minimize it by making provisions for such students to rest at necessary intervals throughout the school day. Some teachers have successfully used a cot or lounge chair in the corner of the classroom for this purpose.

Another important factor related to stability is the progressive nature of some orthopedic impairments. For example, the voluntary muscles of students with muscular dystrophy slowly degenerate until they are totally physically incapacitated. The teachers of these students often are able to detect deterioration of mobility from month to month throughout the school year. In addition to making adjustments in academic and physical activities tailored to the student's capacity, the teacher also has a role in helping students with decelerated mobility and their peers with the social and psychological implications. Suggestions on how to handle these affective concerns are included in chapter 11.

Adaptive Equipment. Students with paralysis will use a variety of adaptive equipment to enhance their mobility. Types of equipment include wheelchairs, braces, and crutches. Teachers who have had no previous contact with orthopedically handicapped students need to learn about the use and maintenance of these devices. The best procedure for teachers is to gather this information from discussions with the student, parents, physical therapist, and occupational therapist. Teachers of young children, who will likely need to assume more responsibility for helping the student maneuver a wheelchair (and for helping peers develop this skill), should ask for demonstrations of how to lock the braces, fold the chair when it is not being used, open it again, remove the arms, and assist the student in moving from the wheelchair to a regular chair or carseat. Examples of other areas of information related to moving around the school grounds include getting up and down curbs and boarding elevators.

Teachers should not hesitate to ask any questions that will help them feel more confident and competent in helping a student with mobility impairments. Further, teachers may be surprised at how much of this information they already possess. Manipulating wheelchairs around the environment is very similar to manipulating baby strollers (Pieper, 1976), and most adults have had this experience.

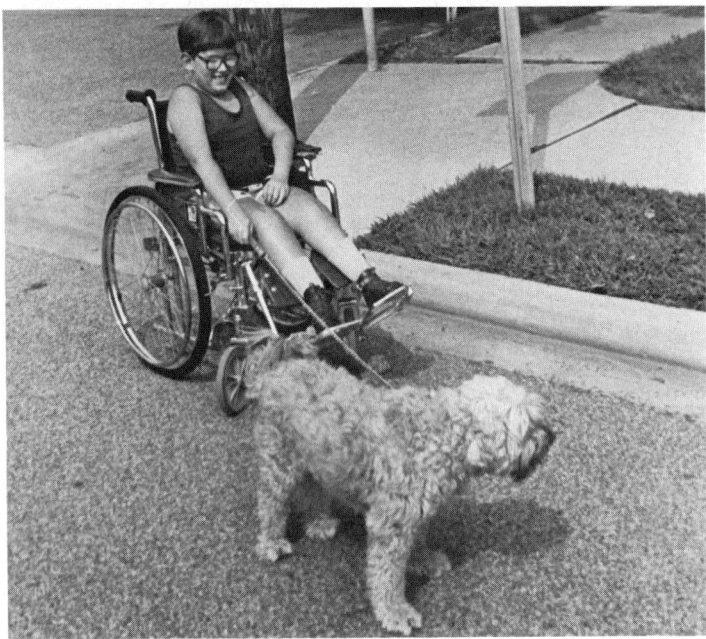

CASE STUDY

Orthopedic Impairments

When we were told that Jason would be in our class we were apprehensive. We had observed him when he was in kindergarten and our impression was that his every motion was painful and lengthy. Frankly, we felt it was an imposition to ask us to have an orthopedically handicapped child in a class with fifty-one first and second graders. We thought it would be a burden; we didn't know how to cope.

Actually, we have been pleasantly surprised this year. Jason is such a delightful, happy child that we feel fortunate to have him in our class. Our chief problem has been that he must be taken to the bathroom by one of us; this requires ten to fifteen minutes away from the class and may mean that we have to leave in the middle of a lesson. His coordination is poor; writing takes him longer. However, he takes his unfinished work home and and his mother helps him, so it's no problem. When he is absent (which is often) his mother helps him keep up. His home situation has been a definite asset.

We have received more help than we expected. Recently we acquired the services of a part-time aide; this helps with the bathroom problem. The special education teacher in our school, who had known Jason previously, reassured us from the beginning and informed us of resources where we could find manipulative materials for children who need special help. We have a high school student who works with Jason in physical education.

Jason is well liked by his peers. They look after him without being protective. For example, during the last fire drill one child reminded us, "Don't forget Jason!" The other children try out Jason's crutches and are very accepting of his problems. They like and respect him.

Jason wants to be treated like everyone else. At cleanup time, he picks up paper and crawls to the wastebasket with it. He is on grade level and is helping his cousin with his reading.

We think it would be a shame to have Jason in a special class; we think it would be harmful to him. We hope to have him in our class next year!

Ms. Norma Allman, Ms. Evelyn McMahan, Team Teachers, Fairview Elementary School.

HEALTH IMPAIRMENTS

Some students have major health problems related to chronic illnesses or conditions. Such impairments can necessitate adaptations in classroom schedules and activities. This category of handicaps is defined by P.L. 94–142 as:

> . . . having an autistic condition which is manifested by severe communication and other developmental and educational problems or having limited strength, vitality or alertness, due to chronic or acute health problems such as a heart condition, tuberculosis, rheumatic fever, nephritis, asthma, sickle cell anemia, hemophilia, epilepsy, lead poisoning, leukemia, or diabetes, which adversely affects a child's educational performance. (*Federal Register*, 1977, p. 42478; *Federal Register*, 1981, pp. 3865–3866[1])

These conditions can vary in age of onset, severity, and prognosis. Some conditions (e.g., asthma) can result in students' going through periods of heightened or decreased symptoms and problems. Other conditions (e.g., tuberculosis) can be cured through proper treatment and others (e.g., epilepsy) can be effectively controlled through medication. Autism is an example of a health impairment that must be managed largely through behavioral, as contrasted to medical, intervention. Finally, some health impairments can be terminal, such as some forms of leukemia. It is particularly important for the teacher to communicate openly with the student, parents, school nurse, and physician to identify the diagnosis, treatment, and prognosis of a student's health impairment. Furthermore, it is important to identify the implications of the health impairment for classroom programming and guidelines on how specific problems should be handled. Some general educational implications of health impairments are reviewed in this section.

1. The definitional change of autism from the category of seriously emotionally disturbed to health impaired is reported in the January 19, 1981, *Federal Register*, pp. 3865–3866.

Educational Implications

Special Schedules and Requirements. The teacher may have to supervise medication schedules, arrange for rest periods, or be aware of special nutritional or diet requirements. All these responsibilities can be handled in the regular class with minimal disruption. The important point is that they should be carefully discussed with the student, parents, and physician.

Many students with health impairments are required to take daily medication. Frequently, schedules can be arranged so that medication is only administered at home; however, in some cases teachers and students will need to assume the responsibility for administering medication at school. In these instances, school nurses or teachers should obtain written instructions from parents or the student's physician about the schedule and written consent from parents for the medication to be given at school. A safe and convenient place must be found at school to store the medication, and it should be carefully labelled. Many schools have the policy that only the school nurse can dispense medication. Teachers are therefore advised to check their local policies. Regardless of the role of the person who dispenses the medication, accurate records of dosage and time of administration should be kept.

The teacher and parents need to maintain frequent communication on how the drug seems to be working and on any unanticipated side effects, such as hyperactivity, nervousness, drowsiness, and physical discomfort. Sometimes it is necessary to change the dosage of a drug; thus, the teacher should report to the school nurse and parents any observations that might indicate a need to re-evaluate the drug prescription.

As suggested in the previous section on orthopedic handicaps, other special requirements such as rest periods can be handled by having a lounge chair in the classroom or using a cot in the school's nursing quarters. The fatigue of students can also be minimized by alternating classroom activities that require mental and physical responses.

Finally, some health impairments result in special nutritional and diet requirements. In these cases, the special requirements need to be discussed with the school dietician. It is necessary to determine whether the student's special needs can be totally met by the food services at school or whether it will be necessary to provide special supplements, as in the case of a student who may be allergic to a wide range of foods.

Seizures. Seizures most often are associated with epilepsy, although they can occur in other conditions. Many teachers are wary of teaching students with seizures because they are afraid they will be unable to handle a student's seizure in the classroom. This is an understandable concern that can be alleviated by adequate information.

When nerve cells in the brain are charged with excessive electricity, the brain may temporarily lose control of functions, such as attention, sensation, perception, and muscle control. This phenomenon is referred to as a seizure. The two most common types of seizures teachers might encounter in the classroom are petit mal and grand mal.

When petit mal seizures occur, a student is likely to appear to be daydreaming. The student might stare straight ahead, blink his or her eyes, drop books or pencils, or nod his or her head for a few seconds. The student does not comprehend classroom information for the brief period of the petit mal seizure. First, the teacher must realize that the student is not just failing to pay attention. A teacher who suspects the possibility of seizures should discuss this concern with the school nurse and the student's family. The teacher's second responsibility is to make sure the student has an opportunity to get the information missed in class. Both the teacher and the student's classmates can help fill the gaps in classroom activities and instruction caused by the occurrence of the seizure.

A grand mal seizure is a more severe manifestation. It is usually preceded by an aura, a strange sensation that can alert the person that a seizure is about to occur. The student probably will stiffen the muscles of the body first and then proceed into a stage of jerking movements. During this period, he will lose consciousness, perhaps emit sounds and/or saliva, and possibly lose bladder and bowel control, which can result in extreme embarrassment to the student. The actual seizure lasts only several minutes and is followed by the need for rest or sleep. Teachers can help to manage seizures that occur at school by following these guidelines.

1. Collect information and plan your classroom response so that you can remain calm when the seizure occurs. Talk with the student, parents, and doctor to make sure your questions about the student's particular seizure pattern are answered. Write the Epilepsy Foundation of America (see Appendix A for address) to obtain pamphlets for classroom teachers on school management of seizures.
2. Try to help the student respond to the aura or warning signal by getting to an open space away from desks and tables. The student should lie on the floor and be free to move around. The teacher should not attempt to restrict movement or place anything in the student's mouth other than possibly a soft handkerchief between the teeth. It is important for the teacher to remember that the seizure is painless to the student.
3. After the seizure occurs, the student may need to sleep (but not necessarily need to be sent home). The teacher should always report the seizure to the student's parents and school nurse.

Most seizures are controlled very effectively by medication and rarely occur in classrooms. Unfortunately, students with histories of seizures are often stigmatized. Teachers have a major responsibility to help classmates understand the nature of seizures, as well as the strengths and talents of students who have seizures. Suggestions for increasing understanding are included in chapter 11.

School Absenteeism. Various types of health impairments often require hospitalization. The educational implication is that some students are excessively absent from school and thus at a disadvantage in keeping up with academic work. Teachers can minimize the disadvantages associated with frequent absences by working with special education personnel in the school system to arrange for these students to have hospital/homebound tutoring. The majority of school systems employ special teachers or contract with other educational agencies to provide this type of instruction. Whatever the particular arrangement, school systems are responsible for providing educational services when students must be out of school on a long-term basis because of chronic health conditions. Teachers may also be able to locate volunteers, in addition to the hospital/homebound teachers, to work with students. In these situations, the classroom teacher must coordinate the instructional program with all persons working with a student, including the hospital/homebound teacher, volunteers, and the student's parents. Weekly or biweekly meetings can be set up to handle this coordination.

To keep an absentee abreast of classroom discussions, a student who excels in organizing major concepts during such discussions can be asked to make a carbon copy of notes. Classroom discussions and various activities can also be taped so that the student who is hospitalized or at home can still share in what goes on at school.

CASE STUDY

Health Impairments

Karl has been a student in my resource room for the last two years. He spends one-half day in the resource room and is mainstreamed into industrial arts, physical education, and music for the remainder of the day. He is currently a senior and will soon be graduating. Karl has two types of handicaps—he has epilepsy and he also has some serious emotional problems.

Karl's epilepsy—petit mal seizures—was not diagnosed until the beginning of his junior year. To tell you the truth, I think his biggest problem was the medication rather than the actual seizures. When he first started taking the medication, he was groggy, had no energy, and practically couldn't function at all. I immediately called his parents and learned that much of the same behavior was going on at home. They worked with the doctor over a three to four month period before the right type and dosage of the medication was finally pinpointed. We have to keep a constant check on his behavior because every several months re-adjustments in the prescription have been needed.

I have talked with Karl's other teachers about his seizures and the effects of his medication. It's interesting that before the seizures were diagnosed his teachers had different reactions to his periods of tuning out. Some would punish him; others stopped expecting much of him and would just roll their eyes and go along with his inattention. The best strategy is to keep him actively involved in tasks. I've noticed that he has the least problem with seizures when he is engrossed in active learning tasks. I also have tried to get Karl to let his teachers know when he has missed important information and to ask for help in catching up on what was missed. I strongly believe that this approach will be vital to his maintaining a job after he graduates. I'll have to admit that it sometimes is still hard to know exactly how to handle the situation when he is staring off in space. His staring periods could be attributable to goofing off, having a seizure, or his medication needing to be re-adjusted. Since his seizures were diagnosed, I think all of his teachers have become more patient with him.

I have spent a lot of time with Karl and his parents who are very caring people. My hope is that Karl will complete a vocational training program after high school. On a good day when Karl gets it all together, it is obvious that he has real potential.

Mr. Lewis Allen, Lawrence High School. (Courtesy of Mr. Lewis Allen)

LEARNING DISABILITIES

Many classroom teachers have had the experience of working either directly or indirectly with students who have significant gaps between their educational achievement and their intellectual potential. These students may experience severe academic difficulty in one or two, but not all, subject areas. They may have difficulty attending to their assigned task, sitting still for seemingly brief intervals, decoding or comprehending in reading, using expressive and receptive language, writing legibly, solving math problems, or generally following instructions. They can be characterized by a large combination of these factors or by only one or two. Frequently, students who fit this description are described as "underachievers," "poorly motivated," and "reluctant learners." An adult with some of these educational disadvantages recalled her school career as a period of being labeled "everything from lazy to crazy," when, in fact, she was part of the population of students who are appropriately referred to as learning disabled.

P.L. 94–142 defines a specific learning disability as:

> . . . a disorder in one or more of the basic psychological processes involved in understanding or in using language, spoken or written, which may manifest itself in an imperfect ability to listen, think, speak, read, write, spell, or to do mathematical calculation. The term includes such conditions as perceptual handicaps,

brain injury, minimal brain dysfunction, dyslexia, and developmental aphasia. The term does not include children who have learning problems which are primarily the result of visual, hearing, or motor handicaps, of mental retardation, or of environmental, cultural, or economic disadvantage. (*Federal Register*, 1977, p. 42478)

To gain a clearer understanding of learning disabilities, a closer examination of four of the component parts of this definition is warranted (Myers & Hammill, 1976).

1. ". . . a disorder in one or more of the basic psychological processes involved in understanding or in using language, spoken or written . . ."

Since the term *psychological processes* is not operationally defined, it is open to different interpretations. Perhaps the most frequent referents are learning modalities, such as visual, auditory, tactile, and motor, in addition to learning processes such as memory, comprehension, and generalization. For these processes, the disorder may result from a developmental lag or impaired functioning. A developmental lag occurs when the learning process becomes refined at a slower rate than that of other students. For example, some students may not have the necessary fine motor skills for successfully learning to write in manuscript in the first grade, but the refinement of these readiness skills may be present one to two years later. Impaired functioning of modalities or processes refers to a basic distortion in interpretation, organization, and/or expression. An example of impaired functioning in the area of language would be a student who routinely is unable to find the words he or she wants to say to respond to an oral or written question. This word-finding difficulty represents impaired functioning of learning processes. It is often difficult for teachers to distinguish accurately between the disorders representing a developmental lag in which remediation might reasonably be expected to occur in the future and impaired functioning in which the possibility exists that the student will always experience difficulty.

2. ". . . which may manifest itself in an imperfect ability to listen, think, speak, read, write, spell, or to do mathematical calculation."

It is these skills that form the core of academic success and in which the learning disability may be evidenced. The majority of questions from classroom teachers revolve around questions concerning methods and materials for teaching these skills to students with learning disabilities. Chapters 3 through 10 respond directly to these concerns.

3. "The term includes such conditions as perceptual handicaps, brain injury, minimal brain dysfunction, dyslexia, and developmental aphasia."

These terms do not have operational meanings, and even experts in the field of learning disabilities do not agree on their definitions. Teachers are wise to develop the habit of discussing characteristics of the student in educational terms such as the specific strengths and weaknesses in subject areas. This information is educationally relevant to classroom teachers. Jargon and labels are superficial and often add more confusion than clarity to the development of a student's instructional program.

4. "The term does not include children who have learning problems which are primarily the result of visual, hearing, or motor handicaps, of mental retardation, or of environmental, cultural, or economic disadvantage."

Learning disabilities are often diagnosed through the process of elimination. When the student's primary handicap is not attributable to other conditions, yet a wide gap exists between achievement and potential, the student often is considered to have a learning disability. The key word in this portion of the definition is *primarily*. The student with learning disabilities may have secondary problems related to other handicapping conditions. Furthermore, students with other handicapping conditions (emotional problems, sensory deficits) may have secondary educational concerns that fit the description of a learning disability. The decision between primary and secondary handicapping conditions is not always clearcut. Again, the important considerations for teachers are pinpointing the student's individual strengths and weaknesses and developing a systematic instructional program geared to the student's needs.

Educational Implications

Academic Difficulty. Students with learning disabilities experience substantial difficulty in school subjects. Frequently they have a peak profile across all school subjects with very distinct abilities and disabilities. Sometimes a student is deficient in only one subject and at other times in a combination of subjects. A student in the sixth grade, for example, might be working on basic addition in arithmetic, which would be significantly below grade level expectations, yet be entirely commensurate with peers in reading achievement. Individual strengths and weaknesses are particularly striking with these students.

When students are impaired in language arts (reading, spelling, and writing), other subject areas are also affected. Special considerations must be made when students are unable to read content area books. Chapter 8 includes suggestions on adaptations teachers can make in regular classes to accommodate these types of educational considerations.

Academic difficulty associated with learning disabilities is an outgrowth of the disorders related to developmental lags or impaired functioning in learning modalities and processes. Teachers should be aware that students can have deficits in one or more learning modalities that make it difficult for them to process information. Some learning-disabled students will respond to a phonics approach to reading instruction, and others will experience tremendous difficulty and frustration in discriminating the differences between isolated sounds. The failure of several instructional methods is not an indication that a student cannot learn. Rather, it is a message to the teacher to keep looking for the instructional technique that provides the best match with the student's learning characteristics.

Other factors that frequently contribute to the academic difficulty associated with learning disabilities are problems in the area of memory and generalization. Both these learning processes are critically important to the development of academic competence in every subject.

Attention. The nature of learning disabilities often results in an impairment in the student's ability to pay attention selectively to the relevant stimuli. A student may be unable to screen out interfering noises like the ticking of a clock, the squeak of desks, and the buzzing of fluorescent lights in the classroom. Sometimes these noises, unnoticed by most teachers and students, significantly impede a learning-disabled student from paying attention to the task at hand. Open classrooms with a large number of students and a lot of movement within the room can be an educational disaster for someone already at a distinct disadvantage in ability to maintain attention. A student having difficulty screening out background disruptions can be seated close to where the teacher most frequently stands to give instructions, have a classroom peer repeat instructions, and/or be given a quiet work center away from more distracting parts of the classroom. Another problem with attention relates to the amount of time a student can work on a given task before becoming restless or getting involved in something else. Short work periods followed by a break are often helpful. These suggestions are discussed in more detail in chapters 4 and 10.

Activity Level. The activity level of students refers to the frequency and intensity of movement in which they engage. Some students handicapped by learning disabilities are described as hyperactive and others as hypoactive. Hyperactivity refers to an activity level significantly above norm expectations. Students who are prone to hyperactivity could be described as distractible, restless, and fidgety. They might be the ones scooting around the classroom while the teacher is trying to lead a class discussion. It is sometimes easy to regard such students as troublemakers and overlook the fact that they may not be able to control some of the disruptions strictly on their own. The classroom management techniques discussed in chapter 10 will be helpful to teachers in controlling hyperactivity.

Drug therapy is an alternative for students with severely excessive activity levels. Teachers should discuss this possibility carefully with the school nurse who could be asked to observe the student in the classroom. On the basis of behavioral observations, the nurse might talk with the student's parents who then should consult the family doctor. Drug treatment is usually recommended only as a last resort. It is encouraging for teachers to remember that excessive activity levels generally decrease with age.

Hypoactivity is the reverse of hyperactivity; its characteristics include lethargic, passive, and quiet behaviors. Students affected in this manner are usually very slow and have low energy levels. They often do not complete their work and sometimes go unnoticed in the classroom. Either extreme of activity levels places the student at a disadvantage in functioning successfully in a regular class.

CASE STUDY

Learning Disabilities

Having Tom in my eighth-grade language arts class means that there is never a dull moment. At the beginning of the year, his capabilities and performance were not easy to figure out. With some students, all the pieces of information fall into place immediately. Tom puzzled me. I knew he had high ability, yet he demonstrated real problems in getting his work done. After observing his behavior closely and talking with the resource teacher in the school, I now seem to have a handle on some of his learning strengths and weaknesses.

In the language arts areas, Tom is able to read just slightly below grade

level. Although he does not have the reading proficiency of most of his classmates, he is able to read his textbooks, rarely needing help with a word. In written assignments, his handwriting can be neat; however, he usually approaches a written task in a harum-scarum fashion, writing quickly to get through as soon as possible. More often that not, his papers are messy and difficult to read. When he gets down to work, he is able to make a passing grade on his spelling test. That is the heart of the problem—"when he gets down to work."

It is basically organization that poses extreme difficulty for Tom. He seems almost constantly distracted, having a difficult time sitting down and getting settled. On some days I think he spends more time wandering around the classroom than sitting in his seat. When he goes to sharpen his pencil, he will look out the window and become captivated watching a bird, or he will pass the magazine rack and flip through several magazines before returning to his seat. He's fidgety, constantly turning in his seat and moving around. As to his work, he often does not complete it. Since it takes him longer because of his attention span, he sometimes will hand in work several days late. With that much delay and his general difficulty with organization, it is not unusual for him to lose assignments that he has started but not completed. I have to watch Tom about taking shortcuts with his work. If he has ten questions to answer, he sometimes will answer the first, a couple in the middle, and the last, and state that he has finished the assignment. Sometimes I purposefully shorten his assignments so that the length is adjusted to his learning pattern. In this way, he can achieve success and demonstrate a mastery of the content without being penalized for his distractibility. Another approach which seems to help him is for me to write instructions for the class period on the board and sometimes even an outline of class discussions. Since Tom does not always generate his own structure, he seems to benefit from as much as I can impose. I have been pleased with the encouragement and direction he gets from the other students in the class. They tell him things like, "Turn around and do your work," or "Come on, Tom, I don't have time to talk to you."

Tom has his good and bad days, just like all of us. He's got the ability, and it's a continual challenge for me to capitalize on his strengths.

Ms. Elaine Allison, Culbreth Junior High School.

SPEECH IMPAIRMENTS

Speech impairments are defined by P.L. 94–142 as:

> . . . a communication disorder, such as stuttering, impaired articulation, a language impairment, or a voice impairment, which adversely affects a child's education performance. (*Federal Register*, 1977, pp. 42478–42479)

Sometimes it is difficult to determine when a difference in speech patterns falls outside the range of normality and adversely affects a child's educational performance. The criterion generally accepted for speech handicaps was specified by Van Riper (1972); "Speech is defective when it deviates so far from the speech of other people that it calls attention to itself, interferes with communication, or causes the possessor to be maladjusted" (p. 29). This definition focuses mainly on the effects of speech. Sometimes speech handicaps are in the eye of the beholder, but for the most part it is the actual production by the speaker that is deficient.

Speech impairments are related to other disabilities. Mentally handicapped students frequently have delayed language development. Conditions related to orthopedic handicaps, such as paralysis, can seriously impede the production of speech. Since hearing-impaired children are at a distinct disadvantage in developing oral communication, these special concerns will be discussed separately. The significant contribution of language impairment to learning disabilities has been highlighted. Almost across the board, speech and language factors are major considerations in every handicapping condition. Aside from the implications of speech and language deficits that are discussed elsewhere in this chapter, the major types of disorders with educational implications that receive attention in this section include stuttering, articulation, and language delays.

Educational Implications

Stuttering. Stuttering is manifested in disruptions in the normal flow of speech (Hull & Hull, 1973). These disruptions may be prolongations or repetitions of sounds and words. Stuttering can vary tremendously as to circumstances, particular sounds or words, location of syllables in words or of words in sentences, fatigue, and emotional comfort. Although a significant amount of research has been conducted on stuttering, resulting in numerous theories of causation, experts debate and disagree over the definitive causes (Brutten & Shoemaker, 1967; Van Riper, 1972). Some people believe it is learned, others that it represents a developmental lag, and still others that it is emotionally and environmentally based. These debates are likely to continue; however, the important consideration for teachers is learning to minimize the educational implications of stuttering in the classroom.

Teachers should remember that normal disfluencies occur in everyone's speech at various times. Also, prolongations and repetitions normally are more frequent in the speech of young children, generally up to the age of eight. Therefore, caution should be taken in interpreting normal disfluencies as actual stuttering. Going back to Van Riper's definition, stuttering becomes a problem when ". . . it calls attention to itself, interferes with communication, or causes the possessor to be maladjusted." In these situations, teachers should refer students to the speech therapist for evaluation and therapy. The therapist should give the teacher and parents particular suggestions of ways to follow through with therapy in the classroom and at home. The following are some general suggestions for the teacher.

Avoid calling attention to the stuttering. Let students finish what they are trying to say and maintain good listening habits, such as eye contact and positive facial expressions.

Make a special note of the classroom circumstances (discussions, oral presentation, free play) and the times of day when the stuttering seems to be the most severe. On the basis of each student's particular pattern, minimize the difficult situations and maximize the situations characterized by more fluency as much as possible.

Talk with the student and parents and cooperatively discuss ways of helping other students in the class react positively to stuttering episodes. Chapter 11 contains many suggestions for conducting such discussions. Classroom peers may resort to teasing and mimicking if they do not know other ways to react positively.

Reduce anxiety over speaking situations as much as possible. If students who stutter are particularly fearful of being called on to answer a question orally in class, the teacher can tell them that they will not be called on unless they volunteer. Often, this strategy can prevent students with stuttering problems from "sweating out" every discussion period.

Articulation. Articulation problems generally refer to consistent mispronunciation of syllables or of the entire word. These mispronunciations occur very commonly among children in the primary grades and frequently disappear as students mature. Other articulation disorders can create significant communication problems. Articulation problems can be categorized as substitutions, distortions, and omissions.

Examples of *substitutions* are wove for love, tite for kite, yeth for yes. Some students consistently substitute at various word positions (initial, medial, and final).

Distortions of sounds can be considered one kind of substitution; however, their distinctiveness comes from being unidentifiable as any other consonant or vowel.

Omissions occur when sounds are dropped from words, such as when h is dropped from *house*. When this problem is severe, language is extremely difficult to understand.

In classroom situations, articulation errors can interfere with the student's performance in the following ways: expressive language can be difficult to understand, phonics training affecting spelling and reading skills can be held back, and the student's social interactions can be influenced. The teacher needs to be alert to these possibilities and to work cooperatively with the student and the school's speech therapist to eliminate these problems to the greatest extent possible.

Delayed Language. Some students are significantly behind chronological age expectations in production of language and/or comprehension of ideas. Sometimes the cause can be pinpointed as mental retardation, hearing loss, severe emotional problems, environmental, or bilingual considerations. In other cases, students can have language delays and it is impossible to identify the origin of the problem. Regardless of the particular cause, handicaps of this nature can put students at a distinct disadvantage in achieving classroom success. These handicaps are characterized by an insufficient vocabulary, difficulty expressing or comprehending complex sentence structures, problems with sequencing ideas or organizing information, or difficulty with inferring the meaning of words or sentences. Speech and language are developmental processes, and some children and youths proceed through the levels of higher-order functioning at slower rates than others.

Specific educational implications could be delays in reading, writing, and spelling since these subjects depend on understanding the language process; difficulty in understanding classroom discussions or mastering concepts in content subjects such as science and social studies; and difficulty in following directions. Helping students overcome language delays and avoid these educational handicaps is the responsibility of teachers and speech therapists. Chapters 5 and 6 offer suggestions on educational approaches for the remediation of these problems.

CASE STUDY

Speech Impairments

Jane is the brightest student in my third-grade class. In every subject area, her achievement is outstanding to the point that every assignment is practically perfect. In contrast to all these strengths, she has a significant stuttering problem. At the beginning of school, it was immediately apparent. I was concerned because I have never before encountered this type of handicap. I was relieved when Jane's mother asked to meet with me during the second week of school. She openly discussed Jane's problem, which helped me understand it. It seems that Jane started talking very early and was using complete sentences long before her second birthday. Around the age of three she started stuttering and went through periods of mild to more obvious disfluencies. She has been receiving therapy since she was five. Since I was unsure how to handle the stuttering in the classroom, she suggested that I listen carefully to Jane, let her finish what she is trying to say, and try to be relaxed about it. I really appreciate being able to talk about this directly with Jane's mother.

As the school year has progressed, the stuttering has become worse. I have noticed that it seems to be very bad during spontaneous conversation in the classroom and during oral reading. Sometimes she jerks her neck and twists her mouth as she is struggling to say something. She seems to stutter less in free-play situations on the playground and with her peers. Lately her stuttering has been so severe that I have difficulty understanding her. I realize that I am having a problem handling the stuttering, because I feel uncomfortable when I see her struggling so much. Sometimes I almost want to skip over her in the reading group. I realize that this is a problem I must deal with.

The other children in the class are very sensitive. They have great respect for Jane's intelligence and would never tease or mock her. She is popular with her peers and very friendly. It concerns me that she rarely discusses her feelings. She's very closed about her personal reactions. Sometimes she looks sad and alone, but during these times she never will open up with me. She seems to be very conscious of the stuttering, yet she never mentions it. Her therapist has suggested that I not call attention to her problem, but I would like to talk with her about it. I operate better when I can be open with the students. I want to talk with him again about the possibility of talking openly with Jane. Since her speech therapist is handling her program, it is important to coordinate things with him. At the same time, it is important for him to be aware of techniques and approaches that fit comfortably into my teaching style.

I will have to admit that I am concerned about Jane. Stuttering is a difficult handicap. I just hope that her problem can be decreased.

Ms. Linda Tully, Ephesus Road School.

VISUAL HANDICAPS

A functional definition of visual handicaps is included in P.L. 94–142.

> . . . a visual impairment which, even with correction, adversely affects a child's educational performance. The term includes both partially seeing and blind children. (*Federal Register,* 1977, p. 42479)

For educational purposes, a partially sighted student is considered one who is able to read large print books, whereas a blind student needs to read braille.

Since students with visual problems traditionally have received their education in residential schools, many teachers have had limited contact with them. Teachers are often understandably uncomfortable about situations for which they have little information. It is sometimes difficult for sighted people to imagine how blind people are able to get around and participate in their environment.

As with all other handicapping areas, the capabilities of blind persons are frequently underestimated. Again, the same condition has a different effect on different people. Some blind people withdraw from involvement and participation, whereas others make their way around busy city streets, engage in advanced academic study, make significant contributions in their career, participate in sports of all kinds, and have a meaningful and enjoyable family life as a husband or wife, father or mother. Readers who would like greater insight into the world of blind persons are referred to *If You Could See What I Hear* (Sullivan & Gill, 1975). Mr. Sullivan shares his lifetime experiences as a blind person. This book expands one's awareness of human adaptability and causes one to question personal perceptions of a handicap.

In the majority of cases, severe visual problems are identified early in the first years of life; however, teachers should be alert to warning signals of visual problems previously undetected. Warning signals (Gearheart & Weishahn, 1976; Kirk & Gallagher, 1979) could include chronic eye irritations, such as encrusted lids, recurring sties, wateriness, or reddened eyelids; excessive blinking, squinting, or facial contortions when reading or doing close work; arranging reading material or classroom charts unusually close or far away; overconcern for establishing awareness of the body in relationship to other students or classroom fixtures, or bumping into peers and fixtures; difficulty in copying from the chalkboard and paper, or writing in general with respect to quality of letter formation, spacing, and staying on the line; tilting the head or shutting one eye while reading; and complaining of headaches, burning eyes, or dizziness.

When teachers suspect visual problems based on these symptoms, they should discuss their concern with the student's parents and the school nurse. The disadvantages associated with visual problems can be drastically minimized through the use of corrective aids (e.g., glasses) and sound educational programming.

Educational Implications

Cognitive Functioning. Visually handicapped students have been found to be within the normal range of intelligence (Bateman, 1963; Scholl & Schnur, 1976). Their school achievement, however, does tend to fall behind that of their sighted classmates (Bateman, 1963; Hayes, 1941; Lowenfeld, Abel, & Hatlen, 1969).

Their underachievement could be attributable to a number of reasons, including slower concept development associated with impaired vision, slower reading rates, and inappropriate instructional procedures. Instructional procedures for teaching visually handicapped students are included in chapters 3 through 10. Problems in achievement resulting from difficulty in concept development are discussed here.

Concept development basically refers to the process of attaching meaning to ideas and clustering them into units of information to form a conceptual framework. A concept can be thought of as the "hook" on which students can attach ideas when they are first perceived. This type of concept formation adds clarity, meaning, and organization to the thousands of inputs students receive each day. Vision contributes significantly to the quality of concept development. It is considered the *unifier* of experience. We can hear an airplane, ride on an airplane, smell an airplane, and listen to a story about an airplane, but the sensory experience that can pull all these bits of information together is actually seeing an airplane. When vision is impaired to the extent that visual sensory input is impossible, teachers must capitalize on the use of other sensory channels, such as listening, feeling, tasting, and smelling. It is also important to use the remaining, useful vision. In many cases, the more the vision is used, the more efficient it becomes.

Another significant aid to concept development is concrete experience. One aspect of concreteness involves touching and manipulating in order to understand concepts of size, texture, and shape. If algae are being discussed in the science class, do not rely just on verbally describing this concept to blind students. Have them feel the side of an aquarium as a more concrete encounter. Real objects and their models can be valuable learning aids. Learning from concrete experiences could involve field trips. These types of experiences are good for all students, not just for ones who are blind or partially sighted.

Some blind students may be able to memorize definitions of words without having any clear understanding of how to relate that information to anything meaningful. A program that starts at a concrete level using practical experiences and a multisensory approach can help students with visual problems move from concrete to abstract levels of understanding.

Orientation and Mobility. Orientation and mobility have similar, yet different, meanings. They are often confused when related to blind and partially sighted people. Orientation is the awareness of one's position in space as related to other objects and people in the environment. Mobility refers to one's movement within the environment as you go from one place to another (Suterko, 1973).

Students with severe visual impairment probably will have started mobility training before entering school. Many students will have an orientation and mobility instructor to work with them, their families, and teachers in helping prepare them to get around the classroom and school independently. The objectives of orientation and mobility training as defined by Apple (1976) include:

1. that the person will be able to orient himself and remain oriented while walking on foot in either familiar or unfamiliar environments;
2. that he will be able to travel safely with a minimal amount of reliance on others and with reasonable ease of movement and physical freedom;
3. that he will develop efficient techniques of physical search and visual scanning; and
4. that he will develop correct techniques for the use of optical and mechanical aids for travel without also developing an incongruous or uncomfortable gait or posture. (p. 138)

Teachers should follow through carefully on the suggestions of the instructor to insure that consistent expectations and guidelines are set for the student.

Here are some general tips for teachers in this area. Have the student spend time in the classroom for a couple of days before the beginning of the school year. Guide the student around the room explaining the layout, learning centers, arrangement of desks, location of special equipment, and other important information. Let the student ask questions and generally spend the necessary time to feel comfortable in moving about. Practice walking to the bathroom, playground, cafeteria, library, and other special areas. Again, explain the layout of each and practice moving about in them. Practice the procedure of exiting the building for fire drills.

When the arrangement of the classroom or parts of the school change, tell the student in advance and provide for practice in relearning orientation and mobility if necessary.

Call the blind or partially sighted student by name (eye contact is impossible) and give explicit directions. For example, if the student is being asked to get a particular library book, describe the location precisely.

Blind students who have attended public schools report on the horror of walking down the steps when a mass of students is thundering down past them. Encourage sighted classmates to take precautions against possible collisions or schedule the blind student's transition time a few minutes earlier or later than other students'.

Adaptations in Classroom Procedures and Equipment. Adaptations in general classroom procedures are necessary for students with visual impairment. Some helpful considerations, depending on the individual student, include seating close to the teacher and chalkboard; avoiding glare by having the student work facing away from a window; keeping doors either opened or closed, since ajar doors can be a potential safety hazard in mobility; providing adequate space for the storage of special equipment, such as braille books and typewriters, and adequate desk space for using it; providing a verbal explanation of board work, filmstrips, or other visual presentations; and alternating periods of using residual vision with other educational experiences to reduce fatigue and strain.

A substantial amount of adapted instructional equipment has been developed for partially sighted and blind students. Two tactual aids for blind students are the braillewriter and the slate and stylus. The braillewriter is a six-key machine that is manually operated to type braille. The slate and stylus can be used to take notes in class. The slate is a metal frame with small openings. Braille dots can be embossed through these openings with the use of a pointed stylus. Aids for partially sighted students include glasses with special prescriptions and magnifiers either held in the hand or attached to glasses. As each curriculum area is discussed in this book, special equipment will be identified and explained. Catalogs of materials and adaptive equipment are available free of charge from the Commission for the Blind in each state. Materials are also distributed free of charge from regional and subregional libraries of the Library of Congress, Division for the Blind and Physically Handicapped (see Appendix A for the address of the Library of Congress). Teachers are urged to write the Library of Congress to obtain reference brochures on these available materials.

CASE STUDY

Visual Handicaps

When I learned that I would have a blind student in my home room and social studies class, my first thought was "What can I do for him?" I had misgivings about things I would say, such as "Look at the board," or "We're going to see a film." After talking with a friend, I decided that the first day I would tell David that I would treat him just like the other students. This worked out well; his attitude made it easy for me and we both relaxed.

David wants to learn more than any kid in my class. He wants to learn because he's behind. He will have to work hard just to finish high school.

Before David came into the class and the home room, I talked with the other students. At first he was a curiosity to them but soon it was evident that the others liked him and wanted to help in any way they could. David talks about his handicap and thus there is no pressure on the other kids; they don't view him as very different.

Actually, David has been an asset to the class. I put him at a table of boys who like him; they are conscious that they must verbalize so David can take part in whatever is going on. As they read or look for answers for questions, they talk about it for David's benefit and they all profit. He has helped the whole class verbalize their feelings and their findings.

I have had to take a good look at my instructional techniques and I am not altogether happy with what I am doing. For one thing, I like showing "war movies"; the kids like them and are motivated by them. But I feel David is cheated when we have movies and that this emphasizes his disability.

Sometimes I feel that I neglect David, and that I need to let him know I'm there. The lack of eye contact makes me feel he may think I have forgotten him.

I have not been easy on David; I feel it would be demeaning to expect less of him than I do of the other students. I have given him tests equal to the ones the rest of the class took. We started with verbal tests, then I asked him to type the answers. He didn't like this, but I required him to do it. I don't feel I've measured his understanding of concepts, such as on the subject of communism.

Next year I will be better prepared for David. The best thing David and I have going is that we like each other. He's helped me more than I've helped him.

Mr. Dewey Rayburn, Fairview Elementary School.

HEARING IMPAIRMENTS

Imagine not being able to hear favorite sounds often taken for granted, such as a symphony, rain on the roof, a crackling fire, the song of a bird, children's laughter, or the voices of loved ones. It is also disconcerting to consider not being able to hear the sounds signifying safety warnings, such as the honking of a horn on a city street, ambulance sirens, fire alarms, weather alerts, and the ring of a telephone. Hearing impairments must also be considered in classroom settings. Some students have difficulty hearing or are unable to hear the teacher's instructions, conversations of their peers, educational television, classroom discussions, the comradely comments on the playground, or even the noise in the cafeteria.

The terms *hard of hearing* and *deaf* are defined by P.L. 94–142 as follows:

> "Hard of hearing" is a hearing impairment, whether permanent or fluctuating, which adversely affects a child's educational performance but which is not included under the definition of "deaf" in this section.
>
> "Deaf" means a hearing impairment which is so severe that the child is impaired in processing linguistic information through hearing, with or without amplification, which adversely effects educational performance. (*Federal Register,* 1977, p. 42478)

A hearing impairment is an extremely complex phenomenon. To explain its influence on a person's development, three factors should be considered (Birch, 1975).

The *nature* of the hearing impairment refers to a person's hearing pattern as it relates to frequency and intensity. Frequency can be thought of as pitch; intensity refers to loudness. Frequency must be considered in terms of the pitch range needed for communication purposes in order to understand the nature of a hearing loss. Some students may be able to hear the majority of sounds, missing those at one extreme of pitch or the other. Students with the greatest educational handicap are those who are unable to hear the pitch range of normal conversation. As for intensity, students vary in their ability to hear different levels of amplification. Some students, unable to hear faint or even conversational intensity, can hear when these sounds are amplified.

The *degree* of hearing impairment is the second important factor. Some students with residual (remaining) hearing benefit from the use of a hearing aid to the extent that total regular class assimilation is effectively accomplished without major adaptations. Other impairments range along every point of the continuum to the point of total deafness. Students who are totally deaf do not benefit from the amplification of hearing aids. Classification systems have been developed that describe the degree of hearing impairment at the levels of mild, moderate, moderately severe, severe, and profound.

The *age of onset* is the third factor for consideration. A hearing impairment creates more significant educational handicaps when it is congenital (present from birth) or when it occurs in the first or second year of development. Early onset is more significant because language has not yet been learned; therefore, the child has no frame of reference for understanding language. When the onset occurs later, for example at the age of ten, the child's vocabulary and syntax of language and reading achievement are developed to the point that continued, steady growth can be strongly anticipated.

All of these factors interact to determine the specific educational handicap of a given student. It is impossible for teachers to be experts in understanding and interpreting the intricate details of specific hearing problems. Again, each student's condition will vary according to these three factors. Teachers are advised to talk carefully with the student's parents, speech therapist, and audiologist to gain information on the educationally relevant influences of the hearing impairment.

Sometimes hearing-impaired students are not identified before entering school. In other situations, hearing problems can follow immediately after diseases or accidents. Upper respiratory diseases, chronic middle ear infection, or infected tonsils and adenoids can create temporary or sometimes permanent hearing loss. The teacher should observe carefully any behaviors indicative of hearing problems. Some of these behaviors (Gearheart & Weishahn, 1976; McConnell, 1973) include turning one side of the head toward the speaker or touching the ears when trying to listen; delayed language; standing very close to someone who is talking; frequently asking for comments or instructions to be repeated; lack of attention; inappropriate responses to questions signaling lack of understanding; and complaints of earaches, runny discharges from ears, sore throat, and constant colds. The teacher who observes some of these symptoms should contact the student's parents and the school nurse. Initial screening of problems might indicate the need for medical, audiological, and educational evaluations.

Educational Implications

Communication. The greatest single educational handicap of deaf and hard-of-hearing students revolves around the development of communication skills. The two basic approaches are referred to as oral and total communication (Birch, 1975). The oral method requires the student with a hearing impairment to use a combination of residual hearing, a hearing aid, and speech reading (the ability to understand another person by watching the lips and face) to comprehend. For self-expression, the student using the oral approach verbalizes. The total communication approach also involves the use of residual hearing, a hearing aid, speech reading, and oral speech. Additionally, this approach includes the use of sign language and the manual alphabet. In sign language, concepts are represented by movement of the hands and arms (signs). As opposed to concept representation, the manual alphabet has a movement for each letter and is often referred to as finger spelling. Words are spelled using particular movements for different letters. The manual alphabet has been likened to writing in the air.

The form of communication a student uses has tremendous implications for the classroom. Although there is some debate over the most advantageous approach, many specialists seem to follow the pattern of intensively stimulating oral communication with hearing-impaired students during preschool and early elementary years (Nix, 1976). If the child has not developed adequate language by the age of nine or ten, consideration is then given to teaching the two forms of manual communication. The oral approach to language facilitates mainstreaming in that the student with a hearing handicap can understand and be understood by classroom peers. When signing is necessary, however, hearing students often enjoy the intrigue of learning signing as a way of communicating with their friends. In some mainstream situations, teachers also have learned signs for basic classroom terminology.

Many students with hearing handicaps have been limited by teachers and parents who excused them from the rigorous requirements of language training on the basis that it was too difficult for them. The capabilities of these students in obtaining language proficiency often exceed our expectations. Specific instructional strategies for developing communication skills are discussed in chapter 5.

Special Equipment in the Classroom. Hearing-impaired students frequently wear hearing aids. Therefore, teachers must have a basic understanding of how hearing aids work and of basic maintenance operations. The hearing aid itself is composed of three parts: a receiver for picking up the sound, an amplifier for making it louder, and a speaker for transmitting the sound to the hearing-impaired person. The aid runs on batteries. Any specific questions about its operation or maintenance, and all major repairs, should be directed to the hearing aid dealer who sold it. General guidelines important for the classroom are discussed in this section (Birch, 1975; Gearheart & Weishahn, 1976).

Hearing aids cannot be assumed to achieve normal hearing. Aids do make sounds, including background noises, louder. Preferential seating should be assigned students wearing aids to accommodate their need to hear classroom discussions and instructions; this will also prevent sounds from being drowned out by loud background noises. Sometimes it is difficult to know the best seating location. Perhaps the special education teacher in the school could offer some suggestions. A good strategy is to start with the "best educated" guess and try students in a particular seating arrangement. Seek feedback from them as to their ability to hear, and also observe their behavior to see if they seem to be straining or missing important information. Make modifications in the seating pattern until the optimal location is identified.

If a hearing aid has been prescribed for a student, it should be worn at all times unless otherwise directed by the student's audiologist. When a student repeatedly tries to remove an aid at school, it may indicate that the aid is not doing the proper job reproducing sounds. The teacher can listen to the aid to get an idea of possible disturbances. Aids should be checked intermittently.

Students who wear a hearing aid should learn early to care for it. When they first detect a change in functioning, they should report it to their parents and teacher. Teachers should keep extra batteries and cords at school. As students advance in elementary years, they usually are able to change batteries or insert cords themselves. Teachers should be knowledgeable in these procedures and carry them out for young children. Audiologists and hearing aid dealers are usually the best people to give teachers and parents detailed information on this type of maintenance.

In addition to hearing aids, some schools purchase auditory training units, which generally have stronger amplification and a wider frequency range than hearing aids. The student wears the trainer, which has the same three parts as the hearing aid—receiver, amplifier, and speaker. Additionally, the teacher wears a portable microphone that transmits the voice directly to the student wearing the auditory trainer. A distinct advantage of trainers is that they can be adjusted to close off all sound except the teacher's voice. With background distractions cut down, the student is able to focus completely on what the teacher is saying. Typically, trainers are used for speech and language development. Hearing aid dealers can give teachers more specific information on the use of auditory trainers.

Adaptations in Classroom Procedures. In considering necessary adaptations in classroom procedures, the teacher must realize that the needs of hearing-impaired students vary according to the details of their particular handicap. Here are some general suggestions for classroom adaptations that might be considered and modified for a particular student in a regular classroom.

If the student needs specialized services to keep up with achievement in the classroom or to develop communication skills, help should be obtained from the resource teacher, audiologist, or speech therapist. The students may receive individual tutoring outside the classroom, or the resource teacher and/or speech therapist might work with the student within the regular class. The total coordination of the program will be a key to success.

The teacher (classroom, resource, or both) may have to introduce the vocabulary of lessons to hearing-impaired students ahead of time, or seek the help of the student's parents in this preliminary preparation for the lesson. This language orientation can facilitate speech reading and understanding. Another helpful hint is to write key words and phrases on the chalkboard as an outline for the student during a class discussion.

The teacher should try to remain stationary when talking and not stand near a window that creates a glare for the student. Light on the teacher's face is most helpful to students with hearing impairments. Of course, it is important to face students when talking. Using an overhead projector rather than the chalkboard can increase the amount of time a teacher faces a class.

Fancy hairstyles, mustaches, beards, and excessive jewelry worn by teachers often create distractions and interfere with the hearing-impaired student's ability to read lips. Other facial obstructions to avoid include pencils, books, cigarettes, and pipes.

Teachers should not exaggerate lip movements, speech rate, or voice volume. Complete sentences should be used so that individual words can be interpreted in the context of their meaning.

Visual aids are extremely helpful. Consider using captioned films, pictures, and the chalkboard.

Students who work very hard to hear in the classroom often tire more quickly than other students. Academic subjects should be interwoven with physical activity and short intervals of free time to minimize fatigue and frustration.

A hearing-impaired student in the class can benefit significantly from having a "hearing buddy" make an outline or carbon copy of notes, repeat directions, clarify concepts, or point out the right page in a book. Hurwitz (1979), a deaf adult, described the note-taking assistance he received during his college years as follows:

> The registrar could not find an academically strong student to work with me, so we settled for a weak-C student who happened to be enrolled in all of my classes. He agreed to help me, since he needed the money which was financed by the Office of Vocational Rehabilitation. At first, he would use carbon copy papers, and I would sit next to him to read his notes. It did not work out well because I was bored. The teacher's lecture was often not relevant to the textbooks I had before me on my desk. My notetaker would take the kind of notes he felt would be useful for me and himself. So we agreed to eliminate the carbon papers and I would copy his notes in the class as he took them. I would try to analyze the notes with my textbooks. Whenever I needed to ask a question, I would write it down on scratch paper and give it to my notetaker to ask the teacher for me. It worked out well. At the end of the academic year my notetaker became an honor student! I did well myself, too. The support services program worked out well not only for myself but also for my notetaker. It enabled him to take better notes for himself too. (p. 51)

Buddies can be rotated on a weekly or biweekly basis. The teacher has to instruct classroom peers carefully on how much help is needed or when help is not needed. Striking the proper balance is an important educational decision.

Sometimes hearing-impaired students make unintentional noises, interrupt conversations, and speak too loudly or not loudly enough without being aware of it. They need guidance in appropriate verbal interactions. Overlooking or excusing these types of behaviors with students who are perfectly capable of appropriate communications skills denies them an opportunity to learn otherwise.

CASE STUDY

Hearing Impairment

My experiences in mainstreaming hearing-impaired children had a terrible beginning and a very happy ending. It all started last year when Dave, a severely hearing-impaired student was placed in my class. Prior to the first day of school with Dave, I had received no training in teaching children with hearing handicaps.

When Dave started in the third-grade class, I thought I could adapt my program to meet his needs. Although I was promised consultation and help from a special education teacher, I received none. Dave's language and reading skills were very low and his handwriting was all done in tall manuscript letters. I shudder now to think of all the mistakes I made with him. For example, we always give standardized achievement tests to students in the third grade. Not knowing any better, I gave him a group test on the third-grade level. Dave scored very low, and I recommended him for possible placement in a special class for mentally retarded children. His mother got very upset and contacted the state department of education. Someone from the hearing-impaired program in the state department called and fussed at me for using a test that required third-grade reading and language skills with Dave. I could then understand that the test was inappropriate for him and that his hearing handicap had penalized his performance. I did not mean to treat him unfairly, but I simply did not know what was best for him. I developed a very negative attitude about teaching Dave.

Just when I was relieved that the school year was over and I had made it through the year, the principal asked me to move up to the fourth grade and teach the same class the following year. This meant another year of having Dave in class. The only hope I had was that a new special education teacher had been hired to work with me and with other classroom teachers. I was very skeptical, but I agreed to give it a try. Ms. Goulding, the new teacher, held a short workshop before school started and gave me lots of suggestions on good instructional tips to use with Dave. I don't want to sound like I am overstating it, but she was truly like a ray of sunshine. All of a sudden I knew help was close by and that she had much to offer. She started working with Dave every day in reading and math. He seemed to do well in programmed series like the Sullivan. Instead of always taking Dave out of the room, she frequently came into my class and worked with him there. She then could remind me of important considerations, like facing the children when I talk, avoiding standing in front of the window, and writing assignments on the board. Even though she had told me these things before, sometimes I would forget and not even realize it. Another thing that I really appreciate is that she always gives me suggestions in such a nice way. There's nothing threatening or negative about them.

I am responsible for the social studies and science portion of Dave's program. I use the overhead projector frequently to introduce vocabulary, and I always try to put new words into context for him. He enjoys captioned films and supplementary library books. Dave always wears an auditory trainer at school. I wear the microphone so that my voice is amplified for him and background noises are screened out. At first he tended to wear his coat over the trainer to hide it, but now it is a normal thing in our classroom. I have never heard any teasing by the other students. One thing that has helped tremendously is that hearing-impaired children have been attending our school for the last ten years. It is nothing new for the other children.

As I look back on this year, I realize that I have made great strides as a teacher. I can honestly say that they key has been Ms. Goulding. The great thing about it is that the techniques I have learned for Dave have benefited all the students. I am excited over what has happened this year. It seems that all of us have made gains in different ways.

Ms. Sandra Fracker, Cary Elementary School.

SERIOUS EMOTIONAL DISTURBANCE

The term *serious emotional disturbance* is defined by P.L. 94–142 as:

> A condition exhibiting one or more of the following characteristics over a long period of time and to a marked degree, which adversely affects educational performance:
> a. An inability to learn which cannot be explained by intellectual, sensory, or health factors;
> b. An inability to build or maintain satisfactory interpersonal relationships with peers and teachers;
> c. Inappropriate types of behavior or feelings under normal circumstances;
> d. A general pervasive mood of unhappiness or depression; or
> e. A tendency to develop physical symptoms or fears associated with personal or school problems. (*Federal Register,* 1977, p. 42478)

There are two important factors to consider in interpreting this definition. First, this is the only definition in P.L. 94–142 that uses the term *serious*. Thus, the population of students who have mild to moderate emotional problems are excluded from this classification. Many of these students were served in special education programs before the implementation of P.L. 94–142 (Yard, 1977). Secondly, many school systems have previously used the classification of *socially maladjusted* to refer to students who exhibit disruptive or antisocial behavior. It has been reported that socially maladjusted students between the ages of ten and seventeen commit more than 50 percent of all serious crimes in this country (Raiser & Van Nagel, 1980). Unless socially maladjusted students are also seriously emotionally disturbed, they do not qualify for special education services under the federal requirements. Professionals have suggested that the definition of seriously emotionally disturbed be carefully reviewed and amended to broaden its application to students with mild and moderate problems and to those who have social maladjustments (Raiser & Van Nagel, 1980; Yard, 1977).

The important point for our discussion is that students with serious emotional problems will be formally classified as handicapped. Students having less serious emotional problems or social problems will not be formally identified as handicapped; however, they still will require some systematic intervention programs to help them achieve success in the regular classroom. Such interventions could involve curriculum modification, classroom management programs, or strategies aimed at helping the student improve personal relationships. Teachers should plan such interventions based on the individual needs of students rather than on formal labels and classifications.

Some behaviors indicative of serious emotional problems may be situational (e.g., related to a family crisis) and others occur over a long period of time. Students considered emotionally handicapped by one teacher in a given classroom may not be so considered by another teacher in a different classroom. Students perform differently in various situations according to expectations, guidelines, responses, and personality traits of teachers. Tolerance is a reciprocal factor between student and teacher. Some teachers are more tolerant of particular student behavior and vice versa. An important educational principle is matching student and teacher characteristics/styles to the greatest degree possible in order to maximize the potential of a "comfortable fit" (Forness, 1981).

Educational Implications

Learning Problems. Students with higher vulnerability to emotional pressures, who are coping with a host of factors that are distracting to goal-directed activity, often encounter academic difficulty. Bower (1969b) reported that emotionally handicapped students scored lower on reading and arithmetic achievement tests than did their nonhandicapped counterparts. Sometimes the problem becomes that of the chicken or the egg. Which came first—the emotional or the learning problem?

> Consider the eighth-grade student who reads on a third-grade level. Such a student is recalled who was expected to function academically with textbooks all on the eighth-grade level. Since he could not read them, he encountered continual failure. He was characterized by his teacher as "lacking in self-confidence, fearful,

depressed, and anxious." As his emotional problems become more pronounced, his achievement came to a halt as he refused to attempt assignments.

This example illustrates the interaction between learning problems and emotional problems, as well as the interaction between student and teacher behavior. Just as success begets success, often failure begets failure. Students who experience difficulty in personal and interpersonal development also often have learning problems. When students get on this type of failure treadmill, they need help in getting off.

How can the teacher help? There are many ways. Motivation and interest have to be established—useful techniques are discussed in chapter 4. To use these techniques, a teacher must be willing to try a number of novel approaches until a successful one for the particular student's difficulty can be identified. Sometimes the initial investment of more individualized teacher time can ultimately be extremely efficient in preventing future classroom disruptions and even more serious emotional handicaps on the student's part.

When motivation and interest have been established, the teacher might begin instruction in a structured, systematic format that stresses the step-by-step development of skills. This instruction should be based on thorough academic assessment. When students know they are making progress and are receiving positive recognition for their gains, they are more likely to be emotionally healthy. In general, teachers will see a substantial reduction in the number of students with emotional handicaps as these students are able to state with confidence, "I can learn. I am competent. Good things happen to me. I make positive accomplishments."

Peer Relationships. Students with emotional handicaps often suffer in silence as they eat lunch alone in a crowded cafeteria, get into arguments in the restroom, or feel excluded immediately before or after school when informal groups occupy the schoolyard. Sometimes the quality of peer relationships is more telling outside the formal classroom situation than within. Loneliness and isolation can exaggerate emotional handicaps. Again, we have the treadmill situation:

- A person engages in annoying or bothersome behavior associated with an emotional problem.
- Peers become irritated with the behavior and reject the individual.
- The individual is hurt by the rejection and loneliness.
- The harder the individual tries to be accepted, the more annoying he or she becomes.
- Greater annoyance leads to further rejection.

Peer relationships are significant aspects of the educational experiences of students. When students within a class are factionalized, effective instructional strategies involving the range of group activities become greatly reduced. The breakdown of peer relationships is a major implication of emotional handicaps and creates significant educational disadvantages. Chapter 11 includes many strategies and resources for enhancing the social integration of students who experience alienation and rejection.

Inappropriate Behavior Leading to Classroom Problems. Some students with emotional problems engage in otherwise appropriate behavior at inappropriate times. For example, rowdy behavior associated with the playground or clowning appropriate in some social interactions might be carried out by some students in the midst of a reading group or math lesson. As a rule, students with emotional handicaps function better when teachers provide structure and clearly set limits to classroom behavior and assignments. Some students who do not personally generate their own stability and orderliness can benefit substantially from teachers who provide this structure. Additionally, when the classroom disruptions of students with emotional handicaps are reduced, all students benefit.

In spite of the teacher's best intentions, it often happens that students who tend to be overly passive, shy, and withdrawn get overlooked in the teacher's effort to respond to the seemingly most demanding aspects of the school day. Acting-out, aggressive behavior almost always requires an immediate response in the best interest of the student relative to safety and personal/interpersonal disruption. When students say nothing, cower from attention, and generally do what is asked of them, they frequently are overlooked in classroom situations.

Severe withdrawn and passive behavior is a clear signal of an emotional handicap. Active intervention in building trust and understanding is required to insure both personal and interpersonal development. Many of the suggestions included in chapter 11 regarding the development of relationships are particularly applicable to these students.

Teachers can request assistance from a variety of resource persons to help them devise intervention programs to enhance the classroom success of the student with serious emotional problems. These resource persons include a special education teacher with expertise in emotional handicaps, guidance counselor, and school psychologist or psychiatrist. Schools that do not employ a psychiatrist frequently can attain psychiatric consultation from community services such as the mental health center or from private medical practices.

CASE STUDY

Serious Emotional Disturbance

I teach a beginning course in Naval Science. In addition to the academic component, the class offers a number of extracurricular activities including military drill, competitive drill, and rifle team. The purpose of the course is to develop informed, responsible citizens, and to provide a theoretical and practical experience in leadership.

Until this year, I had no experience or training in special education. This year Charles, a 17-year-old junior, enrolled in the Naval Science course. At the beginning of the year, Charles was a constant behavior problem in the classroom, speaking out at will, insulting other students, threatening other students, and refusing to cooperate. He seemed to want to solve every problem by "meeting you after school." I informed him of the rules of our program and advised him that it was it was my responsibility to recommend the disenrollment of any student who did not meet these standards. He surprisingly said he wanted very much to stay in the program. I told him that I would recommend him for disenrollment if he did not cease making threats to the other students. He agreed to try.

Charles told me he didn't care what other people thought of him, since most people didn't like him anyway. He told me he was like General Patton (he saw the movie). I agreed that Patton demonstrated one type of leadership—fear and force. I pointed out to him that leadership by personal example and persuasion was much more successful in the long run and certainly more satisfying to the person. I suggested to him that he try a new method, since he was already very good at the Patton way. If the new way didn't work, he could always revert to his old ways. I suggested that the first step to becoming a good leader was to be an accomplished follower.

The entire class was divided into four squads with one person serving as squad leader for about two weeks. No one wanted to be in a squad with Charles. I was able to convince three other students to accept the challenge. After a short conference, Charles agreed to experiment with the new method of personal example and persuasion.

The first week went well with my keeping a close eye on Charles. The day before the first competition Charles turned in his class project. It was very well done, and he received many nice compliments. His squad won first place and he was very proud of himself. The students took turns being the squad leader. The first leader of Charles's squad—Earl—was an experienced drill team member and pushed the other students very hard for perfection. Charles did not take to these harsh measures and began to rebel. I reminded him of his goals and suggested that this student was somewhat like Patton. The next day Charles reported to class limping and informed me that he wanted to be excused from drill. Since his ankle was bandaged, I agreed.

After several weeks, it became Charles's turn to be leader of the squad. I held my breath. He began by explaining to his squad that he had done his best to help them and he now needed their help. He even advised them that, when he found he could not stand Earl, he faked an ankle injury so as not to hurt their chances. With the cooperation of the students, he did very well as their leader and I believe now has at least three people who are much friendlier to him. Charles agrees that the new methods did work but are a lot of trouble. He still thinks it might have been better to punch Earl. He said that with a smile.

Charles and I have developed a close friendship, and he frequently comes to me to discuss problems. He had by no means conquered all. He was disciplined last week for fighting in gym class.

An important part of this year is the beginning success of one student. Another important part has been the education of Charles's teacher. I have learned that success can be achieved—even with difficult students.

Mr. Mike Lavin, Shawnee Mission West High School. (Courtesy of Mr. Mike Lavin)

SUMMARY

After various areas of handicapping conditions are highlighted, common threads can be identified. The most obvious one, language, cuts across almost every handicap in some aspect. Other common threads are attention span, generalization, mobility, lowered academic achievement, and emotional considerations. These characteristics should be approached in light of the particular student with whom the teacher is working. It is impossible to define a set of successful instructional strategies for all learning-disabled or all hearing-impaired students. There is no assurance that what is successful for one student will automatically work with another.

In each curriculum area, basic principles will be discussed with many different possibilities for application in classroom settings. Methods and materials will be suggested for student characteristics or those particular strengths and weaknesses that have educational relevance. Although these characteristics often cluster according to the particular handicapping condition, every student is unique and must be approached on that basis. The characteristics pointed out in each handicapping area in this chapter should help readers direct their attention to correlating remediation strategies discussed in the following chapters.

In summarizing the introduction to handicapped students in school situations, we emphasize several points. All students have various combinations of strengths and weaknesses. It is important for the teacher to be aware of both. Students may possess tremendous ability to overcome disadvantages and compensate for deficits. Handicapped students have far more similarities to than differences from nonhandicapped peers.

Often the most critical educational disadvantage for handicapped students is that instructional strategies are not tailored to their needs. Classroom teachers have both a challenge and an opportunity in developing competency to teach these students. There is no way teachers can be prepared to deal with every possible handicap; they are not expected to be experts in the field. They do need to be alert to problems, familiar with resources, and capable of individualizing instruction. The methods and materials discussed in this book address these needs. These methods and materials are not only useful with handicapped students; they can also enhance the teacher's effectiveness with all students. There are no substitutes for sound educational principles and instruction.

REFERENCES

Apple, L. E. Orientation and mobility of patients with low vision. In E. E. Fay (Ed.), *Clinical low vision.* Boston, Ma: Little, Brown and Co., 1976.

Bateman, B. Reading and psycholinguistic processes of partially seeing children. *CEC Research Monograph,* Series A, No 5. Arlington, Va.: Council for Exceptional Children, 1963.

Belmont, J. M., & Butterfield, E. C. The relations of short-term memory to development and intelligence. In L. C. Lipsitt & H. W. Reese (Eds.), *Advances in child development and behavior* (Vol. 4). New York: Academic Press, 1969.

Birch, J. W. *Hearing impaired children in the mainstream.* Minneapolis, Minn.: Leadership Training Institute/Special Education, University of Minnesota, 1975.

Bower, E. M. A process for identifying disturbed children. In H. Dupout (Ed.), *Educating emotionally disturbed children.* New York: Holt, Rinehart and Winston, 1969.

Brutten, G. J., & Shoemaker, D. J. *The modification of stuttering.* Englewood Cliffs, N.J.: Prentice-Hall, 1967.

Butterfield, E. C., Wambold, C., & Belmont, J. M. On the theory and practice of improving short-term memory. *American Journal of Mental Deficiency,* 1973, *77,* 654–669.

Ellis, N. R. Memory processes in retardates and normals. In N. R. Ellis (Ed.), *International review of research in mental retardation* (Vol. 4). New York: Academic Press, 1970.

Federal Register. Washington, D.C.: U.S. Government Printing Office, August 1977.

Forness, S. R. Concepts of learning and behavior disorders: Implications for research and practice. *Exceptional Children,* 1981, *48*(1), 56–64.

Gearheart, B. R., & Weishahn, M. W. *The handicapped child in the regular class.* St. Louis, Mo: C. V. Mosby Co., 1976.

Grossman, H. J. (Ed.). *Manual on terminology and classification in mental retardation.* Washington, D.C.: American Association on Mental Deficiency Special Publication, Series No. 2, 1973.

Hayes, S. P. *Contributions to a psychology of blindness.* New York, NY: American Foundation for the Blind, 1941.

Hull, F. M., & Hull, M. E. Children with oral communication disabilities. In L. M. Dunn (Ed.), *Exceptional children in the schools.* New York: Holt, Rinehart and Winston, 1973.

Hurwitz, T. A. Reflections of a mainstreamed deaf person. In M. E. Bishop (Ed.), *Mainstreaming: Practical ideas for educating hearing-impaired students.* Washington, D.C.: The Alexander Graham Bell Association for the Deaf, 1979.

Kirk, S. A., & Gallagher, J. J. *Educating exceptional children* (3rd ed.). Boston, Ma: Houghton Mifflin Co., 1979.

Lowenfeld, B., Abel, G., & Hatlen, P. *Blind children learn to read.* Springfield, Ill.: Charles C. Thomas, 1969.

McConnell, F. Children with hearing disabilities. In L. M. Dunn (Ed.), *Exceptional children in the schools.* New York: Holt, Rinehart and Winston, 1973.

MacMillan, D. L. *Mental retardation in school and society* (2nd ed.). Boston, Ma.: Little Brown and Co., 1982.

Myers, P. I., & Hammill, D. D. *Methods for learning disorders.* New York: John Wiley and Sons, 1976.

Nix, G. W. *Mainstream education for hearing impaired children and youth.* New York: Grune and Stratton, 1976.

Pieper, B. The teacher and the child with spina bifida. Unpublished manuscript, 1976.

Raiser, L., & Van Nagel, C. V. The loophole in P.L. 94–142. *Exceptional Children,* 1980, *46*(7), 516–520.

Scholl, G., & Schnur, R. *Measures of psychological, vocational, and educational functioning in the blind and visually handicapped.* New York: American Foundation for the Blind, 1976.

Sullivan, T., & Gill, D. *If you could see what I hear.* New York: Harper and Row, 1975.

Suterko, S. Life adjustment. In B. Lowenfeld (Ed.), *The visually handicapped child in school.* New York: John Day, 1973.

Tjossem, T. D. (Ed.). *Intervention strategies for high risk infants and young children.* Baltimore: University Park Press, 1976.

Turnbull, A. P. Teaching retarded persons to rehearse through cumulative overt labeling. *American Journal of Mental Deficiency,* 1974, *79,* 331–337.

Van Riper, C. *Speech correction: Principles and methods* (5th ed.). Englewood Cliffs, N.J.: Prentice-Hall, 1972.

Yard, G. J. Definition and interpretation of P.L. 94–142: Is behavior disorders a question of semantics? *Behavioral Disorders,* 1977, *24,* 252–254.

Zigler, E., & Valentine, J. (Eds.). *Project Head Start: A legacy of the war on poverty.* New York: Free Press, 1979.

2

Principles of Mainstreaming

The perspective of a parent of an orthopedically handicapped student offers insights into some of the fundamental principles of mainstreaming.

> Sara was mainstreamed before we heard the word; therefore, I wish the same for all other children. I believe very strongly that normal children benefit when they get to know the handicapped children. I think the general public also benefits when there is more awareness of handicapping conditions and the personhood of those whose bodies or minds are less than whole.
>
> I feel that people should be aware that often the worst handicaps are those that are hidden inside the heart, such as hatred, bitterness, resentment. I feel that we all should get our perspectives in better order and our sense of values in better balance. . . .
>
> I think it unwise and unfair to mainstream unless teachers are prepared to handle it and unless resource rooms, special aides, etc., are made available. I also think it is unjust to isolate handicapped children from normal children. How are they to grow up without interaction with "normal" peers? They need models as much as they need textbooks. (Paul & Beckman-Bell, 1981, pp. 149, 151)

Clearly, mainstreaming has many positive aspects; however, both in the literature and in practice there are numerous mainstreaming myths. The very word *mainstreaming* is a red flag to many persons, indicating that teachers are being asked to take on unreasonable responsibility. It is important for educators to consider carefully what mainstreaming is and what it is not. In order to eliminate red flags immediately, let us first consider what mainstreaming is not.

WHAT MAINSTREAMING IS NOT

Mainstreaming is not the total elimination of self-contained special education classes. It does not mean that *all* handicapped students will be placed in regular classes. Further, it does not automatically imply that those handicapped students who are placed in regular classes will be in that setting for the entire school day.

Mainstreaming is not an arrangement that can be accomplished overnight in a school system. Instant change often leads to unstable classroom environments.

Mainstreaming is not just the physical presence of a handicapped student in the regular class.

Mainstreaming does not mean that the placement of handicapped students in regular classes jeopardizes the academic progress of nonhandicapped students.

Mainstreaming does not mean that the total responsibility for the education of handicapped students placed in regular classes will fall to the regular class teacher.

Finally, mainstreaming does not put educators "out on a limb" and expect them to accomplish tasks for which they are not prepared.

WHAT MAINSTREAMING IS

Many different definitions of mainstreaming have been cited in the literature (Blacher-Dixon & Turnbull, 1979; Kaufman, Gottlieb, Agard, & Kukic, 1975; Keogh & Levitt, 1976; Meyen & Lehr, 1980). The definition of mainstreaming adopted in this book is: Mainstreaming is the social and instructional integration of handicapped students in a regular education class for at least a portion of the school day. For a handicapped student to be mainstreamed, this definition requires that two criteria be met: (1) physical inclusion in a regular class (for an unspecified portion of the day), and (2) functional inclusion as evidenced by social and instructional integration with nonhandicapped students (Turnbull, 1982). In light of this definition and the previous statements on what mainstreaming is not, this section focuses on what mainstreaming is.

Mainstreaming Is the Creation of Alternatives

Mainstreaming is the creation of new and different alternatives for handicapped students rather than the elimination of alternatives. Thus, mainstreaming requires the availability of alternatives, the exploration of different strategies, and the flexibility of new ideas.

Awareness of the available alternatives is the first step in determining appropriate placement for each handicapped student. Although there is room for creativity and local strategy in seeking alternatives, the following settings are used in many systems:

1. regular class with no supplementary services,
2. regular class with direct or indirect services,
3. resource room,
4. self-contained special class,

5. special school,
6. hospital-home instruction, and
7. residential school.

These alternatives are illustrated in Figure 2-1.

Regular Class with No Supplementary Services. For some handicapped students, the regular class, with no modifications, is an appropriate learning environment. The nature and degree of the student's handicap and the coping skills demonstrated by the student are factors determining the appropriateness of such a placement.

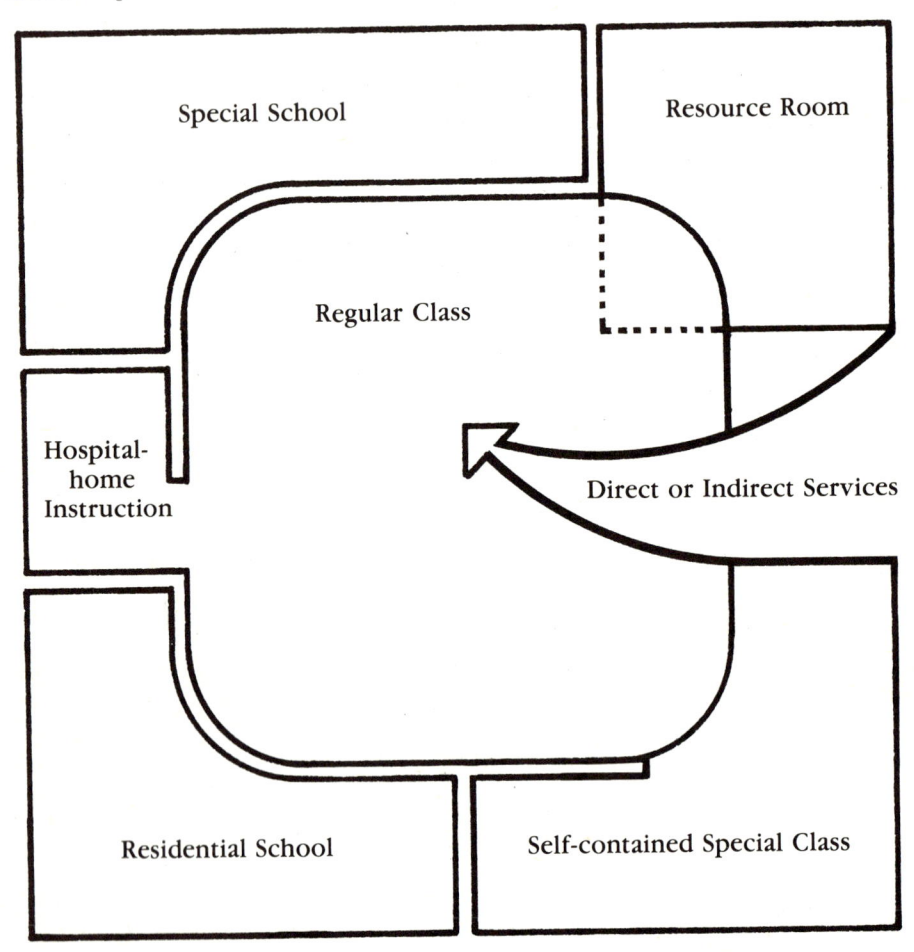

FIGURE 2–1. Placement Alternatives

Regular Class with Direct or Indirect Services. Supplementary services can be added to the regular classroom to enable handicapped students to be instructionally and socially integrated. Among the alternatives are consulting teachers, methods and materials specialists, and itinerant teachers. Supplementary services within the regular classroom can be categorized as direct or indirect.

Direct services can be provided to handicapped students. As an example, the school psychologist may work with students who have behavior problems. With this direct help, students may learn to manage their behavior and to relate to other students within the regular setting. Blind students may receive instruction in braille from a vision specialist within regular classrooms.

Another approach to these problems can be developed through indirect services. To help teachers with students exhibiting behavior problems, psychologists might work with teachers in developing classroom strategies for individual students or the group as a whole. Services for blind students could be provided through the State Commission for the Blind, such as furnishing a tape recorder, a typewriter, tapes, and brailled material. In both cases, handicapped students can remain in the regular classroom on a full-time basis.

Resource Room. Some mildly handicapped students can function well with or without supplementary services in the classroom; others, however, need more support, more specialized services, and individual or small-group instruction. The resource room is designed to fill this need. Handicapped students can receive instruction in resource rooms, which are staffed by a special educator. Time spent in the resource room is determined by the needs of the students. Cooperation between resource teachers and classroom teachers is essential to the success of this model. Scheduling should not penalize students by absenting them from their classrooms during important learning experiences or pleasurable activities.

Self-Contained Special Class. During the early stages of mainstreaming, some people believed that special classes would be abolished. Although many students have been moved from self-contained special classes back to the regular classroom, there are others for whom this is still an appropriate setting. Students who are more severely handicapped or who have unusual curriculum needs may be served better in a special classroom. Special classes have fewer students than regular classes; thus, it is usually possible to provide intensive instruction in these settings.

Another use for the self-contained special class is on a transitional basis. Some students with behavior problems may be so distracting and distractible that they cannot be served in a regular classroom or resource room. After a period of intense training in a structured setting, it may be possible for them to return to regular classrooms on a part- or full-time basis. Blind students may need a specialized setting to acquire mobility and other skills before progressing into the mainstream of regular classes.

Special School. In the continuum of services, there may still be a need for special schools. Facilities may be available at special schools that offer greater opportunities for some students. A school for children who are severely mentally retarded may offer vocational, physical education, or home living programs appropriate to their needs. The trend, however, is toward providing these services in schools attended by nonhandicapped students.

Hospital-Home Instruction. Some handicapped students are absent from school for extended periods of time because of health impairments or medical interventions. In these instances (discussed in chapter 1), a teacher hired by the school system provides special education to the student in the hospital or home setting. This instruction is coordinated with the teacher who typically provides instruction to the student at the school setting.

Residential School. The residential school represents the most restrictive environment in the continuum of services. Even though there has been a concerted national effort toward deinstitutionalization, children and adults still need residential services. Such services may include medical care as well as educational and vocational programming. Two factors usually lead to the choice of a residential placement. The handicapped person may have severe or multiple handicaps or there may not be a suitable living situation available with the individual's family.

Many educators erroneously believe that the state and federal law pertaining to handicapped students requires that all handicapped students be placed in regular classes. Rather than a legal requirement, there is a legal preference for mainstreaming when it is appropriate to the needs of a handicapped student. The legal interpretation of mainstreaming will be highlighted later in this chapter in the discussion of the least restrictive placement principle of P.L. 94–142. The legal preference for mainstreaming is evidenced by the fact that the majority of handicapped students are educated in regular rather than specialized settings (U.S. Department of Education, 1980).

Mainstreaming Is a Systematic Process

To be successful, mainstreaming must be an ordered, systematic, and step-by-step process of moving older handicapped students, formerly segregated in special classes, and first-grade students just entering the school system into regular programs. In many schools, mainstreaming has resulted in some unfortunate situations when handicapped students have been inappropriately integrated into regular programs. The effective implementation of mainstreaming involves accomplishing many tasks, such as the development of a systematic plan, inservice training, acquisition of resources, coordination of services and support personnel, and the development of evaluation procedures (Paul, Turnbull, & Cruikshank, 1977).

Mainstreaming Is the Social and Instructional Integration of Students

Mainstreaming is the social and instructional integration of handicapped students in regular classes; it is not just their physical presence. Social integration involves peer relationships, an opportunity to gain status and acceptance, and feeling comfortable and secure as a member of the classroom group with the corresponding rights and responsibilities of membership. Respect for the strengths and weaknesses of all students is a key aspect of social integration. This concept will be developed in greater detail in chapter 11.

Instructional integration is the involvement of handicapped students in the curriculum of the classroom. Schubert and Glick (1981) identified the following placement criteria as being important, based on observations of successful mainstreamed classes and interviews with teachers and administrators:

- The student was capable of doing work at his grade level to some extent.
- The student was capable of doing work in the regular classroom without much assistance, special materials, or adaptive equipment having to be provided by the regular classroom teacher.
- The student was capable of staying on task in the regular classroom without as much teacher feedback and attention as was available to him/her in the special education setting.
- The student could fit into the routine of the regular classroom.
- The student was capable of functioning socially in the regular classroom, and could profit from the modeling of appropriate behaviors by his/her peers.
- The physical setting of the classroom did not interfere with the student's functioning or could be adapted to his/her needs.
- Scheduling could be worked out between the various classes in which the student was to participate. Schedules could often be altered informally to fit temporary needs or problems, and then readjusted once the need or problem had been met. (p. 12)

The goal of mainstreaming should not be confined solely to a "now" orientation; rather, establishing the appropriate levels of social and instructional integration should be viewed as a means of preparing handicapped students for adult competence and survival in the mainstream of society (Meyen & Lehr, 1980; Zigler & Muenchow, 1979).

Mainstreaming Is a Strategy to Advance Learning—Not to Penalize Nonhandicapped Students

The proper environment for mainstreaming is a classroom that is appropriate to the needs of handicapped students. If classrooms are appropriate and teachers are knowledgeable in a variety of techniques to individualize instruction, there is no basis for concern that the presence of handicapped students will interfere with the progress of nonhandicapped students. If teachers feel that there is interference, they should examine the specific mainstreaming problems and devise a plan to eliminate them. Concerns often center around the amount of individual time required, behavior problems, or lack of appropriate instructional materials. These concerns typically are related to the teacher's need for increased information and skill and the need for wider availability of special education support services. Before a handicapped student is allowed to become the scapegoat for the lack of progress of nonhandicapped peers, the teacher is responsible for trying a variety of techniques and approaches. Creative and persistent teachers are usually successful in eliminating the possibility of peer interference.

When various approaches have been tried and a handicapped student still is unable to be socially and instructionally integrated into a classroom without disrupting the atmosphere and requiring an inordinate amount of time, the appropriateness of the placement should be carefully examined by the committee who developed the student's individualized education program (IEP). A comment included in the federal regulations for educating handicapped students specifically addresses this issue of the impact of mainstreaming on classroom peers:

> . . . it should be stressed that, where a handicapped child is so disruptive in a regular classroom that education of other students is significantly impaired, the needs of the handicapped child cannot be met in the environment. Therefore regular placement would not be appropriate to his or her needs. . . . (*Federal Register,* 1977, p. 42497)

Mainstreaming Is a Shared Responsibility

Mainstreaming requires shared responsibility among all educators in a school.

Larry, a hearing-impaired student in the second grade, typically spends 75 to 80 percent of the school day in the regular class, with his teacher assuming primary responsibility. In addition, he works with the resource teacher on basic academics thirty minutes per day and with the speech therapist on language development for forty-five minutes three days a week. The music teacher at his elementary school has responsibility for the class for thirty minutes every Friday. Occasionally a volunteer from the PTA helps out in the classroom and is particularly interested in spending time with Larry. Larry's parents are eager to be involved in his educational program and to follow up on his language development activities at home. Involvement with Larry is definitely a shared responsibility: the regular teacher, resource teacher, speech therapist, music teacher, PTA volunteer, and his parents all have a direct role to play and responsibilities to assume to insure the success of his mainstreaming.

A word of caution: uncoordinated shared responsibility is self-defeating. If all these persons have different goals with no knowledge of what others are doing, progress will be minimal and Larry will be very confused trying to make sense out of all that is happening to him. Perhaps having all these different resource persons available to work with a student is possible in some systems and totally unrealistic in others. Later in this chapter, we will return to the concept of shared responsibility and suggest a host of resource persons, agencies, and organizations that might have either direct or indirect roles to play in the implementation of mainstreaming.

Mainstreaming Is an Opportunity to Learn New Skills

Mainstreaming does require skills and knowledge different from what many teachers previously acquired in either preservice or inservice training. Many special education teachers primarily emphasize one type of handicapping condition in their training program. They might be extremely competent in the area of learning disabilities but totally at a loss in assessing and planning an instructional program for a blind student. Additionally, many special education teachers work with approximately fifteen students in a self-contained class (sometimes with the help of a teacher aide) of possibly twenty to thirty students throughout the school week in a resource program. This type of student-teacher ratio is an advantage in individualizing instruction. Many special education teachers, for example, have not had to face the complex task of middle school and secondary teachers who teach 120 to 150 students per day for five or six periods of roughly fifty minutes each.

Just as special education teachers recognize the need to expand their skills, classroom teachers find themselves in a similar situation. In pinpointing the particular concerns of teachers in inservice training sessions, it has been found consistently that classroom teachers generally ask for more information on assessing a student's level of achievement, strategies for individualizing instruction, appropriate instructional materials for various student characteristics, and ways to manage behavior problems. Colleges and universities are challenged to prepare *all* education majors for successful mainstreaming practices (Grosenick & Reynolds, 1978). A corollary to the college and university responsibility is the need for school systems to develop inservice training programs for all school personnel. It is not just the teachers who need this information; it is also principals, school psychologists, counselors, special therapists, school-based consultants, and central administrators.

BACKGROUND OF MAINSTREAMING

Reynolds and Birch (1977) describe the history of the education of handicapped students that has preceded their placement in regular classes as characterized by "progressive inclusion." This concept is illustrated by the rough historical breakdown in Table 2–1. A clear trend from more to less restrictive settings is evidenced by Table 2–1. There were some very specific reasons for questioning the value of special class placement for the majority of handicapped students during the seventies. These reasons are outlined briefly.

Efficacy of Special Classes

During the late 1960s and early 1970s, research studies were conducted to assess the academic progress and social adjustment of handicapped students placed in special classes as contrasted to handicapped students who remained in regular classes. Most of the efficacy studies were conducted on mentally retarded students rather than on a broad sampling of children with various types of handicaps. Regarding academic progress, it was found that the achievement of retarded students in special classes was very similar to that of retarded students in regular classes (Bradfield, Brown, Kaplan, Rickert, & Stannard, 1973; Budoff & Gottlieb, 1976). Some studies, however, did indicate slightly higher gains in reading for students attending the regular class program (Carroll, 1967). Research on social adjustment resulted in mixed findings (Budoff & Gottlieb, 1976; Goodman, Gottlieb, & Harrison, 1972; Iano, Ayers, Heller, McGettigan, & Walker, 1974). The trends apparent in the research findings have shown that retarded students generally have low social status whether they are placed in special or regular classes (Corman & Gottlieb, 1979).

Thus, the efficacy studies were interpreted as failing to document specific beneficial outcomes for retarded students in special class placements. During the mid-1970s, these studies added momentum to the parental and court actions (to be discussed subsequently) that placed pressure on the public school systems to curtail the separation of handicapped and nonhandicapped students.

It is paradoxical that after the establishment of legal requirements pertaining to mainstreaming, the efficacy studies have been severely criticized in

TABLE 2-1. Approximate History of Progressive Inclusion of Handicapped Students in Regular Classes

GENERAL TIME FRAME	PREDOMINANT EDUCATION SERVICE
1. Ancient times	No education. Handicapped individuals were generally neglected and abused.
2. 1850–1900	Development of residential schools for the purpose of providing education and training.
3. 1900–1950	Special schools and special classes became more prevalent; residential schools continued to grow and expand.
4. 1950–1970	Special classes became the preferred type of educational service for students with mental retardation, emotional disturbance, and learning disabilities. Residential institutions and special schools flourished for blind, deaf, and physically handicapped students.
5. 1970–1977	Movement toward placement in regular classes of handicapped students who were able to be socially and instructionally integrated (mainstreaming). Development of special classes in public schools for some moderately and severely handicapped students formerly placed in residential institutions and special schools.
6. 1977–present	Major national effort directed to implementing federal and state legislation in providing a free appropriate public education to handicapped students in the least restrictive environment (including mainstreaming a substantial number of handicapped students in regular class settings).

a number of reviews because of methodological problems (Corman & Gottlieb, 1979; Jones, Gottlieb, Guskin, & Yoshida, 1978; MacMillan, Jones, & Aloia, 1974; Meyers, MacMillan, & Yoshida, 1980). The efficacy studies, however, were interpreted in the 1970s as providing empirical justification of mainstreaming.

Minority Imbalance

One of the first major criticisms of special classes regarding minority imbalance was made by Dunn (1968), who pointed out that 60 to 80 percent of the students in special classes are from "low status backgrounds," including Mexican American, Puerto Rican American, black, and poverty-level homes. Such imbalance has largely been attributed to the use of standardized intelligence tests, which have resulted in a disproportionately large number of students from minority backgrounds being labeled as intellectually subnormal and a strikingly small number of these students being considered gifted (Mercer, 1973). Since most intelligence tests generally reflect the culture and language patterns of middle-class Anglo-Americans and are mostly standardized on this population, persons from other socioeconomic groups or backgrounds are automatically put at a disadvantage for performing successfully on these tests.

> *On a frequently used IQ test, one of the general information questions is: "What does the stomach do"? When the psychologist asked this question to Walter, his response was "it growls." Walter was from a low socioeconomic background. He routinely did not have food at home for breakfast and often his only meal was his free lunch a school. Based on Walter's life experience, his response was accurate; although the item was scored as "failed."*

Racial desegregation contributed to focusing attention on special classes predominantly composed of students from minority backgrounds. In carrying out the decision of the Supreme Court in *Brown* v. *Board of Education* (1954), the Office of Civil Rights in the federal government has required some school systems to eliminate special classes that were interpreted to be vehicles for de facto segregation.

Parental and Judicial Action

On the basis of a combination of the foregoing reasons questioning the value and effects of special class placements, many parents of handicapped students began to seek help through the judicial system for what they considered to be educational inequities. They were joined by groups of parents whose handicapped children had been completely denied any type of appropriate free public education. These parents had essentially been told that the schools offered no programs for their children. The National Association for Retarded Citizens, a parent organization, initiated strong advocacy efforts based on the philosophical premise of equal educational opportunities for handicapped students. The first legal suits against schools for failing to provide appropriate educational programs for handicapped students were brought by parent organizations and based on this philosophy.

The precedent for many of the court cases involving educational discrimination of handicapped students was the landmark case of *Brown* v. *Board of Education* (1954). It was argued that special education was a separate and unequal system of education. The court cases resulted in rulings that all handicapped children have a right to an education (*Mills* v. *D.C. Board of Education,* 1972; *Pennsylvania Association for Retarded Children* v. *Commonwealth of Pennsylvania,* 1971, 1972), that students may not be inappropriately evaluated with tests reflecting cultural bias and subsequently placed in special classes based on the results (*Hobson* v. *Hansen,* 1967; *Diana* v. *State Board of Edu-*

cation, 1970, 1973), and that tracking is discriminatory (*Hobson* v. *Hansen,* 1967).

The judicial decisions in these special education cases provided a strong impetus to mainstreaming. The decision of *Pennsylvania Association for Retarded Children* v. *Commonwealth of Pennsylvania* (1971; 1972), the first right-to-education case, provides an example of this impetus.

> It is the Commonwealth's obligation to place each mentally retarded child in a free, public program of education and training appropriate to the child's capacity, within the context of the general educational policy that, among the alternative programs of education and training required by statute to be available, placement in a regular public school class is preferable to placement in a special public school class and placement in a special public school class is preferable to placement in any other type of program of education and training. (334 F. Supp. 1257, 1260, E.D. Pa. 1971)

Court cases involving the right-to-education were brought in almost every state with very similar results. The social context of the 1970s in which these court cases were embedded is important to consider in understanding the widespread judicial preference for mainstreaming. The push to establish rights for handicapped persons was highly consistent with the public sensitivity to establish rights for other groups, such as racial minorities and women who had previously been the targets of discrimination. Thus, it can be concluded that the *primary* judicial rationale for mainstreaming was based on sociopolitical factors rather than scientific-pedagogical ones (Miller & Switzky, 1979; Turnbull, 1982).

The judicial decisions resulted in every state's except New Mexico adopting legislation regarding the education of handicapped students. Readers are encouraged to get a copy of their state legislation on the education of handicapped students from their State Department of Public Instruction, the attorney general's office, or the legislative library. A further result of parental and judicial action was the passage of federal legislation in November 1975, referred to as Public Law 94–142, the Education for All Handicapped Children Act. This legislation sets forth regulations and requires actions by teachers and school systems. These actions can be interpreted as legislative remedies to some of the past failures of schools in providing appropriate education to handicapped students. P.L. 94–142 has a striking correspondence to the legislation of most states regarding the education of handicapped students in terms of legal and educational principles. A summary of the major principles and requirements follows (*Federal Register,* 1977).

LEGISLATIVE PRINCIPLES AND REQUIREMENTS

The provision of a *free appropriate public education* is the central consideration of P.L. 94–142. Six major principles of P.L. 94–142 define the parameters of what is meant by this key phrase—free appropriate public education. These six principles include zero reject, nondiscriminatory evaluation, individualized education, least restrictive environment, due process, and parental participation. These principles will be discussed individually, along with an overview of specific requirements associated with each.

Zero Reject

The principle of zero reject requires public school systems to serve *all* handicapped students, regardless of the type of handicap they have or the level of its severity. In terms of age, handicapped students between the ages of three and twenty-one must be provided with a free appropriate public education. The only exception to this requirement is for the age ranges of three to five and eighteen to twenty-one; states that do not provide educational services to nonhandicapped students in these age ranges are exempt from being required to provide such services to handicapped students.

The zero reject principle prevents both total and functional exclusion of handicapped students. Total exclusion refers to cases in which handicapped students were denied the opportunity of attending school at all in the past. Functional exclusion occurs when handicapped students are allowed to attend school but are provided with inappropriate programs that are not responsive to their special needs. In order to prevent the occurrence of functional exclusion (and thus to insure that handicapped students receive an appropriate education), P.L. 94–142 requires that special education and related services be provided to them. Special education is defined as:

> . . . specially designed instruction, at no cost to the parent, to meet the unique needs of a handicapped child, including classroom instruction, instruction in physical education, home instruction, and instruction in hospitals and institutions. (*Federal Register,* 1977, p. 42480)

In addition to special education, public school systems are also required to provide handicapped students with all related services that they need to enable them to benefit from special education. Related services are defined as:

> . . . transportation and such developmental, corrective and other supportive services as are required to assist a handicapped child to benefit from special education, and includes speech pathology and audiology, psychological services, physical and occupational therapy, recreation, early identification and assessment of disabilities in children, counseling services, and medical service for diagnostic or evaluation purposes. The term also includes school health services, social work services in schools, and parent counseling and training. (*Federal Register,* 1977, p. 42473)

Legislative Principles and Requirements

The legal definition of these services is included in Table 2–2.

It is important for classroom teachers to know that handicapped students in their classes are entitled to special education and related services designed to meet their individual needs. When handicapped students are entitled to such services, it implies that classroom teachers are assured of assistance from special education teachers and related services providers (e.g., speech therapist, school

TABLE 2-2. Related Services in Special Education

Audiology	(a) Identification of children with hearing loss;
	(b) Determination of the range, nature, degree of hearing loss, including referral for medical or other professional attention for the habilitation of hearing;
	(c) Provision of habilitative activities, such as language habilitation, auditory training, speech reading (lip reading), hearing evaluation, and speech conservation;
	(d) Creation and administration of programs for prevention of hearing loss;
	(e) Counseling and guidance of pupils, parents, and teachers regarding hearing loss; and
	(f) Determination of the child's need for group and individual amplification, selecting and fitting an appropriate aid, and evaluating the effectiveness of amplification.
Counseling Services	Services provided by qualified social workers, psychologists, guidance counselors, or other qualified personnel.
Early Identification	Implementation of a formal plan for identifying a disability as early as possible in a child's life.
Medical Services	Services provided by a licensed physician to determine a child's medically related handicapping condition which results in the child's need for special education and related services.
Occupational Therapy	(a) Improving, developing, or restoring functions impaired or lost through illness, injury, or deprivation;
	(b) Improving ability to perform tasks for independent functioning when functions are impaired or lost; and
	(c) Preventing, through early intervention, initial or further impairment of loss of function.
Parent Counseling and Training	Assisting parents in understanding the special needs of their child and providing parents with information about child development.
Physical Therapy	Services provided by a qualified physical therapist.

TABLE 2-2. (Continued)

Psychological Services	(a) Administering psychological and educational tests, and other assessment procedures; (b) Interpreting assessment results; (c) Obtaining, integrating, and interpreting information about child behavior and conditions related to learning. (d) Consulting with other staff members in planning school programs to meet the special needs of children as indicated by psychological tests, interviews, and behavioral evaluations; and (e) Planning and managing a program of psychological services, including psychological counseling for children and parents.
Recreation	(a) Assessment of leisure function; (b) Therapeutic recreation services; (c) Recreation programs in schools and community agencies; and (d) Leisure education.
School Health Services	Services provided by a qualified school nurse or other qualified person.
Social Work Services	(a) Preparing a social or developmental history on a handicapped child; (b) Group and individual counseling with the child and family; (c) Working with those problems in a child's living situation (home, school and community) that affect the child's adjustment in school; and (d) Mobilizing school and community resources to enable the child to receive maximum benefit from his or her educational program.
Speech Pathology	(a) Identification of children with speech or language disorders; (b) Diagnosis and appraisal of specific speech or language disorders; (c) Referral for medical or other professional attention necessary for the habilitation of speech or language disorders; (d) Provisions of speech and language services for the habilitation or prevention of communicative disorders; and (e) Counseling and guidance of parents, children, and teachers regarding speech and language disorders.
Transportation	(a) Travel to and from school and between schools; (b) Travel in and around school buildings; and (c) Specialized equipment (such as special or adapted buses, lifts, and ramps), if required to provide special transportation for a handicapped child.

Source: From *Federal Register.* August 23, 1977, pp. 42479–42480.

counselor) in designing and delivering an appropriate educational program to handicapped students.

Another assurance to teachers to prepare them to provide appropriate educational programs to handicapped students is the availability of inservice training. P.L. 94–142 requires the state education agency to develop and implement *innovative* inservice training programs to insure that teachers are qualified to carry out their responsibilities. Furthermore, incentives for teachers (e.g., released time, payment for participation, options for academic credit, salary step credit, and certification renewal) must be incorporated into the inservice programs according to the legislative requirements.

Nondiscriminatory Evaluation

Federal and state legislative guidelines specify the manner in which evaluations are administered to handicapped students. The following legal definition of evaluation is important to consider.

> . . . procedures used . . . to determine whether a child is handicapped and the nature and extent of the special education and related services that the child needs. The term means procedures used selectively with an individual child and does not include basic tests administered to or procedures used with all children in a school, grade, or class. (*Federal Register,* 1977, p. 42494)

Evaluation is thus used to classify students as handicapped and to plan appropriate educational programs for them.

The timeline for evaluations is an important consideration. An evaluation must be conducted before placing or denying placement of a handicapped student in a special education program or transferring or denying transfer to a student in a special education class to a regular class setting. After students have been initially evaluated and classified as handicapped, they must be reevaluated every three years or more frequently if requests are made by the students' teachers or parents.

Most of the requirements pertaining to the principle of nondiscriminatory evaluation are aimed at assuring fairness in testing procedures, particularly in consideration of racial and cultural factors. Examples of evaluation requirements include:

1. testing specific areas of educational need rather than focusing only on general intelligence;
2. making the decision for educational placement on the basis of giving a minimum of two tests or types of tests;
3. considering information concerning physical development, sociocultural background, and adaptive behavior in conjunction with test scores; and

4. setting up a *team* of persons in the school who possess knowledge about the student being evaluated and the placement alternatives.

In most school systems, responsibility for developing procedures adhering to these legislative requirements regarding evaluation is assigned to one of the central administrators in charge of special education, special services, school psychology, or another related area. Classroom teachers are encouraged to ask for a copy of the system's written policies on evaluation, if this information is not routinely provided. One right of classroom teachers in this area is to have their questions concerning the handicapped students for whom they are responsible considered by the evaluation committee and answered to their satisfaction. Teachers responsible for instructing handicapped students are entitled to complete information on the curriculum implications of these evaluation results, appropriate resource materials, and behavior management programs. Strategies for teachers to use in working with the multidisciplinary evaluation committee are included in chapter 3.

Individualized Education

To assure that educational programs are appropriate to the individual needs of handicapped students, P.L. 94–142 and state legislation require the development of individualized education programs, or IEPs. The IEP requirements can be subdivided into two parts: the IEP document and the IEP meeting.

The components of the IEP document are specified by law (*Federal Register,* 1977):

1. a documentation of the student's current level of educational performance,
2. annual goals or the attainments expected by the end of the school year,
3. short-term objectives, stated in instructional terms, which are the intermediate steps leading to the mastery of annual goals,
4. documentation of the particular special education and related services that will be provided to the student,
5. an indication of the extent of time a student will participate in the regular education program,
6. projected dates for initiating services and the anticipated duration of services, and
7. appropriate objective criteria, evaluation procedures, and schedules for determining mastery of short-term objectives, at least on an annual basis.

The IEP document must be developed for every handicapped student receiving special education. All curriculum areas that must be specially designed to meet the particular needs of the handicapped student should be included on the IEP. In regard to timelines, IEPs must "be in effect" for each handicapped student receiving special education at the beginning of the school year. "Be in effect" is typically interpreted to mean the IEP is less than one calendar year old.

The second aspect of IEP regulations is the meeting held for the purpose of developing the IEP document. The following individuals are required participants at the IEP meeting (*Federal Register,* 1977):

1. a representative of the school system, other than the student's teacher, who has qualifications to provide or supervise special education,
2. the student's teacher,
3. one or both of the student's parents,
4. the student when appropriate,
5. other individuals at the request of the parents or school representatives, and
6. for handicapped students evaluated for the first time, either a member of the evaluation team or another individual (representative of the school system, the student's teacher) who is knowledgeable about the evaluation procedures used with the student and the results of the evaluation.

Parent participation in decision making is an extremely important aspect of the IEP meeting; thus, the legislation requires that parents be notified of the purpose, time, location, and other participants of the meeting. Meetings may be held without parent participation only when school personnel have documentation of their unsuccessful attempts to encourage parents to attend.

Because the IEP document and meeting are so central to the development of an appropriate education for handicapped students, chapter 3 outlines the requirements in more detail and suggests strategies to implement them.

Least Restrictive Environment

The law requires that state and local education agencies set up policies to assure that handicapped students are educated to the maximum extent appropriate in programs with nonhandicapped students and that they be placed in special classes or special schools only when the handicap is so severe that education cannot be satisfactorily accomplished in the regular education program with the use of supplementary aids and services. It is important to recognize that restrictiveness is a relative issue based on the special needs of each student. For some moderately and severely handicapped students, the regular classroom is a highly restrictive environment. Thus, the most normal environment is not always the least restrictive. Two factors must be considered in determining the least restrictive environment for a handicapped student. The first involves identifying the range of placements (e.g., regular class, resource room, special class) in which the student's instructional and social needs could be appropriately met. The second factor is the identification of the particular placement from the range of those identified that provides the handicapped student with the greatest opportunity to interact meaningfully and successfully with persons who are nonhandicapped (Turnbull, 1982).

As discussed earlier in the chapter, school systems are required to include a range of educational alternatives, including instruction in regular classes, resource rooms, special classes, special schools, hospitals and homes, and institutions. In regard to implementing the least restrictive requirement, schools should review the placement of handicapped students at least annually. The placement decision should be based on student IEPs. Unless the IEPs require some other arrangement, handicapped students should be educated in the same school they would attend if they were not handicapped. Further, handicapped students should be integrated into nonacademic and extracurricular activities with nonhandicapped students to the maximum extent appropriate.

Due Process

The principle of due process entitles both parents and professionals to *fair* procedures in the identification, evaluation, and placement of handicapped students. The specific due process requirements comprise a system of checks and balances regarding decisions made by parents and professionals concerning the education of handicapped students.

Prior written notice must be provided to parents of handicapped students whenever a change is proposed or refused regarding the identification, evaluation, or placement of handicapped students. Additionally, prior parental consent is necessary when a student is *initially* evaluated for special education placement with psychological or educational tests that are over and above those routinely given to nonhandicapped students.

A due process hearing may be initiated by parents or school personnel when conflicting points of view exist on the identification, evaluation, or placement of a handicapped student. Examples of such conflicts are whether the student is, indeed, handicapped or whether the student should be placed in a regular or special class. When conflicts cannot be resolved in the IEP meeting and all other attempts to reach a satisfactory resolution are unsuccessful, the school system is responsible for appointing an impartial hearing officer and conducting a due process hearing. At the hearing, both parties have the right to be represented by counsel or by persons having expertise in the area of handicapping conditions and to present evidence and cross-examine witnesses. They are entitled to a written record after the hearing. Either the parents or the school system may appeal the hearing decision from the local school system to the state education agency, and beyond to the appropriate state or federal court. While the proceedings of the hearing are pending, the handicapped student should remain in the current educational placement.

Only a relatively small number of cases involving handicapped students actually progress to the stage of a due process hearing. Thus, the vast majority of teachers will never be involved in such a hearing. It is important, however, for teachers who are involved in due process hearings to be prepared for this role. More detailed information on the hearing and the teacher's role in it can be found in Turnbull and Strickland (1981).

Parental Participation

The last legislative principle is parental participation. Although the five preceding principles are all directly or indirectly linked with parental participation, this principle is considered separately since some parental rights cannot be classified in the other five categories. These rights include the involvement of parents in the development of educational policy and parental access to records.

Parents of handicapped students have the opportunity to participate in the development of educational policy by attending required public hearings on the state's special education plan and serving on local and state advisory panels. Thus, parents can influence program priorities, budgets, and other organizational factors.

Access to educational records is an extremely important parental right. Parents have the right to review *all* educational records maintained on their handicapped child. (The only exception to this right is under state law requirements pertaining to situations involving guardianship, separation, and divorce.) Parents may also request that the contents of their child's records be explained and justified, and they may request that the contents be changed if they believe recorded information is inaccurate or represents an invasion of privacy. Furthermore, no personally identifiable information on a handicapped student may be released to anyone who is not involved with developing or implementing the student's educational program without obtaining the written consent of parents. Thus, parents have the right to control the flow of information on their handicapped child to persons who are not directly involved in the education of their child. Parental decisions, however, can be questioned by school personnel through the proceedings of a due process hearing.

In summary, federal and state legislative requirements have tremendous implications for all teachers. Knowledge of these requirements can help teachers provide appropriate educational programs and insure their own professional behavior in teaching handicapped students. Readers who would like more detailed information on legislative requirements and their educational implementation are referred to Martin (1978); Turnbull and Turnbull (1978); Turnbull, Strickland, and Brantley (1982); and Weintraub, Abeson, Ballard, and Lavor (1976).

SHARED RESPONSIBILITY

The implementation of mainstreaming requires a team approach. In many school systems, classroom teachers have been expected to have all the skills and time to accomplish the successful mainstreaming of students representing the full range of educational handicaps—in most cases an impossible expectation. A sound approach to mainstreaming requires shared responsibility on the part of all educators in the school.

Classroom Teachers

Classroom teachers will undoubtedly be called on to assume major responsibility in the mainstreaming process. As they teach handicapped students for a portion of the school day or in some cases for the entire day, they will coordinate the students' instructional and social integration, which is the essence of mainstreaming. It is very important for these teachers to know where help is available. The following sections briefly outline responsibilities that might generally be shared with other team members. These suggestions are offered as a general guide and must be adapted to the particular staffing pattern of each school.

Special Educators

Resource Teachers. Many handicapped students in regular classes receive individual or small-group instruction from a special education resource teacher. Handicapped students may leave the regular class to receive instruction in the resource room for a specified period of time each day or each week, or the resource teacher may come into the regular class and instruct handicapped students in the everyday setting. To insure maximum educational progress, resource and regular teachers need to coordinate their programs carefully and maintain close communication relative to student performance. Classroom teachers can expect resource teachers to give them suggestions or instructional techniques and curriculum adaptations that are appropriate for students when they are in the regular class.

Itinerant Teachers. Itinerant teachers usually function like resource teachers. They are considered itinerant as they travel from one school to another to work with individual students. This model is usually followed in sparsely populated areas or in schools that have too few handicapped students to justify a full-time resource teacher. Also, many therapists (e.g., speech, occupational, and physical) are employed on an itinerant basis.

Self-Contained Class Teachers. Special class teachers are responsible for working with handicapped students in the self-contained class setting and also for integrating these students into school activities and curriculum blocks as appropriate. Although self-contained class teachers usually do not have the consultative duties of the resource or itinerant teacher, they do share instructional suggestions and materials readily with classroom teachers in many situations.

Special Education Consultants. Larger school systems often employ a special education consultant whose job might be to provide inservice training to classroom teachers and to offer backup support to classroom and resource teachers. Consultants usually have advanced training and are knowledgeable about a variety of instructional strategies. Systems that do not directly employ a consultant are likely to have consultative services available from the Division of Exceptional Children in the State Department of Public Instruction (agency titles vary from state to state) or from a regional educational service agency.

Director of Special Education. School systems typically have either a part-time or full-time director or coordinator of special education. This person is responsible for knowing the legal requirements and for administering, and often supervising, special education services. Classroom teachers who have specific questions about obtaining needed services, resources, or evaluations of handicapped students should consider working through their principal to contact the director of special education.

Principals. Principals have been identified as one of the keys to mainstreaming success (Payne & Murray, 1974). They might be called on to arrange inservice training, consider hiring additional personnel, instigate a volunteer program to help with individualization, locate appropriate instructional resources, and/or work toward the reduction of the student-teacher ratio. Teachers should share their concerns about mainstreaming constructively with principals so that principals can respond most effectively to teachers' needs.

Counselors

Counselors have various roles to play in the implementation of mainstreaming. They often serve as chairpersons of evaluation teams and IEP committees. They might help teachers with problems of social adjustment or coordinate activities associated with parent involvement. Specific responsibilities vary from school to school, but the important thing for teachers to remember is that counselors share in the responsibility for mainstreaming.

School Psychologists

Many schools employ part-time or full-time psychologists. Frequently psychologists, like itinerant teachers, are responsible for serving more than one school. Psychologists typically assume major responsibility in evaluation and placement decisions, in addition to participating in the development of the IEP. Other mainstreaming involvement could be working with teachers on behavior management programs and on ways to individualize instruction effectively.

Librarians

Librarians can be of great assistance in curriculum adaptation, particularly in helping to identify textbooks and a large variety of supplementary materials appropriate to student achievement levels and interests. Many handicapped students who read significantly below grade level need books of a high interest/low vocabulary nature. Librarians are qualified to identify such materials and to make them available to students and teachers.

Therapists

Mainstreaming requires the expertise of many specialists, such as those in speech, physical development, occupational development, dramatics, art, and music. Many schools do not employ therapists in these areas on a full-time basis; however, they may contract for services with mental health clinics, hospitals, special schools, colleges and universities, and state department consultants. When it is documented in IEP conferences that the needs of handicapped students require the expertise of therapists, such help must be made available by the school system. Therapy sessions should be coordinated with the students' academic schedules. Therapists can also train teachers in special techniques that teachers can provide routinely in the regular class.

Paraprofessionals

Paraprofessionals or teacher aides can contribute significantly to the quality and quantity of individualized instruction. Even if their help is available for only a portion of the school day or week, every bit of "extra-hands" time can be helpful. When working with a handicapped student, paraprofessionals should be thoroughly aware of the IEP and the other educational placements in which the student is included (resource program). Suggestions for preparing paraprofessionals to work with handicapped students are provided by Boomer (1980) and Kahan (1981).

Students

Students, both handicapped and nonhandicapped, have a significant role to play in successful mainstreaming. Handicapped students should be involved in the development of their IEPs when appropriate, considering their age and maturity. They should be encouraged to share their perspectives on their social acceptance in the regular class. Problems can often be pinpointed and eliminated in early stages if students bring them to the attention of teachers before they reach a crisis point. Handicapped students often know how to adapt the curriculum or school environment to their needs most effectively. For example, sometimes teachers waste time by trying to second-guess the needs of a blind student. Asking the student directly about when help is needed and when it is not can assist teachers in getting on with the task of appropriate instruction. Mainstreaming should be viewed not as an arrangement to be imposed on handicapped students, but rather as a process involving reciprocal information sharing and responsibility.

Nonhandicapped students often are helpful as "peer tutors" providing instruction to their handicapped friends. This arrangement will be explained more fully in chapter 4. Nonhandicapped students can also help to make instructional materials, for example, taping textbooks or making charts explaining concepts.

Parents

Parents can be tremendous partners to teachers in mainstreaming programs. First, they have a significant responsibility as members of the team developing the IEP. As they participate in specifying priority instructional goals, they help shape the curriculum through which their children will progress. Educational decision making and accountability, therefore, become shared responsibilities with parents. Other participatory involvement of parents might include serving as classroom volunteers in their child's class or in another class in the school; sharing information on helpful hints regarding possible classroom/environmental adaptations or motivational suggestions; making instructional materials to be used at school; reviewing and reinforcing classroom concepts after school; and helping to foster their child's social adjustment.

Community Volunteers

Volunteers from the community have made beneficial contributions to mainstreaming in some school systems by serving, like parents, in the role of classroom volunteers. They might work individually or in small groups with handicapped students needing extra help or might be involved in projects or assignments with other class members in order to free teachers to spend more time with students having special problems. Some communities have organized volunteer programs for the purpose of making instructional materials needed by handicapped students or raising money to purchase equipment, such as auditory trainers for hearing-impaired students, wheelchairs, large-print typewriters, or braille readers. Civic groups and service clubs in many communities have a particular interest in the needs of handicapped persons. One of the best examples of this interest on a national basis is the Lions Club, an organization that has made a tremendous contribution to services for blind persons. Other interested target groups could include college students and retired people. For readers interested in guidelines for recruiting and training volunteers to work with handicapped students, information is provided by Adams and Taylor (1980), Buffer (1980), and Cuninggim (1980).

Professional and Consumer Organizations

Educators involved in mainstreaming should call on the resources of professional and consumer organizations. These organizations are many in number and most have information dissemination as one of their major goals. The names and addresses of some of these organizations are included in Appendix A. Readers with particular interest in a certain type of educational handicap or a focused area of mainstreaming are encouraged to write the organizations with corresponding target groups and concerns. A wealth of information is available from these sources. Additionally, many of these organizations have local and state chapters that can provide "on-site" contributions to the implementation of mainstreaming, such as providing consultants to conduct inservice training, offering specific instructional suggestions for particular handicapped students, or sharing information on appropriate instructional materials.

Team Approach

Mainstreaming requires shared responsibility involving many team members working cooperatively with classroom teachers to provide quality educational programs to handicapped students. Mainstreaming does not mean that classroom teachers must assume all the responsibility; rather, special educators, principals, counselors, school psychologists, librarians, therapists, paraprofessionals, students, parents, community volunteers, and professional/consumer organizations all have responsibilities and opportunities in planning and implementing mainstreaming for handicapped students. Paul, Turnbull, and Cruikshank (1977) provide a more detailed examination of roles and responsibilities of various team members for interested readers. Emphasis again is directed to the need to coordinate all involvement carefully in order to maximize the ultimate benefit to students. Coordination, communication, and cooperation are keys to shared responsibility and successful programming.

REFERENCES

Adams, P. K., & Taylor, M. K. Volunteer help in the classroom. *Education Unlimited,* 1980, *2*(1), 26–27.

Blacher-Dixon, J., & Turnbull, A. P. Preschool mainstreaming: Definitions, rationale and implementation, *Education Unlimited,* 1979, *1*(21), 16–22.

Boomer, L. W. Special education paraprofessionals: A guide for teachers. *Teaching Exceptional Children,* 1980, *12*(4), 146–149.

Bradfield, H. R., Brown, J., Kaplan, P., Rickert, E., & Stannard, R. The special child in the regular classroom. *Exceptional Children,* 1973, *39*, 384–390.

Brown v. *Board of Education,* 347 U.S. 483 (1954).

Budoff, M., & Gottlieb, J. Special class students mainstreamed: A study of an aptitude (learning potential) X treatment interaction. *American Journal of Mental Deficiency,* 1976, *81*, 1–11.

Buffer, L. C. Recruit retired adults as volunteers in special education. *Teaching Exceptional Children,* 1980, *12*(3), 113–115.

Carroll, A. The effects of segregated and partially integrated school programs on self concept and academic achievement of educable mental retardates. *Exceptional Children,* 1967, *34*, 93–99.

Corman, L., & Gottlieb, J. Mainstreaming mentally retarded children: A review of research. In N. R. Ellis (Ed.), *International review of research in mental retardation* (Vol. 9). New York: Academic Press, 1979.

Cuninggim, W. Citizen volunteers: A growing resource for teachers and students. *Teaching Exceptional Children,* 1980, *12*(3), 108–112.

Diana v. State Board of Education, No. C–70–37 RFP (N.D. Cal., Jan. 7, 1970 and June 18, 1973).

Dunn, L. M. Special education for the mildly retarded: Is much of it justifiable? *Exceptional Children,* 1968, *35,* 5–22.

Federal Register. Washington, D.C.: U.S. Government Printing Office, 1977.

Goodman, H., Gottlieb, J., & Harrison, R. H. Social acceptance of EMRs integrated into a non-graded elementary school. *American Journal of Mental Deficiency,* 1972, *76,* 412–417.

Grosenick, J. K., & Reynolds, M. C. (Eds.). *Teacher education: Renegotiating roles for mainstreaming.* Minneapolis, Minn.: National Support Systems Project, 1978.

Hobson v. Hansen, 269 F. Supp. 401 (1967), *aff'd sub nom. Smuck* v. *Hobson,* 408 F. 2d 175 (D.C. Cir. 1969).

Iano, R. P., Ayers, D., Heller, H. B., McGettigan, J. F., & Walker, V. S. Sociometric status of retarded children in an integrative program. *Exceptional Children,* 1974, *40,* 267–271.

Jones, R. L., Gottlieb, J., Guskin, S., & Yoshida, R. K. Evaluating mainstreaming programs: Models, caveats, considerations and guidelines. *Exceptional Children,* 1978, *44*(8), 588–601.

Kahan, E. H. Aides in special education—a boon for students and teachers. *Teaching Exceptional Children,* 1981, *14*(3), 101–105.

Kaufman, M. J., Gottlieb, J., Agard, J. A., & Kukic, M. B. Mainstreaming: Toward an explication of the construct. *Focus on Exceptional Children,* 1975, 7(3), 1–12.

Keogh, B. K., & Levitt, M. C. Special education in the mainstream: A confrontation of limitations. *Focus on Exceptional Children,* 1976, *8,* 1–11.

MacMillan, D. L., Jones, R. L., & Aloia, G. F. The mentally retarded label: A theoretical analysis and review of research. *American Journal of Mental Deficiency,* 1974, *79*(3), 241–261.

Martin, R. The teachers' rights in P.L. 94–142. *Journal of Learning Disabilities,* 1978, *11*(6), 4–14.

Mercer, J. R. *Labeling the mentally retarded: Clinical and social system perspectives on mental retardation.* Berkeley, Calif.: University of California Press, 1973.

Meyen, E. L., & Lehr, D. H. Least restrictive environments: Instructional implications. *Focus on Exceptional Children,* 1980, 12(7), 1–8.

Meyers, C. E., MacMillan, D. L., & Yoshida, R. K. Regular class education of EMR students, from efficacy to mainstreaming: A review of issues and research. In J. Gottlieb (Ed.), *Educating mentally retarded persons in the mainstream.* Baltimore, Md.: University Park Press, 1980.

Miller, T. L., & Switzky, H. N. P.L. 94–142 and the least restrictive alternative: An interim progress report for educators. *Journal of Education,* 1979, *161*(3), 60–80.

Mills v. *D.C. Board of Education,* 348 F. Supp. 866 (D.D.C. 1972).

National Association for Retarded Children. *The educators viewpoint.* New York: NARC, 1954.

Paul, J., Turnbull, A. P., & Cruikshank, W. *Mainstreaming: A practical guide,* Syracuse, N.Y.: Syracuse University Press, 1977.

Paul, J. L., & Beckman-Bell, P. Parent perspectives. In J. L. Paul (Ed.), *Understanding and working with parents of children with special needs.* New York: Holt, Rinehart and Winston, 1981.

Payne, R., & Murray, C. Principals' attitudes toward integration of the handicapped. *Exceptional Children,* 1974, *41,* 132–135.

Pennsylvania Association for Retarded Children v. *Commonwealth of Pennsylvania,* 334 F. Supp. 1257 (E.D. Pa. 1971) and 343 F. Supp. 279 (E.D. Pa. 1972).

Reynolds, M. C., & Birch, J. *Mainstreaming in all America's schools.* Reston, Va.: Council for Exceptional Children, 1977.

Schubert, M. A., & Glick, H. M. Least restrictive environment programs: Why are some so successful? *Education Unlimited,* 1981, *3*(2), 11–14.

Turnbull, A. P. Preschool mainstreaming: A policy and implementation analysis. *Educational Evaluation and Policy Analysis,* 1982, *4*(3), 281–291.

Turnbull, A. P., & Strickland, B. Parents and the educational system. In J. L. Paul (Ed.), *Understanding and working with parents of children with special needs.* New York: Holt, Rinehart and Winston, 1981.

Turnbull, A. P., Strickland, B., & Brantley, J. C. *Developing and implementing individualized education programs* (2nd ed.). Columbus, Ohio: Charles E. Merrill Publishing Co., 1982.

Turnbull, H. R., & Turnbull, A. P. *Free appropriate public education: Law and implementation.* Denver, Co: Love Publishing Co., 1978.

U.S. Department of Education. "To assure the free appropriate public education of all handicapped children." Second annual report to Congress on the implementation of Public Law 94–142: The Education for All Handicapped Children Act. Washington, D.C.: U.S. Department of Education, 1980.

Weintraub, F. J., Abeson, A., Ballard, J., & Lavor, M. L. *Public policy and the education of exceptional children.* Reston, Va.: Council for Exceptional Children, 1976.

Zigler, E., & Muenchow, S. Mainstreaming: The proof is in the implementation. *American Psychologist,* 1979, *34*(10), 993–996.

3

Developing Individualized Education Programs

The IEP document is the written plan that specifies the nature of each handicapped student's instructional program and the degree to which it is specially designed. This chapter provides an overview of the components that comprise the IEP and offers guidelines to classroom teachers for participating with educators, parents, and the handicapped student in the meeting to develop the IEP. In order to understand IEP development, however, it is important to recognize the steps in the special education planning process that must occur before the point of planning the IEP. The total sequence of the special education planning process is outlined in Figure 3–1.

The special education planning process is coordinated within each school by a committee of persons responsible for insuring that appropriate procedures are used to refer, evaluate, and provide special education programs for handicapped students. In different states this committee goes by different names, including the special services committee, school-based committee, placement team, and child study team. In this chapter, it is referred to as the special services committee. The standing members of the special services committee typically include the principal, special education teachers, school psychologist, guidance counselor, and therapists. Classroom teachers are frequently asked to meet with the special services committee when a student they teach is being evaluated for special education programming.

The first two steps of the special education process coordinated by the special services committee are referral and evaluation. These are discussed in the next two sections before focusing on the mechanics of IEP development.

REFERRAL

A referral represents the initial indication that a student has special needs that may be disadvantageous for achieving school success. At this point, a student may be experiencing problems in the classroom but has not yet been formally identified as handicapped and in need of special education programming. Based on an awareness that professional assistance is needed to document whether or not students are handicapped and the extent of their special needs, a referral form is completed for the purpose of requesting formal evaluation. This form can be completed by any member of the school's faculty or by persons outside

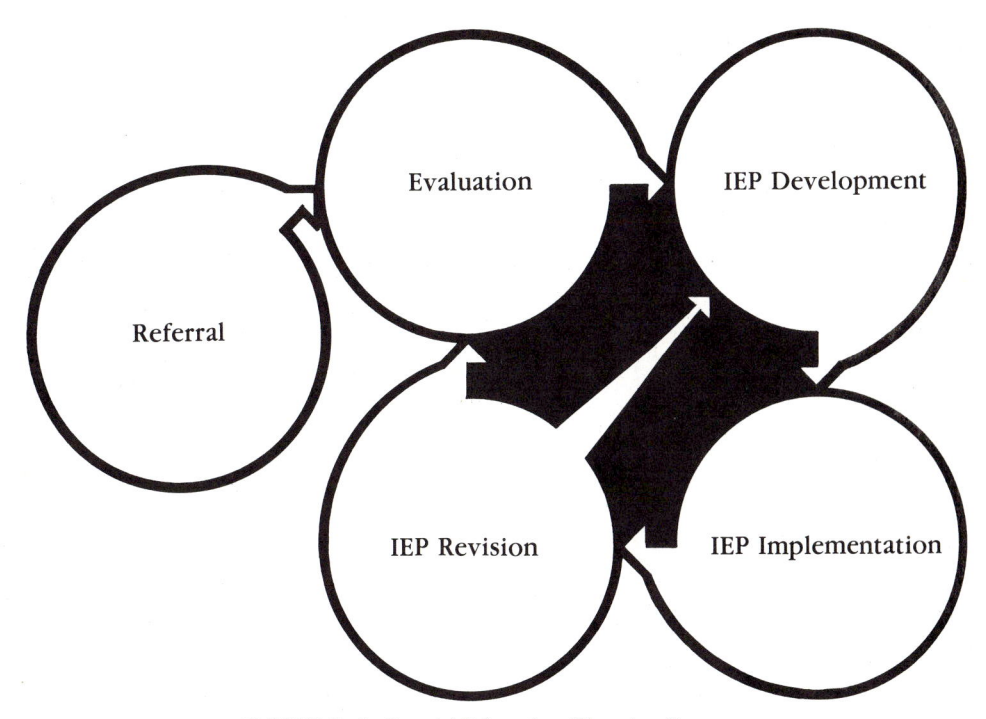

FIGURE 3–1. Special Education Planning Process

the school, including parents, physicians, psychologists, or anyone else concerned with the educational welfare of the student. Classroom teachers play a major role in the referral process, since they have more direct contact with the students in their classes than any other person in the school.

Federal guidelines for the referral process are not specified by P.L. 94–142; however, guidelines are provided in each state's legislation and regulations and in the operating policies of local school systems. Thus, teachers are advised to discuss the specific referral guidelines and their associated responsibilities with their principal or the chairperson of the special services committee. Copies of the actual referral form used in the school should be obtained at that time.

Classroom teachers should be acquainted with *general* referral guidelines that can be applied to the specific procedures in each school. These guidelines are in the areas of identifying, verifying, and reporting the special needs of students.

Identifying Special Needs

Classroom teachers have the responsibility to identify the special needs of students. The characteristics of handicapped students discussed in chapter 1 represent the types of special needs that teachers should identify when such characteristics are manifested by an individual student. It should be remembered that the severity of these characteristics and the number of different characteristics representing special needs will vary from student to student. The major criterion used by teachers should be whether the special needs of students adversely affect their educational performance to the point at which they are placed at a disadvantage for achieving success. To make this determination, teachers should compile information from a variety of sources, including observation of classroom performance, analysis of classroom assignments, review of performance on teacher-made tests and standardized achievement tests, and reports from parents. A careful analysis of this comprehensive information can help insure that special needs are accurately identified.

Verifying Special Needs

Once teachers have compiled and analyzed comprehensive information and have documented their own concern that the special needs of a particular student are interfering with educational performance, it can be helpful to obtain an independent opinion about the concern from a member of the special services committee. Such an independent opinion could be established by having a committee member observe the student in the classroom, review the information compiled by the teacher, and discuss concerns with the teacher. The purpose of this independent opinion is to verify that the degree of the student's special needs warrants the action of a formal referral for evaluation. Such a verification can possibly provide new insights for the teacher in understanding the nature of the referral concerns and can also minimize the possibility that referral is initiated when it is actually not warranted. Some states require a third-party verification before referring a student for evaluation. There are three possible outcomes of verification: (1) referral to the special services committee for evaluation, (2) adaptation of classroom procedures to deal with the problem without referral, and (3) referral to resources outside the school, such as law enforcement agencies or vocational rehabilitation agencies (Turnbull, Strickland, & Brantley, 1982).

Reporting Special Needs

When the decision is made to refer the student to the special services committee, the specific referral guidelines of each school must be followed. Again, teachers are advised to discuss these guidelines with the principal or chairperson of the special services committee. Such reporting typically involves completing a referral form.

It is important to complete referral forms as thoroughly as possible, since the tests and procedures used to evaluate the student will be selected on the basis of this information.

In many states and local school systems, policy requires that the student's parents be notified that a referral is being made to the special services committee. Since many parents are unaware of the purpose and function of referrals and evaluations, this process would need to be explained to them. Frequently, responsibility for parent notification is assumed by the special services committee.

Teachers should recognize that referring students for evaluation to determine whether a handicapping condition exists is a critical step in the special education planning process. Unless special needs are identified, the student may never receive the specially designed instruction needed for optimal progress. Referring students for an evaluation is *not* an indication of a teaching weakness or an inability to individualize instruction. Rather, it represents the fulfillment of an important responsibility of classroom teachers, which is the identification of students with handicaps so that specially designed instruction can be provided to meet their special needs. Once the referral form is completed and forwarded to the special services committee, the second step in the special education planning process—evaluation—is initiated.

EVALUATION

According to P.L. 94–142, there are two major purposes of evaluation:

1. to determine whether or not a student has a handicapping condition (according to the definitions included in chapter 1); and
2. to identify the student's strengths and weaknesses as a basis for instructional planning.

Students must receive a comprehensive evaluation before they can be classified as handicapped. In some cases, the results of the evaluation confirm that fact that students are *not* handicapped, and that their educational problems that initiated the referral must be handled in ways other than special education programming. When students *are* found to be handicapped, the evaluation information collected on strengths and weaknesses serves as the basis for planning the IEP.

As stated in chapter 2, P.L. 94–142 includes many regulations on the nature of conducting evaluations to insure that procedures are fairly administered and interpreted. Thus, federal guidelines exist that pertain to the evaluation process; however, state and local policies must also be followed. Just as teachers should inquire about the referral process in their local schools, they should also investigate state and local evaluation requirements that exceed federal ones. In analyzing federal evaluation requirements from the perspective of classroom teachers, the major areas of concern are personnel responsible for evaluation, type of evaluation procedures, administration of evaluation procedures, and interpretation of evaluation procedures.

Personnel Responsible for Evaluation

As stated earlier, the special services committee in each school is responsible for coordinating the entire special education planning process, including the important step of evaluation. The typical procedure used by special service committees is to appoint a multidisciplinary team of persons to plan, administer, and interpret the evaluation procedures. P.L. 94–142 requires that the team include at least one teacher or specialist in the area of the student's suspected disability. Frequently, this team is comprised of a special education teacher, school psychologist, therapists (e.g., speech therapists, physical therapists) related to the student's needs as specified on the referral form, and a guidance counselor. Since the composition of the team depends on the nature of the student's special needs, membership can vary widely in individual situations. For example, a school nurse would be an appropriate member of an evaluation team for a student with a health impairment, whereas a mobility specialist would be needed for a blind student. It is the responsibility of the special services committee to appoint the appropriate persons to serve on the multidisciplinary evaluation team, based on the areas of concern documented on the referral form.

Classroom teachers are sometimes asked to assist the evaluation team in collecting information on their students. The sources of this information could be tests, class assignments, or observation. Another important role for teachers who initially refer students is to specify the particular questions they would like the multidisciplinary evaluation team to address. Sample questions include:

- What reading level of textbooks would be most appropriate to use in the content areas?
- What concepts has the student currently mastered in mathematics?
- To what extent does the student's difficulty in hearing interfere with the ability to comprehend classroom lectures?
- How long should the student be expected to attend to classroom assignments without a break?
- What classroom management procedures are likely to be successful in decreasing the student's disruptive behavior?

The identification of specific questions increases the probability that the evaluation procedures are appropriately planned and result in relevant, functional findings. Thus, a critical role for classroom teachers is to identify the areas of needed information.

Parents also have responsibilities associated with the evaluation process. Before evaluating the student, the special services committee is responsible for informing parents, through a written notice, why a formal evaluation is being considered. When a student is initially being evaluated to determine whether or not a handicap exists, parents must give their written consent for the evaluation. The only way an evaluation can proceed without parental consent is for school personnel to override the parents' refusal through the proceedings of a due process hearing (see chapter 2).

Parents can also be asked to contribute information to the evaluation process on such topics as the student's adaptive behavior, language skills, cultural background, social and emotional status, and health needs. Obviously, many parents have a wealth of information on their child's past and current functioning that can be extremely helpful to the evaluation team. Although parents are required members of the committee to plan the IEP, their involvement in contributing information during the evaluation process is optional.

Identifying Types of Evaluation Procedures

The multidisciplinary evaluation team is responsible for identifying tests and procedures to determine whether or not a student is handicapped and the nature of specially designed instruction tailored to the student's strengths and weaknesses. As stated earlier, the referral information is carefully considered by the evaluation team as they identify appropriate tests and procedures, as well as legal guidelines.

The evaluation team can choose from among a large number of tests and procedures those most suited to the student's particular areas of concern. The major types of instruments and procedures that are used fall into the general categories of standardized tests, criterion-referenced tests, and observations.

Administering Evaluation Procedures

Once the tests and evaluation procedures have been identified, the multidisciplinary evaluation team begins administering them to the student. The testing should be spread over a minimum of several days to insure that the student is not fatigued by the testing demands and that a variety of testing situations are used to gather a comprehensive view of student functioning. Situational factors, such as time of day, length of sessions, characteristics of the testing materials, and distractions in the environment (e.g., noise, lighting) can influence student performance (Turnbull, Strickland, & Brantley, 1982). Other important considerations include whether or not the student is anxious, the student's motivational level, and the rapport between the examiner and the student.

Classroom teachers can play an extremely important role in helping to prepare students for the evaluation by explaining to them the purpose of evaluation and the procedures that will be followed, as well as helping to build rapport between the student and the evaluation team members.

> *The day before Phillip was to be evaluated, his teacher, Mrs. Henderson, explained to him that he was going to be asked to do some special work as soon as he arrived at school the following morning. The work, she explained, would involve some tests in the areas of reading, language arts, and math. Mrs. Henderson told Phillip that he should try to do his best on these tests, but he would not get a grade on them that would count for his report card. Rather, the tests would be used to help her and his parents decide on how to plan the best possible school program for him. She told Phillip that Mr. Williams, who would be giving him the test, is a really nice person who likes to do many of the same things he likes to do—play basketball, soccer, and softball. She told Phillip that he might like to bring some of his basketball autographs to show Mr. Williams.*

Interpreting Evaluation Procedures

The interpretation of evaluation procedures is an extremely important responsibility of the multidisciplinary evaluation team. General guidelines include the following:

1. Considering test results and observational information from a variety of sources;
2. Recognizing that test scores are estimates of performance under a specified, and rather limited, set of circumstances;
3. Considering alternative interpretations of test scores;
4. Recognizing and documenting the limitations of the tests and procedures used;
5. Identifying whether more information is needed before final decisions are reached and gathering more information if necessary;
6. Adhering to the definitional criteria of handicapping conditions to insure that classifications are accurately made; and
7. Identifying trends of performance in an effort to determine the student's strengths and weaknesses as a basis for instructional planning.

As stated earlier, classroom teachers can help insure the relevance of test interpretation by giving team members a list of questions for which information is needed. When team members meet as a group to analyze and interpret the evaluation data, these questions can direct the attention of team members to functional classroom implications.

The purpose of this interpretation process is to determine the existence of a handicapping condition. If the student is found not to be handicapped, recommendations need to be formulated by the team on strategies for addressing the referral concerns that do not involve special education placement and services. On the other hand, if the student is classified as having a particular handicapping condition, the next step in the planning process is the development of the IEP. The student's strengths and weaknesses as identified by the evaluation team form the foundation for planning the IEP. The team is responsible for preparing a written report describing the evaluation procedures, results, and the recommendations for programming. P.L. 94–142 and state legislation require that a copy of this report be sent to the student's parents. Classroom teachers responsible for teaching the student should also have access to the report, either by reading the copy placed in the student's permanent file or asking for their own copy. Each school system has policies for maintaining evaluation reports on students; thus, teachers need to be aware of these policies and to abide by them.

INDIVIDUALIZED EDUCATION PROGRAMS

An IEP must be developed for each student who is classified as handicapped and in need of special education programming and placement. The development of the IEP is the focal point for planning the student's program and coordinating instruction among the classroom teacher, special education teachers, related services providers (e.g., speech therapist), and parents. As stated in chapter 2, IEP development can be viewed in two parts: the IEP document and the IEP meeting.

IEP Document

The components of the IEP required by federal law were reviewed in chapter 2. Additionally, the legislation of some states requires additional information on IEPs, such as the person responsible for teaching each objective and the special methods and materials that will be used to teach objectives. Although components of the IEP are specified by federal and state legislation, local school systems are free to develop their own forms according to preferred formats. Since there is a tremendous range of formats, teachers are advised to ask for a blank copy of the form used in their system.

In this section, each required component of the IEP will be discussed.

Readers interested in sample IEPs at preschool, elementary, and secondary levels are referred to Turnbull, Strickland, and Brantley (1982). This source also provides an in-depth guide to IEP development.

Current Levels of Performance.   Stating the student's current levels of performance provides documentation of "entry level" skills and concepts and establishes the starting point for planning goals and objectives. The evaluation information can readily be translated into performance level statements. Teachers also need to collect current information on the student's performance. This can be done by reviewing the student's mastery of objectives on the previous year's IEP, administering classroom tests, and observing the student's progress in academic as well as behavioral areas.

A major decision to be made when reviewing evaluation information is the determination of *all* subjects and skill areas (e.g., adaptive behavior) requiring specially designed instruction. These subjects and skill areas will need to be addressed on the IEP. An orthopedically handicapped student who has mobility impairments only in the lower body, and no academic problems, will likely need an IEP only in physical education; a mentally retarded student may need to have all curriculum areas covered by the IEP. Once subject and skill areas have been identified, the student's current levels of performance should be specified for each one. Performance statements should be written by the IEP committee according to the following criteria:

- use of current information,
- use of concise and clear language, and
- identification of specific skills. (Turnbull, Strickland, & Brantley, 1982, p. 137)

Annual Goals.   An annual goal is a statement of the student's expected achievement over a period of one calendar year. Annual goals must be written for every subject or skill area included on the IEP. Since it is impossible for the IEP committee to know in advance exactly how much progress a handicapped student will make, an annual goal represents an estimate of accomplishments.

The National Association of State Directors of Special Education (1976) suggests critical areas to consider in formulating goals:

- What are the priority parental concerns? What are the priority teacher concerns?
- What are the appropriate developmental sequences of tasks or behaviors that the child would be expected to move through?
- What behaviors appear to be the most modifiable, as determined from baseline assessment data including the child's strengths, weaknesses, and learning style?
- Are there any other crucial considerations one needs to make in selecting areas of educational need, such as any problem areas that are truly dangerous for the child, injurious to his or her health, or others? (p. 30)

Annual goals are broad, global statements and should not be confused with more specific instructional objectives. An example of an annual goal is "Sabrina will demonstrate skills in applying for jobs." The short-term objectives would address the particular application skills to be covered and the criteria of mastery to be demonstrated for each. Although there is no set standard, typically IEPs include three or four annual goals per subject or skill area (*"To assure the free appropriate public education of all children,"* 1980).

Short-Term Objectives. Short-term objectives are measurable statements outlining the intermediate steps between the student's current levels of performance and the projected annual goals. Objectives should be sequential, specific in stating desired behavior and criteria, and manageable for both the student and the teacher.

As with goals, the number of objectives is not set by law. Morgan (1981) recommends that *at least* quarterly objectives be written, which would be three or four objectives per year. These quarterly objectives could then be broken down into smaller units as teachers develop monthly, weekly, and daily instructional plans. This process of breaking down objectives is referred to as task analysis and is discussed in the section on curriculum adaptations in chapter 4. IEP objectives represent benchmarks of progress and are not expected to include every skill and concept that the student will be taught throughout the school year.

If criterion-referenced tests have been used to evaluate the student, a list of sequenced objectives is already available for the IEP committee to consider. Other sources of objectives are contained in curriculum guides and in the teacher's manual of many commercial materials.

Some school systems are using computer banks to store objectives. Teachers are given a master copy of objectives for each subject area, and they select by number objectives appropriate for the student. These numbers are typed into the computer and the computer provides a print-out of the selected objectives, saving a great deal of the teacher's time.

Evaluation Procedures, Criteria, and Schedules. A required component of the IEP is the specification of evaluation procedures, criteria, and schedules to be used at least annually to evaluate student achievement of the short-term objectives. Evaluation procedures refer to the type of measures to be used and include any measure that is appropriate for assessing the specified objectives—standardized tests, criterion-referenced tests, observation, teacher-made tests, and a review of classroom assignments.

The criterion for evaluation is the degree of accuracy that the student must demonstrate. If objectives are appropriately written, they will include the necessary criteria. Thus, once the criteria are specified in the objective, they do not have to be restated on the IEP form in the evaluation section.

The third required dimension of evaluation is the schedule that refers to the frequency of student assessment. P.L. 94–142 requires that the student's progress in meeting objectives be evaluated at least annually. Some states and local school systems require a more frequent schedule of evaluations. It is preferable for evaluations to be conducted on a short-term basis—daily, weekly, and monthly—so that teachers have current information on the student's progress and the effectiveness of the methods and materials they are using. In this way, problems the student encounters can be identified quickly and changes in the instructional program can be made. Also, student success can be readily identified and reinforced, which can be an impetus for motivation. The IEP committee must determine the appropriate evaluation schedule and specify that schedule on the IEP.

This evaluation component of the IEP is extremely important since it relates to the difficult task teachers face in grading handicapped students. A more detailed discussion of evaluation procedures, criteria, and schedules is included in chapter 4, with suggestions of how this information can be used to devise individualized approaches for assigning and reporting grades.

Documentation of Special Education Placement and Related Services. Decisions pertaining to the particular special education placement and related services that are appropriate to the needs of a handicapped student are based on current levels of performance, annual goals, and short-term objectives. Thus, the determination of placement and related services is made *after* these curriculum-related decisions are made. As discussed in chapter 2, special education placements can include a variety of educational environments—regular classrooms, resource rooms, special classes, special schools, residential facilities, and hospital/homebound instruction. The placement decision is made based on the environment that will best provide the needed support for the handicapped student in accordance with the guidelines of the least restrictive environment principle of P.L. 94–142.

Related services are defined as developmental, corrective, or supportive services necessary to enable a student to benefit from special education. Definitions of related services were included in chapter 2. In addition to specifying the type of service needed by the student, it is desirable to document the extent of service (e.g., two 30-minute speech therapy sessions per week) and the person responsible for providing the related service. When school systems do not have needed related services available in their program, they can contract with other programs, including neighboring school systems, other public agencies (e.g., mental health clinics), or private service providers (e.g., physical therapists in private practice).

Extent of Time in Regular Education Programs. Because of the legal preference for placing handicapped children in regular classes when appropriate in light of their educational needs, a required component of the IEP is the specification of the extent of time the student will participate in the regular program. Extent of participation can be expressed in a percentage of instructional time or in the actual number of hours spent in the regular classroom on a daily or weekly basis.

This requirement should not be interpreted to mean that all handicapped students must be in the regular classroom for at least some portion of the school day. To the contrary, placement decisions must be made individually on the basis of the educational environment in which the student's IEP goals and objectives can most successfully be taught. Thus, if a student is in a special class for the entire school day, the extent of participation in the regular class would be documented as zero on the IEP.

Dates of Services. The final component of the IEP is the specification of the dates for initiating services and the anticipation duration of services. As previously discussed, school systems are legally required to provide the related services needed by the handicapped student. In some cases, however, there may be an unavoidable delay when the IEP committee must make arrangements to subcontract with other agencies for services. Thus, the initiation date recorded on the IEP should occur either immediately after the IEP is approved or shortly thereafter when necessary arrangements have been made.

The anticipated duration of the service is determined based on the individual needs of the student. A student with a mild articulation problem may need only six months of speech therapy, whereas more severe problems may require much more time. Although some services, such as transportation, may be needed throughout a student's total school career, services on the IEP are typically not documented for more than one year. Since the IEP must be reviewed and revised on an annual basis, extensions of service from one year to the next can be made when the updated IEP is planned.

IEP Meeting

A meeting must be held to develop the initial IEP after a student has been classified as handicapped, and the IEP must then be reviewed and revised on an annual basis. The IEP meeting is discussed here in terms of the participants and the components of the meeting.

IEP Meeting Participants. The legally required participants in the IEP meeting, according to P.L. 94–142, were identified in chapter 2. As with other legal regulations, some states and local school systems require that additional persons attend the IEP meeting (e.g., related service providers). In a national survey of special education directors conducted by one of the authors, the typical number of participants at IEP meetings was found to be five persons.

More than one representative of the school system may attend the IEP meeting, including the principal, director of special education, psychologist, or a special education teacher other than the student's teacher. Particularly when the student for whom an IEP is being planned needs a variety of related services, a system representative attending the meeting should have the authority to commit resources without the concern that this decision will be reversed at a higher administrative level (*Federal Register,* 1981; Morgan, 1981).

Although only one teacher is required to be present, the special education teacher, classroom teacher, or both may attend. Research on IEP meetings has revealed a pattern of minimal to moderate attendance and participation by classroom teachers (Goldstein, Strickland, Turnbull, & Curry, 1980; Pugach, 1982). In a study involving thirty-three regular classroom teachers, Pugach found that 52 percent had attended the most recent IEP meeting for a student in their class. The teachers reported that their most frequent type of involvement was conferring with the special education teachers and reporting current levels of performance. Low levels of involvement were indicated in participation in decisions related to goals, objectives, and related services. A particularly troublesome finding of this study was that 67 percent of the teachers reported that no goals and objectives were written on the IEP for the subjects the handicapped students were taught in the regular classroom. The lack of IEP coverage of the regular program is a major barrier to the delivery of specially designed instruction, since the majority of mildly handicapped students spend a substantial portion of their school day in the regular class.

There are many reasons that the involvement of classroom teachers in IEP meetings has been low and the coverage of the IEP devoted mostly to the portion of the day a handicapped student spends in a resource room or special class. A major reason is that the IEP process is still relatively new—it was instigated in 1977. Thus, many classroom teachers do not have sufficient knowledge of the purpose of the IEP and their important role in its development and implementation. Secondly, since many classroom teachers have been relatively uninformed of the IEP, they have questioned whether their participation in its development was worth the time and effort. A third reason is that the trend toward placing handicapped students in regular classes strongly increased after the implementation of P.L. 94–142; thus, in the past it was far more likely for special education teachers to have primary responsibility for instruction. The concept of shared responsibility among special and regular educators requires new attitudes and skills on the part of everyone concerned. Such changes in roles and responsibilities usually take time and cannot be expected to occur instantly.

The time is ripe for classroom teachers to assume a much greater role in the IEP meeting. Since they are responsible for teaching handicapped students, it is critically important for them to have a strong voice in planning a program that can be effectively implemented in their classroom. The IEP provides the opportunity for classroom teachers to receive necessary information about students, such as an interpretation of their strengths and weaknesses as documented through the multidisciplinary evaluation. Teachers also can contribute important information on evaluation related to the students' daily performance in the classroom. In the area of goals and objectives, teachers have valuable information to share concerning the scope and sequence of the regular curriculum. Typically, special education teachers are not thoroughly trained in teaching content subjects; thus, the expertise of the classroom teacher is particularly important in this area.

Another decision that has vital relevance to the classroom teacher is placement and related services. Classroom teachers need to insure that when students are recommended for placement in their classes, the specially designed instruction required to teach the goals and objectives can realistically be delivered. If special materials (e.g., taped books, auditory trainers, high interest/low vocabulary reading materials) are needed to adapt instructional procedures, the teacher needs to make sure that the school system will, indeed, provide these materials.

Thus, the involvement of classroom teachers can insure that the IEP is appropriate to the needs of the handicapped student and that it guarantees that teachers will receive the assistance they need. It is important to remember that anything seems possible to those with no responsibility for implementation. If classroom teachers are required to provide specially designed instruction to handicapped students, they have both the right and responsibility to share in decisions regarding the nature of the student's program.

Parents are other important members of the IEP committee. The intent of P.L. 94–142 is for parents to be equal participants in shared decision-making with school personnel (*Federal Register,* 1981). Parents have a wealth of information on their child's educational and health history, ways to adapt daily procedures to enhance the success of their child, levels of adaptive behavior, strategies for discipline, likes and dislikes, and the nature of peer interaction outside school. Parents can be extremely helpful in helping educators understand the special needs of their child, and teachers are encouraged to take advantage of the parents' knowledge and perspective.

Although the legal intent was for parents to be equal participants in decision making, research has shown a rather minimal level of parental participation (Goldstein, Strickland, Turnbull, & Curry, 1980; Lynch & Stein, 1982; Morgan, 1982). Some parents of handicapped children are intimidated by the idea of shared decision-making in conferences and believe that educators are experts and know what is best for their child. Accordingly, teachers are encouraged to provide a conference atmosphere that will enable parents to relax, to ask questions that elicit parental perspectives, and to provide feedback to parents that their contributions are helpful and appreciated (Goldstein & Turnbull, 1982; Turnbull, Strickland, & Brantley, 1982).

The student's involvement in the conference is extremely important as well. Too frequently, we talk *about* handicapped students and fail to talk *with* them. In interviews with adolescent students who had been classified as learning-disabled, educable mentally handicapped, seriously emotionally disturbed, and orthopedically handicapped, Gillespie and Turnbull (in press) reported that 75 percent of the students were unaware of their right to participate in the development of their IEP. These students, however, strongly agreed with the concept of student participation and expressed a desire to be included. They stated that they thought they would benefit from participation, in terms of gaining information about themselves and their school program and sharing information about their preferences and their desire to cooperate with teachers and parents. Sample responses of students to the question, Why do you think it is a good idea for you to go to your own IEP meeting? indicate the viewpoints of these students:

> The teachers and parents get everything out and students have feelings and want to get them out too.
> (12-year-old, emotionally handicapped student)
> I could learn more about why I'm in a special class.
> (14-year-old, educable mentally retarded student)

Detailed guidelines for involving parents and students in conferences are available in Turnbull, Strickland, and Brantley (1982) and Gillespie and Turnbull (in press).

IEP Meeting Components. Since there is no one standard procedure for conducting IEP meetings, formats vary among school systems. Despite the differences that exist, there are certain components of IEP meetings with which all teachers should be familiar. These components are:

1. *Preconference preparation*—advanced planning on the part of participants to insure that necessary information is gathered, the meeting is scheduled at a convenient time, and special concerns to be discussed are identified;
2. *Initial conference proceedings*—creating an atmosphere for open communication and a plan for decision making;
3. *Interpretation of evaluation results*—reporting formal and informal evaluation information as a basis for establishing the student's current levels of performance and the subject areas to be covered in the IEP;
4. *Development of goals, objectives, and evaluation methods*—specifying the skills and concepts appropriate to the needs of the handicapped student and the methods to be used to evaluate the student's progress;
5. *Decision of special education placement and related services*—specifying the particular classroom placement for the student, the percentage of time in the regular class, the nature and extent of related services, the dates for initiating services, and the anticipated duration of services; and
6. *Conclusion of the meeting*—synthesizing decisions that have been made

and outlining future actions, such as communication with parents and timelines for reviewing and revising the IEP.

Table 3–1 includes a summary of suggestions for classroom teachers re-

TABLE 3-1. Suggestions to Enhance the Active Participation of Classroom Teachers in IEP Meetings

1. *Preconference Preparation*
   a. Tell the chairperson of the special services committee that you would like to attend the IEP meeting for a handicapped student who is presently in your class or who is being considered for placement in your class.
   b. Insure that the time of the meeting is convenient in light of your schedule.
   c. Reschedule the meeting if the time suggested is inconvenient.
   d. Collect any information that you believe will be helpful at the meeting, such as samples of the student's classroom work, anecdotal records on performance, and/or test papers.
   e. Develop a *draft* list of subjects that you believe require specially designed instruction and any tentative ideas you have on goals and objectives. Take these draft notes to the IEP meeting.
   f. Make notes in advance of potential problems that could arise with the student with which you would like assistance from the IEP committee.

2. *Initial Conference Proceedings*
   a. If you are not introduced at the meeting to any persons you do not know, introduce yourself to all committee members—especially the student's parents.
   b. Ask questions to clarify the particular role of other committee members, if this is unclear to you.
   c. If you have a time limit for the meeting, let other committee members know.
   d. Ask the chairperson to review the agenda for the meeting, if this is not done. If you have concerns that are not already included on the agenda, ask that these concerns be included.

3. *Interpretation of Evaluation Results*
   a. Insure that the resource teacher or psychologist states all tests that were administered and the specific results of each.
   b. You may make notes of evaluation results or ask for a written copy of the student's evaluation report.
   c. Insure that the classroom implications of the evaluation results are identified. Ask questions, if necessary, to insure your understanding.
   d. If any professional jargon is used that you do not understand, ask for clarification. If you do not understand the jargon, it is likely that the parents and student do not understand it.
   e. If you disagree with the evaluation findings in light of the student's previous performance in your classroom, state your disagreement and provide a rationale for your perspective.
   f. Insure that the student's current levels of performance are clearly identified.

TABLE 3-1. (Continued)

- g. State the subjects and skill areas that you believe require specially designed instruction. Insure that performance levels are specified for each one.

4. *Development of the Goals, Objectives, and Evaluation Methods*
   - a. Contribute your own ideas for goals and objectives. If you question the goals and objectives suggested by others at the meeting, ask for justification. Remember that you may be assigned major responsibility for teaching the student.
   - b. Insure that goals, objectives, and evaluation methods for *all* subjects requiring specially designed instruction are included in the IEP.
   - c. Insure that the evaluation methods can be translated into procedures for grading the handicapped student. Discuss criteria for assigning grades and strategies for reporting grades to the student and parent.
   - d. Insure that you understand the nature of the specially designed instruction needed by the student.

5. *Placement Decision and Related Services*
   - a. Suggest the placement (e.g., regular classroom, resource program, special class) that you believe is most appropriate for the student.
   - b. Be sure all necessary related services (e.g., speech therapy, physical therapy, transportation) that you believe the student needs are included. Remember that the school is not obligated to provide related services that are not written into the IEP.
   - c. If the student is to receive instruction from both you and the resource teacher, clarify the manner in which the responsibility for teaching the objectives will be shared.
   - d. Insure that the student has appropriate opportunities to interact with nonhandicapped children (placement in the least restrictive setting).
   - e. If the student is to be placed in your class, clarify with all committee members whether or not you believe you can effectively implement the IEP. Ask for whatever help and support of committee members or other school personnel you believe you will need.

6. *Conclusion of the Meeting*
   - a. If the chairperson does not initiate it, ask for a summary of the meeting to review major decisions and follow-up responsibility. You may want to make a written record of this summary.
   - b. If follow-up responsibility has not been specified (e.g., locating or purchasing specialized materials), ask who is going to be responsible for each task.
   - c. Insure that a tentative date is set for reviewing the IEP on at least an annual basis and preferably more often.
   - d. State in what ways and how frequently you would like to keep in touch with the student's special education resource teacher, related service provider(s), and parents. Discuss mutually preferred strategies for maintaining ongoing communication.
   - e. State your desire and intent to work in close cooperation with IEP committee members to insure that an appropriate education is provided to the student.
   - f. Express appreciation for the opportunity to share in decision making.

lated to enhancing their active decision-making role in each of these six components.

IEP development is a major step in meeting the educational needs of handicapped students, although it is a hollow accomplishment unless the IEP is effectively implemented. Thus, the IEP is a means rather than an end—it is a means of providing systematic instruction. Readers interested in futher information on IEPs are referred to Larsen and Poplin (1980); Morgan (1981); Turnbull, Strickland, and Brantley (1982); and Weiner (1978). The remaining chapters in this book focus on strategies for effectively implementing IEPs through the provision of specially designed instruction.

REFERENCES

Federal Register. Washington, D.C.: U.S. Government Printing Office, 1981.

Gillespie, E. B., & Turnbull, A. P. Involving special education students in planning the IEP. *Teaching Exceptional Students.* In press.

Goldstein, S., Strickland, B., Turnbull, A. P., & Curry, L. An observational analysis of the IEP conference. *Exceptional Children,* 1980, *46*(4), 278–286.

Goldstein, S., & Turnbull, A. P. The use of two strategies to increase parent participation in IEP conferences. *Exceptional Children,* 1982, *48*(4), 360–361.

Larsen, S. C., & Poplin, M. S. *Methods for educating the handicapped: An individualized education program approach.* Boston: Allyn and Bacon, 1980.

Lynch, E., & Stein, R. Perspectives on parent participation in special education. *Exceptional Education Quarterly,* 1982, *3*(2), 73–84.

Morgan, D. P. *A primer on individualized education programs for exceptional children: Preferred strategies and practices.* Reston, Va.: Foundation for Exceptional Children, 1981.

Morgan, D. P. Parent participation in the IEP process: Does it enhance appropriate education? *Exceptional Education Quarterly,* 1982, *3*(2), 33–40.

National Association of State Directors of Special Education. *Functions of the placement committee in special education.* Washington, D.C.: National Association of State Directors of Special Education, 1976.

Pugach, M. Regular classroom teacher involvement on the development and utilization of IEPs. *Exceptional Children,* 1982, *48*(4), 371–374.

"To assure the free appropriate public education of all handicapped children," Second Annual Report to Congress on the Implementation of Public Law 94–142: The Education for All Handicapped Children Act. Washington, D.C.: U.S. Department of Education, 1980.

Turnbull, A. P., Strickland, B., & Brantley, J. C. *Developing and implementing individualized education programs.* Columbus, Ohio: Charles E. Merrill Publishing Co., 1982.

Weiner, B. B. (Ed.). *Periscope: Views of the individualized education Program.* Reston, Va.: The Council for Exceptional Children, 1978.

4

Implementing Individualized Education Programs

Individualized instruction involves the process of tailoring instruction to the educational needs of each student. Such instruction does not require the teacher always to work with a student in a one-to-one situation. Rather, individualized instruction can be delivered in many ways, including large groups and small groups as well as individual formats.

As stated in chapter 2, special education is defined as specially designed instruction. Such instruction is specially designed to meet the unique needs of each student. That is also the essence of individualized approaches—to design instruction specifically according to the performance levels and special needs of the handicapped student.

The development of the IEP is the beginning point for delivering individualized instruction in the regular classroom. The IEP contains vital information for the classroom teacher to use in making instructional decisions. It should be remembered, however, that the IEP is a means to an end—it is a plan for the actual delivery of specially designed or individualized instruction on a daily basis. It is the teacher's responsibility to translate the IEP into daily and weekly lesson plans. To make this translation, teachers must make instructional decisions to answer the following questions:

1. What types of adaptations are needed to adjust the curriculum content to the goals and objectives that have been determined appropriate for the handicapped student?
2. What instructional strategies will be effective for the student and manageable for the teacher in delivering instruction?
3. What procedures will be the most effective in coordinating instruction between the regular classroom and resource room?
4. How can the evaluation procedures as specified on the IEP be implemented in the regular classrooms, and how should grades be assigned?

This chapter addresses each of these questions by suggesting strategies that can realistically be implemented in regular classrooms.

ADAPTATIONS IN CURRICULUM CONTENT

A variety of adaptations can be made to adjust the content of the regular classroom curriculum to the particular needs of a handicapped student. Such adaptations are needed when the handicapped student's current levels of performance are below those of the majority of students. Thus, the goals and objectives as specified on the IEP are ones that most of the other students in the class have already mastered.

> *Kea is in the third grade and has been classified as learning disabled. Math is the subject with which she has the greatest difficulty. She has obtained about 75 percent accuracy on addition and subtraction facts, but she still needs more instruction on solving problems with regrouping. While most of her classmates are successfully mastering multiplication and division concepts, Kea needs more practice on addition and subtraction.*

Below grade-level achievement almost always occurs with students who are mentally retarded and often with students who are learning-disabled. Because of special learning needs, students with sensory handicaps may also have achievement deficiencies.

Determining the Need for Curriculum Adaptations

The first step in making curriculum adaptations is to review carefully the current levels of performance, annual goals, and short-term objectives on the IEP. This information will apprise the teacher of the extent of needed adaptations by comparing the goals and objectives considered appropriate for the handicapped student with the general goals and objectives that comprise the regular curriculum.

A second step in decision making concerning curriculum adaptations is to break down the IEP objectives into the subskills and concepts that are inherent in each. This process is referred to as task analysis. To analyze a task, ask questions such as: What must the learner be able to do to achieve the objective? What kinds of learning are involved? What prior skills are necessary? What specific knowledge is required? What concepts or meanings must be understood? What is prerequisite to ultimate success (Johnson & Johnson, 1970). If objectives are not analyzed before teaching a student, a teacher is often unaware of which prerequisite skills the student has mastered.

> *A student teacher was observed attempting to teach a child to tell time. Her materials were carefully prepared, the child was well motivated, and still the child would respond to 12:15 sometimes as fifteen minutes before twelve and sometimes as fifteen minutes after twelve. An experienced observer immediately identified the problem: the child did not have the concepts of "before" and "after," prerequisite skills to telling time. A similar problem was encountered when an experienced teacher attempted*

to offer typing instruction to a visually impaired child. In dictating simple sentences, she learned that the student had limited phonics and spelling skills. It was necessary, therefore, that he be instructed in basic word-attack skills before typing could be offered.

The determination of how many steps are necessary to master a skill or concept is based on the complexity of the objective and the learner's current abilities. The method of completing a task analysis recommended by McCormack (1976) for a group of learners working toward the same objective, but functioning at different levels, is to construct the instructional sequence for those learners demonstrating the least competence. The task is analyzed into the simplest steps; the more capable learners simply skip steps.

Frank (1973) presents an example of a task analysis that leads to an informal test constructed from the steps. The objective is stated as follows: The child is able to count correctly a specified number of coins handed to him by the teacher. A partial task analysis includes:

1. Identifies a penny and nickel.
2. States that a nickel is equivalent to five pennies.
3. Counts a row of pennies placed in a straight line.
4. Counts pennies placed in scattered fashion.
5. Counts one nickel and several pennies which are placed in a straight line where the nickel is first.

The following items comprise a corresponding test:

Test Item Number	Test Item	Directions Given by Teacher
1	Coins or pictures of coins	Teacher asks child to name each coin as he points to it
2	Same	Teacher asks child how many pennies he can get for one nickel
3–5	Same	Teacher asks child to count the money

After administering the test to each child who will be learning about money, the teacher is able to determine which steps each student needs to master to reach the stated objective.

For some tasks, it is possible to determine the steps by observing and recording the sequential activities of a person performing the task. In most cases, the teacher decides what activities presented in what order will most assist the learner in acquiring the skill (McCormack, 1976).

Task analysis is an important aspect of adapting the content level of the curriculum. An ability to analyze tasks allows the teacher to determine pupil readiness, to teach groups of students with varying skills, and to produce alternatives to instructional failure. It identifies the demands that a task will make on students and allows the teacher to prepare them to meet each demand (Junkala, 1972). Task analysis is a tool that helps to teach the goals and objectives specified in the IEP.

After the IEP has been carefully reviewed and a task analysis of objectives has been completed, several curriculum alternatives are possible. First, the teacher may decide that the goals and objectives for a handicapped student are consistent with the goals and objectives for the majority of other students in the class. Thus, adaptations in content would not be needed. Rather, the student may require adaptations in instructional strategies (e.g., the methods and materials used to deliver the content), which will be discussed in the next section. The other three alternatives include supplementing, simplifying, or changing the regular curriculum (Allen, Clark, Gallagher, & Scofield, 1982).

Supplementing the Regular Curriculum

The skills and concepts comprising the regular curriculum may be generally appropriate for a handicapped student; however, the student may need instruction on some prerequisite skills that most other students have already mastered. Another special need can arise when a handicapped student requires more practice than the rest of the class on the particular steps of a skill sequence.

Individualization can occur in these instances by supplementing the regular curriculum with special materials. The student, in this case, would generally be taught the same curriculum as other students. The adaptation would involve the insertion of additional materials to teach prerequisite skills or to allow for more intense instruction over a longer period of time. Such materials could be acquired from the library; textbooks from a lower grade (in the case of prerequisite skills) could be identified; or supplementary materials could be devised by the teachers, peer tutors, or classroom volunteers.

Simplifying the Curriculum

The goals and objectives for handicapped students in certain curriculum areas may be substantially below those of their classmates. When such deviations occur, the IEP committee must decide the subjects that should be taught in the resource room by the special education teacher and the amount of time that is appropriate for the handicapped student to attend the resource program. For students who have substantial learning problems, it is likely that the instruction in the resource room will not cover all subjects requiring specially designed instruction. In these cases, the classroom teacher will need to simplify the regular curriculum to accommodate the goals and objectives that are appropriate for the student.

> *Sandy, a tenth-grade student who has been classified as mildly mentally handicapped, attends the resource program for two hours each day. During this time, he receives instruction in his areas of greatest needs, which are reading and spelling. The resource teacher also helps him with his homework in the subjects being taught in the regular classroom. These subjects include civics, business arithmetic, and vocational education. He particularly has trouble in these subjects when reading and written reports are required. His classroom teachers have found it necessary to simplify the curriculum in these subjects by task analyzing the objectives and teaching skills and concepts in small steps with special learning aids and materials.*

Teachers can use many techniques to simplify the curriculum. As previously stated, a task analysis of the objectives enables teachers to identify the precise skills and concepts that the student has already mastered and those that require instruction.

Since reading is frequently a problem area for mentally handicapped and learning-disabled students, the adaptation of reading materials is a major area for curriculum simplification. Many strategies can be used for reading adaptation, including using textbooks or library books on a lower reading level, taping books, highlighting pertinent material in textbooks with a colored marker, providing study guides or outlines of major concepts from the textbook, using advanced organizers for reading material that introduce vocabulary and highlight major concepts, and rewriting textbooks at a lower reading level. These strategies are discussed in detail in chapters 6 and 8.

The skills and concepts in a particular subject area can be simplified by using alternative levels of task difficulty. Task requirements for students can be adapted to their level of cognitive thinking. Table 4–1 outlines levels of the cognitive domain based on the work of Bloom and described by Popham and Baker (1970). These levels can be used to formulate objectives and task requirements. The cognitive levels range from simpler ones (i.e., knowledge level) through increasing degrees of intellectual complexity (i.e., evaluation). This model of cognitive thinking is an example of curriculum simplification.

> *Mr. Sims taught the same units to all of the students in his eleventh-grade government class. A wide range of achievement and ability existed in the class. Mr. Sims was aware of the need to simplify his curriculum for the two learning-disabled students. He also had students who were extremely gifted and needed to go beyond the requirements of the majority of the class. Mr. Sims adapted his instruction according to the level of cognitive functioning expected of the students. The learning-disabled students pri-*

TABLE 4-1. Levels of Cognitive Domain

KNOWLEDGE. Knowledge involves the recall of specifics or universals, the recall of methods and processes, or the recall of a pattern, structure, or setting. It will be noted that the essential attribute at this level is recall. For assessment purposes, a recall situation invovles little more than "bringing to mind" appropriate material.

COMPREHENSION. This level represents the lowest form of understanding and refers to a kind of apprehension that indicates that a student knows what is being communicated and can make use of the material or idea without necessarily relating it to other material or seeing it in its fullest implications.

APPLICATION. Application involves the use of abstractions in particular or concrete situations. The abstractions used may be in the form of procedures, general ideas, or generalized methods. They may also be ideas, technical principles, or theories that must be remembered and applied.

ANALYSIS. Analysis involves the breakdown of a communication into its constituent parts such that the relative hierarchy within that communication is made clear, that the relations between the expressed ideas are made explicit, or both. Such analyses are intended to clarify the communication, to indicate how it is organized and the way in which the communication manages to convey its effects as well as its basis and arrangement.

SYNTHESIS. Synthesis represents the combining of elements and parts so that they form a whole. This operation involves the process of working with pieces, parts, elements, and so on, and arranging them so as to constitute a pattern or structure not clearly present before.

EVALUATION. Evaluation requires judgments about the value of material and methods for given purposes. Quantitative and qualitative judgments are made about the extent to which material and methods satisfy criteria. The criteria employed may be those determined by the learner or those given to him.

Source: W. James Popham, Eva L. Baker, SYSTEMATIC INSTRUCTION, © 1970, pp. 32–33. Reprinted by permission of Prentice-Hall, Inc., Englewood Cliffs, N.J.

marily worked on unit tasks requiring them to perform at the knowledge and comprehension *level. For example, in a unit on the branches of the federal government, they were required to identify each of the branches and to state the contribution each of them makes to the establishment of federal policy. On the other end of the spectrum, gifted students contracted for an independent project involving the cognitive processes of* analysis, synthesis, *and* evaluation. *Each of these students selected a particular federal policy. They analyzed legislation related to the policy and the findings of at least two judicial cases that had provided interpretations of the policy. Mr. Sims found that every student in the class benefitted by having options available for them to work at their own individual level.*

A curriculum model (Bailey & Leonard, 1977) using these levels of cognitive thinking has been developed for the target group of preschool children who have been classified as both handicapped (e.g., visually impaired, orthopedically handicapped) and gifted (e.g., intellectual ability or talents). The model is comprised of instructional units with activities at each of the cognitive levels depicted in Table 4–1.

Another strategy for simplifying the curriculum at the secondary level is to insure that the student's courses are carefully chosen each semester. After considering the student's strengths and weaknesses, caution should be taken to avoid an "overload" of heavy courses. In some instances, it may be necessary to reduce the total course load (Allen et al., 1982).

Changing the Curriculum

In some cases, the performance levels of handicapped students differ so markedly from those of their nonhandicapped peers that curriculum must be altered to the point of teaching different content. Rather than working on the same unit with other students, the handicapped student may need to work on a prerequisite unit already mastered by other students. As previously indicated, the teacher first needs to determine the student's entry level for instruction by reviewing the goals and objectives on the IEP and completing a task analysis on the objectives. If it is determined that the student's goals and objectives differ *substantially* from other students, a change in the regular curriculum will be needed to accommodate the delayed achievement level.

In such cases, the appropriateness of placing a particular handicapped student in the regular classes should be carefully reviewed. If the student's needs for specially designed instruction cannot be accomplished within the framework of the regular curriculum, a more specialized setting may be required. In some instances, it may be appropriate to keep the student in a regular class setting and to make substantial curriculum changes.

The instructional strategies discussed in the next section apply to all three levels of curriculum adaptation—supplementing, simplifying, and changing. Because of the extent of specially designed instruction required to teach a modified curriculum, such instructional strategies are essential in these cases.

ADAPTATIONS IN INSTRUCTIONAL STRATEGIES

After the curriculum content of the handicapped student's program has been appropriately modified, the next major consideration is devising instructional strategies to package and teach the content specified by the goals and objectives. Instructional strategies, as used here, refer to methods and/or materials for delivering instruction. When mainstreaming handicapped students in the regular classroom, it is essential that the methods and materials used are not only effective for the handicapped student but also manageable for teachers, in the light of their responsibilities to the other students in the class.

In this section, seven instructional strategies are discussed, including changes in the format of materials, changes in the input and output requirements of tasks, tutorial programs, learning centers, contracts, learning activity packets, and educational technology.

Changes in Format

The special needs of many students can be accommodated by changing the format of materials, directions, or assignments. This is one of the simplest adaptations to make. Examples of special needs that may require format changes are:

- Short attention span—student can maintain attention to task only for relatively short intervals;
- Distractibility—student is distracted or attention is diverted by an overload of stimuli on a worksheet;
- Hypoactivity—Student is slow and lethargic, taking an excessive amount of time to complete an assignment;
- Memory problems—Student has trouble remembering directions and frequently forgets important points.

To accommodate special needs associated with short attention, assignments can be divided into smaller units or reduced in length. This type of adaptation can also help students who are hypoactive. A secondary language arts teacher described the use of such an adaptation.

The note from the Learning Center teacher said, "Very slow worker. Ability higher than you might suppose, like vocabulary." "Very slow" is an understatement. Stephen speaks at about 60 words a minute and he writes correspondingly. My Reading Improvement class uses vocabulary tests as well as individual oral book reports. Stephen is in a class with 23 other students; time was clearly going to be a real problem. After several weeks of trying to give Stephen's vocabulary with the rest of his group, it became obvious that this would not work. So with Stephen, I gave him 10 words and then randomly selected five of them for him to use in sentences instead of all 10. I also explained the reason why his was being done differently. He had often come to me saying "I didn't have time to finish this" or "Can I finish this tomorrow?" By giving him five words, he was able to finish on time and feel successful with having finished his assignment. We still had the problem of Stephen's oral book reports. After one disastrous attempt with his giving me his report during the class hour as the usual procedure, he was embarrassed, waiting students were frustrated, and I was frantically trying to cope with all of this. Sometimes I wonder why it takes me so long to come up with a solution when it is so apparent. I have a study hall 5th hour. Stephen is in the Learning Center 5th hour. The two rooms are next door. Solution: Stephen comes into my study hall and gives his book reports. We have all the time we need; he enjoys the lack of pressure; the other 23 students can have more of my attention during class.

Format adaptations can also be made by providing shorter work periods with more frequent activity changes than are typically used. Teachers can consider several types of work periods for students with short attention spans, such as:

1. warm-up activity—individual activity completed at a learning center;
2. main activity—usually teacher directed; and
3. cool-down—can be done alone or with peers.

Another strategy for breaking up work periods is to schedule preferred and less preferred activities alternately. While working on a less preferred activity, the student can eagerly anticipate completing a favorite activity.

Students who are distractible and have difficulty focusing on a single stimulus item on a worksheet will benefit from an altered format. Such alterations can be made by cutting pages so that fewer items are in view simultaneously or by using a cover sheet to expose a single or reduced number of stimulus items at one time.

Misunderstanding or forgetting directions to tasks, or confusion over the sequence of steps to solve problems, can also be overcome through format changes. Some students benefit from simplified directions or cues that prompt them in a correct response. Such cues are an example of a correct response or an outline of the steps to follow in completing a task. A first-grade teacher finds the following format adaptation successful in insuring that directions are understood and tasks accurately completed.

A student who recently entered my classroom has extreme difficulty transferring work from the board onto paper. He copies what he sees but has no idea of placement. To aid this student, I have found it very helpful if I make a copy of the day's assignment on a piece of paper exactly the way I want it copied. He then can visualize it on paper and know exactly what I expect from him.

When practicing writing, he has difficulty with letter placement, size, and spacing. For this assignment, I use a colored marker to write the letters, words, or sentence on his writing paper. Again, he can see the correct way I want him to write.

Math is another difficult area for this child. When presenting a new concept, I always have a few students come to the board to insure that I have made myself clear. This student is always called on so I can clearly see if and where he is having difficulty. When giving a math assignment, I stand near his table and point out everything on his paper that I am explaining, step by step. After I have given the assignment, I work with him individually, making sure he fully understands what he is supposed to do. When I feel he does understand, I let him finish alone.

Changes in Input or Output Requirements

All students, handicapped and nonhandicapped, have preferred modes of receiving information (input) and expressing known information (output). Alternative input and output modes are depicted in Table 4–2. Five input methods are identified: view/observe, read, listen, smell/taste/touch, and try/do/use. The

TABLE 4-2. Alternative Input and Output Requirements

INPUT/DATA COLLECTION

VIEW/OBSERVE	READ	LISTEN
visuals	books	radio
bulletin boards	comic books	records
banners	pamphlets	TV
posters	posters	speeches
transparencies	newspapers	lectures
slides	bulletin boards	debates
films/filmstrips	flash cards	discussions
flashcards	reports	dramatics
TV	wall graffiti	interpretive readings
graphs	letter	concerts
community events		interviews
field trips	*SMELL/TASTE/TOUCH*	
dramatic presentations	objects	*TRY/DO/USE*
nature/animals	textures	
	foods	games
	temperatures	experiments
	chemicals	exercises
		manipulative materials

TABLE 4-2. (Continued)

OUTPUT/DATA SYNTHESIS

MAKE/CONSTRUCT	VERBALIZE	WRITE
diorama	oral report	theme
collage	panel	research paper
scroll	debate	report
sand painting	discussion	workbook answers
diary	games	blackboard
pictograph	brainstorm	problems
media presentations	oral questions and answers	poems
maps		essays
models	SOLVE	
timelines	puzzles	PERFORM
leaf prints	mazes	simulation
paintings	problems	role play
food	equations	sociodrama
clothing	games	concert
bulletin board	riddles	pantomime
banner		interpretive reading
graph		
work wall drawings		

Source: From Pamela B. Smith & Glee Bentley. *Facilitator manual, teacher training program. Mainstreaming mildly handicapped students in the regular classroom.* Austin, Tex.: Education Service Center, Region XIII, 1975. Reprinted by permission.

five output methods include: make/construct, verbalize, write, solve, and perform. This model suggests that many different instructional strategies can be used to teach the same skill or concept. Table 4–3 uses this model to provide an example of alternative instructional strategies that can be used in a social studies class to teach the concept of democratic decision-making.

In reviewing Tables 4–2 and 4–3, it is obvious that certain input and output modes are more appropriate than others in meeting the special needs of students with different handicaps. Blind students would need input modes other than viewing/observing or reading print; hearing-impaired students, however, could benefit from these modes. Mentally retarded or learning-disabled students may need the output mode of making/constructing; students with mobility impairments may require adaptations in these types of activities.

Much stress is typically placed on the reading, writing, and listening skills of students. From an observational analysis of secondary classes in the areas

Adaptations in Instructional Strategies

TABLE 4-3. Alternative Input and Output Modes for Concept of Democratic Decision-Making

Input Modes

VIEW/OBSERVE	READ	LISTEN
Watch film on voting procedures	Read newspaper account of committee meetings	Listen to tape of political speakers
Observe political candidates and visit their offices	Review results of elections	
	Read books on democracy	TRY/DO/USE
Observe meetings of school committee, school board, and local government	SMELL/TASTE/TOUCH	Practice using voting machine; fill out ballot
		Conduct a mock election
		Participate in club and civic organizations
		Conduct a meeting with Robert's Rules of Order

Output Modes

MAKE/CONSTRUCT	VERBALIZE	SOLVE
Make political posters	Make speeches in favor of or against a candidate or proposal	Compute the percentage of votes each candidate receives
Construct bulletin board displays	Prepare oral questions and answers for school elections	Conduct a poll and compute probability that a candidate will win
Make local voting maps of districts and precincts		
	WRITE	PERFORM
	Write campaign slogans	Set up and hold mock elections
	Write essay on previous elections	Role play committee decision-making process; deal with a classroom problem and propose solution

of language arts, science, and social studies, Moran (1980) found that the predominant input mode is lecture. Teachers rarely asked questions or provided opportunities for students to respond verbally in class. Student output was primarily obtained through written performance. From self-report data collected, it is interesting to learn that teachers perceived themselves as lecturing less and asking more questions of students.

It is clear that many handicapped students can benefit greatly from instructional strategies that are individualized according to their special learning needs. Adapting input and output modes is an excellent strategy for meeting individual needs. As an example, many students with learning disabilities, mental retardation, and visual impairments benefit from using manipulative objects to supplement lessons that might otherwise be abstract for them. It is quite possible for the handicapped student to deal initially with a concept in some concrete way and still participate in class discussions and group projects. A compact, simple way to provide manipulative materials is illustrated in Figure 4–1. Pockets attached to file folders can be used to store concrete learning materials that help in the development of concepts. Such folders can be prepared as supplements to regular textbook or group assignments.

If classroom teachers have questions about the ideal input and output modes to use with handicapped students, they should raise these questions at the IEP meeting and discuss appropriate alternatives with the committee members. It is important for classroom and resource teachers to share information throughout the school year on the success they are having with various input/output modes.

Tutorial Programs

Many different types of tutorial programs can be devised in the regular classroom to provide individualized instruction to handicapped students. Tutors may include peers, paraprofessionals, parents, and community volunteers.

Peer tutoring has become a popular and prevalent strategy in many regular classrooms. In comparing teacher preferences for peer, parent, or volunteer tutors, it has been reported that teachers prefer the use of student tutors (Semmel, Cohen, & Kandaswamy, 1980). Also, students find satisfaction in working together, recognizing that knowledge and skills can be shared in a profitable way. They soon realize that tutor and tutee learn from each other.

The integration of handicapped students into regular classrooms can be facilitated immeasurably by students teaching students. In any classroom, there is always a student asking for help and there is usually one giving it. When this occurrence is used systematically, it becomes a powerful instructional techique.

Debbie, who receives help with math in the resource room, was reviewing multiplication tables. Kevin, who has severe emotional problems, was

Adaptations in Instructional Strategies   111

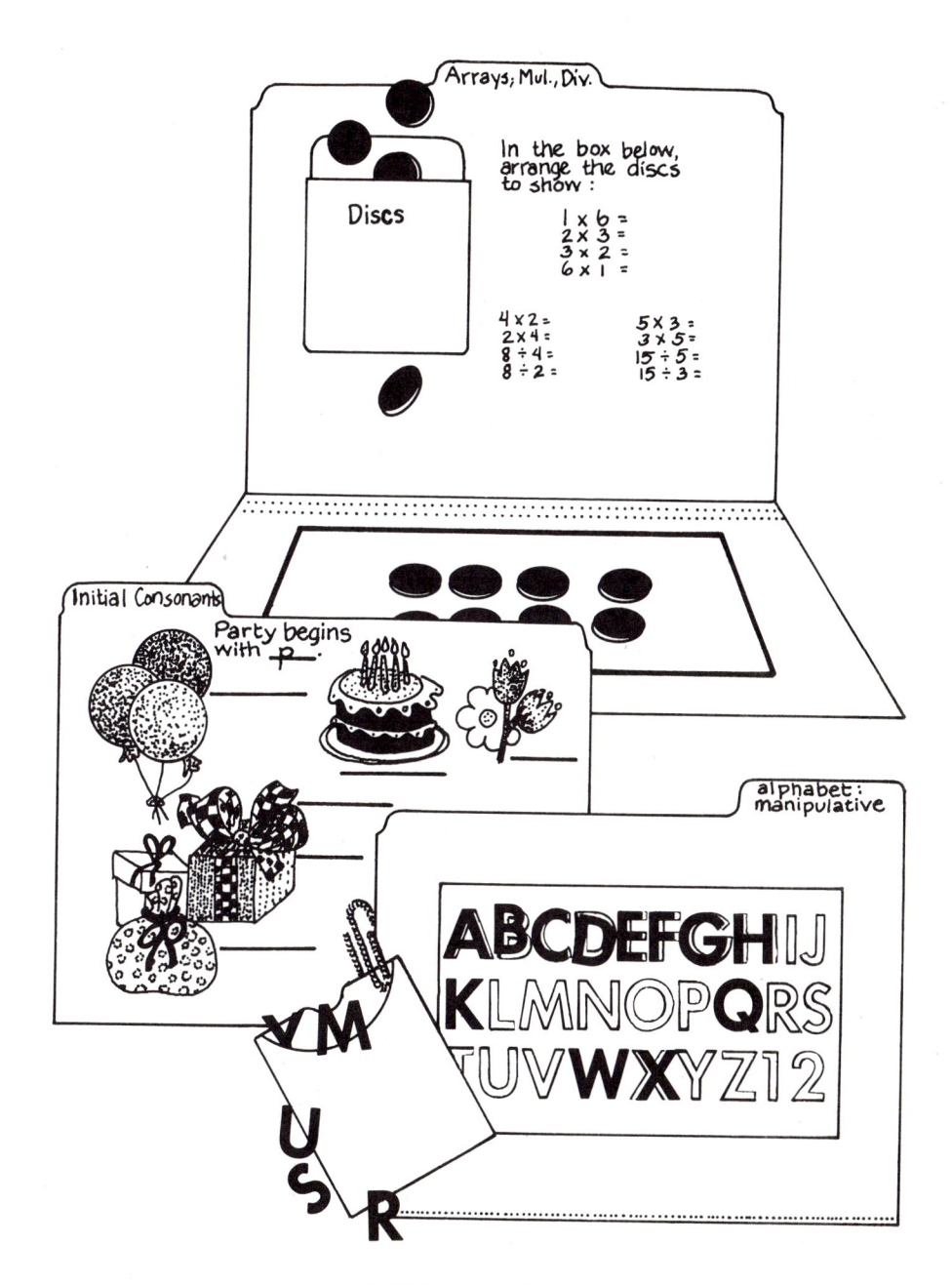

FIGURE 4–1. File Folders

asked to help her. He used drill cards and became the "teacher." His self-image and Debbie's multiplication skills both improved.

Frequently, a nonhandicapped student will help a handicapped schoolmate. The process can and should work in reverse.

David, who is blind, has mastered the use of the Numberaid, a pocket-sized abacus. He was asked to demonstrate its use to a group of fourth graders who were having difficulty with the concepts of place value and regrouping.

Peer teaching can occur in an informal way or in a more structured fashion. Jenkins and Mayhall (1976) describe a program in which peer teachers were trained and supervised by a resource teacher. Results of the one-to-one tutoring indicated an overwhelming superiority over small-group teacher instruction.

Another approach involves the cooperative grouping of students as contrasted with the one-to-one tutoring model. Cooperative grouping involves structuring learning experiences for heterogeneous groups that include handicapped and nonhandicapped students. The group is given a task to complete and required to work together in sharing skills and giving assistance.

A junior high science teacher divided his class into cooperative groups (comprised of nonhandicapped and mentally handicapped students) to complete an array of projects and participate in curriculum-based games. One game involved the teacher's calling out questions for each group to answer. The first persons in the group to raise their hands and answer were not allowed to answer again until everyone else on the team had answered a question. Questions progressed from simple to hard. The outcomes of this game, according to the teacher's report, were very consistent: brighter students tended to coach the mentally handicapped students "for the sake of the team" and brighter students avoided answering easier questions that the handicapped students in the group could answer. The teacher enthusiastically cited a high level of cooperation among students and aid offered to the handicapped students, as well as an impressive percentage of correct responses.

Johnson and Johnson (1980) have conducted extensive research on the outcomes of cooperative learning. Their results indicate that cooperative learning situations promote higher achievement in all students, in addition to more social acceptance and friendships among handicapped and nonhandicapped students. This technique is discussed further in chapter 11.

There are a number of techniques that can be used to initiate peer tutoring. Potential tutors can be identified with the use of a classroom resource bank. The posted directory would include information and resources about each class member. To develop the directory, students can be paired to interview each other to discover "who's good at what." The teacher can encourage active use of the directory at any time by making frequent referrals to it when a student needs help.

Training for students who want to be peer tutors can be made available. One type of training helps students to learn to relate well with younger children or handicapped students. Such instruction focuses on helping the tutored students achieve success and feel important. Sapon-Shevin (1980) has suggested four categories for skill development: asking for help, offering help, accepting help, and refusing help. Another type of training emphasizes the development of teaching strategies in specific content areas.

Paraprofessionals are another source of tutorial assistance to classroom teachers. Pickett (1980) reported that the number of paraprofessionals working with handicapped students tripled during a seven-year period, from 1973 to 1980, to a total of 80,000. Paraprofessionals are typically assigned to work with special education teachers. However, classroom teachers needing extra assistance with mainstreamed students should discuss with their principal the possibility of receiving paraprofessional help.

Finally, parents and volunteers may be interested in working with handicapped students to increase the amount of individualized instruction provided to them. Since tutoring programs involve additional time for planning, training, and supervision, administrators or counselors can help teachers with the logistics of setting up and maintaining tutoring programs (Semmel et al., 1980). The book of Ecclesiastes states the principle of providing tutorial assistance to handicapped students: "Two are better than one. . . . For if they fall, the one will lift up his fellow; but woe to him that is alone when he falleth; for he hath not another to help him up" (4:9-10).

Learning Centers

Individualization can be provided through learning centers or learning stations. The learning center is an area in the classroom where students go to work on facts, concepts, or skills. Here, materials and resources related to a given curriculum are collected and presented in an attractive and well-organized manner.

Learning centers have specific objectives to fulfill. They have multilevel activities and materials requiring various modes of learning to meet individual needs, styles, interests, and achievement levels. Choices and alternatives are offered with clear and simple instructions that a student can follow without constant teacher guidance.

Piechowiak and Cook (1976) describe four types of learning centers:

1. *Basic Learning Skills.* A skills center may utilize close-ended activity cards such as math drill cards, phonics, or sentence scrambles, or open-ended task cards

such as: make a list of all the ways that you can use the number 4. Activity task cards state the main goal, specific objectives, preassessment, and evaluation.

2. *Listening Center.* This is the ideal choice for a teacher who is just beginning to use learning centers. The use of a listening post with multiple headsets enables the teacher to add variety and offer some independence to the class, yet offers little threat to classroom control.

3. *Discovery Center.* This is the place for exploration and discovery. An example would be a science center where the child may float a variety of objects in a large container of water, leading to the discovery that dense objects sink and less dense objects float.

4. *Creative Center.* The creative center includes language arts, art, music, and crafts activities.

The following is a description of a communication skills learning center (see Figure 4-2).

COMMUNICATION STATION

Objectives:

To recognize that people communicate in a variety of ways.
To acquire skills in a new form of communication.

Materials:

Charts of finger spelling, Navy signal flags, and braille. (Other communication systems that could be used are Indian language symbols and foreign languages.)

Activities:

1. Choose a partner. By definition, communication has to be with someone. Skills are acquired and reinforced through use.

2. Together, learn a new communication system. Students choose one of the systems presented or research another one. They may memorize the symbols or prepare a chart to be available when they need it.

3. Find someone who uses this system; see if you can understand each other. This is the real test and the real challenge to the student. For example, if there is someone in the school or community who is deaf and who uses finger spelling, contact that person and carry on a conversation. It would also be interesting to invite him or her to class.

4. Find another system. This step provides an option for the student who (a) was not successful with the first choice or (b) would like an additional challenge.

5. Read about someone who communicates in a different way. Suggestions include *The Story of My Life* by Helen Keller or *In This Sign* by Joanne Greenberg. (Schulz, 1981, pp. 81-82)

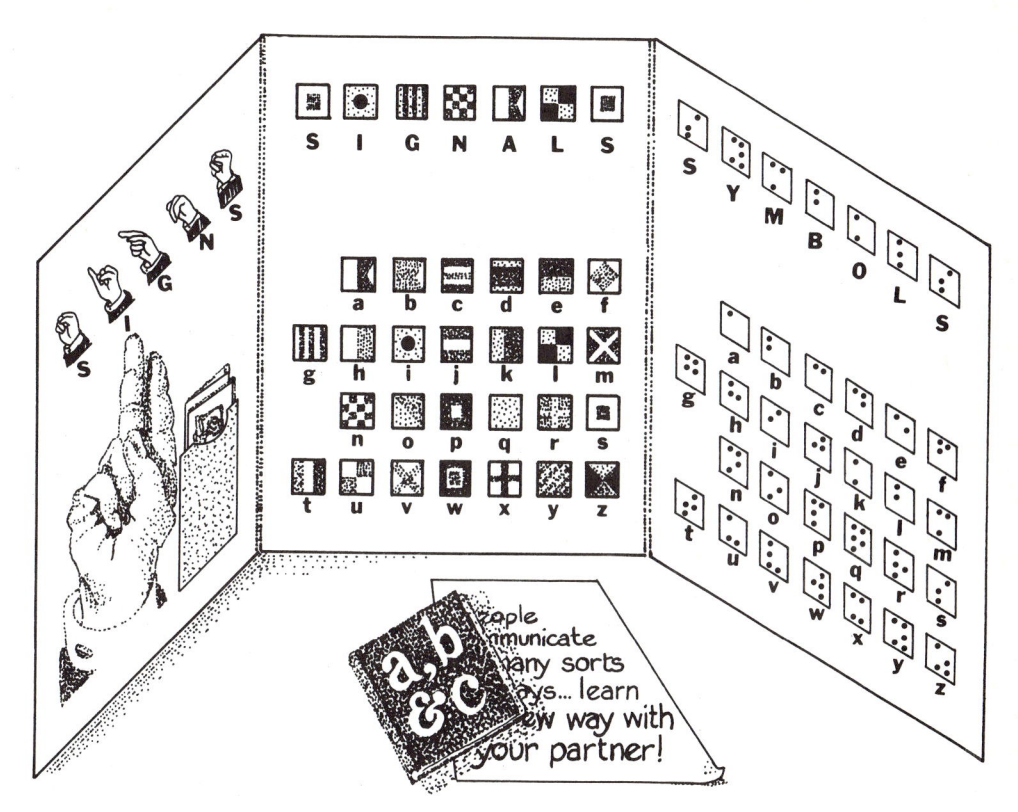

FIGURE 4–2. Communication Station Learning Center (From Jane B. Schulz, Communication station—a learning center for mainstreaming. *Teaching Exceptional Children,* 1981, 13 (2), 81–82.)

Learning centers may be added to the classroom to emphasize materials that support basic skills programs, to relate to a unit of study, or to provide an enriching element to the classroom. On the other hand, the teacher may elect to convert the classroom to a total learning center scheme. A center should prove useful to many students in the class if it fits their maturity, interests, and learning style (Voight, 1971).

Learning centers may be used to provide activities for independent study, follow-up for teacher-taught concepts, activities in place of regular assignments, or enrichment activities. An additional use as a reinforcer is described in chapter 10.

The steps necessary in creating a learning center are to:

1. Select a subject area.
2. Determine the skill or concept to be taught, reinforced, or enriched.

3. Develop the skill or concept into a learning activity, which should include manipulating (such as cutting, pasting, or matching); experimenting (observing, charting, keeping a log); and listening or viewing.
4. Prepare the skill or concept into an applying activity, such as filling in; arranging in order; putting together, taking apart; listing; classifying; matching; tracing; writing; locating or labeling.
5. Incorporate the skill or concept into an extending activity, such as comparing; developing your own; researching; reconstructing; finding what other or deciding what if.
6. Place all the games, worksheets, charts, etc., together in one area of the room for children to use in a self-selected manner.[1]

A major consideration in insuring the smooth operation of learning centers is to devise a student scheduling plan. Braithwaite (1980) suggests a variety of scheduling options, including a rotation schedule set by the teacher, student choice of centers based on needs and interests, and contracting.

Piechowiak and Cook (1976) claim that the learning center approach is humane to students with learning difficulties since they are not pressured to perform at a level exceeding their skill or chastised because they cannot do the work. "When students perform self-selected and self-scheduled tasks, the opportunities for comparison are less frequent. Who can tell if the immature child is still working on math, or if he has just started it later in the day?" (p. 68). Because learning centers contain a variety of activities ranging from simple to difficult and from concrete to abstract, they enable handicapped students to participate in interests shared by classmates. Instructions should be simple and clear; they can be on a cassette tape or pictured rather than written. Learning centers can provide alternatives related to the ability and learning style of each class member.

Contracts

A contract is an agreement written for, by, or with the student. It provides opportunities for a student to learn independently, and usually includes a variety of learning resources, such as tapes, records, books, films, pictures, loops, slides, and games (Dunn & Dunn, 1972). Contracts usually specify the type, amount, and quality of work to be completed by a student as well as the timeline. They cover academic as well as social behaviors and can be specially designed according to the individual needs of handicapped students. Contracts are particularly beneficial for students with emotional problems who benefit from having contingencies clearly identified in advance. Students who are poorly

1. From CHANGE FOR CHILDREN by S. N. Kaplan, J. B. Kaplan, S. K. Madsen and B. T. Gould. Copyright © 1973 Scott, Foresman and Company. Reprinted by permission.

motivated, or who are disorganized and frequently forget assignments, can also be aided by the use of contracts.

Contracts include behavioral objectives, a listing of many kinds of learning resources, and a series of activity alternatives that provide the student choices in applying and reporting gathered information. Contracts may be primarily determined and negotiated by teachers or by students. Blackburn and Powell (1976) define the following types of contracts:

- Structured contracts, in which all components are predetermined by the teacher. The student and the teacher negotiate a contract from these components.
- Partly structured contracts, in which some components are predetermined by the teacher and others are designed and developed by the teacher and the student.
- Mutually structured contracts, in which no components are predetermined; the teacher and the student cooperatively develop and negotiate the contract.
- Unstructured contracts, in which no components are predetermined; the student initiates and develops the parts and negotiates with the teacher.

Teachers should systematically encourage students to assume increasing responsibility for devising their own contracts. Many different forms can be used for contracts, including commercial forms produced by some publishers.

Contracts help remove the time variable from learning and permit students to work at their own pace. With the choices provided, they allow students to achieve independence and to assume responsibility for learning. Contracts also allow the teacher to prescribe activities on individual bases for many students. As students engage in contract activities, the teacher has time to spend with those encountering difficulties or needing assistance. Table 4–4 includes an example of a contract.

Learning Activity Packets

A learning activity packet is a self-instructional unit designed to help students learn one basic concept or idea that is broken down into several components. A learning activity packet is geared to a specific ability level and provides flexibility in the activities students may choose to reach stated goals. Students proceed at their own pace. The format of the learning activity packet is structured in a way that insures its success. The following components are essential:

1. A specific objective or set of objectives.
2. A pretest designed to assess the student's level of achievement relevant to the objective or objectives prior to the instructional experience.
3. A series of instructional activities designed to help the student meet the objective or objectives.

TABLE 4-4. Responsibility Contract: Plant Identification

OBJECTIVE AND ACTIVITIES:	Identify 15 plants in the chart below. You may use plants, labels, seed catalogs, and library reference books. 1. Fill in the plant name. 2. Draw a leaf. 3. Draw the flower if there is one. 4. Identify the plant type (annual, biennial, perennial). 5. Give the use of the plant (potting plant, bedding plant, shrub, tree, etc.) 6. Tell or show how the plant may be propagated (seed, leaf cutting, stem cutting, etc.)
EVALUATION:	100% of activities completed Criteria for grade include accuracy, neatness, and promptness of completion
TIMELINE:	Due one week after contract is signed

DATE SIGNED: _____
STUDENT: _____
TEACHER: _____
DATE CONTRACT COMPLETED: _____

Source: Adapted from John P. Schulz. Simulated work laboratory. Unpublished program of instruction, 1972.

4. A posttest designed to assess the student's level of mastery relevant to the objective or objectives.

5. Remediation procedures for those students who do not demonstrate mastery on the posttest.

The objective or objectives for learning activity packets should be drawn from the student's IEP. Teachers can review the IEP and identify particular objectives that can be appropriately taught through this instructional strategy (Clay & Stewart, 1980).

The pretest should be constructed based on a task analysis of the objective. By assessing the student's performance level on prerequisite skills and the sequence of skills and concepts involved in meeting the objective, the teacher can determine the student's entry level. The pretest may indicate that some activities can be bypassed.

Instructional activities can be as limited or numerous as necessary, depending on the complexity of the topic and the abilities and needs of the student. Regardless of the simplicity or complexity, the activities should be varied and highly motivational.

The posttest can be the same as, or a different form of, the pretest. If the student does not pass the posttest, this may indicate that the objective was not appropriate, that the activities were not relevant to the objective, or that more activities are required for the student to meet the performance criteria.

In the latter case, remediation activities (sometimes called branching activities) are used to approach the task through different input or output modes. After completing these activities, the student again takes the posttest and, if successful, is ready for a new packet.

The learning activity packet is a valuable tool in integrating handicapped students into regular classrooms. It enables students to work at their own speed; it provides additional material to insure learning; it offers alternatives to learning styles; and it allows students to work alone or in groups.

Learning activity packets can be prepared by the teacher, peer tutors, volunteers, or paraprofessionals. In one school, the resource teachers developed a library of packets for classroom teachers to use. Placed in the media center, it is available for anyone's use and contains activities, at many levels of difficulty, in all subject areas. Once prepared, they can be used individually by a student or with the help of a volunteer or peer tutor. Although the packets are planned for individual needs, many students have similar needs. Therefore, a library of various kinds of learning activity packets would assist tremendously in the individualization process.

The following learning activity packet is illustrated in Figure 4-3.

TIE A BOW

Objective:

Student will tie shoestrings at school and at home with no assistance.

Pretest:

Student is instructed to tie shoestring.

Activities:

Follow illustrated task analysis of tying a bow:

1. Tie strings on tennis shoe (colored shoestrings correspond with pictorial directions)
2. Practice with lacing board
3. Tie own shoestring

Branching Activity:

Forty knots—a visual aid for knot tying
Packet is contained in box which ties to close.
Packet may be used at home or at school.

The learning activity packet as a means to individualized instruction has advantages for the learner and teachers:

1. Students learn at their own rate.

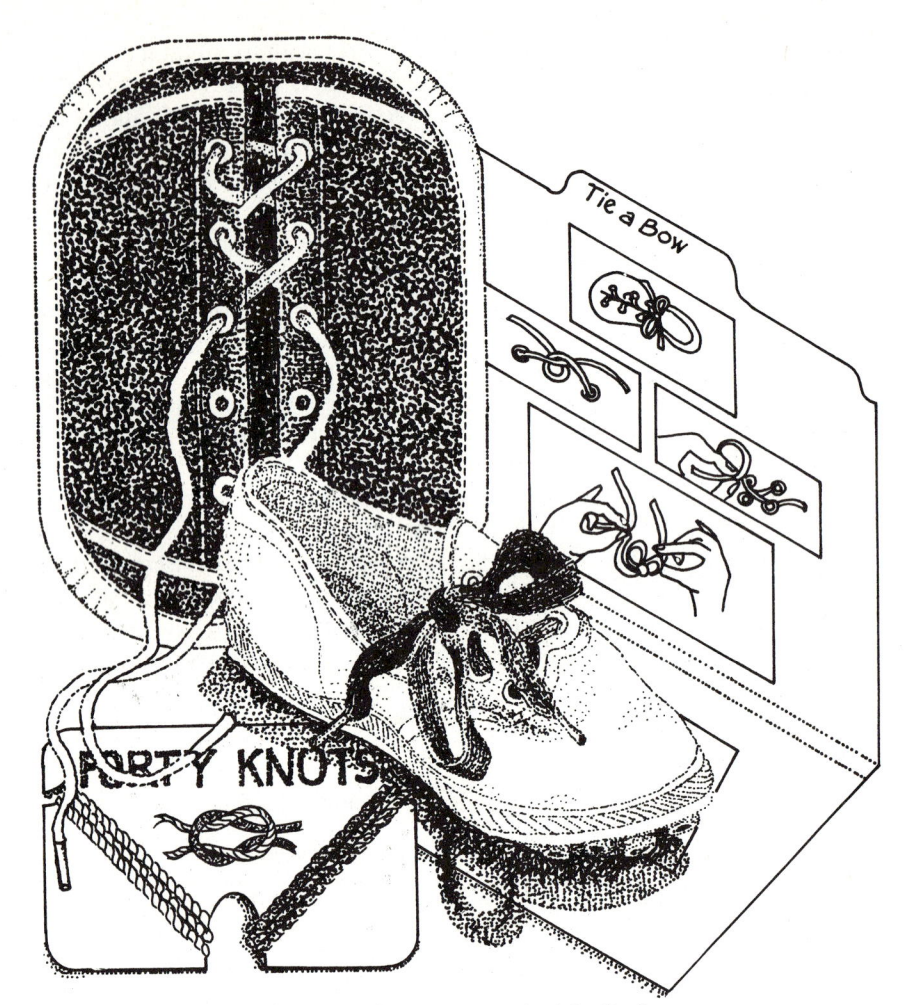

FIGURE 4–3. Learning Activity Packet

2. Students are successful.
3. Students are motivated to learn and to acquire independence.
4. Teachers' time and energy are extended.
5. Students who perform at different levels can work in the same classroom.

Although it is highly structured, the learning activity packet consists of a variety of methods and materials from which the student can choose. Structure is more evident in the instructional objectives, with emphasis on "what you must arrive at" rather than a forced "how you must get there."

Educational Technology

The rapid increase in educational technology has tremendous potential for enhancing the degree of individualized instruction that can be provided to handicapped students. Although the cost of computers has in the past been prohibitive for many schools, the availability of computers is rapidly making computer-assisted instruction an educational reality.

Microcomputers typically use some form of a keyboard for input and a display screen similar to a television for output. Information and program data can be stored permanently on cassette tapes or on a floppy disk, which is circular, thin, and plastic coated. Computer technology has been used effectively to provide individualized instruction. A highly successful project, using the computer language of LOGO, has been developed by Papert at MIT (Weir & Watt, 1980–1981). Based on the work of Piaget, LOGO teaches computer programming, problem solving, and mathematical thinking to handicapped as well as gifted students. The success of these programs with autistic, orthopedically handicapped, and learning-disabled students has been documented. An ongoing project to use LOGO with the learning-disabled population has the following student goal:

> To help mildly to moderately learning disabled students, grades 5–8, who receive remedial services in school Learning Centers, make gains in the areas of motivation, self confidence, basic skills in math, reading, spelling and punctuation,

creative writing, typing logical problem solving, and computer literacy. (Weir & Watt, 1980–1981, pp. 16–17)

Individualized instruction is a key component of this project:

Since the project stresses flexibility of approach, and the integration of computer activities into individual education plans, all students will not be expected to meet all objectives equally. An important aspect of the project will be the development of the best possible integration of individual student needs and project activities in order to meet particular objectives. The project staff and teachers will make use of ongoing evaluation of each child's work to make the best possible match between student needs and project objectives. For example, some students may make extensive use of the text-editor, with reduced emphasis on computer programming. For others the reverse may be true. The overall evaluation will need to take these individual differences into account. (Weir & Watt, 1980–1981, p. 17)

Another computer program, PLATO, has been used in providing individualized instruction to handicapped students. Evaluations of PLATO in teaching number concepts and reading skills (work attack, encoding, decoding, and comprehension) to handicapped students have indicated successful applications (Wieck, 1980).

In addition to its use in teaching concepts and problem solving, the computer is used for drill and practice. Commercial or teacher-made computer programs provide a large bank of questions and answers. When students need more practice on a particular skill or concept, the computer program draws questions from the data bank, presents them to the student, and provides immediate feedback on the accuracy of the student's response (Moursund, 1980–1981). Frequently, handicapped students have a slower learning rate and, consequently, require more practice. Computer-assisted instruction in this area can increase student performance and decrease daily teacher responsibility for locating appropriate worksheets for students. Wieck (1980) has provided a review of computer advances aimed at various types of handicapping conditions.

The selection of software (computer programs) is a key factor in the effective use of computer-assisted instruction. When the goal is to individualize instruction for handicapped students, software must be selected that takes into account the educational characteristics of these students. Grimes (1981) reviews some of these characteristics (attention, visual, memory, and generalization problems) with specific suggestions for the design of software programs. Criteria for selecting software in the areas of learner/teacher needs, instructional integrity, and technical adequacy and utility are presented by Hannaford and Sloane (1981).

The prerequisites to using computers to deliver individualized instruction are to insure that teachers are computer literate and to teach basic computer usage skills to students. Staff development programs on computer literacy have been developed by many school systems. Descriptions of sample programs are provided by Beck (1981) and Diem (1981).

Regarding computer literacy for students, Dahlberg (1980) reviewed an instructional program implemented by a school district that covered grades four through twelve. He described the instructional resources used in this program.

> One hour a day (for approximately one week before the computers are in the classroom) is spent discussing social aspects and the impact computers are having on employment. We use as a text, *What Is a Computer?* by Marion Ball. The last two weeks of the three week period allows a "hands on" programming experience for the elementary school students. The curriculum uses tapes and a handbook to introduce the concepts covered, both of which were developed by district teachers. At the 7th grade level, emphasis is placed on career exploration in nine week "mini courses" which use a text, *Are You Computer Literate?* by Billings and Moursund. (p. 15)

Further guidelines for developing computer literacy training for students are provided by Board of Cooperative Educational Services (1981) and Stevens (1981).

In addition to computers, electronic games can be used successfully in the individualization process. Games such as *Speak and Read, Speak and Spell,* and *The Little Professor* provide entertaining and intensive skill development, as well as problem solving, in the areas of reading, spelling, and mathematics. As an example of the instructional value of these aids, *Speak and Read* (Texas Instruments) provides practice in phonics, sight words, and comprehension. Through the various games that can be played, students have an opportunity to hear, see, pronounce, and spell words by pressing letters. Students can also punch in the letters of unfamiliar words that they encounter during silent reading, and the machine will pronounce the word for them (if the word is in the *Speak and Read* bank). Such individual assistance can free teachers from the disruptions to identify words for students. The cost of *Speak and Read* is between thirty and forty dollars, generally affordable for many schools.

Other electronic games have been devised that are timely, motivating, and filled with instructional possibilities. Drawbacks to some of the games are that the size and type of controls require fine manipulations and that the speed of play may be too fast for some handicapped students. Hughes (1981) has provided excellent suggestions for adapting such games to the particular needs of handicapped students.

The use of educational technology to individualize instruction has many advantages, including high motivational value, novelty, immediate feedback, self-pacing, and active practice. As stated by Wieck (1980):

Advancements in computer based technology during the next decade may be one way to enhance the learning opportunities of all students with handicapping conditions. Only time will define whether educators will accept, reject, or neglect these resources in providing educational opportunities. (p. 27)

COORDINATING INSTRUCTION BETWEEN THE CLASSROOM AND SPECIAL EDUCATION SERVICES

A misconception about mainstreaming is that classroom teachers seem to feel they will have to "go it alone." Actually, the mainstreaming process requires a great deal of ancillary help from special education resource teachers, itinerant teachers, and related service providers, such as speech therapists, adaptive physical education teachers, and occupational therapists. Other support and advice will come from psychologists, social workers, parents, volunteers, college personnel and students, paraprofessionals, and peer tutors (as suggested in chapter 2).

In order to achieve the optimum benefit from special education services provided by resource teachers and related service providers, it is essential to coordinate these services carefully with the regular classroom program. Two important issues of coordination involve scheduling and communication.

Scheduling

When direct services are provided by a resource teacher or related service provider, scheduling student time away from the regular classroom may become difficult. Although proper scheduling requires time and attention, it is extremely important for smoother operation and good working relationships. The classroom teacher should consider several time blocks during which handicapped students could be away from the classroom without jeopardizing their instructional program. Generally, it is wise to schedule special student services during the period of the subject being remediated. For instance, if students are provided with special services in reading, they should be taken from the class during the regular reading period. Thus, they will be absent from class during a time when they do not usually experience success. Also, they will not miss instruction in other important subject areas.

Students typically should not be scheduled for direct services during physical education, music, art, or library classes. Handicapped students usually enjoy and need this instruction; the resource room should not be punitive.

Scheduling preferences of teachers and students can be discussed at the IEP meeting. It is important for classroom teachers to state their preferences and negotiate for a convenient arrangement. If the schedule is in the student's best interest and manageable for both the classroom and resource teachers, the program will more likely succeed. It is extremely important for all teachers to adhere to the determined schedule. From the resource teacher's point of view, every minute counts since students are usually scheduled in short, consecutive blocks. From the classroom teacher's point of view, lack of adherence to the schedule can mean interruptions in group activities. Handicapped students should be taught and expected to assume responsibility for leaving the regular classroom at the appropriate time to arrive punctually for their special services.

Communication

Communication among regular classroom teachers, resource teachers, and related service providers is an essential ingredient of successful mainstreaming programs. This communication should begin at the IEP meeting and continue throughout the school year as the IEP is implemented.

At the IEP meeting, the roles of the various persons responsible for the handicapped student's program should be clarified. It should be specified at that time which teacher or related service provider will be primarily responsible for teaching each objective, providing each service, and meeting the special needs identified as essential in providing the student with an appropriate education. Also, a plan can be devised at the IEP meeting to maintain communication throughout the year. Such a plan could schedule periodic review meetings for teachers to discuss the student's progress, or set up a notebook the student could take back and forth from the classroom teacher to the resource teacher. This notebook would include comments on the student's progress and any special concerns noted by either teacher.

> *Johnny completed his math quiz with 100 percent accuracy today. I am really proud of him. The use of manipulative objects and the practice sheets he has been completing at home seem to be a very successful strategy for him.*

> *Maria had an argument with several of her friends at recess, which resulted in a great deal of anger and frustration. Her work is likely to be affected by her disposition.*

> *Next week we will be starting a unit on erosion. Jason has a list of vocabulary words for this unit in his notebook. I would appreciate it if you would help him with the meaning and spelling of these words. It would give him a head start on keeping up with our unit work. Thanks very much. Your assistance is invaluable to him and to me.*

As instructional strategies are planned and implemented throughout the year, ongoing communication and coordination are vitally important. Many resource programs have failed because the special educator and the classroom teacher did not have time to communicate and to coordinate services. Frequently, the result is that instruction provided in the resource room has no relation to that provided in the regular classroom. Classroom teachers and resource teachers do not have to use identical instructional approaches; however, their approaches should be complementary. It is essential that the classroom teacher and the special educator have established times, convenient for both, to talk, plan, and explore ways of mutually assisting handicapped students in achieving success.

EVALUATION PROCEDURES AND GRADING

A high school social studies teacher, who has been the recipient of several teaching awards during her eighteen years of experience, recently commented, "I believe grading and grade reporting are the most difficult tasks for the classroom teacher." Most teachers would probably agree with her perspective. The evaluation dilemma is even more complex for handicapped students who require specially designed instruction in the regular classroom. The challenge for educators is to devise fair systems that accomplish the purpose of evaluation while considering the interests of both handicapped and nonhandicapped students.

Evaluation is a means of informing students, parents, and teachers of the student's achievement (both strengths and weaknesses) and the areas of needed attention. This type of information should lead to appropriate decision making concerning the nature of the student's educational program and career choices. Thus, evaluating student progress and reporting grades should be a means of enhancing the quality and appropriateness of educational and vocational decisions.

Teachers should never underestimate the impact that grades have on both students and parents. They can strongly influence the student's self-concept, attitude toward school, peer relationships, development of hobbies, and level of motivation. For parents, grades can play a large role in shaping parental expectations, defining priorities for the use of time at home, and influencing the quality of the parent-child relationship. Evaluating student progress and reporting grades thus becomes a major responsibility for teachers.

This section focuses on two aspects of the evaluation process: the individualization of classroom evaluation procedures, criteria, and schedules and methods for assigning and reporting grades.

Individualization of Evaluation

Just as the curriculum should be adapted in light of the special needs of handicapped students, so should the evaluation procedures. The beginning point for planning such adaptations is the IEP conference. As discussed in chapter 3, one required component of the IEP is the specification of evaluation procedures, criteria, and schedules. At the IEP conference, classroom teachers have an opportunity to work with the other committee members in planning for evaluation that reflects the particular student's special needs and the goals and objectives that have been determined appropriate for the student.

Clearly, there is no best evaluation system that can be applied to every mainstreamed student. There are, however, general principles and guidelines that can be helpful in making these evaluation decisions at the IEP conference and implementing them in the classroom.

Evaluation Procedures. Evaluation procedures refer to the types of assessment instruments used. There are two important guidelines to consider. The first is that students should be evaluated on the curriculum they have been taught. Thus, if the student's curriculum has been simplified or changed, evaluation procedures need to be adapted accordingly. Evaluation procedures should be tailored to the content (goals and objectives) of the student's program.

Criterion-referenced tests have a particular advantage since they include a listing of objectives the student is expected to learn, criteria for mastery of the objectives, and test questions keyed to the objectives. By using criterion-referenced tests, the progress of students is assessed in relation to their starting point rather than an arbitrary normative standard. Criterion-referenced tests also are readily transferrable into checklists that can be used to report progress to parents, as discussed in the next section. In addition to criterion-referenced tests, other types of appropriate evaluation procedures include observation, teacher-made tests, review of assignments, and student self-reports.

The goals and objectives comprising the student's program constitutes one basis for selecting evaluation procedures. In addition to goals and objectives, decisions must be made on other areas of evaluation, such as the student's effort, social adjustment, work habits, and peer relationships. Most school districts have written policies on target areas for evaluation. The first step for teachers is to review these policies carefully. If the teacher believes that modifications in the policies are necessary in light of the needs of a handicapped student, such modifications should be discussed with the principal.

The second guideline is that some students will need adaptations in the way evaluation procedures are administered, just as they need adaptations in the way instruction is delivered. The earlier discussion in this chapter regarding changes in the format of materials and directions and changes to input or output requirements applies to evaluation as well as instruction. All the alternative output modes illustrated in Table 4–2 can be translated into evaluation procedures.

It is obvious from reviewing Table 4–2 that many evaluation procedures can be used as alternatives to tests. The performance of some students will increase according to the output mode used. Through a review of the student's performance, and discussion at the IEP meeting, teachers should identify the output mode best suited to the individual student's needs.

When traditional tests are administered, techniques can be used to insure that handicapped students are not at a disadvantage because of their special needs. Techniques in the areas of format considerations, test adaptations, technical aspects, and strategies for minimizing stress and strain are outlined by Regan (1979). Many of these suggestions are also highly appropriate for use with nonhandicapped students.

A secondary language arts teacher described adapted evaluation procedures that she found to be successful:

> *Because of Michelle's cerebral palsy, handwriting is a very slow, deliberate effort. To compensate for this, I attempted to keep her writing tasks at a minimum on tests so that she would not be unfairly penalized.*
>
> *Those parts of tests which were essay in nature posed a particular problem. The best solution was to have her answer the questions orally. Sometimes she answered directly to me and other times she went into an adjoining work room and answered into a tape recorder. I could then play back her responses at a convenient time.*
>
> *When the tests involved theme writing, we again needed to make adjustments. One solution to the problem, which worked well, was to shorten the required length of her themes so that she could do all of the writing herself. She generally preferred to do the same work in the same manner as her classmates so this procedure was particularly effective. Another way we sometimes handled this was by having her use the tape recorder to record her thoughts. I would then write down what she had recorded and she would then go over it and finalize it before turning it in.*

Evaluation Criteria. The evaluation criteria must be specified for each IEP objective. In making decisions pertaining to criteria, a major issue to consider is the referent for the criteria. Will the criteria be based on the norms for progress of nonhandicapped students at the same grade level or on the student's progress in relation to current level of performance? This fundamental decision involves specifying either a norm-referenced or criterion-referenced standard for setting criteria. Consistent with the philosophy of individualization, the criterion-referenced standard of evaluating students according to their progress on IEP goals and objectives is the most reasonable procedure. Particularly in the case of students whose achievement is significantly below grade level, expecting them to meet the standards of nonhandicapped students gives them no option but failure.

> *Don, a student identified as mentally retarded, was mainstreamed into a fourth-grade class for science, social studies, and music. His reading*

skills were at the first-grade level, and he had a great deal of difficulty with concept development. Don's teacher had ignored the IEP objectives and taught him on a fourth-grade level with no adaptations. His teacher used a norm-referenced standard of evaluation. Don tried very hard to do his assignments and worked far more diligently than most students in the class. But his achievement, as compared to others with normal ability, just didn't measure up. On his daily assignments and on his report card, he received an F in every subject. Is it Don who failed or was it really the teacher who failed?

It is important to state the level of mastery that the student is expected to demonstrate on each objective. If an 80 percent criterion is agreed on for a given objective, then the teacher and student are clear about what constitutes an acceptable performance.

In addition to qualitative standards for criteria, quantitative standards can be set. In the development of contracts, as previously discussed, the teacher and student can agree on criteria for determining the successful completion of a project. Quantitative criteria would include the number of books read, worksheets completed, or problems solved. For handicapped students who work more slowly than other students, modifications can be made in quantitative criteria to adjust the level of expectation to their work pace.

Schedules. The schedule or frequency with which handicapped students are evaluated is an important consideration. Some handicapped students, particularly those who have experienced a high level of failure in the past, may benefit from more frequent evaluations to reassure them that they are making progress and to provide them with positive reinforcement. Also, some students who have learning and/or emotional problems may perform at an optimal level if given shorter quizzes on a smaller portion of material rather than longer exams covering an extensive amount of content. Thus, the schedule of evaluations may need to be specially designed to account for the strengths and weaknesses of a given student.

Assigning and Reporting Grades

Based on the classroom evaluations that are conducted on a daily, weekly, and monthly basis, teachers must address the issues of formally assigning and reporting grades to the student and parents and recording grades in the student's permanent file. Again, there is no best system to handle the complexities of grading a handicapped student, particularly those achieving significantly below grade level. As mentioned earlier, teachers need to familiarize themselves with the grading policies and forms of their school system. Some school systems have flexible policies already established, and others have policies that place major restrictions on adaptive procedures. Thus, teachers need to be aware of the negotiable and nonnegotiable aspects in their own school system for individualizing grading procedures.

Another aspect of grading that is typically dictated by system policy is the schedule of reporting grades to parents. Schedules vary from a monthly to a quarterly basis.

This section presents two types of reporting systems—progress checklists and assignment of letter and number grades.

Progress Checklists. The use of progress checklists naturally follows if criterion-referenced assessment and instruction have been used. Based on IEP goals and objectives, this checklist would list skills and concepts taught in each subject area for the period of time covered by the reporting schedule. Columns can be provided for the teacher to check indicating whether each skill or concept has been "mastered" or "still needs improvement." Table 4–5 contains an example of a progress checklist. Space can be provided on the form for written comments pertaining to the student's strengths and weaknesses.

The advantage of such a system is that grading is clearly based on the substance of the student's individualized curriculum. Additionally, parents and students are provided with specific information on skill development indicating the progress the student is making and the areas needing more concentrated effort. Such information can help parents select the skills and concepts to practice and reinforce at home.

Progress checklists also have disadvantages. Many school systems require the use of grades to compute grade point averages. An alternative is to combine features of the checklist with the assignment of letter and number grades as discussed in the next section. Also, many handicapped students want to have report cards similar to those of their peers. Thus, if nonhandicapped students do not receive progress checklists, many handicapped students may be embarrassed to receive such reports.

Letter and Number Grades. A combination of letters and numbers is probably the grading system used most frequently in schools. Two issues need to be resolved—the areas around which letters and numbers are assigned and the criteria used to assign the grades.

The target areas around which grades are assigned and reported should depend on the areas that have been identified as vital to the student's educational program. The two areas routinely included on report cards include achievement and effort.

Achievement grades can be assigned in several ways:

1. Use criterion stated in IEP objective so that if a student masters an objective to 80 percent accuracy, a grade of B would be assigned. The subject grade would then be computed as an average of the objective grades.

TABLE 4-5. Progress Checklist Based on Criterion-Referenced Assessment

OBJECTIVES

MASTERED	NEEDS IMPROVEMENT	LINEAR MEASUREMENT
____	____	1. Identifies the number of inches in one foot with 100% accuracy.
____	____	2. Identifies the number of inches in one yard with 100% accuracy.
____	____	3. Identifies one inch with 100% accuracy.
____	____	4. Measures with 100% accuracy a 6-inch line drawn on paper, with 12-inch ruler.
____	____	5. Measures with 100% accuracy a 4½-inch line drawn on paper, with 12-inch ruler.
		6. Completes with 100% accuracy.
____	____	a. one foot = _____ inches.
____	____	b. one yard = _____ inches.
____	____	c. one yard = _____ feet.
____	____	7. Orders correctly from shortest to longest with 100% accuracy: 1 foot, 1 yard, 8 inches, and 24 inches.
____	____	8. Completes with 100% accuracy numerical problems in addition and subtraction involving inches, feet, and yards. No conversion required.
____	____	9. Completes with 100% accuracy word problems in addition and subtraction involving inches, feet, and yards. No conversion required.
____	____	10. Completes with 100% accuracy numerical problems in addition and subtraction involving inches, feet, and yards. Conversion required.
____	____	11. Completes with 100% accuracy word problems in addition and subtraction involving inches, feet, and yards. Conversion required.
		12. Reads the following words with 100% accuracy.
____	____	a. foot
____	____	b. inch
____	____	c. yard

Source: Adapted from Ann P. Turnbull, Bonnie Strickland, & John C. Brantley, *Developing and implementing individualized education programs* (2nd ed.). Columbus, Ohio: Charles E. Merrill Publishing Co., 1982. Used with permission of the publisher.

2. A more global, IEP-based system could be used according to a scale such as:

   A—the student surpasses the expectations of the IEP

   B—the student meets IEP expectations

   C—the student performs somewhat below IEP standards and expectations

   D–F—the student performs significantly below IEP standards and expectations.

3. Letter grades can be used to indicate the extent of the student's progress in various subject areas.

   S—progress is satisfactory

   I—improving but not completely satisfactory

   N—needs to improve

   U—progress is unsatisfactory

   X—not being evaluated at this time

Reporting grades on the student's effort can also provide helpful information. This can be done using the satisfactory/unsatisfactory scale shown previously, or by using numbers. For example:

1—best effort

2—good effort but could work harder

3—poor effort—needs much improvement

Other areas that can be included in the grading system are social adjustment, work habits, and peer relationships.

An advantage of this system of letters and numbers is that it is likely to conform to the grading system used with nonhandicapped students. Thus, handicapped students would not have a "different" report card setting them apart from their peers or causing extra difficulty in the record-keeping system of the school. Also, the use of multiple grades helps to insure that handicapped students are assessed over a broad spectrum of areas. Thus, they have the opportunity to receive feedback on their strengths as well as weaknesses.

A major disadvantage of letter and number grades that are criterion-referenced rather than norm-referenced is that the grades of handicapped students can be viewed as inflated compared to grades of nonhandicapped students (who have higher standards to meet in some subject areas in line with their higher ability). Some people argue that it is unfair for handicapped students to receive an A when their IEP objectives may be below grade-level expectations. One strategy for addressing this issue on a school district level is to devise a weighting system for academic credits as a basis for formulating grade point averages. The following example of a weighting system uses a 4-point scale, so that for a given class:

1. Student 1, of average ability, does grade-level work and receives a grade of A and an assignment of 4 points;
2. Student 2, who is gifted, does accelerated work and receives a grade of A and an assignment of 5 points;
3. Student 3, a learning-disabled student, does below grade-level work appropriate to his level of achievement and receives a grade of A and an assignment of 3 points.

Such a system enables students who meet grade-level or above expectations to be rewarded without depriving handicapped students of success.

These two strategies of progress checklists and assignment of letter and number grades primarily rely on a written reporting format. Both strategies, however, can be combined with a student and parent conference to explain the basis for grading, to highlight areas of the student's progress, and to pinpoint areas of needed improvement. Verbal communication can clarify areas of misunderstanding and can take into account the special needs of the student.

In summary, providing specially designed instruction to handicapped students requires individualization, and individualization requires creative teaching strategies. It is necessary for teachers to maintain perspective on both the challenge and reality of this task.

> Complete individualization is a goal for educators much as democracy is a goal for Americans or Christianity is a goal for Christians. Everyone in education should strive to reach the goal, knowing that complete individualization is rare, if not impossible. Anytime, however, that the school situation is focusing on the individual student in the teaching-learning process, another step is being made toward the ultimate goal (Musgrave, 1975, p. x).

REFERENCES

Allen, J. B., Clark F., Gallagher, P., & Scofield, F. *Classroom strategies for accommodating the exceptional learner.* Minneapolis: National Support Systems Project, 1982.

Bailey, D. B., & Leonard, J. A model for adapting Bloom's taxonomy to a preschool curriculum. *The Gifted Child Quarterly,* 1977, *21*(1), 97–103.

Beck, J. J. A paradigm for computer literacy training for teachers. *The Computing Teacher,* 1981, *9*(2), 27–28.

Blackburn, J. E., & Powell, W. C. *One at a time all at once: The creative teacher's guide to individualized instruction without anarchy.* Pacific Palisades, Calif.: Goodyear, 1976.

Board of Cooperative Educational Services. Developing computer literacy in K–12 education. *The Computing Teacher,* 1981, *9*(3), 43–48.

Braithwaite, J. Living with learning centers. *Exceptional Teacher,* 1980, *1*(9), 1–12.

Clay, J. E., & Stewart, F. Implementing individualized education programs with contract activity packages. *Teaching Exceptional Children,* 1980, *12*(4), 161–165.
Dahlberg, H. Computer literacy project. *The Computing Teacher,* 1980, 7(6), 15–16.
Diem, R. A. Developing computer education skills: An inservice training program. *Educational Technology,* 1981, *21*(2), 30–32.
Dunn, R., & Dunn, K. *Practical approaches to individualizing instruction: Contracts and other effective teaching strategies.* West Nyack, N.Y.: Parker, 1972.
Frank, A. R. Breaking down learning tasks: A sequence approach. *Teaching Exceptional Children,* 1973, *6*(1), 16–19.
Grimes, L. Computers are for kids: Designing software programs to avoid problems of learning. *Teaching Exceptional Children,* 1981, *14*(2), 49–53.
Hannaford, A., & Sloane, E. Microcomputers: Powerful learning tools with proper programming. *Teaching Exceptional Children,* 1981, *14*(2), 54–57.
Hughes, K. Adapting audio/video games for handicapped learners: Part 2. *Teaching Exceptional Children,* 1981, *14*(3), 127–129.
Jenkins, J. R., & Mayhall, W. F. Development and evaluation of a resource teacher program. *Exceptional Children,* 1976, *43,* 21–29.
Johnson, D. W., & Johnson, R. *Promoting constructive student-student relationships through cooperative learning.* Minneapolis: National Support Systems Project, 1980.
Johnson, S., & Johnson, R. B. *Developing individualized instructional material.* Palo Alto, Calif.: Westinghouse Learning Press, 1970.
Junkala, J. B. Task analysis and instructional alternatives. *Academic Therapy,* 1972, *8,* 33–40.
Kaplan, S. N., Kaplan, J. A. B., Madsen, S. K., & Taylor, B. K. *Change for children.* Pacific Palisades, Calif.: Goodyear, 1973.
McCormack, J. E., Jr. The assessment tool that meets your needs: The one you construct. *Teaching Exceptional Children,* 1976, *8,* 106–109.
Moran, M. R. An investigation of the demands of oral language skills on learning disabled students in secondary classrooms (Research Report No. 1). Lawrence, Kans.: The University of Kansas Institute for Research in Learning Disabilities, 1980.
Moursund, D. Introduction to computers in education for elementary and middle school teachers. *Computing Teacher,* 1980–1981, *8*(4), 7–19.
Musgrave, G. R. *Individualized instruction.* Boston: Allyn and Bacon, 1975.
Pickett, A. L. Roles of paraprofessionals in schools. *Education Unlimited,* 1980, *2*(1), 6–7.
Piechowiak, A. B., & Cook, M. B. *Complete guide to the elementary learning center.* West Nyack, N.Y.: Parker, 1976.
Popham, W. J., & Baker, E. L. *Systematic instruction.* Englewood Cliffs, N.J.: Prentice-Hall, 1970.
Regan, M. K. *Vocational education inservice training: Training modules* (Vol. 1). Kansas City, Kans.: Department of Special Education, University of Kansas, 1979.
Sapon-Shevin, M. Who says somebody's gotta lose? Competition as an obstacle to mainstreaming. *Education Unlimited,* 1980, *2*(4), 48–50.
Schulz, J. B. Communication station—a learning center for mainstreaming. *Teaching Exceptional Children,* 1981, *13*(2), 81–82.
Schulz, J. P. Simulated work laboratory. Unpublished program of instruction, Columbus, Ga., 1972.
Semmel, M. I., Cohen, D. A., & Kandaswamy, S. Tutoring mainstreamed handicapped pupils in regular classrooms. *Education Unlimited,* 1980, *2*(4), 54–56.
Smith, P. B., & Bentley, G. *Facilitator manual, teacher training program. Mainstreaming mildly handicapped students in the regular classroom.* Austin, Tex.: Education Service Center, Region XII, 1975.
Stevens, D. J. Computers, curriculum, and careful planning. *Educational Technology,* 1981, *21*(11), 21–24.

Turnbull, A. P., Strickland, B., & Brantley, J. C. *Developing and implementing individualized education programs* (2nd ed.). Columbus, Ohio: Charles E. Merrill Publishing Co., 1982.

Voight, R. C. *Invitation to learning.* Washington, D.C.: Acropolis, 1971.

Weir, S., & Watt, D. Logo: A computer environment for learning-disabled students. *The Computing Teacher,* 1980–1981, *8*(5), 11–17.

Wieck, C. Computer resources: Will educators accept, reject, or neglect in the future? *Education Unlimited,* 1980, *2*(3), 24–27.

5

Teaching Language Arts: Listening, Speaking, Writing

The language arts are the communication arts. All aspects of a pupil's world are constantly interacting; communication is a vital part of that interaction. Thus, the language arts, or communications skills, comprise a larger part of the school curriculum than any other subject area.

The tools of communication are essential to social and academic development. Communication is related not only to every area of school but also to every area of life. The person who is deficient in communication skills is unable to follow directions in school (or on the job), is unable to gain information from textbooks (or from news media), and is limited in interacting with other children (or adults).

A hierarchy of development helps to explain the relationship of the elements of the language arts (see Figure 5–1). It is necessary to identify commonalities between these elements in order to develop an instructional program that is oriented toward total communication skill development (Cohen & Plaskon, 1980).

One difficulty in teaching language arts involves the variety of skills that, although taught independently, must be well integrated in language arts performance (Cohen, 1980). For example, writing includes the related skills of vocabulary, expression, spelling, and handwriting.

Another problem is associated with most people's natural use of the language arts. In normal development, one skill flows into another, with little awareness of the transition on the part of the child or the teacher. The integration may be more difficult with handicapped students; frequently, each step in the developmental process has to be taught separately. It may be necessary to examine each component to be sure a foundation exists for the next step.

LIFE EXPERIENCES

Communication is based on total, multisensory experiences. Through interaction with the environment and people, students develop the ideas, concepts, and relationships on which language and other communication skills are built.

Depending on the nature of their problem, many handicapped students may be limited in their life experiences. Students with sensory handicaps, for example, miss many visual and auditory stimuli that provide other students with information about their surroundings; students who are physically im-

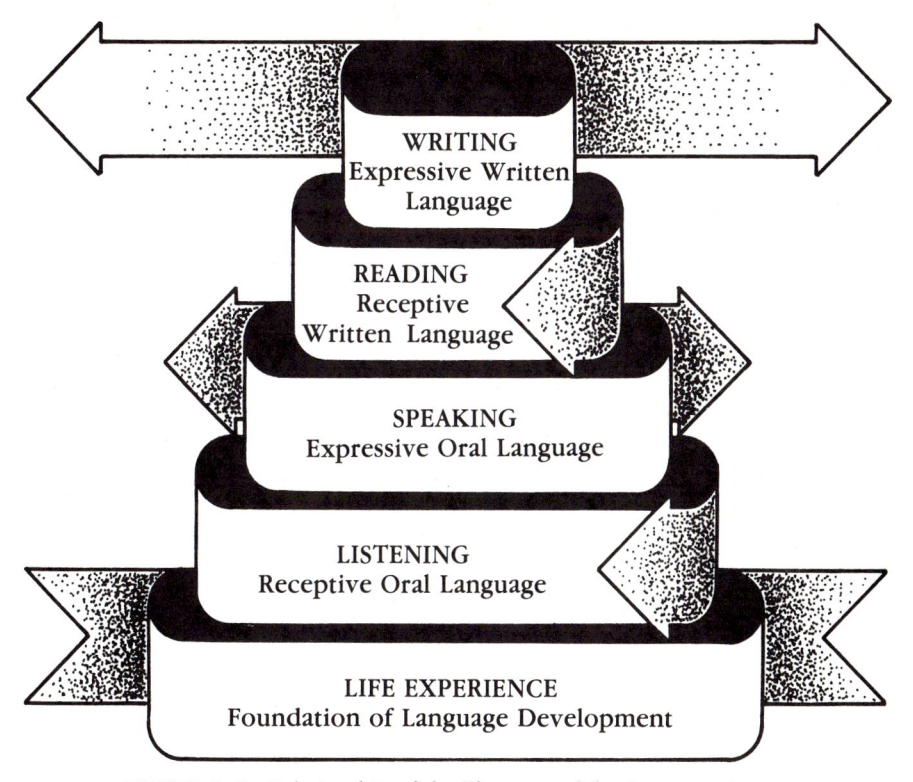

FIGURE 5–1. Relationship of the Elements of the Language Arts

paired may have limited experiences in exploring their immediate environments through such motor activities as crawling, climbing, and exploring; and students who are intellectually handicapped may lack the ability to interpret the information and experiences to which they are exposed.

Craig (1980) indicates two tasks required of the teacher in the experiential realm. The first requirement is to familiarize oneself with the individual experiences of the students and to use those experiences to plan basic thinking, talking, writing, and reading materials. The second task is to structure classes to enable students to begin their learning with concrete, direct, meaningful experiences. Direct experiences provide the background and the motivation to listen, talk, read, and write.

LISTENING

Fritz, a curly-haired, snaggled-tooth "outdoor" boy, had trouble controlling his "indoor" behavior. After a particularly rough day, Fritz's kindergarten teacher was talking to him about her expectations of him in the classroom. After the serious talk, the teacher asked, "Now, Fritz, do you have any questions?" "Yes, teacher. Why do you wear green on your eyes?"

Not listening may be a natural defense against the reception of undesirable or useless information that constantly assaults the ear, or it may be the result of limited auditory perception or training.

Although special concern for instruction of speaking and reading is common, until recently students were expected to acquire the ability to listen without special instruction. And yet, listening is the foundation of all language growth; the pupil deficient in listening skills is handicapped in all the communication skills (Lerner, 1976).

Investigations of listening in the elementary classroom led to the discovery that 57.5 percent of class time was spent in listening (Taylor, 1973). Much of this listening is meaningless and, therefore, inefficient. Lack of ability and inattention in students may indicate failure on the part of the pupil and the teacher to identify the purpose of the listening. The process should not be one-way; students should do more talking and listening to each other and to the teacher instead of just listening to the teacher.

Taylor (1973) describes the process involved in translating sound into meaning:

> *Hearing* designates the process by which speech sounds in the form of sound waves are received and modified by the ear.
> *Listening* refers to the process of becoming aware of sound sequences. In listening to speech, the person first identifies the component sounds and then recognizes sound sequences as known words through the avenues of auditory analysis, mental reorganization, and/or association of meaning.
> *Auding* refers to the process by which the continuous flow of words is translated into meaning. Auding involves one or more avenues of thought—indexing, making comparisons, noting sequence, forming sensory impressions, and appreciating.

Factors involved in the total process are hearing, attention, auditory discrimination, mental reorganization, association of meaning, sensory impressions, and thinking skills. Obviously, many handicapped students have deficits in some or all of these areas.

Lerner (1976) identifies the listening skills that contribute to the process:

1. Auditory perception of non-language sounds.
2. Auditory perception and discrimination of isolated single language sounds.
3. Understanding of words and concepts, and building of a listening vocabulary.
4. Understanding sentences and other linguistic elements of language.
5. Auditory memory.

6. Auding or listening comprehension:
    a. Following directions.
    b. Understanding a sequence of events through listening.
    c. Recalling details.
    d. Getting the main idea.
    e. Making inferences and drawing conclusions.
    f. Critical listening. (pp. 222–223)

She claims that listening is a basic skill that can be improved through training and suggests teaching strategies for each level of listening.

Listening as a skill is particularly valuable for handicapped students. As suggested in several chapters of this book, the use of audio-visual materials is frequently necessary for poor readers. The ability to listen and to comprehend is vital if such materials are substituted for reading.

Obviously, deaf or hard-of-hearing students cannot develop speech and language through avenues of casual hearing or listening. Specific auditory training is necessary to help develop limited hearing into listening skills.

Visually impaired students depend on listening to a greater extent than any other students. Not only their education, but also their safety and existence depend on their ability to listen to sounds in their environment.

If listening is to be learned, it must be taught. The reasons for teaching it are clear: students spend a large proportion of time listening; listening requires different skills than other forms of communication; and listening may be a substitute for reading. The objectives of a listening program include helping students use listening for varied purposes, increasing the efficient use of listening as a mode of learning, understanding the interdependence of the listener and the speaker, and increasing awareness of listening as an active skill (Tiedt & Tiedt, 1978).

Assessment of Listening Skills

Several areas of listening can cause deficiencies: not paying attention, thinking about how to respond while attempting to concentrate on what is being said, and neglecting to ask questions when clarification is needed (Otto & Smith, 1980). Specific areas of difficulty can be evaluated by using formal and informal tests. Two standardized tests suggested by Burns (1980) are Sequential Tests of Educational Progress (STEP), for grades four through twelve, and The Cooperative Primary Tests. Both are published by The Educational Testing Service.

Teacher-made listening tests, close observation by the teacher, and self-checking by the student are likely to produce the best assessment of listening skills and habits. Two facets of the listening process should be evaluated constantly. The student's ability and motivation to listen should be determined, and the teacher's responsibility for evaluating and teaching listening skills should be established.

The assessment procedure for the student should examine the categories of auditory short-term memory, auditory discrimination, auditory recognition, and auditory comprehension. The following activities suggested by Cohen and Plaskon (1980) provide information in each of these areas:

- *Short-term auditory memory:* Have the child listen, eyes closed, to the sound that the teacher makes (clapping hands, tapping foot, or humming a short tune) and repeat the pattern and sound.
- *Auditory sensitivity:* Play a sound-effects record and ask the child to identify as many sounds as possible.
- *Auditory discrimination:* Present two sounds in sequence and ask the child to distinguish between them. Tap a pencil on a desk top, then a pen, and ask the child which sound was the pen and which was the pencil.
- *Auditory recognition:* Identify for a child a particular sound, such as the sound that /s/ makes in /snake/. Present a series of sounds that include the /s/ sound. Each time the child hears the /s/ sound, an object can be placed in a container. At the end of the session, the objects can be counted to determine the degree of recognition.
- *Auditory comprehension:* Ask the pupil to follow a specific set of directions, such as completing a puzzle, coloring a picture, or designing an art project.

If no specific problems are found and there still seems to be an attentional deficit, an informal checklist to help determine the student's overall listening behavior may be of value (see Table 5–1).

Classroom situations provide many opportunities to assess a student's listening performance. The requirement of a verbal response or some specific behavior lets the teacher know whether or not the student is following the speaker's message. Some situations in which this can be done are:

Give the class oral directions for an unfamiliar task and see which students do not follow them. For example, "Please put your arithmetic book and your social studies book on your desk. Put your arithmetic book on top of your social studies book so I can see only your arithmetic book as I walk down the aisle." Notice which students do not comply and which seek a repetition from you or a classmate.

While engaged in individual social conversation or instruction, ask a student to repeat your last sentence in his or her own words.

Say something absurd in the course of talking to a class, small group, or individual and notice who does not react to the absurdity.

Use a nonsense word while giving directions to an individual and observe his or her reaction. For example, "Put the book on the framler when you finish."

Ask a question that calls for an obvious answer but is out of context in the present discussion. For example, "By the way, who can tell me what the day after tomorrow is? Those who can tell me, raise your hands."

TABLE 5-1.

A Simple Checklist of Listening Behavior

NAME	YES	NO
1. Does the child consistently request to have directions repeated?	___	___
2. Does the child appear to be easily distracted when presentations are being made in class?	___	___
3. Does the child appear to understand what is expected when assignments are given?	___	___
4. Does the child frequently participate in class discussions?	___	___
5. Is the child able to pick out inconsistencies in the conversations of others?	___	___
6. Does the child frequently complete the wrong pages in the workbook, or do inappropriate homework assignments?	___	___
7. Are requests, messages, or informational items orally presented to the child frequently misinterpreted resulting in misinformed parents or guardians?	___	___
8. Does the child not hear you so often that it has become annoying?	___	___
9. Are the other children in class complaining about the child's behavior in small group activities because the child does not seem to "listen"?	___	___
10. Does the child consistently have problems on the playground with peers because of misinformation regarding the rules for a particular game?	___	___

Source: From LANGUAGE ARTS FOR THE MILDLY HANDICAPPED by Sandra Cohen and Stephen Plaskon. Columbus, Ohio: Charles E. Merrill Publishing Company, 1980, pp. 179–180. Reprinted by permission of the publisher.

Play a short, tape-recorded story and ask students to summarize the story in their own words when it is finished. Do not tell them beforehand that they will be asked to do this.

Play a musical selection, the title of which is obvious from the lyrics (for example, "My Favorite Things" from *The Sound of Music*). Ask the students to write the obvious title of the selection when it is concluded.

After a short speech ask the students to (1) describe the speaker's appearance and mannerisms and (2) tell the major ideas the speaker presented. Note which aspect the students attended to more carefully.

Read a ballad, short story, or news article that moves to an obvious ending. Stop reading before the ending and ask students to supply the obvious ending. Do not tell them ahead of time that they will be asked to do this.[1]

---

1. Otto-Smith: CORRECTIVE AND REMEDIAL TEACHING, Third Edition, pp. 306–307 and 350–351. Copyright © by Houghton Mifflin Company. Used by permission.

These assessment techniques also provide activities to improve listening ability at the secondary level.

The evaluation of teachers' procedures in teaching listening is an imporant consideration. The following questions can alert the teacher to this responsibility:

- Do I provide a classroom environment (emotional and physical) that encourages good listening?
- Am I a good listener and do I really listen to the pupils?
- Do I use appropriate tone, pitch, volume, and speed in my speaking?
- Do I vary the classroom program to provide listening experiences (films, discussions, debates, reports) which are of interest to the children?
- Am I aware of opportunities for teaching listening throughout the day?
- Do I help pupils see the purpose for listening in each activity?
- Do I help children see the importance and value of being good listeners?
- Do I build a program in which listening skills are consistently taught and practiced?[2]

Creative, alert teachers will use a combination of techniques to discover the listening levels at which their students are functioning. At the same time, they will realize the importance of using this information to develop a sequential program.

Improving Listening Skills

With the growing awareness of the importance of listening is also the realization that listening skills can be taught and that listening instruction produces improvement in reading and language use. Because learning depends on listening and because most students are not accomplished listeners, a developmental listening improvement program is recommended by many educators.

Listening is a process that is learned in conjunction with experiences. Unless students learn to listen and attend to the activities in their environment, they cannot learn maximally from that environment.

The following activities help the younger child to listen, to retain, and to recall auditory information.

Learning to Listen
1. Several times a day, play a game of being quiet and relaxed with eyes shut. The voice and the whole body should be quiet so that not a sound is made.

2. ASSESSMENT AND CORRECTION OF LANGUAGE ARTS DIFFICULTIES by P. C. Burns. Columbus, Ohio: Charles E. Merrill Publishing Company, 1980, p. 113. Reprinted by permission of the publisher.

2. Once they can maintain reasonable quiet for 30 seconds or more, whisper children's names and have them rise quietly and come to you. As the child's listening ability improves, give simple directions in the same whispered voice and move to different areas of the room.

3. To encourage children to listen and to prevent them from shouting, make a habit of using a low, quiet tone of voice when presenting tasks or play items that the children really enjoy.

Actions Performed from Auditory Clues

1. Give simple one sentence, one action commands.
2. Increase number of words and commands.
3. Use clues other than words for starting and stopping an activity. The activity may be a simple motor movement, a game, or a task. The task may be as simple as sitting still until a buzzer sounds.

Developing Auditory Memory

1. Have the child repeat unrelated words.
2. Have the child repeat digits and/or letters after you.
3. Increase the length of time between naming of the digits, words, or sounds, as the child demonstrates competency.
4. Read or tell a short, simple story containing two or more elements in a sequence.
   a. Ask the child to retell the story.
   b. Ask the child "What did I say first . . . last?" (adapted from Chaney & Kephart, 1968, pp. 69–74)

The use of listening centers meets the needs of students at many ages and ability levels. Following the basic requirements of learning centers (see chapter 4), a listening center could include tapes, manipulative materials, radios, records, and books.

As educators have become more aware of the importance of auditory training for many children, commercial programs have become available. The following programs are designed to improve auditory perception.

- *Auditory Perception Training.* Tapes and spirit masters designed to provide sequential training for auditory memory, auditory motor, auditory figure-ground, auditory discrimination, and auditory imagery. Developmental Learning Materials.

- *Learn to Listen.* Cassette tapes and duplicator activity sheets designed to help children discriminate and classify sounds and their possible causes. Mafex Associates, Inc.

Auditory Training for Hard-of-Hearing Students

Hard-of-hearing students who are trained to use their residual hearing to the fullest extent develop better understanding of relationships between sounds and objects, sounds and actions, and sounds and people. Techniques in auditory training are designed to stimulate responses to sound and to improve the children's overall responses to their environment. The training is more effective when combined with lip reading, speech preparation, and other activities. The four major steps of auditory training are:

1. Development of awareness of sound.
2. Development of gross discrimination.
3. Development of broad discrimination among simple speech patterns.
4. Development of finer discrimination of speech.

Auditory training programs should be planned by the speech clinician and audiologist and implemented with the cooperation of the resource teacher and the classroom teacher.

If a child has a hearing loss, steps can be taken to improve hearing conditions in the classroom. Since noise should be kept at the lowest level possible, classrooms in noisy locations may need acoustical treatment according to suggestions of the audiologist.

The use of individual learning stations or study carrels reduces noise, and they can also be useful for other students in reducing visual distractions and providing better illumination.

Creating a Good Listening Climate

Many improvements can be made in the listening skills of all students by carefully inspecting the quality of the listening climate. A re-evaluation of teaching methods may lead to a greater variety of listening situations, including independent activities, pupil-team learning, and greater use of audio-visual approaches.

Teachers provide a model for listening. When they listen to students with interest, they help to establish an environment in which listening is valued.

The skills of listening are important for all students. Although many students acquire the skills incidentally, the teacher of handicapped students cannot assume that such acquisition is taking place. The development of listening skills is a prerequisite to speaking and should be programmed accordingly.

SPEAKING

> We walked down the path to the well-house, attracted by the fragrance of the honeysuckle with which it was covered. Some one was drawing water and my teacher placed my hand under the spout. As the cool stream gushed over one hand she spelled into the other the word water, first slowly, then rapidly. I stood still, my whole attention fixed upon the motions of her fingers. Suddenly I felt a misty consciousness as of something forgotten—a thrill of returning thought; and somehow the mystery of language was revealed to me. I knew then that "w-a-t-e-r" meant the wonderful cool something that was flowing over my hand. That living word awakened my soul, gave it light, hope, joy, set it free! (Keller, 1954, p. 36)

Although oral language is identified as the primary form of language, instructional practices in both regular classrooms and special classes do not always reflect the relationship between oral and written language (Lerner, 1976). Language has two specific functions for the individual. It serves as a cognitive tool to help organize and categorize the information conveyed by the senses. It also provides for interactions between people, enabling individuals to give and receive information, thoughts, and ideas (Cole & Cole, 1981).

Language acquisition is a special problem for many students. Most of the students referred to in chapter 1 have some language deficits. Therefore, language must be a critical part of their educational plan. Students' success in their social and academic environments depends largely on how they use language. Their ability to express language (speech) and to use language interpersonally (communication) must be increased through activities built into the educational program (Schiefelbusch, Ruder, & Bricker, 1976).

Miller and Yoder (1972), in discussing the language behavior of mentally retarded persons, conclude that the retarded child develops language in the same order as children without intellectual deficits, but at a slower rate. Gearheart and Litton (1975) assert that this idea is a common misconception. They contend that the variety of physical problems present in many retarded children causes them to follow different developmental patterns. Regardless of the pattern, the fact remains that there are no developmental sequences established for retarded and other handicapped persons; the content for language training must be taken from the data available on language development in normal children.

Three major components are necessary for language development in children: cognitive-perceptual development, linguistic experience, and nonlinguistic experience. In order to acquire the language system, children must be capable of perceiving objects, events, and relationships in the environment; they must be exposed to the linguistic system used to express those recognized objects, events, and relationships; and they must have direct experience with those objects, events, and relationships in the environment (Bloom, 1970). Consequently, children who have cognitive, perceptual, physical, and emotional deficits frequently have difficulty achieving normal language development.

Students with language problems do not display consistency in the severity of their various deficiencies. A student with a mild problem may have good comprehension of language yet produce relatively unintelligible speech. Another student may possess all the tools for becoming a competent speaker and listener but lack the communicative skills to comprehend or to use language appropriately in a learning environment (Schiefelbusch, Ruder, & Bricker, 1976). Therefore, individual assessment is necessary for good program planning. Since language assessment is based on comparisons with normal children, teachers must understand normal language development.

Normal Language Development

Communication, an exchange of ideas and information, can be nonverbal (facial expressions or gestures) or verbal (spoken language). Speech is uniquely human and is a part of a larger system of symbols that carry meaning.

Phonemes, the basic vowel and consonant sounds, are the raw materials of the spoken language. During the babbling period, infants produce sounds that form the basis of language. Typically, they speak their first word about the end of the first year. At this time, the use of single words standing for whole sentences begins; at about eighteen months, the child's earliest "sentences" begin. These sentences are abbreviated adult sentences, consisting largely of essential nouns and verbs. The adult sentence "I see a dog" is said as "See dog." These first sentences occur in all cultures and express a broad range of meanings. Slobin (1973) finds that language everywhere consists of utterances performing a universal set of communicative functions, expressing a universal set of underlying semantic relations, and using a universal set of formal means.

As children's sentences become longer and more complex, they add prepositions, articles, plurals, and possessives. Children make enormous progress in the comprehension and production of language during the preschool years and continue to make important advances throughout childhood (Mussen, Conger, & Kagan, 1974). By age six, the average child can tell what several words mean, answer questions, respond to pictures, and speak sentences of six to seven words.

Because langauge is so distinctively human, because it is so important in social interactions, and because it plays such a prominent part in cognitive functioning, many attempts have been made to explain its acquisition. There is lack of agreement on how language is acquired, but it is generally recognized that despite the many individual differences, children follow established patterns in speech and language development.

Assessment of Language Development

Language is a complex process involving many skills. It involves the ability to receive (receptive language) and the ability to transmit (expressive language). In oral language, information is received by listening and expressed by speech; in written language, information is received by reading and expressed by writing (McLoughlin & Lewis, 1981).

Formal Assessment. Diagnostic instruments used to assess aspects of receptive and expressive language are described by Faas (1981).

> *The Peabody Picture Vocabulary Test (PPVT)* provides information about the auditory reception and comprehension of orally presented words. Its use of nonverbal responses makes it well suited for remedial readers and for those who are speech impaired, cerebral palsied, withdrawn, or mentally retarded. American Guidance Service.
>
> *The Test for Auditory Comprehension of Language (TACL)* consists of 101 items. The stimulus for each item contains three line drawings. One drawing contains the correct answer, one the opposite or negative of the correct answer, while the third drawing serves as a decoy item. The child points to the correct picture following the reception of the examiner's orally produced stimuli. Teaching Resources Corporation.
>
> *The Carrow Elicited Language Inventory (CELI)* consists of 52 items. Each item ranges in length from two to ten words. The sentences are lengthened by increasing the number of semantic relations, expanding phrases, and increasing the number of grammatical morphemes. Teaching Resources Corporation.
>
> *The Northwestern Syntax Screening Test (NSST)* consists of two parts. The first part contains twenty pairs of items that assess comprehension of sentences containing various grammatical structures and forms including subject-verb agreement, gender, voice, negatives, and interrogatives. The second part of the test contains twenty pairs of items that assess the child's ability to produce sentences that contain different types of grammatical structures. Northwestern University. (pp. 232–236)

Another instrument for assessing language is the *Illinois Test of Psycholinguistic Abilities*. Initially, the ITPA was used primarily with children designated as learning disabled. As concepts of prescriptive education have grown in popularity, it has been applied more broadly (Chinn, Drew, & Logan, 1975). Hammill and Bartel (1975) point out a major shortcoming in the ITPA's omission of subtests for linguistic abilities (syntax, phonology, or transformations). They consider the ITPA valuable when the examiner is concerned with such variables as memory or closure, or with receptive, associative, or expressive performance.

A limitation of formal assessment is that it frequently indicates whether or not the child possesses a certain structure but gives little indication of where to begin training. To be maximally beneficial, the assessment instrument should have relevance for the development and implementation of the student's IEP.

Informal Assessment. Informal assessment is a valuable part of the total language evaluation. In its simplest form, it is the parent's or teacher's report of the student's language capacity or their impressions of the language problem (Ruder & Smith, 1974). A somewhat more structured assessment by the teacher may include the following features:

Receptive Language
1. Awareness or attention: include items that require observable responses to sound or speech (e.g., eye contact).
2. Discrimination: ability to respond differently to sound or speech sounds.
3. Understanding: speech accompanied by
   a. gestures
   b. situational clues (e.g., "Turn on water" while in bathroom)
   c. speech alone

Expressive Language
1. Imitating
2. Initiating
3. Responding

Samples may be taken of the pupil's interaction with persons and reactions to elicited speech, such as "Tell me about the picture." Such language samples are useful in planning IEPs.

The importance of informal observation is stressed by Black (1979), who claims there is more to evaluation than hearing students verbalize in formal settings. Communication can be seen and assessed by observing a student's use of language in a variety of social contexts.

Teachers encounter many difficulties in assessing language. Among them are the realization and understanding that background differences influence language, that the course of language development is uneven, that data collection and transcription are difficult, and that students respond to various listener characteristics (Cohen & Plaskon, 1980). To obtain and interpret useful information, the help of a speech therapist is valuable. Cooperative effort is necessary in determining the needs of handicapped students.

Assessment procedures built into language development programs will probably be most useful to the teacher. Such procedures provide for pupil placement in a particular phase of a training program and provide feedback concerning the relevance of a particular training sequence and the prerequisite behaviors required to enter particular stages of a program (Ruder & Smith, 1974).

Speech and Language Problems

The purpose of assessing and identifying language and speech disorders is to plan relevant programs for students. In determining which students should be considered as having a communication disorder, McLean (1974) compares the pupil's language with the standard language form of the culture and with the language of other students at the same age level. He categorizes the most common problems as nonverbal children, language-disordered children, and speech-impaired children. He states:

> Because language is learned behavior, it can be affected by the factors which affect any learning. Factors like intellectual ability, motivation and/or good models of the behaviors to be learned can all affect language acquisition. Because language models are received in the auditory mode, the auditory sensory channel is critical to natural language learning. Because the natural language production mode is a motor behavior, disrupted or diminished motor systems can affect language acquisition. Because language is connected with the child's world and learned within relationships in that world, a child's emotional status can be a factor. Language carries the marks of whatever problems have affected the child. (p. 474)

The most critical factors in poor speech and language development are related to physical, sensory, intellectual, and environmental differences in the student.

Orthopedic Handicaps. Orthopedically handicapped students, particularly those with cerebral palsy, frequently have speech and language problems (see chapter 1). Molloy and Witt (1971) state that a child's speaking mechanism is usable for speech if he or she is able to swallow, suck, maneuver the tongue by controlling its action, and employ some speed in tongue action. Exercises for developing and strengthening the muscles involved can be prescribed and demonstrated by a speech clinician.

Sensory Deficits. Sensory deficits refer to hearing and visual problems. Hearing provides contact with the environment and with other people. It permits the learning of spoken language and plays a major role in the development of abstract concepts and temporal sequences. The hard-of-hearing student misses much of this association of sound with experience (Lowell & Pollack, 1974).

Hearing students learn the sound, shape, and sense of their language through their auditory modality; the hearing-impaired student depends on vision to learn about language. Comparisons of the written language of the deaf and the hearing suggest that the deaf are significantly inferior in all aspects of language development and facility (Moores, 1972). Adler (1964) suggests that when hearing is faulty, the development of speech is likely to be retarded or imperfect. The student learns faulty interpretations of sound or learns to substitute other senses for hearing. Gestures tend to replace speech as a method of communication.

Because of limited interaction with the environment, the hearing-impaired child has difficulty acquiring concepts. A speech therapist described a sequence of steps necessary for a particular hearing-impaired student to develop an understanding of the word *mammals:*

> *The student was asked to use a dictionary to find meanings of words she did not know and to write a sentence with the words to demonstrate her understanding of their meaning. She found that the dictionary defined mammal as any class of animals that nourishes its young with milk. Her first sentence read "I don't want to go to mammal today." The therapist asked the student what the meaning of mammal was. The student replied that it was a class and that the sentence meant that the student didn't want to go to class today.*
>
> *After discussing the entire meaning of the word with the student, the therapist asked her to write another sentence. The second sentence read "The puppy is mammals its mother." The definition of the word was discussed again and again and examples given. When the student presented her third sentence, it read "My kitten is a mammal."*

The hearing-impaired pupil has a limited vocabulary and experiences difficulty with words that have more than one meaning. Prefixes and suffixes added to words may be confusing. Word order is often improper, prepositions and articles may be omitted from sentences, and syntax is generally poor.

The results of a recent study (Brenza, Kricos, & Lasky, 1981) reveal a deficit in the comprehension of semantic concepts by severely and profoundly hearing-impaired students, aged thirteen and fourteen. It is suggested that in mainstreaming hearing-impaired students, teachers need to evaluate and teach basic concepts before moving on to more advanced concepts.

The visually impaired pupil suffers much of the same experiential deprivation as the hearing-impaired pupil and has similar problems with concepts.

> *A blind child was in a language arts group playing the game Password. The word to be discovered was* room. *In giving a clue, the boy who was blind gave the word* box. *While he may have used models to help develop spatial concepts, he had a poor understanding of* room.

The following suggestions for the classroom teacher are applicable to both the hearing-impaired student and the visually impaired student:

- The student should be given preferential seating in class, sitting close to the teacher at all times.
- A classmate "buddy" should be assigned to the student. The buddy should

be a responsible youngster who will assure that the hearing-impaired student understands the ongoing activity at any given time, has the correct place in reading, or knows and understands an assignment.
- The teacher can give assignments verbally and also write them on the board. After the assignment is given, it should be reviewed and understanding determined.
- If a film is shown in class, remember that the student who wears a hearing aid will experience some distortion in picking up sound from another mechanical device (the speaker from the projector). The topic of the film should be discussed with hearing-impaired and visually impaired students so they will be "set" for its content. After the film, a review and simple questioning will help insure understanding.
- To help in concept development, many visual aids for the hearing-impaired student and many auditory aids for the visually impaired student should be used. Tactile experiences should be provided whenever possible.
- Questions or messages should be rephrased if the student does not appear to understand them in their original form.
- The student and, if necessary, the parents should be given a preview of topics to be discussed the next day or week so they can prepare at home for coming topics. The resource teacher can assist in coordinating this procedure.

Intellectual Deficits. Intellectual deficits have a strong bearing on language acquisition since, as Bloom (1970) states, "the acquisition of language is a complex process that is crucially related to the child's cognitive-perceptual growth and his interaction in an environment of objects, events, and relations" (p. 1). The cognitive prerequisites for the development of grammar relate to the meanings and the forms of language; the first linguistic forms to appear in a child's speech are those that express meanings consistent with the child's level of cognitive development. Miller and Yoder (1972) conclude that "children do not talk in the absence of something to talk about" (p. 9).

The mentally retarded student frequently exhibits delayed language. Data available on language development in normal children can be used to plan language training.

Children first learn aspects of language within the scope of their current cognitive development; as they develop cognitively, they gradually learn to use more complex linguistic formulations (Clark, 1974). Miller and Yoder (1972) suggest that children's target language behavior should have some functional relevance to their environment and to their personal and physical needs. They present the following procedures and constructs essential in coordinating implementation of content with teaching strategies in developing programs for language training:

- Before children become language users, they have to have something to say (concepts) and a way to say it (linguistic structure).
- Throughout the entire program the teacher works from comprehension to production.
- New words and syntactical relationships are best established by supplying the underlying concepts through environmental manipulation and experience.
- For the child who is mentally retarded, as for other children, language is acquired through interaction with the environment. Language is part of the child's mental development and should not be isolated. (p. 10)

Environmental Differences. Environmental differences can prevent optimal language development. The pupil may not need to talk, may have inadequate stimulation in the home, or may have such poor models that his or her language will be inadequate in relationship to more standard language forms. Homes in which no one listens to another can also frustrate language learning (McLean, 1974). Other factors limiting verbal communication are a lack of communication with adults in large families, the frequent absence of fathers, the poor quality of child care when mothers work outside the home, and crowded conditions that force children out of doors (McConnell, Love, & Clark, 1974).

In describing the inner-city child, Lerner (1971) says, "It is estimated that a good beginning reader at age 6 has a speaking vocabulary of 2,500 to 8,000 words; whereas the inner-city child at age 6 has been judged to have a speaking vocabularly of less than 500 words, which is equivalent to that of an average 3-year-old in a more favored environment" (p. 145). She offers two solutions: help children secure a broad oral language base before introducing them to more complex language skills, such as reading, and change learning media and materials—teach them to read by using the child's own language as the basis for initial readers.

In relation to dialects, one viewpoint is that the problems stem from differences rather than from deficiencies (Goodman, 1969). Persons concerned with cultural differences caution teachers to be careful how they treat the language children bring to school, not only because of self-image but also because their language makes it possible for them to communicate with people in their environment. If teachers attack the students' language, they cut them off from their world. Houston (1973), for instance, finds that black students anxiously cover their flair for language to please teachers who feel that black English is inferior.

Promoting Language Use

An effective curriculum designed to promote language use has several purposes. As described by Klein (1979), the curriculum design consists of talk purposes, talk contexts, and talk planning. Talk purposes are to inform, to move to action, to inquire, to enjoy, and to conjoin. Talk contexts are settings or environments in which language use takes place. Talk planning refers to processes attended to while preparing to talk, while talking, while taking in the talk of others, and after talking. Talk opportunities should be consciously structured into the curriculum to encourage students to use talk in a wide variety of contexts and purposes.

Language is a tool to be used, not a subject to be studied. Experience and purpose are the key factors in language learning; they are guides for planning instruction aimed at promoting language usage (Winkeljohann, 1981).

For most students, language evolves naturally as they interact with their environment, family, and friends. For students who do not acquire language naturally, this interaction may have to be provided by the classroom teacher. The experiences provided will be most effective if they are related to each pupil's life—to the home background, to experiences in and out of school, and to past and future learning.

Activities for Language Development

Language develops as children become aware of their surroundings. Awareness of the environment can be developed through experiences that stimulate the senses.

Language is stimulated in a classroom where experiences are encouraged and promoted. Pasamanick (1976) states that this means organizing and equipping the room with materials that stimulate language, drama, and thought. She suggests materials for a Language Center that will enrich the possibilities for dialogue.

- A round table and perhaps one or two others to house language games.
- Storage shelves and a comfortable chair, rug, or mats.
- A good supply of blank pages bound into books for students' original stories. Some of these might be precut into different animal and geometric shapes.
- A good stock of colorful magazines—*Woman's Day, Family Circle, Ebony, Sports Illustrated.*
- A picture file of interesting "trigger" pictures on various subjects chosen for the stimulation they offer to concept development and problem solving. Pictures evocative of emotional reaction are very valuable, too. Be sure to include pictures of many different people: black, Indian, Chinese, old, young, urban, and rural. All pictures could be trimmed, mounted on stiff bright paper, and covered with transparent Con-Tact to insure their longevity.
- Language games such as lottos, alphabet letters of various kinds (sandpaper, felt, wood), small and large flannelboards and felt pieces. Your ditto sheets and task cards (simple ones with more drawing than words) belong here, too. So do sequence cards and other homemade language materials.

- Crayons, felt markers, fat pencils, and scissors stored in attractively covered or painted cans should be placed beside stacks of paper for writing and drawing.
- Small "treasures" or doll figures (such as are often found in penny-candy machines); figures of animals, people, vehicles, and furniture are often stimulants to story making. Store them in transparent containers alongside trays for manipulation.
- And finally, there's the primer typewriter. This is a distinct asset to letter recognition and word building. If you possibly can, get one and keep it, along with an abundant supply of paper.[1]

Pets in the classroom offer opportunities for observation and description. Gerbils, hamsters, rabbits, guinea pigs, snakes, lizards, and fish are attractive and provocative choices.

Language can be stimulated through play activities in which children enact pretend or real-life situations. Doll houses, puppets, household centers, and "dress-up" clothing facilitate such experiences.

Instructional Materials

Many of the materials suggested can be made from inexpensive products. For example, puppets can be made from wooden spoons, paper plates, popsicle sticks, and paper bags (Deen & Deen, 1977). Many commercial products also are available. The following list suggests appropriate materials:

- *Language Big Box.* Designed to promote the acquisition of basic language skills, the materials reinforce auditory and conceptual skills by building on the student's existing language strengths. The Big Box includes 170 activity cards for lesson planning and twenty-four products to be used for language development. Developmental Learning Materials.
- *Caption Cards.* Designed for creative writing and language development, the cards are cartoons without captions that form the basis for learning activities. All cards have a situation and a verbal action. The idea is to design verbal interaction displayed in the picture. Educational Design Associates.
- *Developmental Syntax Program.* A programmed approach to the development of syntax, this program is designed to teach the child the grammatical and morphological structure of language. The most common syntactical structure errors have been selected and sequenced to reflect a developmental sequence. Learning Concepts.
- *Language Development Pak.* Develops language skills, including word formation, contractions, phonics, classification, dictionary skills, and others.

1. CHILDHOOD LANGUAGE DEVELOPMENT RESOURCE by Judith Pasamanick. © 1976 by Center for Media Development, Inc. Reprinted by permission of the publisher.

Includes open-ended, multilevel spirit masters and perforated worksheets. Love Publishing Company.

- *Peabody Language Development Kit.* Designed to stimulate oral language development, activities are highly motivating. The kits include lesson plans, stimulus cards, hand puppets, taped stories, transistorized, battery-operated intercommunication sets, and cards to stimulate imagination and continuity in story telling. The kits require no special training, can be used effectively in large or small groups, and are effective in promoting oral language expression. American Guidance Service.

- *Language Making Action Cards and Stickers.* Sets of pictures designed to make the teaching of communication skills easier and more effective. The cards in the set are action verb pictures and designs for teaching color, number, and plural concepts. Also included are pictures helpful in teaching prepositions, personal expression modifiers, polars, comparatives, and multiple attributes. Other cards contain sequence pictures for verb tense illustration and story telling. Word Making Productions, Inc.

READING

Reading, as receptive written language, is an integral and interwoven part of the language arts. The importance of reading as a vehicle for learning in all curriculum areas, the present societal concern for people who have not learned to read, and the complexity of teaching students to read make it necessary to deal with this topic in a separate chapter (chapter 6). However, it is important to remember the relationship that reading has in the language arts schema.

WRITING

As indicated in Figure 5-1, writing is the most advanced of the language arts components. The goal in teaching written language skills is the ability to communicate thoughts that are legible and meaningful.

The three aspects of written language to consider are handwriting, spelling, and written expression. These areas are complicated because they involve many subskills, such as auditory and visual sequential memory, motor control of writing utensils, eye-hand coordination, phonetic knowledge, organization of thoughts, and application of grammatical rules (Piazza, 1979).

Even though the interactive nature of language arts skills can be an advantage in instructional planning, Reid and Hresko (1981) point out a disadvantage for handicapped students. Having had uncomfortable or failing experiences with reading, they may be less than enthusiastic about written compositions, spelling, and handwriting. However, just as students' oral language expression can be improved with appropriate experiences and instruction, their written communication can also be facilitated.

Handwriting

Handwriting is the most concrete of the language arts; it can be observed, evaluated, and used to provide a permanent record of the child's productive efforts. Although largely a motor skill, handwriting also requires visual ability.

Handwriting is not as important in the curriculum as it once was. Beautiful handwriting used to be the mark of a scholar; although the end product was admired, it was difficult to attain and left little room for individual expression (Hofmeister, 1981). The present goal is the use of functional, efficient handwriting. Although it is viewed as a means of expression rather than an end in itself, instruction in the mechanics of writing should not be neglected.

Assessment. Screening criteria are not as clear in handwriting as in other areas. Classroom teachers may not agree on the criteria because of differing emphases on the importance of speed, legibility, and form. Although individual differences in handwriting style are generally accepted, the primary criterion is the response to the question, Can it be read with ease?

Criteria for legibility can be established by each teacher as a base for assessing manuscript and cursive writing. The following checklist is an example of a form used in analyzing and evaluating handwriting:

_____ Appearance of writing

_____ Margins

_____ Slant of writing

_____ Quality of pen or pencil line

_____ Letter forms

_____ Size of writing

_____ Alignment of letters

_____ Figures

_____ Proportion

Areas needing improvement can be indicated and instructional procedures initiated. An ongoing assessment can be maintained through handwriting samples. The student may be asked to write such sentences as "This is a sample of my handwriting on October 1." The difficult part of assessment is deciding on the minimum standard of acceptance.

The Zaner-Bloser Evaluation Scales (1979) provide a standard method of collecting and rating handwriting samples. The student's handwriting is judged for letter formation; vertical strokes in manuscript; and slant in cursive, spacing, alignment and proportion; and line quality.

The *Test of Written Language* (Hammill & Larsen, 1978) has a subtest that is scored only if the student has written in cursive. The most important consideration in this subtest is legibility; letter slant, spacing, and size are not stressed.

Objectives. The handicapped pupil, like the normal pupil, is expected to identify forms and to make movements producing forms. The forms include manuscript and cursive letters, punctuation marks, Arabic numerals, conventions for arrangement and spacing, and conventions for margins and headings (Blake, 1974). The objective for handwriting is legibility. To meet this goal, an effective program should be based on the following principles and conditions:

1. Handwriting instruction is direct and not incidental.
2. Because handicapped students exhibit a diverse range of handwriting achievement, instruction is individualized.
3. The handwriting program is planned, monitored, and modified on the basis of assessment information.
4. Successful teaching and remediation depend upon the flexible use of a wide variety of techniques and methods.
5. Handwriting is taught in short daily learning periods during which desirable habits are established.
6. Skills in handwriting are overlearned in isolation and then applied in meaningful context assignments.
7. Teachers stress the importance of handwriting and do not accept, condone, or encourage slovenly work.
8. Effective handwriting instruction is dependent upon the attitudes of both student and teacher.
9. The instructional atmosphere is pleasant, and motivation is promoted through incentives, reinforcement, success, and enthusiasm.
10. Teachers practice lessons prior to presentation and are able to write a "model" hand.
11. Students are encouraged to evaluate their own handwriting and, when appropriate, actively participate in initiating, conducting, and evaluating the remedial program.
12. Although students do develop personal idiosyncrasies, the teacher helps them maintain a consistent, legible handwriting style throughout the grades.[1]

Beginning Instruction. Three groups of experiences lead to writing readiness. The first group, manipulative experiences, is designed to strengthen

---

1. From Graham, S., & Miller, L. Handwriting research and practice: A unified approach. *Focus on Exceptional Children, 13*(2), 5–6. Copyright Love Publishing Company. Used by permission.

muscles needed for writing and to gain control over writing tools. The second group is designed to increase the pupil's oral use of language. Students have to be able to express their ideas orally before learning to write. The third group of experiences is designed to give practice in the basic movements of writing itself.

Students with learning problems may be unable to control movements well enough to hold a pencil. Exercises may be needed to develop coordination and strengthen the muscles involved in grasping. Spring clothespins can be used for this purpose—the student squeezes the pins to open them and places them on the edge of a box. Strong tactile feedback may be needed to monitor movements. Such experience can be provided through tracing with finger paint or tracing letters made from sandpaper, felt, velvet, or clay. Frostig and Maslow (1973) suggest that kinesthetic feedback provided from tracing soft, warm materials may be more effective for many students than tracing sandpaper letters.

The small muscles of the hands can be developed by playing with toys, dialing the telephone, setting the table, putting puzzles together, cutting with scissors, and modeling clay. The first writing exercise should be with chalk on the board or with crayons on large pieces of paper.

Pasamanick (1976) combines manipulative experiences with experiences to increase the use of language. In her early childhood language development resource book, she presents the idea that every activity and experience has a language component.

Practice in the basic movements of writing begins with variations of the circle, the curved line, and vertical, horizontal, and oblique lines. Verbal cues have been used successfully in teaching manuscript writing to mentally retarded students (Vacc & Vacc, 1979). These basic verbal cues provide a guide when making a writing stroke: touch, pull; touch, cross; touch, slant; touch, slide; and touch, dot. Used in a variety of combinations, the verbal cues strengthen the student's visual skill development.

Handicapped students may benefit from tracing exercises. Tracing paper or a plastic cover can be placed over the forms to be traced. Commercial vinyl overlays are available for this purpose, but inexpensive page covers or even the plastic inserts found in bacon packages work just as well. The initial pattern may consist of lines and simple geometric forms oriented in different positions in space and drawn in a constantly varying assortment of colors. The primary purpose of the exercise is to supply practice in visual motor perception. The next step is to copy the pattern on paper without the aid of tracing.

One variation uses strips of modeling clay to form patterns or the letters of the alphabet. A very distractible pupil often benefits from copying forms with a stylus in modeling clay rolled out on the bottom of a shallow pan or meat tray. The modeling clay affords resistance, which helps to strengthen the kinesthetic perception.

The position in writing is important. The pupil should sit in a comfortable chair, the table should be a proper height, and the paper should be properly placed. For manuscript writing, the paper is not slanted; for cursive writing it should be tilted approximately sixty degrees from the vertical to the left for right-handed students and to the right for left-handed students. A strip of tape can be placed at the top of the desk to indicate position; some students may need the paper taped to the desk. The proper position for paper is illustrated in Figure 5–2.

Left-handed students require different instruction than their right-handed peers because their handwriting problems are more numerous and severe. Suggestions for teaching left-handed students are to:

- Group left-handed children together for handwriting instruction.
- Provide them with a good left-handed model—a teacher, aide, parent, or another student.
- Give them readiness exercises to develop left to right directionality.
- Encourage a fuller movement of the writing arm by having them practice at the chalkboard.
- Teach them to hold their pencils about 1½ inches from the point, slant their papers to the right, and turn their bodies to the right when they write.
- Encourage them to eliminate excessive loops and flourishes in their writing.

FIGURE 5–2. Paper Position for Right-handed and Left-handed Writers

- Teach them to write vertically or with a slight backhand slant; do not insist on a slant to the right.
- Provide each child with a model cursive alphabet showing left-handed writing. They can use this instead of the usual right-handed model to evaluate and self-correct their handwriting.[1]

Manuscript Writing. Children are usually taught to print in kindergarten or first grade, with the transition to cursive writing occurring during the second or third grade. Recently, educators have suggested omitting cursive writing. Kean and Personke (1976) state the rationale to this position: some research indicates that manuscript print can be produced as rapidly as cursive writing once the individual has practiced it; manuscript printing may be more legible than cursive writing; manuscript print has received acceptance in business and commercial contexts; and a printed signature has the same legality as one written in cursive.

Even though the acceptance of individuality in writing may permit the continued use of manuscript, many students feel the importance of learning "real writing," and many parents and teachers see it as an indication of progress. If cursive writing is taught, the transition should be demonstrated (see Figure 5–3) and practice sessions scheduled.

Students should be permitted to choose their modes of writing for spelling, tests, and expressive writing.

Cursive Writing. Although students are taught to print before learning cursive

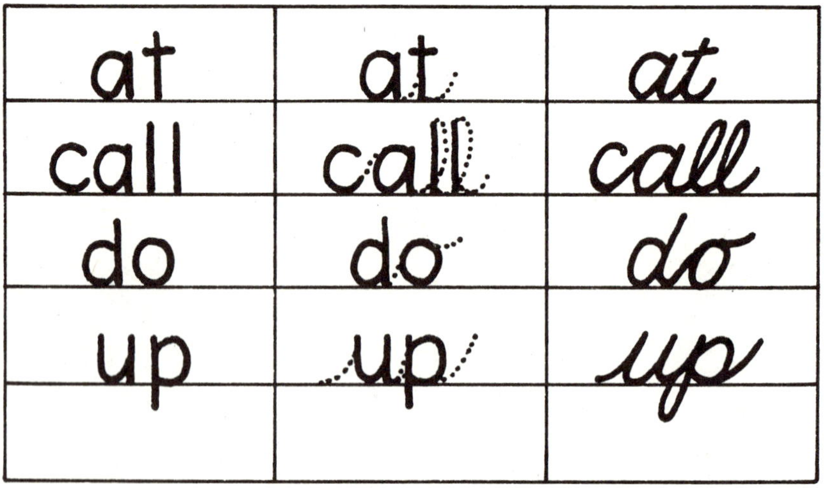

FIGURE 5–3. Transition from Manuscript to Cursive Writing

1. S. Harrison, "Open Letter from a Left-Handed Teacher: Some Sinistral Ideas on the Teaching of Handwriting." *Teaching Exceptional Children,* 1981, *13*(3), 117. Reprinted by permission.

because the letters are easier to form and more closely resemble book print, printing is not the easiest form for some students to reproduce. Cursive writing may be easier because of its connective lines, which indicate the order, position, and grouping of letters (Bigge, 1976).

The flow of cursive writing may help students to establish a smooth left-right progression and to avoid reversals; it helps them to experience words as wholes. It is usually quicker and less laborious, and it helps establish spelling patterns (Frostig & Maslow, 1973).

Strauss and Lehtinen (1947) advocate an early start in teaching cursive writing to students with perceptual or neurological problems. They believe that learning two alphabets (one for writing, one for reading) is an advantage. The knowledge that a word can be written in different letter forms may assist them in making the generalization that it is the order and sound of letters that is significant. This approach avoids the inflexibility resulting from extended use of only one type of alphabet. Recent research indicates that cursive writing may be a necessary alternative to manuscript (Graham & Miller, 1980).

Students who experience difficulty forming the letters in cursive writing may profit from the Alpha-Line (Lectro-Stik Corporation) shaping cord and writing card. The cards are printed with cursive letters numbered to insure proper form sequence; the cord adheres to the letters when the child follows the proper sequence. This inexpensive device provides individual practice and requires little teacher direction.

If the child is unable to indicate the line on which letters should rest, the use of cues may help, such as outlining the major writing space with color or heavy black crayon. The use of felt tip pens also adds color and contributes to the ease of writing.

Handwriting Problems. Handicapped students may be unable to perform the motor movements required for writing or copying; they may be unable to transfer visual information inputs to motor outputs; and activities requiring motor and spatial judgments may be difficult for them. The shortcomings that contribute to such problems are poor motor skills, unstable and erratic temperament, faulty visual perception of letters, and difficulty in retaining visual impressions (Lerner, 1976).

The student with poor motor skills due to orthopedic handicaps may experience difficulty holding a pencil, pen, chalk, or crayon. A commercial pencil grip or a ball of clay or sponge molded around the pencil (see Figure 5–4) will prevent the fingers from slipping; if the problem is severe, pencil holders or mechanical devices may be needed. Care must be taken to equip persons with the adaptations to fit specific functional problems (Bigge, 1976).

Since handwriting is a visual as well as a motor task, visually impaired students need special accommodations. Even if braille is used, the pupil needs some method of communicating with sighted persons in writing. Letters, spelling words, and signatures can be written with the aid of an APH signature guide

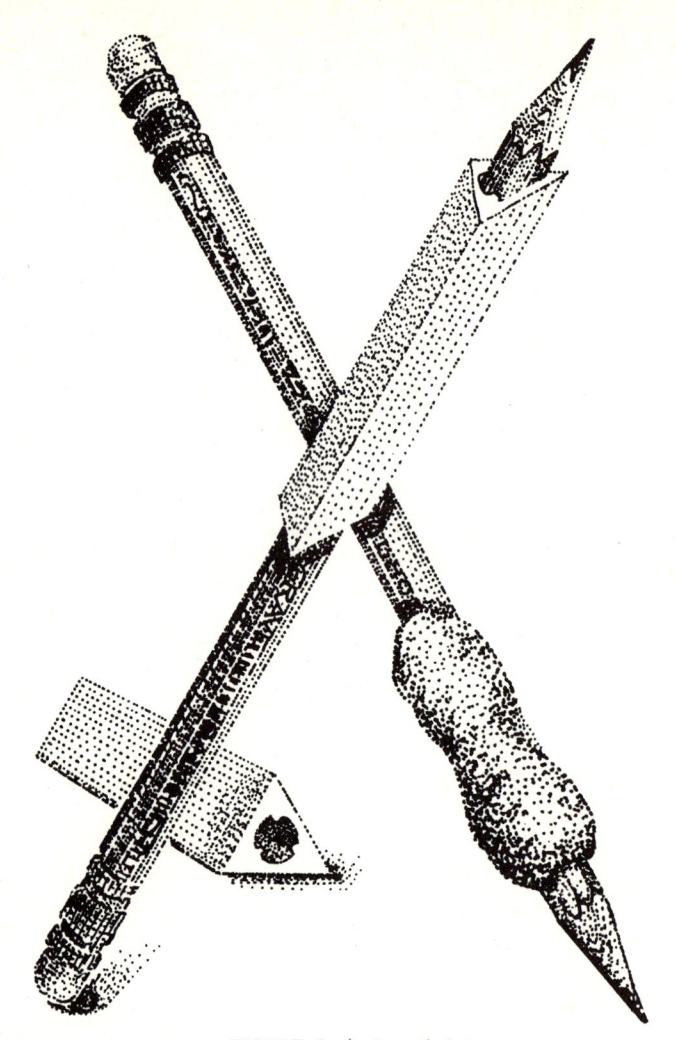

164   CHAPTER 5   *Teaching Language Arts: Listening, Speaking, Writing*

FIGURE 5–4. Pencil Grips

(American Printing House for the Blind). The guide, which is made of metal or cord, provides tactile lines that fit over a paper on a clip board. A small signature guide easily made from tagboard or plastic can be carried in the wallet (see Figure 5–5).

The visually impaired pupil will need dark-lined paper and may need to use large pencils past the primary grades. Writing in sand and in clay will help develop writing ability. The American Printing House for the Blind (see Appendix A for address) has published numerous writing aids, such as a raised-

FIGURE 5-5. Signature Guide

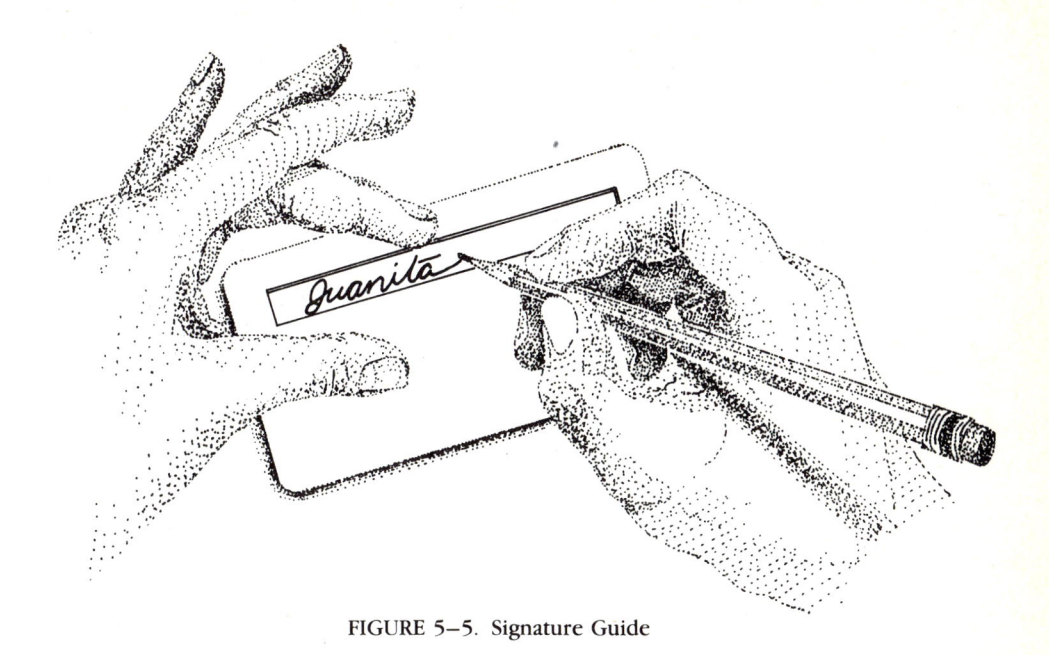

line checkbook, a cursive writing kit, script-letter sheets and boards, bold-lined writing paper, and embossed pencil writing paper.

For visually impaired students and those who write slowly, typewriting may be a useful skill. An electric typewriter would facilitate written expression for the pupil with severe motor difficulties. The secondary student may be integrated into the regular typing class.

An additional problem in handwriting is poor instruction. Hofmeister (1973) cites five common instructional errors in teaching writing: massed practice without supervision, no immediate feedback, emphasis on rote practice rather than on discrimination, failure to provide good models, and no differentiation between good and poor work. Frequently for students, the consequences of trying to improve their handwriting are the same as not trying when there is inadequate instruction and feedback.

Hofmeister (1973) presents a progressive approximation approach using work sheets with a model at the top and space for practice lines below. In the steps outlined, the student completes the first line and informs the teacher; the teacher corrects by overmarking with a "high-lighter" only those letters needing improvement; the student erases incorrect portions of the letters and traces over the teacher's markings; then the student moves to the next line, repeating only the letters that were incorrect on the preceding line.

With knowledge of the developmental aspects of handwriting, regard for individual needs and differences, and skill in instructional procedures, the classroom teacher can provide activities to initiate and improve handwriting for handicapped as well as for nonhandicapped students.

Spelling

Spelling and handwriting have both been neglected in the development of innovative curriculum strategies. Consequently, teachers have little information to build on regarding types of spelling errors, kinds of instruction available, or strategies for task modifications (Reid & Hresko, 1981). This lack of help is especially critical since evidence indicates that poor spelling is increasing at the elementary, secondary, and college levels. There are, in fact, programs at the college level that start out with the same words introduced at the elementary level (Rivers, 1974).

Many poor spellers are also deficient in other language abilities (Otto & Smith, 1980). Therefore, special help should be given in conjunction with other language arts instruction.

Spelling is necessary for daily written communication. Although there is a paucity of recent research on methods for teaching it, spelling does occupy a large portion of school instructional time. The inability to spell carries with it a social stigma and complicates efforts at written communication.

Proficient spellers use three kinds of knowledge when writing words. They use language knowledge, which enables them to assign meaning to sounds to use prior knowledge in order to help determine word structures and to spell related words. Another knowledge, internalized rules, enables them to predict and write the most probable spelling for words. The third kind of knowledge is visual association, which helps in developing automatic spelling and in verifying written words (Nicholson & Schachter, 1979).

Lerner (1976) identifies the many subskills and abilities demanded in the spelling process. Students must be able to read the word, they must be knowledgeable and skillful in certain relationships of phonics and structural analysis, they must be able to apply the appropriate phonic generalizations, be able to visualize the appearance of the word, and have the motor facility to write it.

Since handicapped students may have problems in visual and auditory discrimination, in making generalizations, and with motor skills, spelling success may be difficult to achieve. And yet, there are many instances in which handicapped students have succeeded.

Larry, Libby, James, and David comprise a spelling group that comes to the resource room daily from the sixth grade. The resource teacher and the classroom teacher have worked out a weekly list of ten words, taken from the sixth-grade spelling book, for this group to learn. After several months, this group became the best spellers in their class, sometimes even scoring well on the twenty words given to the whole class. Larry and Libby are mentally retarded, James is learning-disabled, and David is blind.

The resource teacher used a combination of discovery and drill. One of the most effective drill methods was to have one of the students dictate the words to David, who brailled them on cards. He could then drill the others orally, since they could not read his cards.

Assessment. Standardized survey tests assist the teacher in screening students who need help with spelling. Such tests as the *Iowa Tests of Basic Skills* (Houghton Mifflin), the *Metropolitan Achievement Tests* (Harcourt Brace Jovanovich), and the *Stanford Achievement Tests* (Harcourt Brace Jovanovich) have age and grade norms and are based on word counts and lists of general utility. *The Test of Written Spelling* (Larsen & Hammill, 1976) is a norm-referenced standardized measure of spelling skills. It is appropriate for both elementary and junior high students. In addition to formal tests, a number of informal assessment procedures can be used. Some suggested procedures are:

- *Analyzing written work,* including test papers. Are there defects in handwriting that are causing errors? Can the spelling errors be classified as to type? Is there evidence that the student doesn't know important spelling rules?
- *Analyzing oral spelling.* Is pronunciation of the words clear, as well as articulation and enunciation? How does the child spell the word orally (as units, by letter, by digraphs, by syllables)? Is the student able to spell plural forms and derivatives? When the child describes his thought process while studying new words, is it evident that he has a systematic method of study? Does he or she know several different ways to study spelling words?
- *Interviewing the child.* Here questions would be asked regarding knowledge of important spelling rules, his or her attitude towards spelling, and perhaps extent of using the dictionary.[1]

Observation of students' written work offers the best assessment tool for the teacher, for the ability to spell in context is the ultimate goal of the spelling program. Since the purpose of assessment is remediation, the teacher should note the nature of spelling errors, determine any pattern presented, and plan a program to help students overcome the errors. This process is demonstrated in Table 5–2.

Objectives. The major goal of the spelling program for mildly handicapped students is to develop writers who can communicate without a number of spelling errors. There are three major objectives for the student:

1. ASSESSMENT AND CORRECTION OF LANGUAGE ARTS DIFFICULTIES by P. C. Burns. Columbus, Ohio: Charles E. Merrill Publishing Company, 1980, p. 186. Reprinted by permission of the publisher.

TABLE 5-2. Selecting Remedial Procedures

SPELLING ERRORS	PROBABLE CAUSE	REMEDIAL PROCEDURE
"bad" for "bat" "cown" for "clown"	poor auditory discrimination	Give practice in hearing likenesses and differences in words that are similar. Have the student look at a word as it is pronounced to hear all the sounds and see the letters that represent them. Play rhyming games.
"enuff" for "enough" "clim" for "climb" "krak" for "crack"	poor visual imagery	Expose words that are not entirely phonetic for short periods of time and have the child reproduce them in writing from memory. Have child trace words with his finger and write them from memory.
"comeing" for "coming" "happyly" for "happily" "flys" for "flies" "payed" for "paid"	pupil has not learned rules for formation of derivatives	Stress visual imagery. Teach generalizations of forming tenses and adding suffixes.
"form" for "from" "abel" for "able" "aminal" for "animal" "mazagine" for "magazine"	poor attention to letter sequence in certain words	Have pupil pronounce words carefully. Stress sequence of sounds and letters.
"there" for "their" "peception" for "perception" "sasifactry" for "satisfactory"	carelessness	Discuss the importance of good spelling for social and vocational purposes. Encourage careful proofreading of all writing.
"hires" for "horses" "bothry" for "brother" "meciline" for "medicine"	lack of phonics ability	Use a multisensory approach whereby the student sees the word, says the word, spells the word orally, and copies the word.

Source: Otto-Smith: CORRECTIVE AND REMEDIAL TEACHING, Third Edition, pp. 350–351. Copyright © 1980 by Houghton Mifflin Company. Used by permission.

1. To accurately spell the most frequently used words that the child needs to write now and in the future.
2. To develop self-correction skills for adjusting spelling errors.
3. To develop the ability to locate the correct spelling of unfamiliar words. (Cohen & Plaskon, 1980, p. 328)

Spelling, like other areas of learning, is individual. Therefore, the programming objectives must be based on each pupil's abilities and needs. Each pupil should be aware of the relationship of the spelling program to other areas of the curriculum. Clanfield and Hannah (1961) suggest development of the following concepts:

- The purpose for learning to spell correctly is to be able to say something in writing in a way that other people can read.
- Pronouncing words correctly in speaking and oral reading contributes to correct spelling.
- Carefully observing words in reading enables pupils to spell many words without further study.
- Phonics learned during the reading period will be helpful in spelling many words.
- Learning about roots, suffixes, prefixes, homonyms, antonyms, contractions, syllabication, and so on, in reading and language classes are aids to spelling.
- One of the important reasons for learning to use the dictionary is to be able to increase one's spelling power.
- There is a group of important words that is used over and over in writing and should be mastered as quickly as possible.
- Handwriting plays an important part in spelling because letters must be formed correctly for readers to be able to interpret the writing.

Instructional Techniques. Some authors advocate the development of spelling readiness through discrimination training, memory training, sound blending, and auditory closure (Tiedt & Tiedt, 1978; Lerner, 1976). Reid and Hresko (1981) claim that this type of prespelling instruction is inefficient. The best spelling readiness system is probably a broad language development program that integrates reading, writing, listening, and speaking skills.

Gentry (1981) suggests the "immersion of the learner in a language environment" (p. 380) as a factor in learning to speak and to spell. Good spellers form a spelling consciousness through writing, augmented with formal spelling study.

Boyd and Talbert (1971) suggest the *test-study-test* plan as an effective method for teaching spelling. In this plan, students are tested on assigned words and study the words misspelled. It consists of the following features: a preliminary test to determine the general level of spelling achievement; a test on each week's assignment before instruction is begun on that assignment; words that pupils misspell become their study lists; students use a series of steps in learning to spell each word; and one or more tests are given to determine the degree of word mastery. Spelling exercises and activities are used throughout the week. Each pupil keeps a progress chart and words missed on the final test of the week are added to the following week's list.

The *study-test* plan is organized in much the same way, except that the pretest is omitted and all the words in the lesson become the study list for each pupil. Various activities, such as defining the words, writing sentences with the words, working crossword puzzles, and playing spelling games are usually assigned.

Kean and Personke (1976) advocate the use of the *corrected test,* a procedure in which students correct their own tests. With this approach, students are tested on the words of a lesson either before the words have been introduced or any time thereafter. Students correct their own tests, either independently or in a group. They receive immediate, positive feedback and correct their errors immediately.

A *discovery* approach to spelling allows students to discover and apply spelling generalizations rather than memorize individual words. Usually, the teacher decides on a generalization to be taught and guides the students to discover the generalization for themselves (Kean and Personke, 1976). On an independent level, the lesson might be presented to a student in the following way:

future	manage	captain
mixture	average	fountain
adventure	message	curtain

How is each group of words alike?

Form a rule about the spelling of each group.

The *cover and write* method has been advocated for slow learners and mentally retarded children because of the overlearning feature. The following steps are included:

1. Look at the word; say it.
2. Write the word two times while looking at it.
3. Cover the word and write it one time.
4. Check your spelling by looking at the word.
5. Write the word two times while looking at it.
6. Cover the word and write it one time.
7. Check the word.

8. Write the word three times while looking at it.
9. Cover the word and write it one time.
10. Check the spelling.

This approach is useful in making an initial breakthrough with poor spellers, which is motivating in itself. However, it becomes dull if used too often.

A procedure that supports the importance of active teacher involvement during spelling instruction is presented by Stowitschek and Jobes (1977). Instruction is provided through a process of imitation training; teachers model spelling words, orally and in writing, for students to imitate. This direct, tutorial approach has been successful where previous spelling instruction has failed and would be useful if volunteer help or paraprofessionals were available.

Other programs are outlined in teachers' editions of spelling series and in other sources. The plans described are adaptable to the classroom that includes handicapped students. The words can be chosen to fit each pupil's needs and the plan carried out with the help of a resource teacher or with peers. Learning Activity Packets (see chapter 4) are useful in providing practice and motivating activities that can be done on an individual basis.

Activities. For children who need a multisensory approach to spelling, the Language Master is an effective tool. An audiovisual instructional system (Bell & Howell), the Language Master provides visual, auditory, and some kinesthetic experiences for the child. Programmed cards are available, as well as blank cards that can be programmed by the teacher. The blank cards can be reused if the top portion is laminated so that the spelling words can be erased or changed. The blank cards also permit the teacher to add clues, such as pictures or tactile stimulation (e.g., letters in yarn or sandpaper).

The typewriter offers many benefits to the language arts program, such as:

1. Primary children quickly learn the uppercase and lowercase forms of the alphabet letters.
2. Punctuation marks are easily mastered.
3. The left-to-right and top-to-bottom movements of the typewriter carriage help in reading readiness activities.

Exploring words and patterns improves spelling and is highly motivating. An example is a puzzle in which one letter is changed at a time until the top word is changed into the bottom word.

L O V E	Deep affection
_ _ _ _	Existing
_ _ _ _	Numeral following four
_ _ _ _	Flames

```
_ _ _ _            Texture—not coarse
_ _ _ _            Discover
W I N D            Strong breeze
```

Concrete poetry is another example of the exploration of words and patterns. Using a typewriter, pen, or pencil, students arrange a word in as many different patterns as possible.

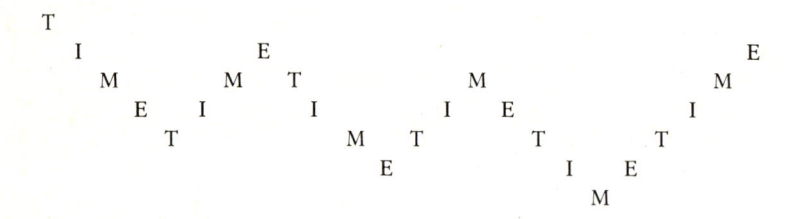

```
T
  I              E                                        E
    M      M   T          M                         M
     E  I    I       I   E                       I
      T         M   T       T                 T
              E               I   E
                                M
```

(Latta, 1977)

Additional activities for promoting spelling appear in teachers' magazines, children's weekly newspapers, and children's magazines. Although many commercial games are available for this purpose, some of the most successful ones have been created by children and teachers.

It must be remembered that spelling is a tool for communication. It should be integrated with writing instruction and activities at all levels of instruction. The best motivation in spelling is the student's need to use particular words. Words identified as particularly useful for handicapped students are referred to as "survival" words.

Written Expression

In describing the current "writing crisis," Wheeler (1979) states that "students who find reading a chore will find writing difficult. When students enjoy reading, they gain not only a familiarity with language but respect for writing" (p. 3). Again, it is apparent that students who have difficulty in one language arts area are at a disadvantage in related areas.

The quality of student writing may be further limited by the scope of their ideas and by the extent of their vocabulary. Their writing usually reflects the level of language they hear at home and at school. A wealth of language experience is needed to enrich the structure and purpose of spoken and written language.

Many people believe that writing is neglected in today's schools. Albert (1977) attributes much of the problem to teachers who place "an uncontrollable, abnormal dependence on blank-filling and labeling exercises which eat away at vital time for learning to write" (p. 43).

This criticism may be particularly applicable to teachers who have worked with handicapped students. In an effort to provide control, models, and structure for students with learning problems, teachers may not have emphasized creative endeavors. Thus, many students have not acquired skills that help them to communicate, to express themselves, and to learn to think.

Assessment. To evaluate a student's written performance, the teacher should be aware of the purpose of evaluation, the components of written language to be assessed, and the variety of assessment techniques available (Cohen & Plaskon, 1980). Even though achievement tests may provide information about the student's performance in spelling and handwriting, they do not assess sentence and paragraph structure or creative expression.

McLoughlin and Lewis (1981) identify three standardized tests that assess composition skills:

- *The Test of Written Language* (Hammill & Larsen, 1978)
- *The Test of Adolescent Language* (Hammill, Brown, Larsen, & Wiederholt, 1980)
- *The Picture Story Language Test* (Myklebust, 1965)

Work sample analysis is frequently used to evaluate written products for syntax, semantics, productivity, handwriting, spelling, and writing mechanics. Different skill areas can be analyzed to identify student strengths and weaknesses.

Informal assessment is valuable in providing diagnostic information and in determining appropriate instructional strategies. Before informal assessment of written expression, the teacher should know the scope of necessary skills, the requirements of the specific writing task, and the characteristics of the student being assessed as they relate to the developmental nature of the student's language system (Poteet, 1980).

A number of checklists are available for assessing written language. An example is *Checklist of Written Expression* (Poteet, 1980). Criterion-referenced tests, such as the *Brigance Diagnostic Inventory* (Brigance, 1977, 1978, 1980), are valuable in determining the needs of handicapped students. The Brigance assesses several written language skills and, at the secondary level, features survival skills, such as completing applications and tax forms and writing letters (McLoughlin & Lewis, 1981).

Objectives. Expressive writing is either functional or creative. Functional writing refers to letters, reports, and other means of relaying information in a structured form. Creative writing permits the author to express, through poetry or prose, personal thoughts, experiences, and observations in a unique fashion.

Functional Writing. Letter writing is a valued social as well as business skill.

As with handwriting, this is an area in which many students (including those who have not been successful academically) can excel.

> *Robert, who is mentally retarded, has been writing thank-you notes since he was quite young. At first, he told his mother what he wanted to say; she wrote it and Robert copied it. As he acquired a small sight vocabulary, his mother put the words he used most frequently on small cards. With her help, he could form sentences from the cards and copy them into letter form. Last year, following his high school graduation, Robert wrote all his notes to thank friends and relatives for graduation gifts.*

Classroom teachers can encourage letter writing in many ways. Noar (1972) suggests the use of individual mailboxes. These can be made from milk cartons, with the top cut off and a sign bearing the owner's name. The teacher can put into the mailboxes welcome back notes for absentees and notes to go home. Children can put in birthday cards, friendly notes to classmates, and notes to the teacher and to parents.

If the teacher wishes to plan a program in letter writing, a visit to the post office could be a starting point. The post office has a writing kit that can be obtained for classroom use. One teacher (Brokamp, 1976) has a post office in her classroom. She writes to two or three students each evening and places the letters in the class post office. The students answer the letter with one of their own and drop it in the box the next day.

Forms of writing should be introduced as vehicles for conveying information rather than as rigid models or patterns to be imitated. Since writing is a very personal and individual production, the handicapped child should not be at a disadvantage. Leeson (1977) describes a project in which eighth-grade students assisted third-grade students in the composition, revision, and evaluation of their writing projects. Both groups improved their use of grammar and spelling, learned to proofread and read aloud clearly, and developed admiration for the other's accomplishments. A similar plan could improve the writing skills of handicapped students and their nonhandicapped peers.

Cooperation between the classroom teacher and the resource teacher helps the handicapped student achieve success in writing. Melissa, a second-grade student, was unable to complete a writing assignment in class. Assisted individually by the resource teacher, she produced her letter (Figure 5–6).

The teaching of writing skills is an important aspect of mainstreaming mildly handicapped students in secondary English classes (Sargent, Swartzbaugh, & Sherman, 1981). Writing instruction can be applied to traditional language arts activities and to practical exercises, including letters of request, complaint letters, personal letters, telephone messages, descriptive essays, and note taking for other classes. The use of a combination of literature-related assignments and practical application assignments keeps instruction in line with

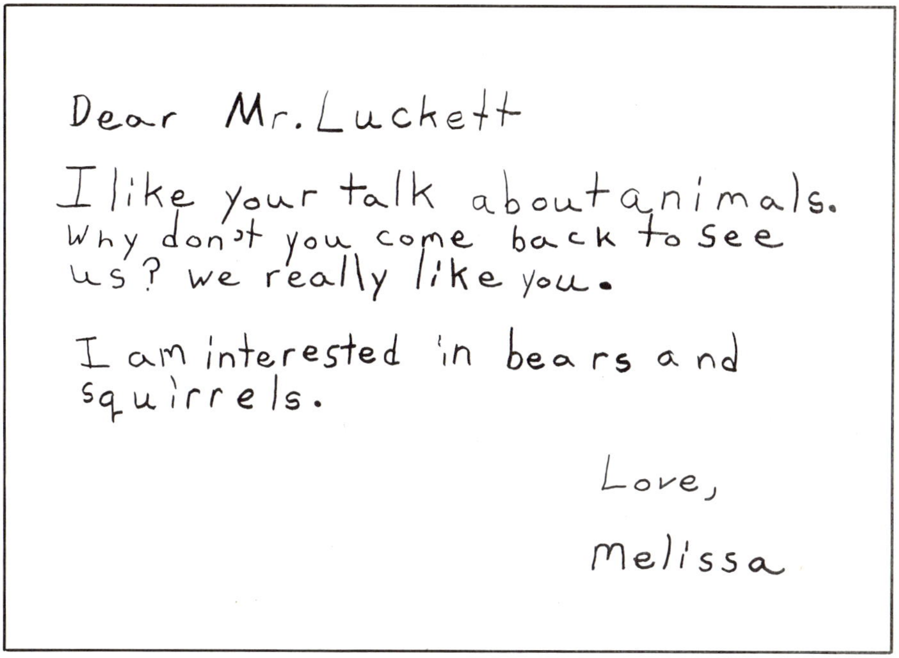

> Dear Mr. Luckett
>
> I like your talk about animals. Why don't you come back to see us? we really like you.
>
> I am interested in bears and squirrels.
>
> Love,
> melissa

FIGURE 5–6. Functional Letter Writing

requirements of the regular English curriculum and meets the needs of handicapped students.

Creative Writing. Writing is a threat to many people. For students who view reading, spelling, and school as areas in which they have failed, writing may seem impossible. Yet it may be the vehicle for expression and growth vital to their intellectual and emotional development.

A program in creative writing for students with learning disabilities (Cady, 1976) demonstrated the value of writing and contributed some excellent techniques for teaching it to students whose reading skills were below the level at which written expression is usually introduced. The topic was introduced to the class by the teacher's reading aloud each day. In addition to such classics as *Charlotte's Web* and *The Story of My Life* by Helen Keller (1954), she read stories and poems written by students of all ages. The students were instructed to write as if they were talking and were provided with copies of *The Spelling Reference Book* (Developmental Learning Materials). Topics were chosen with or without the students' help, and they were free to write at any suitable time, provided a story was completed or a reasonable beginning was made on a particular day. On completion, the students shared their stories. Their pleasure in hearing each other's stories suggested that "real communication occurred and that some of the isolation of struggling with a learning disability was diminished" (p. 29).

In the early stages of writing, it is important not to restrict students by emphasizing the mechanics of writing. Even though editing is important, concern with punctuation may be inhibiting. The classroom climate should permit students to feel free to dare and to explore.

Students who have never written may feel less inhibited if they are granted privacy in their early endeavors. Kohl (1967) used this technique effectively in introducing writing to children of the ghetto. The students were encouraged to write about their lives and were assured that the teacher would see their products only if they wished. The results were moving experiences that helped the teacher understand the children and their problems.

Instructional Techniques. Writing, like other language arts skills, is built on observation and experience. Schiff (1979) suggests that opportunities for prewriting observation should have a manipulative component, such as:

- field trips to museums where visitors can operate the exhibits;
- visits to farms where students may participate in the care of animals;
- tours of historical restorations where students can try out craft implements (spinning wheels, butter presses, blacksmithing equipment);
- school/neighborhood walks on which pupils can work the public address system or plant a flower at a nearby nursery;
- examination of objects with moving parts which students can touch, turn, prod, and pull (kitchen utensils, treadle sewing machines, typewriters). (p. 754)

The earliest expressive student writing originates from their little bits of news, their journals, their personal accounts of experiences, or a class activity. Early writing can begin with the teacher as a scribe, helping students attempt writing by themselves as soon as possible. Teachers who accept "invented" spelling find that students are willing writers (Clay, 1982). During the early stages of drafting, students should not be concerned with punctuation. In pointing out that learning to write takes a long time, Albert (1977) feels that as teachers

> We expect . . . students to spell perfectly before they grasp sound-letter relationships. We expect them to punctuate correctly before they tune into the pauses that commas and periods symbolize. We expect them to adhere to a flawless format before they find something worthwhile to say. (p. 48)

For students who lack adequate background experiences, story starters can stimulate ideas. Within the same classroom, students of varying ability can respond to the same starter. In a fifth-grade class, the teacher provided the starter "I was sitting alone in my room last night when suddenly . . ." and asked the students to complete the story. The task was carried out differently by Cassi (Figure 5–7) and by Nathan (Figure 5–8).

For students who will not write, who do not have the skills to write, who are visually or physically impaired so they cannot write, and/or who still need to express themselves, the tape recorder is an excellent medium. The teacher can provide a list of topics or pictures from which to choose or students can

> I was sitting alone in my room last night when suddenly my cat came in and scolded me for not doing my homework. So I got up and finished my homework.
> When I was done I decided to read, but then 3 rotton eggs came in and told me to go to the kitchen to do the dishes. So I got up again and did the dishes.
> When I was done I was ready to go to bed but a robot came in and threw garlic and rotton tomatoes at me and said, "That's what you get for not taking a bath beep, beep." I decided to get up and take a bath.
> Now I'm in bed waiting for something to happen, but I been thinking, Could I be watching too much T.V.?
>
> by Cassi

FIGURE 5–7. Expressive Writing

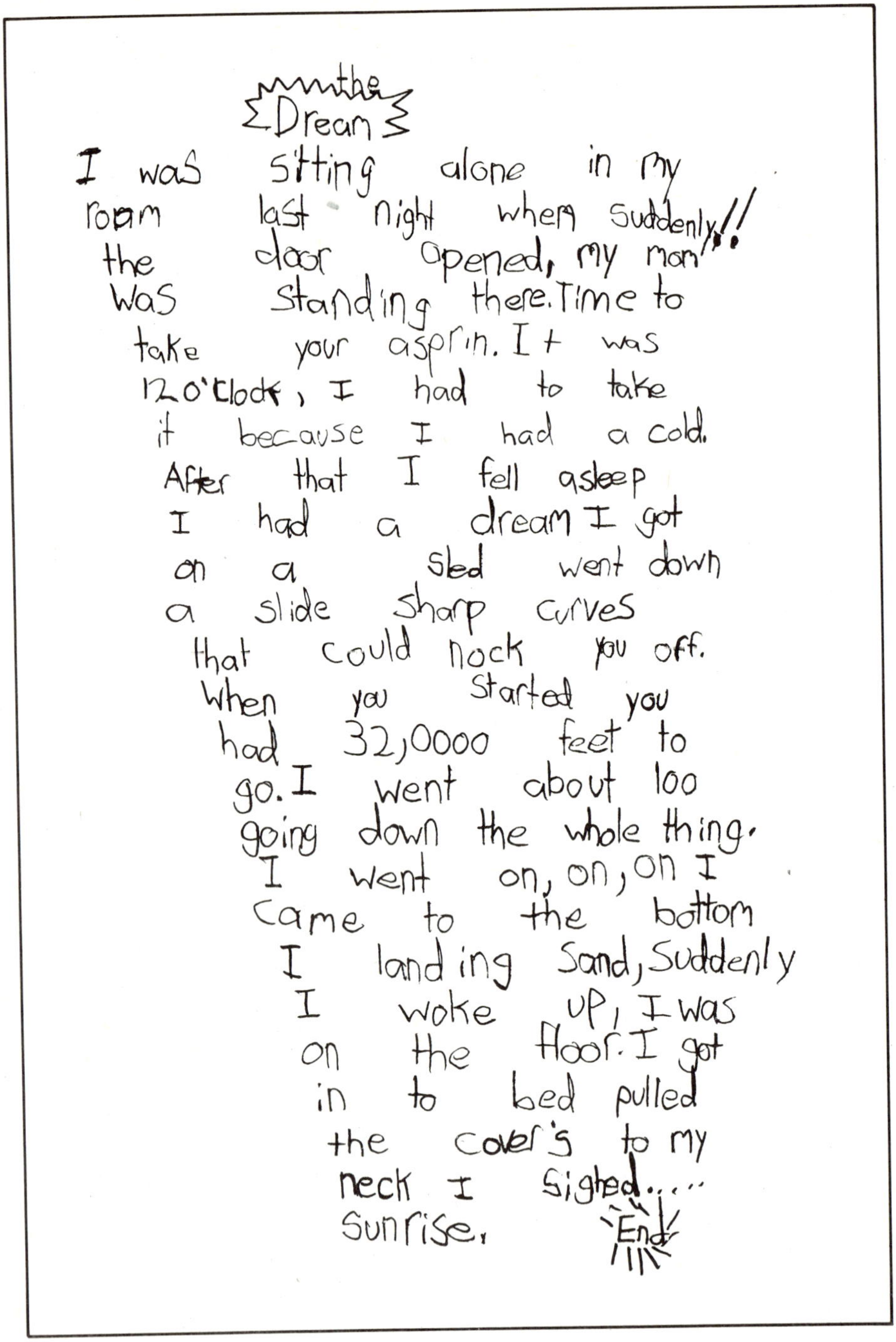

the Dream

I was sitting alone in my room last night when suddenly!! the door opened, my mon was standing there. Time to take your asprin. It was 12 o'clock, I had to take it because I had a cold. After that I fell asleep I had a dream I got on a sled went down a slide sharp curves that could nock you off. When you started you had 32,0000 feet to go. I went about 100 going down the whole thing. I went on, on, on I came to the bottom I landing Sand, Suddenly I woke up, I was on the floor. I got in to bed pulled the cover's to my neck I sighed..... Sunrise. End

FIGURE 5–8. Expressive Writing

select their own topics. When left alone, many students use the tape recorder with a great deal of creativity. One teacher placed the tape recorder on a table with a folder beside it and the following instructions written and recorded: "The pictures in this folder are illustrations for stories. Select one you like and write a story to go with it. You may use the tape recorder if you wish to tell your story. I will write it down later."

A number of pictures cut from magazines were placed in the folder. As taped stories were written by the teacher and read to the class, the students began to read their own as well as others' stories. One student, who had never written a story, chose a picture showing an old house on a hill. This is his story.

> Three ole men were standing in the street. This old preacher guy walked by and they were talking about this old haunted house up on the hill. This old man and woman lived up there years ago and was dead and nobody ever knowed what happened to them. The old preacher was talking and wanted to know who would go up there and stay all night. That old preacher was talking that he'd go up there and stay all night. He went home and got his Bible and a little lamp. And that night, after he went up there, he was sitting there, reading his Bible and he heard something upstairs rattling a chain; he said "Whoooo's up there?" It hushed and after a while he heard something coming down the stairs and he looked up and saw a ghost up there with his eyes hooked back in his head and he said, "That preacher left a new door in the side of that house!" He went down through there and he sat down on a log and that thing sat down beside him and he said, "Tight race, huh?" He said "It's gonna be a dang sight tighter the way he went!"
>
> He tore down the door and went home and his wife told him, "I thought you were going to stay all night." He said, "NO MORE!"
>
> By Larry

There are other alternative writing-related activities for students who have difficulty writing. Referred to as "writing without a pencil" (Tompkins, 1981), activities include forming letters and words in sand or on a flannelboard, or using words cut from newspapers; making letter cookies; using magic slates; using blocks and foam letters, marshmallows, clay, snow, and letter stamps. Drawing filmstrips and using the flannelboard to tell stories are also effective means of expression.

Writing can develop in the same natural way as spoken language if learning conditions are similar (Cohn, 1981). These conditions include a stimulating environment, encouragement, and a relaxed adult attitude.

The Language Experience Approach. The communication skills of listening, speaking, reading, and writing are closely interrelated. In the language experience approach, students develop certain fundamental concepts about themselves and communication so that they have a framework on which to hang the skills they find functional and meaningful.

1. What a child thinks about he can talk about.
2. What he can talk about can be expressed in painting, writing, or some other form.
3. Anything he writes can be read.
4. He can read what he writes and what other people write.
5. As he represents his speech sounds with symbols, he uses the same symbols (letters) over and over.
6. Each letter in the alphabet stands for one or more sounds that he makes when he talks.
7. Every word begins with a sound that he can write down.
8. Most words have an ending sound.
9. Many words have something in between.
10. Some words are used over and over in our language and some words are not used very often.
11. What he has to say and write is as important to him as what other people have written for him to read.
12. Most of the words he uses are the same ones which are used by other people who write for him to read. (Lee & Allen, 1963, pp. 5–8)

These principles are evident in classes where the language experience approach is practiced. Children are eager to express and record their experiences.

A university teacher was visiting in a kindergarten class. She had just observed a little boy as he completed a building with blocks. She commented on the beauty of the production and was directed by the child, "Write it!" Since the teacher obviously did not understand, the boy took her by the hand and led her to a large tablet on an easel. Under his direction, the teacher wrote about the block building which had been constructed.

At a very early age, students are aware of the importance of the written word. It is exciting for them to see their own experiences and words written down. The language experience approach has no age limits; it is as valuable to the high school student as it is to the young child. It may be especially effective for the student who has not learned to read and write by other methods.

Mike, a fifteen year-old, was embarrassed because he could not read. Discovering Mike's interest in camping, his teacher brought in several camping magazines. She pasted several pictures on paper and asked Mike to tell a story about them. She wrote the stories beneath the pictures and

Mike could read them: they contained words in his own vocabulary and were based on his interest.

Language experience stories can be written by the whole class or by one person. A class experience may be interpreted in many different ways by the participants. The important factor is the experience. Many students have a background of experiences to draw from, but some have to be provided with experiences in school.

Me and my daddy are going coon hunting tonight. When I started to go my dog had pups.
Tommy

We went on the nature trail. We heard cows. We seen dogs. I found a acorn. I found some tree limbs. Jake climbed a tree. We saw trees turning colors. Marty and Lewis and Tommy saw doves. We heard a jeep.
Edward

We saw gerbils having babies. The babies didn't have no hair yet. We seen that other gerbil running around that wheel. The father was happy. The gerbils was pretty. I seen the daddy gerbil washing his face. The gerbils had brown fur and black eyes.
Lewis

We drew a big funny nose. We drawed the eyes. We drawed the mouth. The teacher cut the pumpkin. We ate some pumpkin. We pulled out guts. We put the candle in it. We lit it up. We sat down and watched it burn. We saved the seeds. We might plant them. We might eat them.
Sue

The language experience approach illustrates the interrelatedness of all the language arts. Based on the prerequisite skill of oral language expression, it adds skills of spelling, writing, and reading to create a total communication process. As a method of teaching reading, it is only a beginning (see chapter 6). As a bridge from speaking to reading, it is an excellent tool.

REFERENCES

Adler, S. *The non-verbal child.* Springfield, Ill.: Charles C. Thomas, 1964.
Albert, B. Are you giving writing its due? *Instructor,* 1977, 87 (3), 41–48.
Bigge, J. L. *Teaching individuals with physical and multiple disabilities.* Columbus, Ohio: Charles E. Merrill Publishing Co., 1976.
Black, J. K. There's more to language than meets the ear: Implications for evaluation. *Language Arts,* 1979, 56 (5), 525–533.
Blake, K. A. *Teaching the retarded.* Englewood Cliffs, N.J.: Prentice-Hall, 1974.

Bloom, L. Language development: Form and function in emerging grammars. *Research Monograph No. 59.* Cambridge, Mass.: M.I.T. Press, 1970.

Boyd, G. A., & Talbert, E. G. *Spelling in the elementary school.* Columbus, Ohio: Charles E. Merrill Publishing Co., 1971.

Brenza, B. A., Kricos, P. B., & Lasky, E. Z. Comprehension and production of basic semantic concepts by older hearing-impaired children. *Journal of Speech and Hearing Research,* 1981, *24* (3), 414–419.

Brigance, A. H. *Brigance diagnostic inventory of basic skills* (2nd ed.) N. Billerica, Mass.: Curriculum Associates, 1977.

Brokamp, M. Good morning, Mr. Mailman. *The Elementary Teacher's Ideas and Materials Workshop* (November): 8, 1976.

Burns, P. C. *Assessment and correction of language arts difficulties.* Columbus, Ohio: Charles E. Merrill Publishing Co., 1980.

Cady, J. L. Pretend you are . . . an author. *Teaching Exceptional Children,* 1976, *9,* 26–31.

Chaney, C. M., & Kephart, N. C. *Motoric aids to perceptual training.* Columbus, Ohio: Charles E. Merrill Publishing Co., 1968.

Chinn, P. C., Drew, C. J., & Logan, D. R. *Mental retardation.* St. Louis: C. V. Mosby Co., 1975.

Clanfield, M., & Hannan, C. *Teach spelling by all means.* Palo Alto, Calif.: Fearon, 1961.

Clark, E. V. Some aspects of the conceptual basis for first language acquisition. In R. L. Schiefelbusch and L. L. Lloyd (Eds.), *Language perspectives—Acquisition, retardation, and intervention.* Baltimore: University Park Press, 1974.

Clay, M. M. Learning and teaching writing: A developmental perspective. *Language Arts,* 1982, *59* (1), 65–70.

Cohen, S. B. Using learning strategies to teach the language arts. *Exceptional Teacher,* 1980, *1* (7), 1–15.

Cohen, S. B., & Plaskon, S. P. *Language arts for the mildly handicapped.* Columbus, Ohio: Charles E. Merrill Publishing Co., 1980.

Cohn, M. Observations of learning to read and write naturally. *Language Arts,* 1981, *58* (5), 549–556.

Cole, M. L., & Cole, J. T. *Effective intervention with the language impaired child.* Rockville, Md.: Aspen Systems, 1981.

Craig, L. *Language experience approach.* Northbrook, Ill.: Hubbard Scientific Co., 1980.

Deen, B., & Deen, F. Oral language development. *Elementary Teacher's Ideas and Materials Workshop,* March, 1977.

Faas, L. A. *Learning disabilities: A competency based approach* (2nd ed.). Boston: Houghton Mifflin Co., 1981.

Frostig, M., & Maslow, P. *Learning problems in the classroom.* New York: Grune and Stratton, 1973.

Gearheart, B. R., & Litton, F. W. *The trainable retarded.* St. Louis: C. V. Mosby Co., 1975.

Gentry, J. R. Learning to spell developmentally. *The Reading Teacher,* 1981, *34* (4), 378–381.

Goodman, K. J. Let's dump the uptight model in English. *Elementary School Journal,* 1969, *70* (1), 1–13.

Graham, S., & Miller, L. Handwriting research and practice: A unified approach. *Focus on Exceptional Children,* 1980, *13* (2), 1–16.

Hammill, D. D., Brown, V. L., Larsen, S. C., & Wiederholt, J. L. *Test of adolescent language.* Austin, Tex.: Pro-Ed, 1980.

Hammill, D. D., & Bartel, N. R. *Teaching children with learning and behavior problems.* Boston: Allyn and Bacon, 1975.

Hammill, D., & Larsen, S. *Test of written language.* Austin, Tex.: Pro-Ed, 1978.

Harrison, S. Open letter from a left handed teacher: Some sinistral ideas on the teaching of handwriting. *Teaching Exceptional Children,* 1981, *13* (3), 116–120.

Hofmeister, A. M. Let's get it write. *Teaching Exceptional Children,* 1973, *6* (10), 30–33.
Hofmeister, A. M. *Handwriting Resource Book.* Allen, Tex.: Developmental Learning Materials, 1981.
Houston, S. H. Black english. *Psychology Today,* 1973, *6* (10), 45–48.
Kean, J. M., & Personke, C. *The language arts.* New York: St. Martin's Press, 1976.
Keller, H. *The story of my life.* Garden City, N.Y.: Doubleday, 1954.
Klein, M. L. Designing a talk environment for the classroom. *Language Arts,* 1979, *56* (6), 647–656.
Kohl, H. *36 children.* New York: New American Library, 1967.
Larsen, S. C., & Hammill, D. D. *Test of Written Spelling* (TWS). Austin, Tex.: Pro-Ed, 1976.
Latta, R. Creative spelling activities. *Elementary Teacher's Ideas and Materials Workshop,* May, 1977.
Lee, D. M., & Allen, R. V. *Learning to read through experience.* New York: Appleton-Century-Crofts, 1963.
Leeson, J. Language arts: Story partners. *Teacher,* 1977, *94* (9), 68–69.
Lerner, J. W. *Children with learning disabilities.* Boston: Houghton Mifflin Co., 1971.
Lerner, J. W. *Children with learning disabilities* (2nd ed.). Boston: Houghton Mifflin Co., 1976.
Lowell, E. L., & Pollack, D. B. Remedial practices with the hearing impaired. In Stanley Dickson (Ed.), *Communication disorders.* Glenview, Ill.: Scott, Foresman, 1974.
McConnell, F., Love, R. J., & Clark, B. S. Language remediation in children. In Stanley Dickson (Ed.), *Communication disorders.* Glenview, Ill.: Scott, Foresman, 1974.
McLean, J. Language development and communication disorders. In N. G. Haring (Ed.), *Behavior of exceptional children.* Columbus, Ohio: Charles E. Merrill Publishing Co., 1974.
McLoughlin, J. A., & Lewis, R. B. *Assessing special students: Strategies and procedures.* Columbus, Ohio: Charles E. Merrill Publishing Co., 1981.
Miller, J. F., & Yoder, D. E. On developing the content for a language teaching program. *Mental Retardation,* 1972, *10* (2), 9–11.
Molloy, J. S., & Witt, B. T. Development of communication skills in retarded children. In J. H. Rothsteubm (Ed.), *Mental retardation,* New York: Holt, Rinehart and Winston, 1971.
Moores, D. Language disabilities of hearing-impaired children. In J. V. Irwin and Michail Marge (Eds.), *Principles of Childhood Language Disabilities.* Englewood Cliffs, N.J.: Prentice-Hall, 1972.
Mussen, P. H., Conger, J. J., & Kagan, J. *Child development and personality* (4th ed.). New York: Harper and Row, 1974.
Myklebust, H. R. *Picture story language test.* New York: Grune & Stratton, 1965.
Noar, G. *Individualized instruction: Every child a winner.* New York: John Wiley and Sons, 1972.
Nicholson, T., & Schachter, S. Spelling skill and teaching practice—putting them back together again. *Language Arts,* 1979, *56* (7), 804–809.
Otto, W., & Smith, R. J. *Corrective and remedial teaching* (3rd ed.). Boston: Houghton Mifflin Co., 1980.
Pasamanick, J. *Talkabout.* Little Neck, N.Y.: Center for Media Development, 1976.
Piazza, R. *Language and writing disorders.* Guilford, Colo.: Special Learning Corp., 1979.
Poteet, J. A. Informal assessment of written expression. *Learning Disability Quarterly,* 1980, *3,* Fall, 88–98.
Reid, D. K., & Hresko, W. P. *A cognitive approach to learning disabilities.* New York: McGraw-Hill, 1981.
Rivers, C. Spelling: Its tyme to du somthing. *Learning,* 1974, *3* (3), 72–78.

Ruder, K. F., & Smith, M. D. Issues in language training. In R. L. Schiefelbusch and L. L. Lloyd (Eds.), *Language perspective—Acquisition, retardation, and intervention.* Baltimore: University Park Press, 1974.

Sargent, L. R., Swartzbaugh, T., & Sherman, P. Teaming up to mainstream in English: A successful secondary program. *Teaching Exceptional Children,* 1981, *13* (3), 100–103.

Schiefelbusch, R. L., Ruder, K. F., & Bricker, W. A. Training strategies for language-deficient children: An overview. In N. G. Haring and R. L. Schiefelbusch (Eds.), *Teaching Special Children.* New York: McGraw-Hill, 1976.

Schiff, P. M. . . . Stand up, sit down, write, write, write! *Language Arts,* 1970, *56* (7), 753–756.

Slobin, D. I. Cognitive prerequisites for the development of grammar. In C. A. Ferguson and D. I. Slobin (Eds.), *Studies of child language development.* New York: Holt, Rinehart and Winston, 1973.

Stowitschek, E. E., & Jobes, N. K. Getting the bugs out of spelling. *Teaching Exceptional Children* (Spring), 1977, 74–76.

Strauss, A. A., & Lehtinen, L. E. *Psychopathology and education of the brain-injured child.* New York: Grune and Stratton, 1947.

Taylor, S. E. *Listening.* Washington, D.C.: National Educational Association of the United States, 1973.

Tiedt, S. W., & Tiedt, I. M. *Language arts activities for the classroom.* Boston: Allyn and Bacon, 1978.

Tompkins, G. E. Writing without a pencil. *Language Arts,* 1981, *58* (7), 823–833.

Vacc, N. N., & Vacc, N. A. Teaching manuscript writing to mentally retarded children. *Education and Training of the Mentally Retarded,* 1979, *14* (4), 286–291.

Wheeler, T. C. *The great American writing block.* New York: The Viking Press, 1979.

Winkeljohann, R. How can teachers promote language use? *Language Arts,* 1981, *58* (5), 605–606.

Zaner-Bloser Evaluation Scales. Columbus, Ohio: Zaner-Bloser, 1979.

6

Teaching Language Arts: Reading

An eighth-grade student approached his teacher the first day of school with the declaration, "My dad says if I don't learn to read this year, I'm all washed up."

Parents, teachers, and citizens in general are concerned about the lack of literacy among the nation's students. Low reading ability is not a new problem; Wolfthal (1981) reports that in 1926 reading failure was the major cause of nonpromotion. Although progress has been made in identifying problems and developing successful strategies in reading, educators are still a long way from realizing the reading potential of every child.

The greatest concern in mainstreaming centers around reading—at the elementary and secondary levels, in subject matter areas, and in vocational training. Hargis (1982) describes students in intermediate, junior high, and high school who can barely read and claims that they usually do not survive secondary education programs. Frequently, these are students who have not benefited from reading instruction because of the disparity between the curriculum provided and their actual learning rate and readiness.

Success in all academic areas depends on success in reading; all teachers are responsible for teaching reading. The first step in the process is assessment, an essential element that helps the learner and the teacher.

ASSESSMENT

There are five important purposes for reading assessment: (1) to determine when children are ready to begin reading instruction or to enter the next instructional level; (2) to identify students who have problems in reading; (3) to identify the causes of reading problems; (4) to derive information for instructional decisions; and (5) to determine accountability (Hargis, 1982).

There is national interest in and emphasis on accountability and assessment at all levels of instruction. The thrust is particularly strong in the area of reading, since attention has been called to the number of nonreaders in the schools and those graduating from high schools. Reading programs funded by the Office of Education require evaluation in terms of student achievement.

The accountability emphasis in most school districts includes three basic requisites. In order of priority they are: a statement of objective outcomes for reading instruction; specification of learning conditions leading to the outcomes; and selection of measurement instruments to evaluate the degree to which the objectives have been achieved (Ruddell, 1974). Because of the pressure resulting from accountability requirements, this priority may be altered, with the selection of measurement instruments determining the objectives of instruction.

Venezky (1974) stresses the idea that "assessment, whether done by formal testing or informal observation, is an integral component of any instructional program and is legitimatized by the need to make decisions at various points during the program's use" (p. 24). The decisions to be made are based on evaluation of programs, materials, and children.

Much recent development of the evaluation concept has resulted from decision-making requirements of the Elementary and Secondary Education Act (ESEA). The initial development focused on evaluation as a tool for administrators. Although such evaluation is necessary and appropriate, it should be remembered that evaluation within the classroom permits the most important decisions concerning instruction for individual children (Farr & Brown, 1971). Instructional needs are determined through the diagnostic process.

The Diagnostic Process in Reading

The diagnostic process in reading can be organized into three levels: the survey level, the specific level, and the intensive level (Otto & Smith, 1980). The achievement tests described in chapter 3 provide information at the survey level concerning the general success of the reading program from year to year, general information for groups of students, and identification of students who are having problems.

At the survey level, screening should include reading-related areas, such as vision, hearing, language development, and intelligence. Symptoms relating to these problems are discussed in chapter 1. Even though general health screening is conducted annually in many schools, it may be necessary for the teacher to request it from the school or from the local health department.

At the specific level, diagnosis is used to check a tentative diagnosis made at the survey level and to identify strengths and weaknesses as a basis for planning instruction. Intensive diagnosis is used to determine the causes of severe reading problems and becomes necessary only when information gathered at the specific level does not result in reading success. Intensive diagnosis usually requires a multidisciplinary team approach.

The level and amount of assessment individual students require should be proportional to their needs; poor readers should receive more extensive assessment than better readers. A sequential assessment plan for testing reading subskills of students who vary widely in ability is suggested:

Step 1. At the beginning of the year, each student is assessed on oral reading, using a one-to-two minute passage drawn from materials encountered after about the first month of school.

Step 2. Children who had no difficulties in oral reading would be tested no further but would be observed informally, depending on how much differential instruction they could be given. Students who did extremely poorly would be assessed with several finer procedures, beginning with basic word attack skills. The middle group would be assessed on oral reading again, but with easier materials.

Step 3. If any uncertainty existed over the abilities of any of the lower groups of students, even finer assessment procedures would be used, starting with prereading skills assessment. By using this procedure, the best readers spend only a few minutes each in assessment, whereas the poorest readers may receive as much as an hour each (Venezky, 1974).

Handicapped students will, in many cases, require intensive reading assessment. The resource teacher, who has a background in diagnostic testing, should work cooperatively with the classroom teacher to determine the needs of each student.

Classroom diagnosis relies on school records, teacher observation, interviews with students and parents, and test results (Wilson, 1981). The diagnostic process is facilitated by standardized reading tests, criterion-referenced tests, and informal reading inventories.

Standardized Reading Tests. In planning reading instruction for handicapped students, group testing has little value.

During a schoolwide testing program, Tommy was observed by a monitor, who noticed that his test booklet was closed. The monitor pointed out to him that his booklet should be in use. Tommy replied, "Oh, I don't need it; I was the first one through." Tommy, who does not read, scored a reading grade level of 3.5.

Achievement tests, used for academic screening purposes, provide relatively global information about students' skill development. Diagnostic tests provide data to help teachers pinpoint skill development strengths and weaknesses, leading to appropriate educational planning (Salvia & Ysseldyke, 1981). Achievement and diagnostic tests frequently used in reading programs are listed in Table 6–1.

Myers (1975) claims that an alliance of the U.S. Office of Education and the publishers of standardized tests dominates reading programs in most American schools. Standardized reading survey tests were not constructed as instruments intended to indicate with maximum accuracy the reading level achieved by particular students (Durost, 1971).

Even though standardized group reading tests may be ineffective, the teacher can use various sections of standardized individual diagnostic reading tests for

TABLE 6-1. Diagnostic Instruments

DESIGNED TO ASSIST IN EVALUATION OF:

NAME OF TEST	FORMS	TYPE	RANGE	APPROXIMATE ADMINISTRATION TIME, READING SECTION	SPEED	COMPREHENSION	VOCABULARY	WORD ATTACK	SPELLING	AUDING	OTHER	PUBLISHER'S CODE
ACHIEVEMENT												
Botel Reading Inventory Revised	2	Individual and Group	6-18	15-30 min.				X	X			FOL
California Achievement Tests	2	Group	6.5-7 7-9 9-11 11-14 14-17	2 hrs. 2 hrs. 2½ hrs. 2½ hrs. 2½ hrs.		X	X	X	X		Language, Math Reference Skills	CAL
Dolch Basic Sight Words	1	Group	Prim.	80 min.		X	X			X		GP
Durrell Listening Reading Series	1 1	Group	Prim. 6-8 Inter. 9-12	80 min.		X	X			X	Compares Listening Ability with Reading Achievement	HBJ
Gates MacGinitie Reading Tests	2*	Group	6-7 7-8 8-9 9-11 11-14 14-17	40 min. 40 min. 50 min. 45 min. 44 min. 44 min.	X X X	X X X X X	X X X X X					TC
Iowa Test of Basic Skills	2	Group	8-14	70 min.		X	X				Language Work-Study Arithmetic	HMC
Metropolitan Achievement	4	Group	6-8 9-12 12-18	50 min.		X	X	X		X	Science Language Arithmetic Social Studies	HBJ

189

TABLE 6-1. (Continued)

NAME OF TEST	FORMS	TYPE	RANGE	APPROXIMATE ADMINISTRATION TIME, READING SECTION	SPEED	COMPREHENSION	VOCABULARY	WORK ATTACK	SPELLING	AUDING	OTHER	PUBLISHER'S CODE
Stanford Achievement Tests	4	Group	6-8, 8-9, 10-12, 12-15	45 min.	X	X					Arithmetic Study Science Social Studies	HBJ
The Test of Reading Comprehension	1	Group	7-14			X	X				Syntactic Similarities Content Area Vocabularies Reading Directions	PE
DIAGNOSTIC												
California Phonics Survey	2	Group	13-20	40 min.				X				CAL
Diagnostic Reading Scales	1	Individual	6-14	1 hr.		X	X	X		X		CAL
Diagnostic Reading Tests	2-4	Group and Individual	5-13	Varies	X	X	X	X				CDRT
Diagnostic Reading Test (Bond-Balow-Hoyt)	1	Group	8-14	90 min.				X		X		LC
Doren Diagnostic Reading Test	1	Group	8-12	3 hrs.			X	X				ETB
Durrell Analysis of Reading Difficulties	1	Individual	6-12	40-60 min.	X	X	X	X	X			HBJ
Gates-McKillop Reading Diagnostic Test	2	Individual	6-12	1 hr.	X	X	X	X	X			TC

Gilmore Oral Reading Test	2	Individual	6-14	15 min.	X X X X	HBJ
Gray Oral Reading Test	4	Individual	6-18	15 min.	X X X X	B&M
Monroe-Sherman Group Diagnostic Reading Aptitude and Achievement Tests	1	Group	8-14	90 min.	X X X X X Arithmetic	NEV
Reading Versatility Test	2	Group	11-15 16-Adult	25 min.	X X	EDL
The Rosewell-Chall Diagnostic Reading Test of Word Analysis Skills	2		7-12	5-10 min.	X	EP
Standard Reading Inventory	1	Individual	6-14	40-50 min.	X X X	PP

Source: From DIAGNOSTIC AND REMEDIAL READING FOR CLASSROOM AND CLINIC by Robert M. Wilson. Columbus, Ohio: Charles E. Merrill Publishing Company, 1981, pp. 430-433. Reprinted by permission of the publisher.

*There are three forms for age levels 9–11 and 11–14.

prescriptive purposes. Such tests offer more information than do standardized group reading tests. However, several limitations are particularly important: these tests give grade levels that are of little diagnostic value to the teacher because of the lack of correlation of levels between tests and reading materials; they are time consuming; they require considerable practice and study by the teacher; and they do not provide diagnostic information that is necessary in developing a program for the pupil (Gillespie & Johnson, 1974).

Diagnostic reading tests do provide the classroom teacher with a systematic analysis of strengths and weaknesses in reading (Salvia & Ysseldyke, 1981). Although grade scores, stanines, and percentiles shown on standardized tests are of little value in program planning, careful analysis of performance on individual test items can provide useful information.

Criterion-Referenced Tests. Standardized tests do not reveal what a pupil can do relative to a predetermined criterion or mastery level; yet this concern is the basis of most instructional decisions that teachers make. Writers of test items for criterion-referenced tests begin with a definition of desired behaviors, from which test items are derived. Because they are based on well-defined instructional objectives, criterion-referenced tests are more compatible with instructional alternatives than are norm-referenced tests (Venezky, 1974).

The proponents of criterion-referenced testing in reading consider it useful in evaluating the effectiveness of a teacher's instruction and in making decisions concerning appropriate instructional programs for students. Prescott (1971) states the three assumptions underlying the criterion-referenced approach: (1) mastery is a reasonable criterion; (2) each item in a list has inherent worth; and (3) a definite hierarchy of skills and knowledge exists in any skill or content area.

Criterion-referenced testing needs a base of reference. The decision to place a task at a certain chronological or mental age level implies that a certain response is expected from the pupil. The general lack of agreement as to what steps are necessary to insure reading success makes the establishment of a hierarchy of skills difficult.

Because criterion-referenced tests are specific, a careful analysis of tasks to be learned is needed. Reading skill objectives are identified in student reading texts, reading curriculum guides, and skills lists, such as Basic Reading Skills List (Barbe, 1960).

Through criterion-referenced testing, efforts are being made to explore the segments of the reading task and to systematize the learning skills. One recent development is the use of management systems to assess reading skills. Described in detail by Schmidt (1976), a management system analyzes a student's reading proficiency at different developmental points. It provides the teacher with prescribed instructional objectives to use in assessing a student's strengths and weaknesses in reading skills and in planning supportive instructional activities. From a selection of appropriate skills, a list is ordered and posted on each student's reading skills progress chart. As students successfully pass competency tests for each skill, they paste markers under their names. In addition to encouraging students to achieve mastery in many skills, the charts help them manage their own learning activities. This system would help to integrate the handicapped reader into the regular classroom, since it provides for a wide range of abilities. It would also free the teacher to spend time with individual students, to provide immediate feedback, and to assist with problems.

One canon for developing program-related assessment presented by Venezky (1974) is that "The content of assessment should be compatible with the content of instruction" (p. 9). Educators, not test designers, should decide on the content of reading instruction. Assessment procedures and assessment instruments can be designed or selected on the basis of the content. Criterion-referenced testing permits this compatibility.

In addition to the product and its use, the very process of developing and validating criterion-referenced reading tests is valuable (Ogle & Fritts, 1981). Teachers involved in such a task learn to define their teaching goals more precisely, to specify the reading level of material, to give clear directions, and to understand the interaction between test items and students.

Informal Reading Inventories. An informal reading inventory (IRI) is a teacher-implemented testing procedure used to determine the student's reading level, specifically the independent level, the instruction level, or the frustration level. The criteria in Table 6–2 are used to determine whether or not material is appropriate for instruction.

To build an IRI, the teacher chooses a well-graded series of readers that the child has not used. Two selections are chosen from the first part of each book, one for oral reading and the other for silent reading. Selections from the preprimer through the second readers should contain from 60 to 120 words; for grades three to six, 100 to 200 words. The teacher then prepares three to five comprehension questions, avoiding those that can be answered yes or no. To check sight vocabulary, a word list can be prepared using every third or fourth word from the word list in the reader. A checking system similar to those used in standardized individual reading tests is useful (Gillespie-Silver, 1979). An example of a teacher-developed IRI is shown in Table 6–3.

Many textbook publishers provide informal reading inventories containing stories similar to those in the publisher's reading series. Although the commercial IRI is a time saver, teacher-developed inventories tend to relate more closely to the instructional materials and practices being used (Jongsma & Jongsma, 1981). They also enable the teacher to select materials and plan instruction appropriate to each student's level of reading performance.

GOALS AND OBJECTIVES

The development of goals and objectives in teaching reading depends on the interpretation of the reading process itself. Common to recent definitions is

TABLE 6-2. Informal Reading Inventory Scoring Criteria

INDEPENDENT LEVEL	WORD RECOGNITION	COMPREHENSION	FLUENCY
A level at which a student reads with obvious ease as illustrated by reading accuracy.	97% or more accuracy	80% or more accuracy	Smooth
INSTRUCTION LEVEL			
A level at which the student has some difficulties in one or more of the three areas. The difficulties supply the teacher with specific skills deficiencies.	92%–96%	60%–70%	Lacking
FRUSTRATIONAL LEVEL			
A level at which the student is unable to perform instructionally because of the lack of numerous skills.	91% and lower	50% or lower	Poor

the conviction that reading, thought, and language are closely related (Gillespie-Silver, 1979), and that reading is a communication process (May, 1982).

For years, educators have debated whether reading instruction should emphasize decoding or comprehension. May (1982) stresses that reading is not an either-or proposition and suggests a rationale for teaching components:

1. For children who are first learning how to read there has to be more emphasis given to specific decoding and comprehension *subskills* than there needs to be given for children who have already jumped over the first hurdles.
2. At the same time, teachers who neglect to help children perceive "reading as communication" from the very first stage of reading instruction will probably give them the wrong perception of reading and thereby risk slowing up their progress in becoming good readers.
3. A child who learns to read for the purpose of communicating with an author normally becomes a good reader. The teacher who attempts to help children read in this manner normally becomes a good teacher of reading.
4. A child who has learned all of the subskills involved in reading has not necessarily learned to read. (pp. 9–10)

TABLE 6-3. Informal Reading Inventory

SERIES: Keys to Reading
PUBLISHER: The Economy Company, 1980
BOOK TITLE: *Maybe a Mile* (Preprimer 3)
STORY: Time to go on down the road
PAGE NUMBERS: 44–47
NUMBER OF WORDS in selection: 95
INDEPENDENT LEVEL: Word recognition—97% or more
　　　　　　　　　　Comprehension—80% or more
INSTRUCTIONAL LEVEL: Word recognition—92% or more
　　　　　　　　　　Comprehension—60–70%
FRUSTRATIONAL LEVEL: Word recognition—91% and lower
　　　　　　　　　　Comprehension—50% and lower

This is Sue.
"This is my truck," said Sue.
"A lot of fruit is in my truck.
And it's time to go."

Sue must get the fruit to us.
Fruit can soon go bad.
So Sue must get in the truck.
She must go down the road.

Sue will go and go.
Soon it's time to fill up.
This is a truck stop.
Sue will fill up the truck here.

COMPREHENSION QUESTIONS
1. What is the woman's name? (Sue)
2. Why must she get the fruit to us? (fruit can go bad)
3. Why does Sue have to fill up the truck? (run out of gas)
4. What is the place to fill up trucks with gas called? (truck stop)

Independent—word recognition 1–4 errors, comprehension 0 errors
Instructional—word recognition 5–8 errors, comprehension 1 error
Frustrational—word recognition 9 or more errors, comprehension 2 or more errors

For beginning or unsuccessful readers, reading as a communication process is a distant goal. The more immediate goal is to develop the concepts that (1) reading is a meaningful process, (2) a relationship exists between their own oral language and reading, and (3) ideas, when written, are built of words (Greenslade, 1980).

The affective aspect of reading should not be overlooked. Otto and Smith

(1980) assert that even children who find reading difficult can learn that reading can change personal values and be a pleasant experience. Forgan (1977) states that "It is important not only to teach the skills and knowledge that enable children to read, but also to help children develop positive attitudes toward reading by valuing it as a source of information and pleasure" (p. 3).

Basic reading objectives should include:

1. Development of a basic sight vocabulary based on the student's existing speaking and listening vocabulary,
2. Development of consistent methods for word attack appropriate for each student,
3. Development of ability and desire to read independently for information, pleasure, and personal satisfaction, and
4. Development of an adequate level of reading ability to permit effective social and vocational participation in society.

Approaches to meeting these objectives are discussed as they pertain to prereading skills, word recognition, comprehension, and functional reading.

INSTRUCTIONAL APPROACHES

Prereading Skills

Reading readiness has frequently been reserved for five- and six-year-olds and has been the responsibility of kindergarten and first-grade teachers. Within the concept of individual differences, it is apparent that many older students will not have the skills necessary for reading. In order to read, the learner must pay attention to and integrate (1) visual attention to print, (2) directional rules about position and movement, (3) talking like a book, and (4) hearing sounds in words (Mass, 1982).

Regardless of a student's age, prerequisite skills must be evaluated and/or developed.

> Prerequisites common to success in beginning reading are an adequate background of experience, concepts, and general information; visual and auditory discrimination ability; oral language facility (in terms of both production and comprehension); physical and emotional intactness; reasoning ability; interests in learning to read; and, of course, a degree of native intelligence that will permit learning to take place. (Edwards, 1966, p. 358)

By definition, handicapped students lack many of the prerequisites considered essential to reading. Teaching them to read requires recognizing, assessing, and remediating or compensating for problems related to vision, hearing, language, intelligence, emotional development, and physical factors.

Vision. There are three categories of visually handicapped children: the blind, the partially sighted, and those who have visual defects. Since a reader reacts visually to graphic symbols, the visually impaired student is at a tremendous disadvantage. Provisions must be made for an adequate alternative method for the input of information or for an adequate method to develop the student's seeing ability.

In the case of the blind student, a complicated skill must be acquired—learning to read by touch. Braille, a system of six embossed dots arranged in two vertical rows of three, is used for this purpose (see Figure 6–1). These dots can be covered simultaneously by the pad of the finger tip. Grade-one braille is written with full spelling; grade-two braille makes use of contractions and short forms.

The readability of the dots representing the letters of the alphabet is related more to their formation than to their number. Good readers use a uniform pressure in reading braille. Although touch reading is much slower than normal reading, a good braille reader can read as many as ninety words per minute (L'Abate & Curtis, 1975).

Classroom teachers may feel that the responsibility of teaching students to read braille is overwhelming. Even though braille is difficult to learn by touch, using it visually is quite simple. Sighted students are curious about it and view it as a code to be broken (see chapter 4). Teachers and students can decode braille very easily by referring to Figure 6–1.

In most cases, the classroom teacher is not responsible for teaching braille, but rather for content in the total curriculum and any problems in the student's reading that may influence performance. The resource or itinerant teacher assumes responsibility for the specifics of braille reading and the selection of suitable books and reference material. A special reading teacher may be paid for by the State Commission for the Blind or by the local Department of Social Services.

Partially sighted students are unable to perform tasks ordinarily requiring detailed vision without using special aids, such as magnifiers, special lighting, or large type. They usually have limited distance vision but frequently can see objects and materials held a few inches from their eyes (Ward & McCormick, 1981).

A majority of partially sighted students, including those identified as legally blind, read print rather than braille materials. Many partially sighted students can read regular size print, particularly at the first- and second-grade levels where the print is rather large. With appropriate teaching approaches, they can use many of the same materials as their peers and achieve comparable levels of attainment.

The quality of print is an important determinant of legibility. Teachers

198 CHAPTER 6 *Teaching Language Arts: Reading*

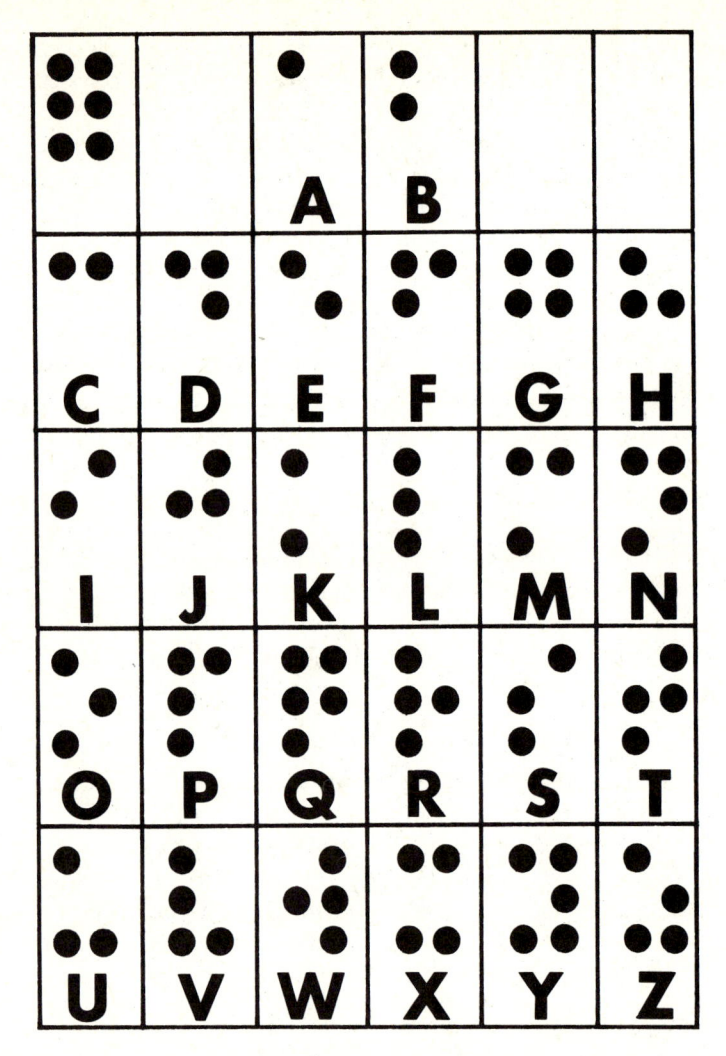

FIGURE 6–1. Braille Alphabet

should do everything possible to insure that print materials are clear, attractive, and meaningful. Reading materials that display the greatest contrast between the print and the paper are the easiest to see. Black print on white paper with fairly large letters and good spacing is best; purple ink used in commercial duplicating is often difficult to see. Teachers should make duplicated copies on white paper and give the darkest, clearest copies to the visually impaired student. Readability can be improved by using black masters and primary type with good spacing. Elite or fancy type, handwriting, crowded letters, colored paper, and blurred or faint copies all add to the difficulties for visually impaired students (Davis, 1981).

Visual defects affect visual acuity. The most common disorders are: *astigmatism,* which causes a generalized blurring of the vision and is often the result of irregular corneal curvature; *myopia,* or nearsightedness, in which sight is clear in proximity but blurred at far distances; and *hyperopia,* or farsightedness, in which sight is clear at a distance but blurred in proximity. Referred to as *refractive* errors, these defects can usually be corrected by glasses, which can help the eye to focus and lower eye strain but may fail to provide normal vision. When corrected by glasses, these errors do not constitute handicaps.

Visual Discrimination. Wallace and Kauffman (1973) state that "Many children who have normal visual acuity experience difficulties in differentiating, interpreting, or remembering different shapes, letters, or words" (p. 166). They suggest that students with visual skill deficiencies should learn to:

1. Discriminate sizes and shapes
2. Discriminate specific letters
3. Discriminate the directionality of specific letters
4. Remember letter names and words
5. Remember particular words learned mainly by sight
6. Recognize structural parts of words. (p. 166)

According to Spache (1964), visual discrimination or perception is derived from or based on physical handling of objects. The student learns shapes and spatial relationships first with the hands and later with the eyes. During the preschool years, when vision is developing, the child learns to explore, recognize, and discriminate objects or forms by tactile and visual approaches, with gradually greater dependence on visual clues.

Evidence of the lack of sufficient tactile and visual experience with objects, forms, and spatial relationships may be described by the teacher as (1) lacking visual discrimination or perception; (2) lacking hand-eye coordination; (3) lacking orientation to left and right; (4) inability to attend to near-point tasks; (5) lack of concentration or attention span; and (6) pointing or using a marker while reading.

According to Cravioto and DeLicardie (1975), the ability to make gross discriminations among visually perceived figures, although a necessary component ability, does not constitute a sufficient refinement of perceptual skill for a task such as reading. In addition to making gross discriminations, a student must respond to more differentiated forms to learn to read.

The student's failure to respond to the spatial orientation of a visual form can result in confusing a number of letters identical in form but distinguishable by their spatial positioning. Letters such as *b, p, d,* and *g,* or *N, Z, W,* and *M,* represent equivalent shapes and depend on the student's ability to respond to shape and to orientation in visual space.

Typical errors of visual perception made by students with learning disabilities indicate the confusion of similar letters and lack of discrimination between words in which the form is similar *(said* for *and, you* for *yes,* and *pretty* for *puddle).* The student's inability to organize letters accurately in their spatial sequence is responsible for many errors, such as *stop* confused with *spot, three* with *there,* and *of* with *for.* Reversals are common, such as *was* for *saw* and *no* for *on* (Strauss and Lehtinen, 1947).

Reading demands such visual discriminations and perceptions as orientation to left and right, up and down, front and back; accurate binocular shifts from point to point; accurate focus and accommodation to distance; and a fine degree of parallel or coordinated action of both eyes. To read, the student must be able to note similarities and differences among words by the clues given by the shapes of their beginning and ending letters, by letters that ascend and descend above the line, and by the patterns or outlines formed by combinations of these elements of words (Spache, 1964).

Formal tests, such as the Bender-Gestalt Visual Motor Test and the Huelsman Word Discrimination Test, will help the teacher to identify the problem of visual discrimination. Getman (1961) suggests that the observant teacher will be more clinically accurate than any test devised.

> If she sees a child stumbling and reversing, losing his place or skipping lines, the chances are very great that this child does not have the ocular motilities he needs for reading comprehension. If she sees him reversing and confusing similar letters of words in his writing and spelling, the chances are very great he does not have the tactual perceptions of directionality that should underlie the visual perceptions of likes and differences that he needs for comprehension. (p. 2)

Visual discrimination exercises can be found in many reading instruction books. Wallace and Kauffman (1973) offer a variety of suggestions. The following are examples of exercises that can be used in any classroom:

- The child finds like objects (such as circles) that are a part of a total picture.
- The child finds "hidden objects" in a picture.
- The child estimates the distance between objects (spatial discrimination). Say, "Place these as far apart as those." A harder task requires the child to place two objects as far apart as the length of a desk or the width of a doorway.
- The child matches silhouettes of an object to the actual picture of that object.

- Use "what's-missing pictures" that require careful observation of details. For example, a picture of a child may show that he is ready to play in the snow, but has forgotten to put on one sock and shoe.
- Many commercial products, such as Etch-a-Sketch and Dot Pictures, are effective developmental and remedial tools.

Hearing. Auditory acuity refers to the ability to hear. Children who are auditorily handicapped may be classified as either deaf or hard-of-hearing. The acquisition of language is frequently used to determine the difference.

Learning to read is one of the most important and most difficult tasks faced by deaf pupils (and their teachers). Hart (1963) expresses the need and the problem:

> The printed form represents the only medium of communication in which the deaf person meets intact language patterns in exactly the same form as anyone else. Therefore, reading would seem to be a lifeline of communication to the world of intellectual stimulation for the deaf. But the nature of the reading process is such, that despite the desire of the child to master this most attractive avenue of communication, his road is fraught with difficulty. (p. 1)

Reading, or written language, is derived from spoken language. In order to understand the symbols reading represents, the pupil must have a background of language patterns that the symbols represent. Deaf students do not have this knowledge of auditory symbols. Dale (1967) states the situation in an interesting way.

> When you read the word *korero* you probably have no idea of its meaning, i.e., the language is quite unfamiliar to you. If the word was placed in a sentence the context is not a great deal of help unless one knows most of it. For example, *Korero te wahine e te tamaiti* does not make the meaning of *korero* a great deal more clear. If one has more vocabulary, however, one might be able to read the above sentence as: "The woman korero the boy." Now it is possible to guess that korero is a verb and may mean "spanked" or "kissed" or "washed" or something like that. In other words, the unknown word takes on *some* meaning. (*Korero* incidentally is the Maori to "talk" or, in this case, "talked to.") (pp. 174–175)

Deaf students are at a double disadvantage. They cannot easily convert written symbols into oral symbols, and their language grows so slowly that many of the words they are trying to identify in written form have no meaning to them in any form.

In general, a young deaf child requires experiences, and the language and concepts of such experiences, before learning to recognize printed symbols. The deaf child who, instead of being given language, speech, and reading drill, is encouraged to participate actively in the events and activities of school life, will in fact learn language, speech, and reading. Such skills will have more meaning if they grow out of direct experiences (Hart, 1963).

Since young deaf children have little or no place in their world for language, they experience the world visually. Thus, in their formal reading program they may learn the concrete words that name the objects and visible things in their environment and fail to understand the intangible and abstract words. It is advisable, therefore, to delay the formal program until the child has acquired some meaning of sentence structure.

The language-experience approach to reading (described in chapter 5 and referred to later in this chapter) is suggested by many educators for deaf and hard-of-hearing students. As students advance in language and reading ability, the vocabulary and the type of sentence presented can become more complex.

The camera has been suggested as a teaching aid to enable deaf students with limited or no spoken language to recall experiences. Other suggestions are field trips to provide experiences, visual aids to help fill in gaps in the pupil's experiential background, and a constant supply of books and periodicals at all levels. A simple type of individual reading activity that stresses sentence comprehension is matching sentences to pictures. Another language development activity is building stories around pictures. Most reading activities suitable for hearing students are adaptable for deaf students. Manson (1982) found that constant exposure to print and many opportunities to write contributed to the development of successful readiness skills in deaf preschool children.

Hard-of-hearing, as well as deaf, students should be provided adequate alternative modes of reception (input) and expression (output) of information to compensate for their hearing limitations. To live as normally as possible, hard-of-hearing students must, to the best of their abilities, be able to convey their ideas verbally. They may need auditory amplification and training to make use of their residual hearing.

Loss of hearing can aggravate reading deficiency. The auditory factor is especially important when there is a severe hearing loss, when the specific hearing loss involves high-tone deafness, or when instruction puts a premium on auditory factors. The exclusive use of the phonic method with a student who has suffered a hearing loss may prevent achievement in reading (Dechant, 1970).

Early identification of children who have hearing impairment is crucial to educational growth. Any child who shows symptoms of hearing deficiencies should be screened with an audiometer.

Classroom teachers can do a great deal to develop the hearing-impaired pupil's auditory discrimination skills. They must train the child in the awareness of sound; in making gross discriminations, as between the sounds of a bell and a horn; in making discriminations among simple speech patterns, as differences between vowels; and in the finer discriminations necessary for speech.

Norwood (1976) reports that educational media are being recognized as a tremendous but relatively untapped resource for deaf and hard-of-hearing persons. The Captioned Films for the Deaf (Appendix A) program is a free loan service of subtitled motion pictures similar in nature to the free loan service of Talking Books for the Blind.

The regular classroom teacher can stimulate the development of reading skills of hearing-impaired students. Vocabulary development can be facilitated by using a new word in a sentence and then asking related questions about it. Comprehension may cause difficulty for the student with limited hearing. Making comparisons and determining differences can be facilitated with questions, such as "What does it look like? How are cats and dogs similar? How are they different?"

Auditory Discrimination. In referring to auditory skills in reading, Wallace and Kauffman (1973) state that "Children with auditory skill deficiencies may have normal hearing acuity. However, they experience difficulties in differentiating, synthesizing, and remembering the sounds of different letters and words" (p. 176). They claim the child must learn to discriminate among sounds, discriminate initial and final letter sounds, synthesize letter sounds into words, and remember the sounds of letters and words.

Wepman (1975) states that readiness to read can be safely assumed from the evidence to be as closely related to auditory perceptual factors as to visual. The three auditory perceptual processes—discrimination, memory span, and sequential recall—have been found to have a positive correlation to reading, writing, and spelling achievement.

Auditory discrimination is the ability to discriminate between the sounds or phonemes of a language, essential to success in reading. Students who cannot *hear* sounds correctly, usually cannot *speak* them correctly. If they confuse sounds in speech, it may be impossible for them to associate the correct sound with the visual symbol.

According to Spache (1976), the goal of discriminating letter sounds and words is founded on many types of listening exercises. Students must first be able to discriminate pitch, loudness, duration, and rhythmic patterns or sequences of sounds, which are auditory cues to letters and words. Her suggestions for auditory memory and discrimination include the following exercises:

Children pretend they are in a cave where echoes bounce from wall to wall. The leader of the expedition makes various sounds, words, sentences. The followers repeat each one, trying to use the same inflections, pitch, and so forth, as an echo.

When children are waiting in line, the teacher says, "Raise your hand if . . ."

your name begins like Billy.
you're wearing something green (or other color).
your birthday is in _____ (month).
you got up before 7:00 this morning.

Children are given dittoed sheets marked with a large circle in which a path of squares has been drawn. Give each child a marker of some sort. The teacher claps two or three times, and children move their markers through the squares according to the number of claps they hear. Children who finish too soon or too slowly need further practice to improve these skills.

The children listen while you pronounce several unrelated words, such as *deer, candy, pencil, ring.* Students try to remember these words and supply the correct ones when you say "something sweet," "something to wear," "made of wood," "has four legs."

Tape voices and let members of the group listen to the tape and identify the voices they hear.

Record a collection of sounds on a tape recorder. After a small group listens to one sound, take time to discuss what it might be. (pp. 42–45)

Several screening tests are available that enable the teacher to determine a student's ability to recognize fine differences between sounds in words. One is the Wepman Auditory Discrimination Test (1958); another is the Goldman-Fristoe-Woodcock Test for Auditory Discrimination (1970). If a weakness is indicated in this area, the teacher should use exercises to strengthen it and should provide reading instruction that is not related to phonics until the auditory skills are developed.

Language. Although oral communication skills for handicapped students were discussed in the previous chapter, their relationship to the reading process should be emphasized here. Since reading is, as one child put it, "wrote down talking," the skills of reading are based on the skills of speaking.

Evidences of delayed and immature speech can be seen in the deaf pupil, the blind pupil, the mentally handicapped pupil, the learning-disabled pupil, and the culturally disadvantaged pupil, as well as in the pupil whose primary difficulty is a speech problem. Therefore, any reading program designed for handicapped students must strongly emphasize language stimulation.

The two most important resources for learning to read and write are competence in oral language and the ability to learn language as it is needed for new functions (Mass, 1982). Authorities in reading and in speech pathology agree that reading is a language-based skill (Shipley & McFarlane, 1981).

The interrelatedness of oral language and reading should be recognized by all teachers. Hall (1970) states the sequence of the relationship: "As children listen they are building their stock of words and knowledge. As children speak their powers of communication are sharpened. As they read they are drawing upon their previous knowledge of words and adding new thoughts and concepts" (p. 3). Thus, when asking why a pupil has difficulty learning to read, the teacher should first determine whether the pupil possesses the sensory experiences and the verbal background to which the written words refer (Ross, 1976). The reading readiness program for deaf students, for example, consists of the use of language association with immediate activities. As the understanding and use of language develop, the pupil will be able to get ideas from written as well as spoken language (Hart, 1963). Blind pupils who have had limited experiences will need structured opportunities for language development. Sequential types of experiences in which verbal communication is increased will have to be offered.

For students who are unable to speak clearly because of sensory, cognitive, or motor handicaps, reading and writing can accelerate speech and language growth (Geoffrion, 1982). Programs like the language-experience approach and related activities are particularly appropriate for nonvocal students.

Intelligence. There is a cause-effect relationship between intellectual ability and reading ability. Although controversy exists on the degree of the relationship, the correlations between scores on intelligence tests and scores on reading tests are usually high (Savage & Mooney, 1979). The degree of the relationship varies with grade level and tests used. On the Wechsler Intelligence Scale for Children (1974) there are few items requiring reading, but reading-related items, such as picture completion and picture arrangement, are included. Picture completion measures the ability to visualize essential from nonessential detail and to identify familiar stimuli from school and home. Picture arrangement measures the ability to see a total situation based on visual comprehension and organization, as well as on environmental experiences.

On group intelligence tests, pictures are used in the primary forms; from the fourth grade on, most questions are in printed form. Thus, poor readers are at a distinct disadvantage and might indicate an intellectual level more in keeping with their reading level.

There is a substantial relationship between mental age and learning to read. However, present evidence does not justify the establishment of an absolute dividing line at any one mental age. The progress of the pupil depends on the difficulty of the material used, the speed required, the specific methods used, and the amount of individualized help. However, most children who fail to learn to read in the first grade have mental ages below six years. More mature children not only learn more easily but also retain what they learn better than less mature children.

Wilson (1981) claims that intelligence is related to causes of reading difficulties only in relation to the ability of the school to adjust the program to meet the abilities of various types of students. Thus, it is not intelligence—or lack of it—that prevents students from reading to their potential, but rather the inadequacy of school programs.

The use of group readiness tests and group and individual IQ tests in the first grade makes it possible to locate the child whose rate of mental growth is below average. The reading program for such children can be adapted by prolonging the readiness program, extending the period of reading readiness activities, and gearing the pace of reading instruction to their learning rates.

Experience and maturation alone do not guarantee success in reading; the pupil needs certain intellectual skills. Reading requires perceiving likenesses and differences, remembering word forms, and possessing thinking skills. It requires telling stories in proper sequence, interpreting pictures, making associations and inferences, and thinking on an abstract level. A review of the educational characteristics of mentally handicapped students (chapter 1) suggests that the absence of many of these intellectual and sensory skills impedes reading progress. In considering the learning characteristics of mentally handicapped students, one becomes aware that several deficits are particularly relevant to the reading process: memory, reasoning skills, language acquisition, perceptual development, and cultural factors.

Memory can be discussed as a factor in reading in relation to auditory memory, visual memory, and sequential or serial memory (Gillespie & Johnson, 1974). The acquisition of a sight vocabulary, the ability to remember details of stories, and the use of skills previously acquired depend on a good memory. Games and activities can be used to increase visual and auditory memory skills.

Visual:
Present a picture with missing parts; ask the child either to draw in the missing part or tell which part is missing.

Printing words with a rubber stamp set calls attention to the sequence of letters.

Cut apart cartoon strips and paste them on oak-tag; ask the child to reassemble the cartoon in the correct order.

Auditory:
Tape or clap out rhythm patterns; have the child repeat the pattern.

Ask the child to repeat a sentence or phrase that you have said to him.

Present a series of movements to a small group of children and have them follow the sequence. For example, "Jump, hop, clap, and skip." (Wallace & Kauffman, 1973, p. 181)

Reasoning skills have been linked with reading comprehension. Reading may be interpreted as a thinking process in which reading comprehension involves solving problems, suspending judgments, and employing concepts (Gillespie & Johnson, 1974). The retarded pupil's inability to deal with abstract relationships may hinder the ability to draw inferences from and make evaluations of the material that is read. Newspapers are valuable aids in increasing these skills.

- Select the key sentence in a newspaper article; underline it.
- Prepare a headline for an article.
- Answer the questions Who? Where? When? in each of several articles.
- Remove the ending from an exciting story; have the student supply one.
- Ask: Why did they do that? What would you do if? What would happen if they did?

Many students who are developmentally retarded are also delayed in language development. It is essential that speech and language stimulation form the basis for the reading readiness program and that reading expectations relate to the student's level of language development.

Many mentally handicapped students also have social, cultural, and economic disadvantages. Frequently, they come from homes in which reading material is lacking and academic achievement is not valued highly. A reading teacher working with a fourth-grade child was alarmed to find him reading two years below grade level. She made a home visit, telling his mother, "John is reading at a second-grade level." The mother was delighted. She then revealed that John was the only one in the family who could read at all. One problem confronted by students from disadvantaged homes is the nonrelevance of much of the reading material they encounter. Kohl (1973) suggests the use of the following materials:

1. A stamp set. Students can make their own signs and posters, play with designing a page of print, make poems, and so forth.
2. Stencils. Some students who don't have the patience to do elaborate work with stamps take to stencils.
3. A Dymo label maker. Label makers provide good practice for someone learning to read. Label the chairs in the room "The hot seat," "A funny chair," or "The seat of power."
4. Plastic or wooden letters. These come with little magnets and a metallic board and may be used to illustrate how words and sounds vary.
5. Scissors, index cards, rubber cement, old newspapers, and magazines. Pupils can make up interesting card games and "found" poetry from headlines, phrases, and sentences discovered in the printed material.
6. Cartoons. Cut cartoons from old magazines and newspapers, remove the captions, and paste the pictures on cardboard. Pupils make up their own captions, which can be printed and used as reading material.
7. Free and inexpensive reading material, such as billboard sections, telephone books, old ads and signs, posters and buttons of all sizes and shapes, street signs, comic books, and catalogues.

Emotional Development. Students who cannot read or who cannot read as well as their age group are marked as failures. They are reminded of their failure every day. Even the skilled classroom or corrective reading teacher often cannot restore their confidence in themselves, since their classmates and worried parents often magnify their deficiencies (Schiffman, 1966).

The incidence of maladjustment among poor readers is greater than among good readers. As indicated in chapter 1, it is difficult to establish a causal relationship; it is not known whether emotional maladjustment causes reading failure, or whether reading failure causes maladjustment. Not all emotionally handicapped pupils are poor readers, nor are all poor readers emotionally handicapped students.

Success in school is impossible without success in reading. Poor reading ability threatens social acceptance and leads to feelings of inadequacy. Poor readers, rejected by others and feeling themselves unsuccessful, may become shy, antagonistic, self-conscious, nervous, inattentive, defensive, discouraged, irritable, fearful, frustrated, defiant, indifferent, restless, and/or hypercritical. They may stutter, be truant, join gangs, and engage in destructive activity (Dechant, 1970).

Emotional problems may precede reading failure and cause inadequacy in that area. Because reading is the first academic subject to be systematically taught to children, it becomes the first major educational issue in which problems become apparent. Because successful reading requires application and sustained concentration, emotional problems that prevent children from concentrating and paying attention can also prevent them from learning to read (Harris, 1961).

Frequently, students who fear academic activity because of past failure can be stimulated to learn by presenting different materials in an unusual manner. Methods that are presented in a structured learning situation and that guarantee success can insure progress. The most productive approach, however, is one of prevention. Emotional problems are less likely to occur in a classroom where differences in ability are accepted and where the value of each student is assured.

Physical Factors. Learning to read begins when parents or others read to very young children and allow them to handle books. Children develop spatial relationships, discover that people begin at the front of the book and turn pages, hold the books and play with the books, and try out behaviors they have experienced while in a reading situation (Hoskisson, 1979). Reading does require some degree of physical ability. However, this seems to be less relevant than other factors.

Students who have health impairments (diabetes, glandular dysfunction, nutritional and circulatory problems), who fatigue easily, and who are ill for prolonged periods of time may have difficulty with any academic skills. There is no evidence that any specific reading disabilities occur because of such physical problems. If a pupil is absent from school for a long period of time, the teacher has to insure the acquisition of readiness and word attack skills that were missed.

Maturation as a factor in reading has been widely discussed. Many people believe that children can and should read as early as they talk (Melcher, 1973). However, a review of the research (Dechant, 1970) suggests the following conclusions:

1. Younger children make less progress than older ones of the same intelligence when they are exposed to the same program.

2. The best age for beginning reading is dependent upon the materials used, the size of the class, the pacing of the program, and teacher expectancies (p. 51).

The preference for beginning instruction later is stated by an experienced teacher who asks:

"Why is there such a hurry to have children read at five or six? At eight, children take to the three R's like ducks to water. As an informal experiment, I gave first-grade readers (books) to a class of eight-year-olds who had just started to learn to read. They read in a week what the six-year-olds had been struggling with for a month." (Cooper, 1977, p. 46)

Summary. Students need prereading skills to serve as a foundation in learning to read. Prereading instruction is the responsibility of every teacher and should be carried on at all age and grade levels. Group instruction moves too quickly for poor readers (Speckels, 1980). For them, the reading process should be carefully analyzed and slowed down; often, they are simply beginners. Since reading readiness can be a function of vision, hearing, language, intelligence, and emotional and physical development, teachers should consider these factors in planning and implementing prereading activities.

Word Recognition

Reading can be defined as a two-step process of translating the written medium to language and translating the language to thought. The translation of writing is *recognition;* the translation of language to thought is *comprehension.* Word recognition (decoding) skills enable a reader to translate printed letters into speech sounds (May, 1982). The four subskills of this process are sight vocabulary, phonetic analysis, structural analysis, and context clues. The following section presents instructional approaches for each of these subskills.

Sight Vocabulary. Most children start school knowing many words. A problem occurs when they do not know the "right" words. Such children do not know how to read for school; presumably, they have brought no prereading experiences with them.

Billy's mother had been told that he would never learn to read, that his intellectual functioning would not permit it. One day in the grocery store, Billy went to a carton he had seen on television many times, pointed, and said, "Geritol." His surprised mother pointed out other items and heard the responses, "Colgate," "Dentyne," and "Bayer."

People in our culture are constantly exposed to the written word through billboards, television, packages, product labels, street signs, and graffiti. The beginning level of reading should incorporate what the learner knows informally and add other skills.

The successful classroom environment is conducive to sight recognition of words. In such a classroom, materials are available for every purpose and every age level. There are props for house play and dramatic play; materials that encourage exploration and spark interest; and articles provided to feed an ongoing project or interest. Books of all kinds and levels are everywhere, including telephone books, magazines, recipe books, and books made by the students. Many things in the room require reading: a sign on the bathroom door indicating that it is vacant or in use; activity charts or lists that indicate choices or specify who has selected particular activities; experience charts recording shared activities; recipes that have been used for cooking; records or graphs recording plant and animal growth or behavior changes; and maps, reference books, and diagrams.

The selection of words to present requires thought and should be adapted to the particular needs of the pupils. Words on standardized lists, such as the Dolch Word List and the Kucera-Francis List, are valuable both as diagnostic instruments and in content development. However, for handicapped students the lists are formidable and do not offer much hope for total success.

Kolstoe (1976) claims that sight words should be taught in the context of meaningful activities. He suggests selecting words and listing them by categories.

Action words

| stand | come | bend | whisper | laugh |
| draw | kneel | sit | go | hop |

wave	touch	clap	run	jump
skip	fly	walk	nod	scratch
cry	write			

Objects

chair	wagon	plate	cow	pencil
telephone	table	truck	knife	horse
book	kettle	basket	block	fork
dog	crayon			

Prepositions

These were taught by pantomime.

up	out	behind	right	bottom
from	down	across	before	left
beside	beneath	in	around	on
top	under	between (p. 108)		

Using cards on which the words are written, games can be played that require students to act out or pantomime the word.

Ashton-Warner (1963) states the philosophy simply: first words must mean something to a child. She finds that if words are chosen accurately, they prove to be "one-look" words. In selecting the appropriate words, she asked the Maori children she taught such questions as: Whom do you love most in the world? What is something that scares you? What did you dream about last night? The answers resulted in such words as *Daddy, Mummy, ghost, bomb, kiss, brothers, butcher, knife, love, dance,* and *wild piggy.* The words were written on large, tough cards and given to the children to read. They became the children's own words.

This procedure of using personal (organic) words has been adapted frequently to strengthen students' reading vocabularies. Brown (1981) offers key points to implement this strategy. First, the word must come from the student and not be imposed or suggested by an adult. Second, teachers must accept the pupil's word without judgment. Third, if students cannot read their words, the words are removed from their books and placed into the class word box.

Another adaptation of this method permits students to select words they want to learn from passages that interest them (Noble, 1981). When students select the words they want to learn, they are more apt to practice the words and remember them.

At first, sight words may be keyed to pictures. Mitchell (1974) used children's first names and the words *sad, mad, glad,* and *is* to make sentences. The sentences were: Mark is sad. Jim is mad. Ricky is glad. Donna is sad. Each sentence was followed by the picture of a face. Other words, with illustrations, were gradually introduced in teacher-made books. This technique (sight repetition and the use of context clues) was successful with mentally retarded students.

Old reading books can be used to advantage in building sight word vocabularies. Key words can be cut from a book and chosen by the pupil in the correct usage. This exercise also helps the pupil to learn to use context clues.

Many high-frequency structure words are difficult to remember because they cannot easily be represented by pictures. Houghton (1974) states that only thirty-two words make up one-third of the words used by a child (or adult). These words are: *a, and, he, I, in, is, it, of, that, the, to, was, all, as, at, be, but, are, for, had, have, him, his, not, on, one, said, so, they, we, wish,* and *you.* The list should include *she, her,* and *hers.* These words should be used frequently in language experience stories, in captioning stories, and in classroom signs. Specific drill on them will help to assure success in beginning reading.

For words that seem impossible for some readers to learn, such as *were, with, what, this, that,* and *them,* a drastic strategy may be needed (Cunningham, 1980). One system requires putting the word on an index card; using it repeatedly in a story; having students make up stories using the word; cutting the word card into letters and having the students reassemble it; writing the word on the board, and instructing students to close their eyes, visualize it, and then write it on paper; and finally, providing the students with printed material in which the word is underlined. Although this procedure is time consuming, its use can establish a learning pattern for students.

Even after specific practice, students may have problems reading these difficult words aloud. Jolly (1981) suggests daily recreational reading to sharpen students' total reading accuracy.

For handicapped students who have limited reading and/or speaking vocabularies, survival words and phrases will comprise the sight vocabulary list. *Men, women, danger,* and other specific words that are essential to safety should be selected.

For students who have visual discrimination problems, the Language Master provides auditory imput to help build a sight word vocabulary. It is also useful with hyperactive students, since it requires some manipulation. With young children, teachers can use large blank cards for picture clues or even manipulative objects. With older students, the standard printed or teacher-made cards permit a variety of clues to be used. The Language Master is a valuable instructional tool that can be placed in the regular classroom and used by handicapped students, with or without earphones.

Some students may require tactile input to learn a sight vocabulary. A clay pan, referred to in chapter 5, is useful in learning words through touch. Tracing activities of all sorts are helpful and applicable in any classroom. Laminated sheets, prepared by the resource or classroom teacher, can be kept in the handicapped pupil's folder for use at any time. The clues can be faded gradually until the pupil can write and read the words without help (see chapter 10 for a discussion of fading techniques).

The appearance of a word affects the reading of it. To provide opportunities to play with words, to become comfortable with them, and to enjoy knowing them, teachers can encourage students to "draw" words the way they feel about them, or to put words instead of people into their pictures. Such drawings provide attractive displays or mobiles for the room and offer additional stimulation for the entire class.

FIGURE 6–2. Word Pictures

Students can also produce visual effects using the letters of the word in phrases. Examples are: giant step; waves, waves, waves; walking in circles; railroad train; and running downhill (Hennings & Grant, 1981).

Phonetic Analysis. The process of analyzing unknown words on the basis of letter-sound relationships is called phonetic analysis (Savage & Mooney, 1979). Auditory discrimination skills are essential to successful phonics instruction; do not assume prior learning in this area with handicapped readers.

Generally, students are ready for phonics instruction when their sight vocabulary is fairly large, when they begin to notice word "families," and when they recognize that words consist of different letters and sounds that they see in other words.

Otto, McMenemy, and Smith (1973) combine the various phonics systems into two approaches: word-family phonics and single-letter phonics. The word-family approach avoids the need for blending individual letter sounds by making use of "families," such as *an, at, in,* and so forth. Usually this approach emphasizes the initial consonant change (e.g., *c*at, *h*at, *r*at). Speckels (1980) stresses the importance of emphasizing the auditory constant (*at*) by printing it in a bright color.

Single-letter phonics consists of blending individual consonant and vowel sounds from the very beginning. Four general rules are suggested for teaching this important skill: provide a great deal of practice in auditory perception; insure that sounds are smooth and continuous; proceed from the whole word to its parts; and keep phonic and blending instruction brief.

Some students seem to learn sound letter correspondence and even phonic rules. They can sound out words letter by letter but are not able to blend the sounds. P-u-t remains p-u-t. To help the student learn to blend sounds, the teacher may briefly present words of two or three letters, pronouncing them. A brief span of time prevents the student from reading the word letter by letter. An extension of this method would be the use of a tachistoscope. The Language Master can be used to introduce new words, so the student sees and hears them simultaneously (Frostig and Maslow, 1973).

Kohl (1973) describes a way to master most of the phonics regularities with little effort. It is easier to think of syllables than of isolated sounds. One way is to start with a list of words generated by the students and modify them:

	kill	love	nation
which can be transformed to	will spill fill	dove but not stove which brings up an exception	station situation

(p. 56)

Students can learn to make transpositions, change letters, reverse letters, and keep one element constant while varying the others.

Word wheels can be used for drill in initial sounds, word families, final sounds, prefixes, and suffixes. Commercial word-building charts, flip cards, and word attack games are available at reasonable prices.

If children have poor auditory discrimination abilities, a program should be chosen that permits the use of visual and kinesthetic word attack skills. At the same time, efforts should be made to improve their auditory discrimination skills in a separate instructional program. There are a number of commercial programs available that help to develop auditory discrimination, auditory sequencing, and auditory memory.

Structural Analysis. The process of identifying meaningful units in words is called structural analysis. It usually begins with the identification of independent word parts in compound words and extends to the recognition of other units from which words are built (Savage & Mooney, 1979). It requires the ability to identify base words, plural and possessive forms, prefixes, suffixes, and syllables.

Although there is a continuing debate as to the advisability of teaching students to identify the syllables in printed words (Groff, 1981), the ability to break words into pronounceable bits is likely to help them deal with multisyllabic words (Otto & Smith, 1980). The use of this and other structural analysis skills, along with contextual clues, will greatly facilitate the decoding of unknown words by students (Parks, 1982).

Context Clues. Using the surrounding language to figure out what an unknown word may be is a useful word recognition skill. Reading a variety of materials is the best way to learn to use context clues.

All the word recognition skills operate together in the total act of reading. Still, certain students who possess the subskills have some difficulty using them. Wilson (1981) suggests teaching a strategy to be used consistently when approaching a new word:

1. Read on and look for clues.
2. Frame the word.
3. Try the first sound.
4. Divide the word into smaller parts.
5. Consult. (p. 300)

Comprehension

During a reading workshop, the instructor asked teachers at different levels to state their chief problem in teaching reading. The primary teachers indicated building a sight vocabulary; the intermediate teachers, word attack skills; and the advanced teachers, with one accord, comprehension. The instructor asked the teachers to consider the premise that if comprehension were given major consideration at all levels, perhaps it would not be a problem at the advanced level.

Reading programs may put too much emphasis on word recognition skills and neglect comprehension. Certainly, many students have reading problems because of difficulties in word attack sequences, which should be taught at every level. However, the ultimate goal of reading is comprehension; word recognition is a means to this end.

Otto and Smith (1980) describe two characteristics of students who have trouble with comprehension. First, they are usually able to comprehend oral communications; they have no disabilities that make them incapable of understanding. Second, their problems are not limited to complex passages; they also have problems with simple and straightforward structures. These characteristics suggest that the problem is a lack of a systematic approach to extracting meaning from printed materials.

To deal with this problem, teachers need to develop a repertoire of strategies that will help handicapped students improve comprehension and organization of reading materials. The following techniques can be used before, during, and after silent reading:

Before Reading:

1. *Develop an advanced organizer.* Stress important concepts and the logical relationships in the material to be learned. Present it in a graphic, schematic form. Key words and phrases can be connected with lines and arrows to show relationships like sequence, cause/effect and comparison/contrast. Pyramids can be used to show concepts/subconcepts, topics/subtopics and main idea/details. Either give a completed organizer to the students and go over it with them or develop it on the blackboard or overhead with the group. Be prepared with relevant questions. Have the final format in mind before you begin. Keep the advanced organizer accessible to the students while they are reading. They need to be able to refer to it as a way of organizing information and concepts.

2. *Preteach new and subject area vocabulary.* Stress roots, prefixes and suffixes. This information can be transferred to new words. Develop lists of related words. Emphasize the relationship of the meaning of the words to the concepts to be developed. This strategy fits in neatly with the advanced organizer and provides labels for categorizing and recalling information later.

3. *Establish objectives.* This will focus the reader's attention and also indicate the kind of reading strategy he should use. "Read the chapter to learn all the dates in the Civil War" and "Read the chapter to learn the reasons why the South lost the Civil War" will produce very different reading and study strategies. In fact, if you add the words "I'm going to give you a test on . . ." you will also change the strategies used. So, choose carefully and vary your objectives.

4. *Ask questions.* This focuses attention on whatever you have determined to be important, particularly for a conceptual type of question. Readers seem to pay

less attention to information not highlighted, so be careful choosing your questions. Limit factual questions to especially important information.

5. *Make statements to be accepted or rejected.* Now, the reader is looking for pro and con evidence, and you are requiring that he evaluate information.

During Reading:

1. *Intersperse questions in the text.* Missing important facts and ideas in a long selection has a snowballing effect. Give students questions that will focus attention and comprehension as they read.

2. *Encourage questions from students.* Don't let students struggle over a word they cannot decode or a sentence they cannot decode or a sentence they cannot comprehend. During silent reading tell them to raise their hands while you walk around and give individual help where needed. Keep the reading process moving.

After Reading:

1. *Ask questions.* This is your chance to bring out inference and develop critical thinking by the questions you ask and the way you sequence them. Ask two questions about facts and a third about an inference that can be drawn from the facts, or a third asking for an evaluation of a possible inference. Don't hesitate to add to or delete from the list of questions at the end of the chapter. Tailor the questions to your students and what you want them to learn.

2. *Provide feedback.* This is one of the most important things you can do. Encourage discussion by the group about the reasons for their answers and opinion. Bring up alternatives for the group to attack or support. Locate supporting data in the material. Relate to other material read previously. Refer back to the advanced organizer.

3. *Develop a post-organizer.* Have the group list all facts and concepts they deem important. Be ready with relevant questions if needed. Then, together develop a schematic representation showing the concepts, facts, and their relationships. You will also find this a good chance to review vocabulary.[1]

Since comprehension is built on the understanding of concepts, on memory, and on generalization and interpretation, it is particularly difficult for students who have deficits in these areas. Teachers working with handicapped students need to stress comprehension at every level.

It is important for students learning a sight vocabulary to know the meanings of the words. Some of the suggestions made in the previous section emphasize this idea: using action words; pantomiming concepts such as "under"; using personal words (as in the Ashton-Warner method); and using pictorial clues.

Following directions is a valuable skill in itself; it also indicates sentence

---

1. French, J. N. Organizing for comprehension: Strategies for teachers and students. *Education Unlimited,* 1981, *2* (2), 33–35.

comprehension. With students who do not follow directions well, give one direction at a time; for example, "Open your book to page 30." After the direction is followed, give another: "Read the title of the chapter." When students can follow one direction at a time, give them two to follow consecutively: "Open your book to page 30 and read the title of the chapter." The directions must be clearly stated and in the students' realm of understanding (Burmeister, 1974). This technique can be used by the classroom teacher to get the students to read more in content areas such as mathematics, social studies, and science. As skills develop, lists of directions to follow in these areas can be given.

Exercise in reading for meaning can be provided through folders designed to provide sources of information. Questions that require comprehensive reading can be asked: What can you order with box tops from this cereal package? How do you order it? What are the ingredients listed on this label? How would you use it? What is the address on this match cover? What sort of place did it come from?

Students of all ages enjoy dramatizing stories. The imitation of characters, situations, and settings requires understanding of the story. Students who grasp the idea of dramatization will be able to write and dramatize their own stories.

The following activities are designed to improve comprehension skills.

Find the Answer. From a chart or folder containing pockets marked "Questions" and "Answers," the student selects a card containing a question and matches it with the card containing the answer.

Form Sentences. An envelope is prepared that contains a series of word cards. The student arranges the words to form a sentence.

Newspaper Questions. The student selects a newspaper clipping and reads to find the answers to the four questions that appear on the chart or folder: (Who) was concerned with the event? (What) happened? (When) did it happen? (Where) did it happen?

Old Reading Books. Old reading books can be used to help build comprehension skills. Remove some of the pictures and have students illustrate the stories using blank paper; or, remove the story and have students write a story to go with the pictures.

Some handicapped students may not advance beyond literal comprehension; some will develop understanding of nonliteral language and will acquire critical reading and study skills. Regardless of their reading levels, children should read for meaning, for enjoyment, and for knowledge.

Functional Reading

Functional reading skills enable students to use reading in adapting to societal demands. These skills are used to avoid danger; to understand symbols and abbreviations; to read maps, diagrams, and charts; to develop study skills; to develop living skills; and to enjoy reading as a recreational activity.

For handicapped students, the key to functional reading is relevance. Reading instruction should be relevant to their abilities, their interests, and their needs.

At the elementary level, instruction can be adapted to various abilities through multilevel materials, language experience stories, and various expressive areas previously discussed. At the secondary level, the curriculum should provide educational content, without using reading as a principal information-gathering tool, as well as skill building in reading (Wiseman & Hartwell, 1980). To be more relevant, reading material may need to be rewritten by cutting sentence length, eliminating complicated sentence structure, and reducing word difficulty.

To insure that instruction is relevant to students' interests, teachers should use interest inventories and their own observation skills. Some handicapped students need to develop interests and should be encouraged to investigate peer interests.

Instruction should also be relevant to the emotional, educational, and career needs of handicapped students. Functional reading packets can be developed around vocational terminology, seed packages, real estate brochures, and even clothing labels.

For some handicapped students, functional reading may be the primary goal of instruction. Reading in everyday, adult pursuits necessitates the ability to read directions and phone books, fill out forms, and read newspapers (Wiseman & Hartwell, 1980). A relevant curriculum addresses the functional reading needs of handicapped students.

Functional reading achievement, as well as other reading skills, are part of the competency testing program in many states. Functional areas assessed are: reading labels, store directions, signs, want ads, and schedules; following directions and completing forms and applications; recognizing the meaning of common abbreviations; and distinguishing fact from opinion. Modules designed to teach functional skills are available in *Reading for Survival in Today's Society* (Adams, Flowers, & Woods, 1978).

MATERIALS AND TECHNIQUES

The Reading Teacher's Dilemma[1]

I know I.T.A.,
I use SRA,
A knowledge of phonics is mine.
I've assigned my troops

---

1. Reprinted with permission of R. G. Larson and the International Reading Association.

To ability groups
I think basal readers are fine.

Linguistics are cool.
My class likes to fool
Around with experience charts.
My kids play Scrabble,
And I often dabble
In reading aloud, with two parts.

My tape recorder,
When not out of order,
Is ready to catch every word.
Earphones on one's head
While stories are read
Means words are seen as they're heard.

Individualize?
I've tried that for size.
I've set up a reading corner,
I let children use
Nasty words that *they* choose,
A la Sylvia Ashton-Warner.

Drill sheets are stellar
(Stored in my cellar
Are all of the Dittos I need).
One problem I find
Drives me out of my mind:
A lot of my students can't read!

Handicapped students, like other students, do not always respond to teacher-designed procedures. Some handicapped students will be able to use the same reading materials as other class members; others will need special materials and techniques to reach their full potential. The use of informal materials, the language experience approach, and special reading programs should be considered.

Informal Materials

Through the use of informal materials, students can relate more readily to their environment and therefore to printed material. Kohl (1973) suggests such materials as the telephone book, *TV Guide,* bus and plane schedules, catalogs, menus, advertisements, instructions included with appliances, price lists in supermarkets, newspapers, campaign literature, posters, buttons, and "how to" manuals. As teachers recognize their students' interests, they can put together packets of material that will appeal to almost anyone.

One of the least expensive and most relevant reading materials is the local newspaper. Frequently, publishers will furnish newspapers free of charge for a specified period of time. Papers can be used to teach many areas besides reading and to focus on specific reading problems, such as sequencing, locating, and memorizing (Fenholt, 1980). The following activities are suggested; the possibilities are unlimited:

- Using pictures from the newspapers, have students discuss what they think is happening in the picture, and then make up their own captions.
- Read a short article to the students; have them retell the story in the proper order.
- Introduce new words from the newspaper. Keep the list on the bulletin board. Have students learn the meaning and spelling of the words.
- Block out some well-chosen nouns, verbs, and adjectives from a story. See how effective your students are at selecting words to fill these slots.
- Write a news summary of the front page of today's newspaper.
- Use news stories or pictures to launch discussion of the forces that change the earth's surface, such as flood damage, hurricanes, earthquakes.
- Design a large calendar for the month. Clip and post news on the calendar for each day. At the end of the month, have the students choose the one item they think is most important and include it on a yearly calendar.

Fairleigh (1977) describes an excellent learning center in which the newspaper is the focus. Activities are suggested that use advertisements, the index, advice columns, and other sections to build reading comprehension, classification, and analysis. With directions and materials in a file folder format, students at many levels use the same center.

The alert teacher will find many environmental items of interest to the student. Reading can be motivated and strengthened using baseball and football cards, greeting cards, joke books, bumper stickers, and cereal and other food boxes.

Local Chambers of Commerce can provide teachers with many materials describing geographic areas, vacation points, and historical places, as well as with maps of the city and state. Many magazines provide addresses to which the teacher or students can write for materials about quarter horses, the trucking industry, or almost any topic of interest. Materials files can be built to provide a number of reading levels and topics.

Language Experience Approach

The language experience approach was presented in chapter 5 and mentioned briefly in this chapter. Many readers who have not succeeded with other methods of instruction respond well to this approach. The essential characteristic of the language experience approach is that students learn to read or to improve their reading by using material that they have dictated and the teacher has written.

As a means of introducing young children to reading, there are several advantages:

1. The language experience approach uses the child's own experiences and oral language as the basis for development of reading behaviors.
2. The flexibility of the language experience approach is well-suited to the diverse needs and abilities of young children.
3. The language experience approach can be incorporated into most programs in a gradual, meaningful, and natural manner. (Jensen & Hanson, 1980, p. 61)

The language experience approach appeals to older students who have negative attitudes toward commercial reading materials. Secondary students with serious reading problems sometimes respond positively to stories, essays, plays, and commentaries of their own creation (Otto & Smith, 1980).

Special Reading Programs

In addition to the basal readers, programmed instruction, trade books, and other series, some unique programs have been designed for students with special problems. If other systems have failed, the teacher will want to investigate the following programs and others that are available.

Edmark Reading Program. The Edmark Reading Program teaches a vocabulary of 150 words and provides activities to use reading skills and to develop comprehension and language. Activities include word recognition lessons, direction books, picture-phrase matching, and storybooks. Pretests and review tests are provided throughout the program to confirm the student's progress. This program is designed for students with extremely limited skills. For information, write to Edmark Associates (see Appendix B).

Distar. The Distar program (Engelmann & Bruner, 1969) was designed to teach beginning reading to culturally deprived and slow-learning children. The program incorporates the teaching of skills considered necessary for beginning to read, such as sequencing, left-right progression, and association of sound with symbol (Gillespie-Silver, 1979). Lessons are highly structured, with teacher instructions for reinforcement, pacing, and correction.

The New Streamlined English Series. Developed by Dr. Frank C. Laubach (1945) to teach adults with no reading skills, this program is being used increasingly with students for whom other methods have proved ineffective. The method uses pictures with letters superimposed on them. The lesson format guarantees success by eliciting the correct response from the student and reinforcing it. Each lesson includes phonics, reading sight words, comprehension checks, structural analysis, and vocabulary development. Information can be obtained from New Readers Press, Division of Laubach Literacy, Inc. (see Appendix B).

High-Interest Books. Pickering (1977) suggests the series of books listed in Table 6–4 for students who are reading below their grade level expectations. The interest level is geared to the chronological age of the reader rather than to reading ability.

Techniques

In evaluating reading instruction, a frequent question is, What reading program gets better results? The question should be, What is it that more successful teachers do that less successful teachers do not do? A number of studies indicate

TABLE 6-4. High-Interest Books for Slower Readers

SERIES	PUBLISHER	READING GRADE LEVEL	INTEREST GRADE LEVEL
American Adventure Series	Harper & Row	2–6	4–9
Checkered Flag Series	Field Educational Publications	2	6–10
Cowboy Sam Books	Benefic Press	1–3	1–4
The Deep Sea Adventure Series	Field Educational Publications	2–4	3–9
Discovery Books	Garrard Publishing Co.	2–4	3–6
The Interesting Reading Series	Follett Educational Corp.	2–3	4–9
Morgan Bay Series	Field Educational Publications	2–4	4–9
Sprint Library 1	Scholastic Book Ser.	2	3–8
Sprint Library 2	Scholastic Book Ser.	2	3–8
Sprint Library 3	Scholastic Book Ser.	3	3–8
Sprint Library 4	Scholastic Book Ser.	3	3–8
The True Books	Children's Book Centre	2–3	2–8

Source: From Pickering, C.T. *Helping children learn to read.* New York: Chesford, Inc., 1977, 109–110. © 1977 by C. Thomas Pickering. Reprinted by permission of Chesford, Incorporated, New York, N.Y.

that more successful teachers individualize reading and spend more time in reading instruction (Cohen, 1971).

The integration of handicapped students into the reading program of the regular classroom requires individualization and a great deal of time. When the reading program is totally different for one or several students, specific techniques are helpful. Rewriting material, peer tutoring, tape recording, and using games are techniques that have been successful.

Rewriting. In referring to the creation of reading materials by the English teacher, Fader (1968) writes:

> Stories, plays and essays written by the teacher who knows what his students' vocabularies really are, rather than what they should be; who knows particular facts rather than patent generalizations about their background, environment and aspirations; who knows, in short, his students as individuals rather than types—such reading materials can be of unequaled value in involving students in the process of reading and writing. (p. 90)

Teachers who are concerned about students at the secondary level who are reading at a second- or third-grade level find it profitable to create new material and to rewrite textbook material, magazine and newspaper articles, and even questions on the board at a lower readability level.

To rewrite material, select an article that is worthwhile, pertinent to topics being discussed in class, and interesting to the students. A word list (such as Dolch), broken into approximate grade levels and containing high frequency words, is a basic tool.

Craig (1977) suggests a rewriting procedure:[1]

1. Read the article or textbook passage and jot down the main ideas. This will help keep your re-written version short and to the point.
2. Look over the main ideas, checking those you especially want the students to get from reading the article. This step will help you focus on why you want this particular article read, and it will also help you keep the passage short and to the point.
3. Make a list of the specialized vocabulary and important concepts that are difficult, not on the lists you are using, but that you feel you must include. When you rewrite, try not to use more than five of the specialized vocabulary words or difficult concepts per 100 words.
4. When you are ready to begin writing, you might have a little trouble getting started—refer to your word lists to give you some ideas of words to use.
5. Follow some of these rules:

    Avoid polysyllabic words.

---

1. L. C. Craig, If it's too difficult for the kids to read—rewrite it! *Journal of Reading*, 1977, 21 (3), p. 213. Reprinted with permission of L. C. Craig and the International Reading Association.

Use words that are easily sounded out, like "black."

Use common nouns.

Underline proper names. Tell them to the students before they read the article. Also, underline any specialized vocabulary you wish to remain in the passage but that you plan to preteach before assigning the material. (Remember to preteach these difficult words in context.)

Limit sentence length to a maximum of ten words. Short sentences of five or six words are best.

Use as many common "kid" or slang terms as possible, for example, "right on." (Both of those words are on the Dolch List).

Turn written numbers into numerals, for example, "ten" into "10."

Use simple sentence construction and present tense verbs as much as possible.

If you know how to check the reading level of your rewritten material with a readability formula, compare it with the reading level of the original.

When you have finished writing the article, type it with the largest type available, preferably a primary typewriter. Double space, and make sentences one line long, if possible.

This technique is particularly useful in helping students to read in content areas. For example, the same procedure can be used to rewrite science and social studies textbook chapters.

Peer Teaching. Reading instruction permits the good reader to help the poor reader and the poor reader to help the younger reader. The programs described in the previous section can be taught by students who have been instructed in the simple steps. Good readers can read to small groups of students and help them understand and react to the stories.

Cross-grade matching enables the poor reader to help younger children learn to read or learn to listen. Several children from a fourth grade were asked to read to a small group of kindergarten children. They had never been asked to read before; they wanted to be perfect. Practice sessions, tape recording, and prolonged preparation preceded the experience. Reading skills were improved; self-concepts were lifted!

Studies of cross-age tutoring at the high school level have also been encouraging. In addition to enhancing reading achievement, peer-assisted learning improved self-concept, frequency of social interaction, social adjustment, classroom behavior, and attitude toward school (King, 1982). It is a good option for the teacher concerned with providing as much individual help as possible to pupils with special needs.

Tape Recording. A great deal of material from the regular curriculum can be recorded. Passages from science, social studies, language arts, math, or any other material the student is expected to read can be taped and listened to at a learning station or with earphones. Books and articles of interest to the student can be taped and placed with the written material; the student can follow the print while listening. This amount of recording is time consuming, but the teacher can usually find help. Smitherman (1974) suggests asking a friend (perhaps one who is convalescing) to record. College and high school students, individually or through service clubs, can help.

Directions can be tape recorded for students who do not read well. At the start of a reading lesson, key words can be presented with directions for follow-up exercises. This can be accomplished at a listening station and can accommodate a number of students at different levels. As described by Yates (1969), this technique has several advantages: (1) Most disadvantaged students have a positive attitude toward audiovisual equipment; (2) the lesson can be carefully structured to provide success and reinforcement; (3) the students are not just listening, but are "doing" as well; and (4) they can turn the teacher off—literally—until they catch up or understand.

Computer-Assisted Instruction. Computer-assisted instruction (CAI) is not a separate approach to teaching reading; it can interface with any approach. Students can use computers for reading drill and practice, tutorial instruction, problem solving, and games and simulations (Thompson, 1980). Teachers can use the computer to assist with diagnostic, prescriptive, and evaluative tasks related to reading.

Mason (1980) enumerates some disadvantages in using computers to teach. The initial cost, the purchase of printers, terminals, and other hardware, and software expenses require that the instruction serve a large number of students to be cost effective. Another disadvantage is the difficulty of reading the text on the computer screen. This would be a definite problem for students who have visual defects. The final disadvantage is that the computer program is preset. The computer cannot listen to someone read and help that person improve in fluency or oral interpretation.

At the present time, most public schools use computers to score teacher-administered tests and to generate prescriptions. A number of organizations have developed management systems for these purposes. Before purchasing such systems, school personnel should ask the following questions:

1. Do we have available most of the reading instructional materials listed in the memory of the computer serving this program?
2. Will the prescriptions reliably be returned to our teacher fast enough to be of value?
3. Are the skills to be tested the ones which children actually use as they read at their instructional levels?
4. Are we prepared to spend money on training the teachers to use the program as well as on purchasing the program? (Mason, 1980, p. 20)

Computer-assisted instruction is highly motivating and can be valuable in teaching reading to handicapped students. Finding and selecting appropriate software is a key factor in assuring its success.

Games. The drill necessary to acquire word attack skills can be dull unless presented in creative ways. The use of games offers unlimited variety. In addition to skill-building properties, games provide excellent opportunities for peer teaching and interaction.

Numerous reading games are commercially available. One source, Little Brown Bear Learning Associates, Inc. (Appendix B), lists a key for selecting the appropriate game as determined by the reading skill goal and prerequisite skills. Kits for making games provide dice, plastic markers, and flexible boards to be used in many situations.

Games for teachers to make are found in the following sources:

- Fretz, Peggy. *Reading Games that Teach: Words—Phrases and Sentences.* Monterey Park, Calif.: Creative Teaching Press, 1969.
- Hall, Nancy A. *Rescue.* Stevensville, Mich.: Educational Service, 1969.
- Keith, Joy L. *Word Attack Joy.* Naperville, Ill.: Reading Joy, 1974.
- Mallett, Jerry J. *Classroom Reading Games Activities Kit.* New York: Center for Applied Research in Education, 1975.
- Pierros, Betty. *How to Create Reading Centers.* Carson, Calif.: Educational Insights, 1974.
- Platts, Mary E. *Spice.* Stevensville, Mich.: Educational Service, 1973.

REFERENCES

Adams, A. H., Flowers, A., & Woods, E. E. *Reading for survival in today's society.* Santa Monica, Calif.: Goodyear, 1978.
Ashton-Warner, S. *Teacher.* New York: Simon and Schuster, 1963.
Barbe, W. B. Basic reading skills list. Reprinted from *Educator's guide to personalized reading instruction.* Englewood Cliffs, N.J.: Prentice-Hall, 1960.
Brown, B. Enrich your reading program with personal words. *The Reading Teacher,* 1981, *35* (1), 40–43.
Burmeister, L. E. *Reading strategies for secondary school teachers.* Reading, Mass.: Addison-Wesley, 1974.
Cohen, S. A. Dyspedagogia as a cause of reading retardation: Definition and treatment. In B. Bateman (Ed.), *Learning disorders* (Vol. 4). Seattle: Special Child Publications, 1971.
Cooper, T. T. Following a child's lead. *Teacher,* 1977, *94* (8), 46–47.
Craig, L. C. If it's too difficult for the kids to read—rewrite it! *Journal of Reading,* 1977, *21* (3), 212–214.
Cravioto, J., & DeLicardie, E. R. Environmental and nutritional deprivation in children with learning disabilities. In W. W. Cruickshank & D. P. Hallahan (Eds.), *Perceptual*

and learning disabilities in children (Vol. 2). Syracuse, N.Y.: Syracuse University Press, 1975.

Cunningham, P. M. Teaching were, with, what and other "four-letter" words. *The Reading Teacher,* 1980, *34* (2), 160–163.

Dale, D. M. C. *Deaf children at home and at school.* Springfield, Ill.: Charles C. Thomas, 1967.

Davis, P. A. Teaching partially sighted children. *Teacher,* 1981, *98* (7), 39–41.

Dechant, E. V. *Improving the teaching of reading* (2nd ed.). Englewood Cliffs, N. J.: Prentice-Hall, 1970.

Durost, W. N. Accountability: The task, the tools, and the pitfalls. *The Reading Teacher,* 1971, *24* (4), 291–304.

Edwards, T. J. Teaching reading: A critique. In J. Money (Ed.), *The disabled reader.* Baltimore: Johns Hopkins Press, 1966.

Engelmann, S., & Bruner, E. C. *Distar reading: An instructional system.* Chicago: Science Research Associates, 1969.

Fader, D. N., & McNeil, E. B. *Hooked on books: Program & proof.* New York: Berkley Publishing, 1968.

Fairleigh, R. A. Extra! extra! the newspaper center. *Teacher,* 1977, *94* (6), 50–58.

Farr, R., & Brown, V. Evaluation and decision making. *The Reading Teacher,* 1971, *24* (4), 341–346.

Fenholt, J. Good news! *Exceptional Teacher,* 1980, *1* (7), 5.

Forgan, W. W., Jr. *The reading corner.* Santa Monica, Calif.: Goodyear, 1977.

French, J. N. Organizing for comprehension: Strategies for teachers and students. *Education Unlimited,* 1981, *2* (2), 33–35.

Frostig, M., & Maslow, P. *Learning problems in the classroom.* New York: Grune and Stratton, 1973.

Geoffrion, L. D. Reading and the nonvocal child. *The Reading Teacher,* 1982, *35* (6), 662–669.

Getman, G. N. Visual success is reading success. *Journal of the California Optometric Association* XXIX (Reprint), 1961.

Gillespie, P. H., & Johnson, L. E. *Teaching reading to the mildly retarded child.* Columbus, Ohio: Charles E. Merrill Publishing Co., 1974.

Gillespie-Silver, P. *Teaching reading to children with special needs.* Columbus, Ohio: Charles E. Merrill Publishing Co., 1979.

Goldman, R., Fristoe, M., & Woodcock, R. *Test of auditory discrimination.* Circle Rines, Minn.: American Guidance Service, 1970.

Greenslade, B. C. The basics in reading, from the perspective of the learner. *The Reading Teacher,* 1980, *34* (2), 192–195.

Groff, P. Teaching reading by syllables. *The Reading Teacher,* 1981, *35* (6), 659–664.

Hall, M. A. *Teaching reading as a language experience.* Columbus, Ohio: Charles E. Merrill Publishing Co., 1970.

Hargis, C. H. *Teaching reading to handicapped children.* Denver, Colo.: Love Publishing Co., 1982.

Harris, A. J. *How to increase reading ability.* New York: David McKay, 1961.

Hart, B. O. *Teaching reading to deaf children.* Washington, D.C.: Alexander Graham Bell Association for the Deaf, 1963.

Hennings, D. G., & Grant, B. M. *Written expression in the language arts.* New York: Teachers College Press, 1981.

Hoskisson, K. Learning to read naturally. *Language Arts,* 1979, *56* (5), 489–496.

Houghton, C. Reading for the beginner: Open but deliberate. *Learning,* 1974, *3* (1), 90–94.

Jensen, M. A., & Hanson, B. A. Helping young children learn to read: What research says to teachers. *Young Children,* 1980, *36* (1), 61–71.

Jolly, H. B., Jr. Teaching basic function words. *The Reading Teacher,* 1981, *35* (2), 136–140.

Jongsma, K. S., & Jongsma, E. A. Test review: Commercial information reading inventories. *The Reading Teacher,* 1981, *35* (6), 697–705.

King, R. T. Learning from a PAL. *The Reading Teacher,* 1982, *35* (6), 682–685.

Kohl, H. *Reading, how to.* New York: E. P. Dutton, 1973.

Kolstoe, O. P. *Teaching educable mentally retarded children* (2nd ed.). New York: Holt, Rinehart and Winston, 1976.

L'Abate, L., & Curtis, L. T. *Teaching the exceptional child.* Philadelphia: Saunders, 1975.

Larson, R. G. The reading teacher's dilemma. *The Reading Teacher,* 1974, 27 (6), 588. Reprinted with permission of R. G. Larson and the International Reading Association.

Laubach, F. C. *The silent billion speak.* New York: Friendship Press, 1945.

Manson, M. Explorations in language arts for preschoolers (who happen to be deaf). *Language Arts,* 1982, 59 (1), 33–39.

Mason, G. E. Computerized reading instruction: A review. *Educational Technology,* 1980, *20* (10), 18–22.

Mass, L. N. Developing concepts of literacy in young children. *The Reading Teacher,* 1982, *35* (6), 670–675.

May, F. B. *Reading as communication.* Columbus, Ohio: Charles E. Merrill Publishing Co., 1982.

Melcher, D. Johnny still can't read. *School Library Journal,* 1973, October 15, 79–87.

Mitchell, J. R. Getting poor readers ready to read. *Teaching Exceptional Children,* 1974, *6* (2), 103–110.

Myers, M. Uncle Sam's a reading puppeteer. *Learning,* 1975, *4* (3), 368–388.

Noble, E. F. Self-selection: A remedial strategy for readers with a limited reading vocabulary. *The Reading Teacher,* 1981, *34* (4), 386–388.

Norwood, M. J. Captioned films for the deaf. *Exceptional Children,* 1976, *43* (3), 164–166.

Ogle, D., & Fritts, J. B. Criterion-referenced reading assessment valuable for process as well as for data. *Phi Delta Kappan,* 1981, *62* (9), 640–641.

Otto, W., McMenemy, R. A., & Smith, R. J. *Corrective and remedial teaching.* Boston: Houghton Mifflin Co., 1973.

Otto, W., & Smith, R. J. *Corrective and remedial teaching* (3rd ed.). Boston: Houghton Mifflin Co., 1980.

Parks, B. H. Acquiring syllabication skills: A simplified approach. *Teaching Exceptional Children,* 1982, *14* (5), 186–187.

Pickering, C. T. *Helping children learn to read.* New York: Chesford, 1977.

Prescott, G. A. Criterion-referenced test interpretation in reading. *The Reading Teacher,* 1971, *24* (4), 347–354.

Ross, A. O. *Psychological aspects of learning disabilities and reading disorders.* New York: McGraw-Hill, 1976.

Ruddell, R. B. Preface. In R. L. Venezky, *Testing in reading.* Urbana, Ill.: ERIC Clearinghouse on Reading and Communication Skills and National Council of Teachers of English, 1974.

Salvia, J., & Ysseldyke, J. E. *Assessment in special and remedial education* (2nd ed.). Boston: Houghton Mifflin Co., 1981.

Savage, J. F., & Mooney, F. F. *Teaching reading to children with special needs.* Boston: Allyn and Bacon, 1979.

Schiffman, G. B. Program administration within a school system. In J. Money (Ed.), *The disabled reader.* Baltimore: Johns Hopkins Press, 1966.

Schmidt, T. Make your own reading management system. *Teacher,* 1976, *93* (5), 60–62.

Shipley, K. G., & McFarlane, S. C. Facilitating reading development with speech- and language-impaired children. *Language, Speech and Hearing Services in Schools,* 1981, *XII* (2), 100–105.
Smitherman, D. W. A hand-up for slow readers. *Learning,* 1974, *3* (3), 87.
Spache, E. B. *Reading activities for child involvement* (2nd ed.). Boston: Allyn and Bacon, 1976.
Spache, G. D. *Reading in the elementary school.* Boston: Allyn and Bacon, 1964.
Speckels, J. "Poor" readers can learn phonics. *The Reading Teacher,* 1980, *34* (1), 22–26.
Strauss, A. A., & Lehtinen, L. B. *Psychopathology and education of the brain-injured child.* New York: Grune and Stratton, 1947.
Thompson, B. J. Computers in reading: A review of applications and implications. *Educational Technology,* 1980, *20* (8), 38–41.
Venezky, R. L. *Testing in reading.* Urbana, Ill.: ERIC Clearinghouse on Reading and Communication Skills and National Council of Teachers of English, 1974.
Wallace, G., & Kauffman, J. M. *Teaching children with learning problems.* Columbus, Ohio: Charles E. Merrill Publishing Co., 1973.
Ward, M., & McCormick, S. Reading instruction for blind and low vision children in the regular classroom. *The Reading Teacher,* 1981, *34* (4), 434–44.
Wechsler, D. *Wechsler intelligence scale for children—revised.* New York: Psychological Corp., 1974.
Wepman, J. M. *Auditory discrimination test.* Chicago: Language Research Associates, 1958.
Wepman, J. M. Auditory perception and imperception. In W. M. Cruickshank & D. P. Hallahan (Eds.), *Perceptual and learning disabilities in children* (Vol. 2). Syracuse, N.Y.: Syracuse University Press, 1975.
Wilson, R. M. *Diagnostic and remedial reading* (4th ed.). Columbus, Ohio: Charles E. Merrill Publishing Co., 1981.
Wiseman, D. E., & Hartwell, L. K. The poor reader in secondary schools. *The Education Digest,* 1980, *XLVI* (2), 56–59.
Wolfthal, M. Reading scores revisited. *Phi Delta Kappan,* 1981, *62* (9), 662–663.
Yates, J. R., Jr. Use of a listening station for introducing a reading lesson to disadvantaged EMR junior high school students. *Education and Training of the Mentally Retarded,* 1969, *4* (1), 29–31.

7

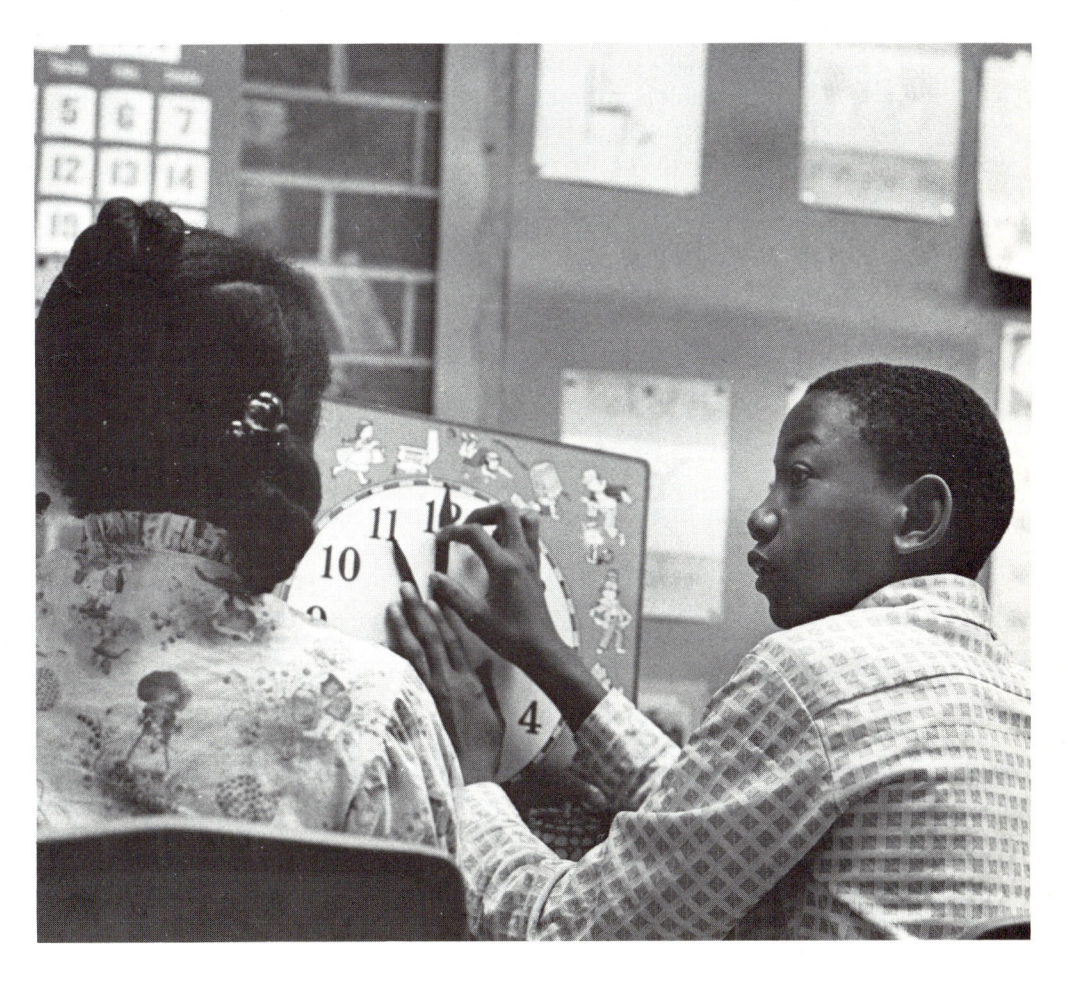

Teaching Mathematics

Many handicapped students mainstreamed in regular classes are at a significant disadvantage in math. Some types of handicapping conditions have a higher probability of interfering with math achievement than others. Students handicapped by mental retardation, learning disabilities, and sensory losses (visual and auditory) are likely to need adaptations in the math curriculum to achieve maximum gains. Orthopedically handicapped students—for example, those with impairment only in their lower limbs—probably need no special adaptations. However, all students, handicapped and nonhandicapped, need some individualization to accommodate their particular strengths and weaknesses. Systematic instruction based on individual needs, as discussed in chapter 4, provides the framework for a math program.

ASSESSMENT

In order to plan a math program, the teacher must answer two questions (Lowenbraun & Affleck, 1976): What is the student's level of functioning in the sequence of math skills? What skills should the student learn next? The selection of assessment tools is the first step in answering these questions. Appropriate assessment tools fall into the categories of standardized tests, criterion-referenced tests, and structured observations. Regardless of the type of tool used, some general guidelines apply in math assessment.

Assessment should occur before math instruction is initiated—at the beginning of the school year for most students. If new students transfer into the school during the year, the teacher should determine immediately the student's repertoire of math skills.

Math assessment tools that are correlated as much as possible with the student's preferred mode of response should be used. As discussed in chapter 4, many alternative output modes can be considered (e.g., constructing, verbalizing, writing, and solving) when assessing student performance. Often, a handicapped student's weakest response mode is paper and pencil; yet this mode is used almost exclusively for diagnosis. Diagnostic techniques should involve more than paper and pencil tests. Many students are more accurate if they respond verbally or use a calculator.

Assessment should be on-going. Sometimes students are nervous or lack self-confidence when tested at the beginning of the year. Errors related to these factors could be misinterpreted by the teacher as lack of skill development. The possibility of unreliable information is minimized as teachers continue to check the student's progress.

An in-depth analysis of all assessment data should be made. Considering only the number of correct and incorrect responses is a superficial way to interpret student performance. Teachers need to observe closely the types of errors a student makes and the reasons that seem to contribute to the errors. This type of information leads directly to remediation. Error analysis is discussed in greater detail later in the chapter.

Assessment should not be the sole responsibility of the classroom teacher, but should be shared with other educators in the school. Math assessment should be included as an area of focus in the multidisciplinary evaluation when it has been documented that a handicapped student has difficulty with math. Special education resource teachers and school psychologists are frequently involved in assessing math skills.

Standardized Tests

The standardized math assessment tools are usually achievement tests and diagnostic tests. Achievement tests generally provide an overview of math achievement by sampling a variety of skills with a limited number of items per skill. The results of achievement tests are typically reported in the form of grade equivalent scores. For example, the Wide Range Achievement Test profile might indicate that a student in the fifth grade is on a 3.4 grade level in mathematics. This means that the student performs on math tasks similarly to the average student in the fourth month of the third grade. At first glance, this type of score seems to provide information to answer the crucial assessment questions: What is the student's current level of functioning in the sequence of math skills? What skills should the student learn next?

However, when the meaning of a 3.4 grade level is analyzed, the precise sequence of skills that need to be introduced next is still not pinpointed. Two students scoring 3.4 are not at the same level, because they probably missed different items. An analysis of items on achievement tests will indicate the strengths and weaknesses of the class as a whole but produces limited information on an individual student's level of functioning. Teachers need to realize that quantitative scores do not provide the assessment information necessary to develop a systematic instructional program.

The second type of standardized assessment is the diagnostic test. Although diagnostic math tests vary widely, they tend to be more specific and precise than achievement tests. Usually, they provide more in-depth analysis of several components of math, such as computation, reasoning, fractions, and application. This type of profile is more likely to result in the identification of individual strengths and weaknesses. One math diagnostic test that is systematically and comprehensively constructed is the KeyMath published by American Guidance Service, Inc. The KeyMath is individually administered and requires only minimal writing responses. It is appropriate for use in kindergarten through sixth grade. The manual includes an instructional objective for each test item, which promotes the generalization of test results into the identification of specific skills for the IEP. The test is designed so that teachers or teacher aides can administer it. Other achievement and diagnostic tests frequently used to assess math skills are identified and briefly described in Table 7–1. More detailed information on the nature and uses of these tests is available from Algozzine and McGraw (1979), Howell and Kaplan (1980), and Salvia and Ysseldyke (1978).

The minimum competency tests currently being implemented or considered in the majority of states (Gallagher, 1979) are diagnostic tests. Although states differ widely in some aspects of their minimum competency testing programs, a standard component of these programs is the inclusion of basic and functional math (Linde & Olsen, 1980).

The guidelines for competency test administration and scoring are developed by states and, in some cases, local education agencies. These guidelines, reviewed by Smith and Jenkins (1980), continue to change as states refine their policies and procedures. Teachers are urged to inquire about the policies and procedures for assessing math competencies in their schools. A major consideration for teachers is to insure that the student's math curriculum and vocabulary are consistent with the assessment questions and criteria on the minimum competency test. In many states, the receipt of a high school diploma is contingent on passing the competency test. Thus, high value is placed on a student's performance. In specifying goals and objectives for the student's IEP, consideration should be given to the state's minimum competency requirements.

Criterion-Referenced Tests

The distinguishing characteristics of criterion-referenced tests are a sequential arrangement of tasks and the specification of criteria the student is expected to reach in order to attain proficiency. Teachers can develop criterion-referenced tests that insure a direct link between assessment and instruction in math. Teachers should adhere to the following procedure in developing these tests:

1. Specify which math skills the student should know;
2. State the desired criteria to indicate proficiency;
3. Develop test questions to assess the skill; and
4. Record student's performance.

An example of a teacher-constructed, criterion-referenced test in the area of multiplication processes is presented in Table 7–2. In constructing criterion-

TABLE 7-1. Standardized Tests—Mathematics

TITLE:	Peabody Individual Achievement Test
PUBLISHER:	American Guidance Service, Inc.
	Circle Pines, Minnesota 55014
DESCRIPTION:	This test measures achievement in several areas, including mathematics. It yields grade equivalents, age equivalents, standard scores, and percentile ranks.
TITLE:	SRA Achievement Series
PUBLISHER:	Science Research Associates, Inc.
	259 East Erie Street
	Chicago, Illinois 60611
DESCRIPTION:	This achievement test is useful for testing children in grades two through six. It measures skills in the areas of concepts, reasoning, and computation.
TITLE:	Stanford Diagnostic Arithmetic Test
PUBLISHER:	Harcourt Brace Jovanovich, Inc.
	Test Department
	757 Third Avenue
	New York, New York 10017
DESCRIPTION:	This test is provided in two forms that overlap and cover the second through the eighth grades. The test gives information in the form of stanines, percentiles, and grade level equivalents. Also this test can be scored by a computer with a programmed readout for interpretation and recommendations.
TITLE:	Metropolitan Achievement Tests
PUBLISHER:	Harcourt Brace Jovanovich, Inc.
	Test Department
	757 Third Avenue
	New York, New York 10017
DESCRIPTION:	This test is given to children in the third through the ninth grades and offers two scores: computation and problem-solving concepts.
TITLE:	California Achievement Tests
PUBLISHER:	California Test Bureau
	McGraw-Hill Division
	Del Monte Research Park
	Monterey, California 93940
DESCRIPTION:	The subtest for arithmetic gives three scores: reasoning, fundamentals, and total tests. It may be used in grades one through nine.
TITLE:	Wide Range Achievement Test
PUBLISHER:	Western Psychological Services
	12031 Wilshire Boulevard
	Los Angeles, California 90025
DESCRIPTION:	The WRAT is provided in two forms; the range is from kindergarten to college level. The arithmetic sections on both forms are designed virtually to eliminate reading. The test is individually administered and can be completed within 10 minutes.

TABLE 7-1. (Continued)

TITLE:	Los Angeles Diagnostic Tests
PUBLISHER:	California Test Bureau
	McGraw-Hill Division
	Del Monte Research Park
	Monterey, California 93940
DESCRIPTION:	These tests are used with children in grades two through nine and measure skill in the four basic computational areas and in reasoning.
TITLE:	Diagnostic Arithmetic Tests
PUBLISHER:	California Test Bureau
	McGraw-Hill Division
	Del Monte Research Park
	Monterey, California 93940
DESCRIPTION:	This test measures skill development in the four computational areas: weights, percentages, measures, and fractions.
TITLE:	Pattern Recognition Skills Inventory
PUBLISHER:	Hubbard Press
	2855 Shermer Road
	Northbrook, Illinois 60062
DESCRIPTION:	This instrument is for use with children between the ages of five and ten years. It analyzes the development of pattern recognition ability and the relationship of this ability to the development of other cognitive concepts. The inventory enables teachers to understand why students display knowledge of certain concepts and not others.

Source: From Gearheart, Bill R.: Teaching the learning disabled, St. Louis, 1976. The C. V. Mosby Co. Reprinted by permission of the publisher.

referenced tests, it is important to include at least three test questions per item to help distinguish between random and substantive errors.

There are several ways to develop criterion-referenced tests for repeated use. One approach is to mimeograph skill sequences in checklist form and develop a laminated index card file of test items keyed by skill number to the checklist. Different students can follow the same sequence, and the mimeographed copies of skill checklists provide an individual record for each student. Skills can be dated as they are mastered. The laminated index cards enable the test items to be used repeatedly without any extra teacher preparation, beyond the initial organization. Test construction can be time consuming. The substantial benefit to the teacher is that the assessment sequence is the same as the instructional sequence. Behavioral objectives are the natural by-product of criterion-referenced tests. As teachers master the task of specifying skill sequences in math, this systematic approach to math programming will facilitate the progress of all students.

Some school systems are using microcomputers to generate criterion-referenced tests. These computers can print up to 10 or 15 test items for the

TABLE 7-2. Criterion-Referenced Test in Multiplication Processes

SKILLS (PARTIAL LISTING)	CRITERIA	SAMPLE TEST QUESTIONS	
1. Multiplies a 2-digit multiplicand with a 1-digit multiplier, involving no carrying in equations and word problems.	90%	(a) 23 × 2	(b) If there are 11 groups of people with 6 people in each group, how many people are in all the groups?
2. Multiplies a 3-digit multiplicand with a 1-digit multiplier, involving no carrying in equations and word problems.	90%	(a) 123 × 3	(b) A school has 123 classrooms with each having 3 erasers. How many erasers are in the whole school?
3. Multiplies a 4-digit multiplicand with a 1-digit multiplier, involving no carrying in equations and word problems.	90%	(a) 2314 × 2	(b) There are 4 schools in the district. Each school has 1021 children. How many children are in the school district?
4. Multiplies a 2-digit multiplicand with a 1-digit multiplier, involving carrying in equations and word problems.	90%	(a) 35 × 3	(b) If a car goes around a 25-mile track 5 times, how far has it traveled?
5. Multiplies a 3-digit multiplicand with a 1-digit multiplier, involving carrying to the 10's place in equations and word problems.	90%	(a) 128 × 2	(b) There are 4 piles with 217 rocks in each pile. How many rocks are in all the piles?
6. Multiplies a 3-digit multiplicand with a 1-digit multiplier, involving carrying to the hundred's place in equations and word problems.	90%	(a) 384 × 2	(b) If 5 trucks each have 141 boxes, how many boxes are in all the trucks?

objectives selected as appropriate for the assessment. The use of such technology can be efficient for teachers and motivating for students.

Observation

In every math lesson, teachers have the opportunity to identify math strategies and activities that students appear to enjoy and use to achieve success. Seatwork, workbooks, games, large-group activities, and small-group activities, in addition to teacher-constructed tests, can provide a teacher valuable assessment information on a continuous basis during the student's normal classroom routine. Although this type of observational assessment is more informal than are standardized or criterion-referenced tests, the insights available to teachers can be invaluable.

Error Analysis

Standardized tests, criterion-referenced tests, and observation enable teachers to analyze students' errors in order to identify the types and causes of errors. Howell and Kaplan (1980) state that "errors are not just the opposite of corrects" (p. 245). They suggest three reasons:

1. There's more than one way to make an error.
2. The answer you get depends on the question you ask.
3. Nothing happens by accident. (p. 246)

Systematic error analysis involves the identification of response patterns and the student's rationale for the response as a basis for instructional planning. Reisman (1972) has developed an error analysis chart, which provides examples of frequent computation errors with a brief statement indicating the possible cause of each error. A portion of her comprehensive chart is included in Table 7–3.

It is also possible to carry out error analysis in the area of math reasoning. In solving word problems, errors may be related to any of the following factors: lack of attention; poor reading comprehension; inability to recognize words; overlooking important cues, such as "how many all together," that indicate which computational process to use; inability to disregard irrelevant numbers included in the problem; writing down the problem incorrectly on paper; lack of knowledge of the correct computation process; lack of concept development; and general carelessness.

Fowler (1978) suggests that teachers sometimes need to go beyond written work and inquire into a student's thinking processes to pinpoint reasoning errors. She states:

TABLE 7-3. Error Analysis Chart

ANALYSIS	EXAMPLE
1. Lacks mastery of basic addition combinations.	3 2 +4 3 7 4
2. Lacks mastery of basic subtraction combinations.	3 8 −2 5 1 2
3. Lacks mastery of basic multiplication combinations.	3 2 × 3 86
4. Lacks mastery of basic division combinations.	35 ÷ 5 = 6 6 9)56 −56 0
5. Subtracts incorrectly within the division algorithm.	3) 73 R1 70 3)230 −21 10 ⟵ −9 1
6. Error in addition of partial product.	432 × 57 3 0 24 21 6 0 24 0 24
7. Does not complete addition: a. Does not write regrouped number.	85 +43 28
b. Leaves out numbers in column addition.	4 8 2 + 3 15 ⟵
8. Rewrites a numeral without computing.	↘72 +15 ⟶ 77 ⟶ 32 × 3 ⟶ 36
9. Does not complete subtraction.	582 −35 47

TABLE 7-3. (Continued)

ANALYSIS	EXAMPLE
10. Does not complete division because of incompleted subtraction.	$\begin{array}{r} 1\,)\,41 \\ \underline{40}\,) \\ 7\overline{)397} \\ \underline{-280} \\ 7 \\ \underline{7} \end{array}$
11. Fails to complete division: stops at first partial quotient.	$\begin{array}{r} 50 \\ 7\overline{)370} \\ \underline{350} \end{array}$
12. Fails to complete division; leaves remainder greater than divisor.	$\begin{array}{r} 80\ \mathrm{R}9 \\ 9\overline{)729} \\ \underline{720} \\ 9 \end{array}$

Source: From A GUIDE TO THE DIAGNOSTIC TEACHING OF ARITHMETIC by Fredricka K. Reisman. Columbus, Ohio: Charles E. Merrill Publishing Company, 1972, pp. 131–132. Reprinted by permission of the publisher.

Granted, individual interviews take time; however, the results of two minutes of discussion can often provide insight into the cause of the difficulties. This is time better spent than time by the student in working problems incorrectly under the same misapprehension and time spent by the teacher in marking them as incorrect. (p. 24)

Each type of error is different and, therefore, requires a different approach to correction. Error analysis is important for all students, but it is particularly relevant for assessing students handicapped by mental retardation, learning disabilities, or sensory impairments. Students who experience substantial difficulty in math make the most systematic progress when errors are consistently identified and then eliminated.

GOALS AND OBJECTIVES

Once math assessment has been completed and the teacher has identified the skills already mastered, the next step is to develop the student's IEP. At this time, goals and objectives are specified based on the handicapped student's current level of performance.

A major decision related to goal setting is what to teach, that is, identifying the specific body of math concepts and skills important for a handicapped student to know. For example, assessment may reveal that a fourth-grade student with significant learning problems has the following skills:

- counts to 100 by ones, two, fives, and tens, but cannot go past 100;
- computes basic addition facts and column addition with no carrying and is ready to learn two-digit addition with carrying;
- tells time only by the hour;
- counts change to 25 cents;
- measures feet and inches, but is unfamiliar with even the vocabulary of the metric system; and
- identifies various geometric figures, but is unable to use a compass to construct a circle or angle.

(Goals and objectives based on these skills are identified later in Table 7–4.)

Where does the teacher start? One of the first considerations is that the majority of handicapped students who achieve significantly below grade level in math will never completely catch up with grade-level expectations. These students may have handicaps attributable to mental retardation or a learning disability, and they probably will master fewer math concepts and skills than the majority of other students. Therefore, teachers need to identify the most *relevant* math curriculum to serve as the core for setting annual goals. This means leaving out some skills that are unessential for daily living situations.

To begin pinpointing relevant skills, ask yourself what math skills you have used in the last twenty-four hours. You might consider noting the math skills you use over the next several days. Also, identify jobs that handicapped students might be likely to have as adults, and list the math skills associated with success on that particular job. The fundamental nature of daily math requirements is often surprising.

As previously discussed, another consideration in defining the content appropriate for handicapped students is the group of competencies that comprise minimum competency tests in various states. When appropriate, these competencies should be incorporated in the student's IEP. It is also important that the student's parents have the opportunity to define goals and objectives as they participate in the development of their child's IEP. There may be math deficiencies the parents would like remediated. Further, handicapped students, depending on their age and maturity, might also help to define the math curriculum in terms of what they would most like to learn. The responsibility and accountability for goal setting should be shared by all members of the IEP committee.

When one realizes the importance of individual differences and that guidelines differ for all students, a general framework for planning math instruction for students with significant learning problems can be constructed that includes: (1) number concepts, (2) facts and processes, (3) money, (4) time, and (5) measurement.

These math subcomponents are tied directly to everyday living skills. Working within this framework, a teacher can establish an annual goal for each subcomponent and then break down the goal into short-term objectives. For the fourth-grade student whose profile was presented earlier, examples of annual goals and objectives (Turnbull, 1976) are shown in Table 7–4.

After the goals and objectives have been identified, teachers must establish the content sequence for teaching the various math subcomponents. The question here is *when* to teach the specified skills and concepts. Students handicapped in their learning potential and/or achievement realize more systematic success when they can practice concepts and skills to the point of proficiency before moving on to something new. For example, when the concept of place value is introduced the student should solidly master each objective before moving to the next objective representing an increased level of difficulty. Success at each step insures the development of a strong foundation in math.

Some students find it frustrating to work routinely on one or more subcomponents (e.g., facts and processes, money, time) during the first part of the week and another subcomponent (e.g., measurement) during the latter part of the week. When learning is more difficult for students, constantly expecting them to "change gears" can be an ineffective instructional strategy. Teachers should consider units of instruction, with each unit focusing on separate subcomponents. There must also be periodic reviews of objectives that were mastered previously.

After teachers decide when to teach the specified goals and objectives comprising the math curriculum for a handicapped student, they can introduce the objectives systematically. As pointed out in chapter 4, many objectives must be broken down into a series of steps. This task analysis applies to the subject of math. Teachers should carefully analyze the prerequisite skills involved in mastering each objective and teach these skills step by step. This ordered approach to teaching enhances successful achievement for handicapped students. Many students with handicaps are further penalized in schools when teachers assume they know certain skills, expect them to make huge leaps in skill development, or expect that they will learn skills incidentally. Classroom success will increase if teachers accurately assess what students have learned and what they need to learn next, provide step-by-step instruction in a sequenced format, and actively teach the skills and concepts to handicapped students.

INSTRUCTIONAL APPROACHES

The instructional adaptations discussed in this section are directly related to some of the educational characteristics of handicapped students identified in chapter 1. These characteristics are associated with various types of handicapping conditions and are likely to interfere with mathematics achievement unless curriculum accommodations are made. The learning characteristics included relate to attention, concept development, memory, generalization, delayed language, and fine motor problems.

TABLE 7-4. Sample Goals and Objectives

1. NUMBER CONCEPTS

A. Current level of performance: Can count to 100 by ones, twos, fives, and tens, but cannot go past 100.
B. Long-term goal: By the end of the academic year, the student will be able to read, write, and manipulate numbers from 101 to 500.
C. Short-term objectives:
  (1) Rote counts beginning with any three-digit number from 100 to 200 up to a designated number, 200 or below.
  (2) Reads any number from 100 to 200.
  (3) Writes from memory any number from 100 to 200.
  (4) Tells the missing number in an incomplete oral sequence using the numbers 100 through 200.
  (5) Writes the missing numbers in an incomplete written sequence using the numbers 100 through 200.
  (6) States, both verbally and using the appropriate mathematical symbols (> and <), whether a given number is less than or greater than another number, for numbers between 100 and 200.
  (7) Rote counts beginning with any three-digit number from 200 to 500 up to a designated number, 500 or below.
  (8) Reads any number from 200 to 500.
  (9) Writes from memory any number from 200 to 500.
  (10) Tells the missing number in an incomplete oral sequence using the numbers 200 through 500.
  (11) Writes the missing number in an incomplete written sequence using the numbers 200 through 500.
  (12) States, both verbally and using the appropriate mathematical symbols (> and <), whether a given number is less than or greater than another number, for numbers from 200 to 500.

2. FACTS AND PROCESSES

A. Current level of performance: Has mastered basic addition facts and column addition with no carrying; is ready to learn two-digit addition with carrying.
B. Long-term goal: By the end of the academic year, the student will have mastered carrying in two- or three-digit numbers and will begin learning basic subtraction facts.
C. Short-term objectives:
  (1) Adds a two-digit and a one-digit number with carrying.
  (2) Adds a two-digit and a two-digit number with carrying.
  (3) Solves column addition with three two-digit addends with carrying.
  (4) Adds a three-digit and a one-digit number carrying to the ten's place.
  (5) Adds a three-digit and a two-digit number carrying to the ten's place.
  (6) Adds a three-digit and a three-digit number carrying to the ten's place.
  (7) Solves column addition with three two- or three-digit numbers carrying to the ten's place.

TABLE 7-4. (Continued)

- (8) Adds a three-digit and a two-digit number carrying to either the ten's or hundred's place.
- (9) Adds two three-digit numbers carrying to either the ten's or hundred's place.
- (10) Solves column addition with three two- or three-digit numbers with carrying to either the ten's or hundred's place.
- (11) Solves subtraction problems using real objects with basic facts 0 through 9.
- (12) Solves subtraction problems using pictures with basic facts 0 through 9.
- (13) Subtracts any two one-digit numbers.

3. *TIME*
   A. Current level of performance: Is able to tell time only by the hour.
   B. Long-term goal: By the end of the academic year, the student will be able to tell time to the minute.
   C. Short-term objectives:
   - (1) Points to and understands the function of the hour and minute hands.
   - (2) States that 60 minutes equals one hour.
   - (3) Tells time by the hour.
   - (4) Understands that 30 minutes equals one-half hour.
   - (5) States that when the minute hand is pointing to six, it is the half-hour.
   - (6) Tells time by the half-hour.
   - (7) Uses the terms *past* and *after* to tell time in five-minute intervals between 12 and 6 o'clock.
   - (8) Uses the terms *before, to,* and *till* to tell time in five-minute intervals before the new o'clock hour.
   - (9) Reads and writes time equivalents.
   - (10) Tells time by the minute.

4. *MONEY*
   A. Current level of performance: Can count change to 25 cents.
   B. Long-term goal: By the end of the academic year, the student will be able to count coins to one dollar and bills to 20 dollars.
   C. Short-term objectives:
   - (1) Recognizes the cent value of all coins.
   - (2) Recognizes the monetary relationships of all coins to each other up to 50 cents (e.g., 5 nickles = 1 quarter, 2 quarters = one-half dollar).
   - (3) Counts coins to 50 cents.
   - (4) Solves addition and subtraction problems with sums to 50 cents.
   - (5) Writes monetary values using the cents sign or dollar mark.
   - (6) Recognizes and counts bills representing one, five, ten, and twenty dollars.

TABLE 7-4. (Continued)

    (7) Recognizes the monetary relationships of all coins to each other up to one dollar.
    (8) Counts coins to one dollar.
    (9) Solves addition and subtraction problems with sums to one dollar.
    (10) Counts to one dollar using a variety of coin combinations.
    (11) Makes correct change from purchases up to one dollar.
    (12) Counts change and bills for amounts up to 21 dollars.

5. MEASUREMENT

A. Current level of performance: Can measure in feet and inches but is unfamiliar with even the vocabulary of the metric system.
B. Long-term goal: By the end of the academic year, the student will be able to use a metric ruler to make a measurement in centimeters.
C. Short-term objectives:
    (1) States the history of the metric system.
    (2) Uses the metric vocabulary related to linear measure.
    (3) Uses a metric ruler to measure classroom objects in approximate terms.
    (4) Recognizes and uses the measure of a centimeter.
    (5) Can identify objects whose length can be measured in centimeters.
    (6) Can identify the relationship of meters and centimeters to feet and inches and can convert from one measure to another.
    (7) Uses a meter stick to measure in whole and fractional parts.
    (8) Can estimate the approximate length of objects in meters and centimeters.

6. GEOMETRY:

Assessment revealed that the student can identify various geometric figures, but is unable to use a compass to construct a circle or an angle. This area seems to have the least relevance to everyday mathematics skills, and the teacher might decide not to include goals and objectives in geometry as part of the student's math curriculum. Rather than teaching concepts related to geometry as a formal part of the math curriculum, the teacher could integrate these concepts into art activities. For example, the student might identify and draw geometric forms in use, such as a bicycle, roof, and house. It is difficult to know where to trim the curriculum; however, curtailment is necessary for students whose achievement is significantly below grade level and whose learning rate will likely be slower than the majority of students in the class. While classroom peers are working on geometry during math periods, handicapped students with significant lags in achievement can pursue the mastery of the specified objectives in the other subcomponents of their program. (It should be remembered that all handicapped students do not achieve below grade level. Students with orthopedic, sensory, and emotional handicaps may not need adaptation in curriculum content. These students, however, may require adaptation in the method of instruction, which will be discussed in the next section.)

Attention

Some handicapped students may fail to pay attention during math because they do not understand the lesson content or the directions for a particular assignment. If assessment and IEP planning have been done properly, students should be working on tasks commensurate with their achievement. When the materials are too complex, the teacher should back up in the sequence of skills. Readjustment of objectives is often necessary before the exact achievement level is pinpointed. Making sure that students understand the task directions helps increase their attention to them. Helpful suggestions include:

1. Use consistent language easily understood by the student.

1. *Example:* When the vocabulary of the metric system is introduced, be sure the student understands one term before another is introduced.

2. Use routine formats for seatwork assignments.

2. *Example:* If math contracts are used, they should be set up in a routine way with standard organization for identifying activities, materials, and requirements.

3. Use a peer tutor to explain directions to a handicapped student.

3. *Example:* If the student is expected to work ten problems on page 38 of the math workbook, have a peer check to see if the student understands and finds the right page. If not, the peer can explain directions.

4. Use the tape recorder to provide a more detailed explanation to the handicapped student.

4. *Example:* If the student is assigned a task on number concepts and the teacher believes that review or a thorough explanation is necessary, a message can be put on the tape recorder. The student can refer to the message as often as necessary.

Another problem associated with focusing attention appropriately is that many math textbooks and workbooks are distracting in terms of page content. On a given workbook page, there may be ten addition, subtraction, and multiplication problems placed around various examples, charts, written directions, and pictures. The print may be in several different scripts and use three or four different colors. For some students, this diverse composition is intriguing; for many handicapped students it is a significant obstacle to focusing attention properly. Faced with so many different stimuli, some students become frustrated and distracted. Teachers should be aware that some students will perform better if their math textbooks and workbooks have problems representing a single or limited number of concepts on each page and a controlled number of "distractors." Also, the required response should be consistent on each page rather than varied (e.g., supplying a missing addend; computing the sum of a problem).

> *Ronnie, a learning-disabled, fifth-grade student, seemed to feel defeated before he even started assignments in his math workbook. His teacher made a tachistoscope for him to use so that only the problem he was working on at a given time was exposed. This approach was easy to implement. The length of time Ronnie was able to attend to his work substantially increased.*

As teachers identify instructional strategies that motivate the student, they should be capitalized on and expanded in order to minimize the disadvantages of students' attention problems.

Another problem is related to attention span or the length of time a student can maintain attention to a given task. Many math periods in regular classes range from thirty minutes to one hour; many handicapped students have much shorter attention spans. For a student whose attention span is ten minutes, the teacher might plan three ten-minute math tasks. After each task is completed, the student might have two to five minutes of free time. A seventh-grade teacher describes her approach:

> *During the first month of school, Carla seemed to never finish an assignment. She would work for 10 to 15 minutes and then be off in a daze. I decided to give her several 10- or 15-minute assignments. I got a math workbook, and cut up the pages to make shorter assignments. I pasted the sections of workbook pages on tagboard. The pride Carla felt in finishing one short assignment seemed to be an incentive for her to begin working on the next one.*

Another option is to arrange periods of structured math assignments interspersed with games, such as Monopoly, Concentration, or Dominoes. Games are often less taxing on attention capabilities, yet are valuable approaches to learning skills. Interesting lessons can boost the length of a student's attention span.

Sometimes the topic of a lesson is the differential factor. If a student is highly motivated to learn to count money but is having a difficult time attending to lessons on place value, the teacher should take advantage of the student's interest. Place value concepts can easily be taught in the context of monetary values. In other cases, students might be more attentive to math lessons involving a manipulative rather than written response. The student might have an increased attention span when using the abacus, rather than paper and pencil, to solve subtraction problems.

The use of microcomputers, calculators, and electronic games can capitalize on student interest; they offer an alternative for students who have difficulty attending to paper and pencil tasks. Microcomputers and calculators are discussed in more detail later in the chapter. An example of an electronic game that can capture the attention of students is Little Professor (Texas Instruments). It presents math problems in addition, subtraction, multiplication, and division on four levels of difficulty. It contains 50,000 preprogrammed problems and is accompanied by an activity book of math games. A major advantage of computer and electronic games is that they typically provide immediate feedback on the correctness of answers. Such feedback encourages students to maintain attention to their work.

Other strategies can be used to provide feedback and, consequently, to increase attention. Students can check their own work by using calculators, or peer tutors can help to provide frequent feedback. Lambie (1980) suggests another strategy for providing feedback:

> The teacher writes the answers directly in the workbook or text in yellow ink. Before looking at the page, the student places a transparent red plastic sheet, like a theme cover, over it, which neutralizes the answers. The student writes answers on a separate sheet of paper one at a time, after which he or she unmasks the correct answers to see if they match. This is a fairly quick and easy process when only a few students and books are involved (p. 8).

Concept Development

A significant component of math instruction for handicapped students is the development of concepts and problem-solving skills. Because of many handicapped students' learning problems, teachers sometimes believe that these students are incapable of higher level conceptualization leading to problem solving. This is an unfounded assumption. Handicapped students can understand higher-order concepts and solve problems if they are systematically taught these skills. The math problems of handicapped students often relate to the facts that computation and problem solving were taught before the students developed the foundation for understanding numbers (Hammill & Bartel, 1978) or that instruction was based on rote learning. Piaget (1952) has described concepts central to the development of understanding numbers. These concepts are briefly described in Table 7–5 with an example of an instructional activity for each concept.

It is essential that handicapped children master these basic concepts, which are precursors to higher-order math functioning. Many problems will arise later if this developmental foundation is weak. In teaching these basic concepts, teachers should start with activities employing real objects and opportunities

TABLE 7-5. Piagetian Concepts and Instructional Activities

CONCEPTS	ACTIVITY
1. Classification Grouping objects according to distinguishing characteristics	1. Group objects of different shapes, verbally identifying the shape of each.
2. One-to-One Correspondence Recognizing the relationship that one object in a given set is the same number as one object in a different set, regardless of dissimilar characteristics.	2. Match each ball in a set of three balls with a bat in a set of three bats.
3. Seriation Ordering objects according to a distinguishing characteristic, such as size, weight, or color.	3. Order Cuisenaire rods (discussed later in the chapter) according to height.
4. Conservation The number of objects in a set remains constant regardless of the arrangement of the objects.	4. Make two identical balls of play dough. Have the student roll one out into a "rope" and state whether the objects contain the same amount of play dough.
5. Reversibility Objects in a set, regardless of their rearrangement, can be returned to their original position without changing their relationship.	5. Pictorially depict the following equations with plastic chips: $4 + 2 = 6$ $6 - 4 = 2$ $4 + 2 = 6$
6. Developing Number Concepts Associated with Numerals Recognition of the number of objects corresponding to a particular numeral.	6. Place the number of clothespins, corresponding to the numerals, on tagboard cards.

for manipulation, proceed to the use of pictures, and finally work toward the more abstract level of paper and pencil and verbal responses. Initial introduction should also include a minimum of objects or distinguishing elements and move gradually to more complexity as the student's concept development increases.

Cawley and Vitello (1972) have developed a comprehensive model specifying components of the math instructional system for handicapped students. The four major units included in the model are learning set, interactive, verbal information processing, and conceptual processing. The interactive unit includes an excellent framework for teachers to use in developing instruction for handicapped students (Smith, 1974). First, the unit is divided into sections: input (the teacher) and output (the student). These sections can be categorized into three cells: do, see, and say. Table 7–6 illustrates math programming according to all the combinations of presenting and responding to curriculum content.

The "do" level basically involves manipulation of objects and pictures in tasks employing constructing, ordering, arranging, and other similar skills. The "see" level involves responding to pictures or a visual model by pointing or marking. The "say" level emphasizes spoken or written language. As depicted in Table 7–6, there are nine combinations of these cells. This model can be a helpful guide in teaching concepts to handicapped students. Generally, the sequence of difficulty is from the "do-do" combination (the easiest level) to "see-see," and finally to "say-say."

The following activities related to teaching place value and multiplication concepts, which are often areas of particular difficulty for handicapped students, illustrate the "do," "see," and "say" levels of instruction for student output.

Place Value

"Do"

1. Use the abacus to represent numbers by moving the correct number of beads illustrating values of the one's and ten's places.
2. Have students make a place-value box or chart with compartments representing the one's, ten's, and hundred's places. Sort the appropriate number of plastic chips, straws, sticks, or other small objects into the compartments to represent numerical values.

"See"

1. The teacher or peer tutor presents the student with two bundles of ten sticks each (on the left) and three individual sticks (on the right). The student is asked to point to the numeral on a worksheet that has the same number of tens and ones as represented by the sticks: 29   23   32.
2. The teacher or peer tutor calls out a number between 11 and 19. The student points to the number of dimes and pennies that represents the numerical value.

"Say"

1. A game is played in which one student describes a number by stating how many hundreds, tens, and ones. Other students must call out the number that corresponds to the description.
2. Cards are flashed with numbers having two or three digits. The teacher or peer tutor ask various questions, such as, "Which number is in the one's place?" Students must respond verbally.

TABLE 7-6. The Interactive Unit of Cawley's Arithmetic Program

	DO	SEE	SAY
INPUT			
OUTPUT			

EXAMPLES OF EACH OF THE NINE POSSIBLE COMBINATIONS:

MODE COMBINATION			
INPUT	OUTPUT	TEACHER BEHAVIOR ILLUSTRATED	STUDENT BEHAVIOR ILLUSTRATED
Do	Do	The teacher has three toy cars and three balls. She says, "Watch me." She groups the three toy cars into a set and the three balls into another set. She says, "Now you do what I did."	The child has the same kind and number of toy cars and balls. He is expected to group the objects into two sets similar to his teacher's groups.
Do	See	The teacher lays seven pieces of string on a table. All of the pieces are of the same color and texture, three are five inches shorter than the other four, all of which are the same size. She separates the three short ones from the four longer ones—making two sets.	The child is shown four pictures, only one of which contains two sets. The child is asked to point to the picture that is like the display which the teacher constructed.
Do	Say	The teacher combines three sets of blocks, each of which contains two blocks.	The child is asked to write the algorithm that describes what was done and to solve the problem.
See	Do	The teacher presents the following stimulus to the child: 8 − □ = 6	With a group of blocks, the child is asked to solve the problem by stacking the number of blocks that belong in the box.
See	See	The teacher presents the following problem: 3 + 2 − 1 =	The child is asked to point to the correct response among the following alternatives: 5 1 2 4 6 0

251

TABLE 8-2. (Continued)
EXAMPLES OF EACH OF THE NINE POSSIBLE COMBINATIONS:

MODE COMBINATION

INPUT	OUTPUT	TEACHER BEHAVIOR ILLUSTRATED	STUDENT BEHAVIOR ILLUSTRATED
See	Say	The child is presented with the following stimulus and asked to tell what time it is: (clock showing 3:00)	
Say	Do	The teacher says to the class, "With your Cuisenaire Rods, prove that 6 + 2 is the same as 4 + 4 and that both are different from 5 + 4."	The children manipulate the rods so that they have a combination of rods for each of the three algorithms. They place the three groups side-by-side to prove the relationships which the teacher requested.
Say	See	The teacher presents the following problem in written form: "Bill has four dogs, Bertha has two cats, and Mark has a hamster. How many more animals does Bill have than Bertha and Mark together?"	The child points to one of the following alternatives: 7 1 3 5 2
Say	Say	The teacher says, "How many ways can you think of to make six?"	The child responds verbally with as many ways as he can generate.

Source: From Smith, Robert M. *Clinical teaching: Methods of instruction for the retarded.* New York: McGraw-Hill Book Co., 1974. Reprinted by permission of the publisher.

Multiplication

"Do"

1. Arrange poker chips to find the answer and understand the concept of 4 fives.
2. If the student already understands basic monetary relationships, arrange the combination with coins (two nickels equal one dime) to illustrate that 2 fives equal 10.

"See"

1. The teacher presents the student with various cards representing domino patterns. The student points to the cards representing the concept of 3 twos.
2. The teacher presents strips with sets depicted, such as . . . . The student points to the correct number of sets that indicate the value of 3 threes.

"Say"

1. A card game similar to Go Fishing is played. The student asks for a card by indicating the multiplication combination, such as 4 ones. The student being asked must respond by stating the correct answer, as well as by indicating whether or not he has the card.
2. Flashcards can be used with peer tutors or among small groups of students to reinforce combinations, after understanding of multiplication concepts has been mastered.

Some students are unable to receive or respond to information in certain ways. Blind students cannot perform at the "see" level; therefore, teachers should capitalize on "do" and "say." Orthopedically handicapped students unable to use their hands and arms may be blocked in the output responses of the "do" channel, but they are fully capable of benefiting from instruction with the "see" and "say" combinations. On the other hand, deaf students might favor "do" and "see" approaches rather than "say."

Teachers should also consider that students able to receive or respond to information at all levels may have preferred methods of learning. Some students respond to one approach more successfully than another or benefit from a combination of approaches. This model can capitalize on the strengths and minimize the weaknesses of the handicapped student and can help teachers greatly in programming math and analyzing classroom tasks.

Another area of conceptualization is verbal problem solving or "word problems." Handicapped students should be taught verbal problem solving in conjunction with computational and process skills. Additionally, verbal problem solving should accompany skill development in the areas of money, time, and measurement. When problem solving is sequenced according to the skill hierarchy, it becomes an integral aspect of the math curriculum. One way to organize this instruction is to compile an index file of word problems keyed according to the sequential order of skills. Problems can be written in different colors to depict the various skill levels. For example, see the sequence in Table 7–7.

The teacher or a volunteer can prepare five to ten cards, with one problem per card, at each level of difficulty. Answers can be put on a separate card to provide for self-correcting. This type of system encourages individualization and independence, since the student can proceed without the teacher's always having to find word problems at the appropriate level. For handicapped students unable to read, the problems can be put on a cassette tape, or a peer

TABLE 7-7. Skill Sequence of Math Problems

SKILL	COLOR	PROBLEM
1. Basic facts—sums 0 to 5	Red	1. Mary has two books. Bill has three books. How many books do Mary and Bill have all together?
2. Basic facts—sums 6 to 10	Yellow	2. There are six girls and three boys in the class. How many children are there in all?
3. Column addition—three addends	Green	3. Jane has three apples. Joe has four apples and Sam has four apples. How many apples do Jane, Joe, and Sam have all together?
4. Two-digit and one-digit addition without carrying	Blue	4. There are 22 pennies in Sally's bank. She puts 5 more pennies in the bank. What is the total number of pennies in Sally's bank?
5. Column addition with three two-digit numbers without carrying	Orange	5. Jay earned 12 stars, Amy earned 11 stars, and Kate earned 16 stars. Find the sum of the stars the children earned all together.
6. Three-digit and one-digit addition without carrying	Brown	6. There are 112 seats in the auditorium. Six more chairs can be placed in front of the stage. What is the total number of people who can be seated in the auditorium?

tutor can read the problems to the student. The peer tutor or a volunteer can also prepare the tapes.

Another strategy for teaching problem solving is to develop learning activity packets (LAPs) as described in chapter 4. The LAPs can be programmed so that real objects or pictures are available for students to manipulate as they solve the problems. The reference dictionary (described in the next section) can be used to help handicapped students focus on cues that help indicate the appropriate process to use in solving a word problem (e.g., find the sum; how much all together?). Goodstein (1973) warns against teachers' promoting mechanical rather than conceptual understanding by teaching the student to scan the word problem for cue words. Teaching word cues should be incorporated in the total process of teaching comprehension of verbal problems. Teaching problem comprehension should include an instructional sequence that: uses problems with extraneous information; categorizes information as a step in problem solving; uses problems with more than one operation involved; and leaves out essential information and has the student identify the necessary missing elements. Again, successful problem-solving instruction must proceed from the simple to the complex in a step-by-step fashion.

Calculators and microcomputers are excellent resources to use in teaching problem solving. Frequently, such technological aids are considered appropriate only to provide drill and practice for students; however, they can greatly assist students in developing problem-solving skills. Calculators allow students to solve problems that they might otherwise avoid because of the computation demands. Some handicapped students may not have the computation skills to complete the problems; other students may have writing problems that interfere with their ability to complete long computations by hand. Since calculators now cost less than ten dollars, their use is generally affordable for handicapped students and adults.

Calculators have been used successfully with handicapped students. Russell (1982) reported on a research study that involved teaching mentally retarded students at the elementary level to solve problems in addition, subtraction, and multiplication. Besides learning to use the calculator, other positive results occurred:

> The motivation and interest level shown by the students was very high as was expected. They were eager to receive their problems each day. The tapes showed that students often worked problems several times. When asked about this, they responded that it was "fun" to use the machines. (p. 6)

Russell described two types of difficulties encountered by the students. The first difficulty was forgetting to clear the calculator after each calculation. Repeated instructions were necessary to eliminate this operational error. The second area of difficulty was failure to estimate the correct answer to a problem.

When students failed to clear the calculator and their answers were totally unrealistic, they rarely recognized their mistakes. Russell stresses the need to teach students "to check answers for reasonableness and sensibility" (p. 6).

In selecting and purchasing calculators for handicapped students, several features are important. Students with learning problems generally benefit if print-out tapes are available; their problem-solving steps can be checked by the teacher or a peer tutor. Calculators with large, well-spaced keys are easier for students with coordination problems to use. Finally, for partially sighted students, the read-out display must be large and clearly legible. A calculator that talks (speech+) is available for visually impaired students (Wieck, 1980). Such a calculator would also be helpful for students who function better with auditory input.

Computers have also been used successfully in teaching problem-solving skills to handicapped students (Beck, 1982; Burns & Bozeman, 1981). The outcomes of two programs (LOGO and PLATO) with handicapped students were reviewed in chapter 4. Another computer program aimed at mathematical problem solving is available from Milton Bradley (Robin, 1982). Developed for use with the Apple II microcomputer, this package has three math units for grades six to eight. The math units are division skills, mixed numbers, and decimal skills. Four language units are also available.

Memory

Attention and concept development are necessary ingredients of memory. In order to remember, a student must first actively attend; therefore, the strategies to aid attention included in the previous sections also apply to memory improvement. Memory is greatly enhanced if the material to be learned is meaningful. Math concepts become meaningful as they are understood through systematic instruction programmed at the "do," "see," and "say" levels. Many memory problems associated with math are eliminated, therefore, when students selectively pay attention to the relevant cues and fully understand the concepts.

Memorization plays a vital role in mathematics proficiency. Number recognition, rote counting, basic facts, time equivalents, measurements tables, and monetary relationships are only a few of the math areas that require some kind of memorization to attain mastery. Many handicapped students are at a disadvantage in remembering information. As pointed out in chapter 1, strategies that systematically improve the memory skills of handicapped students can be used.

One fundamental aspect of the math curriculum is memorizing the basic facts in addition, subtraction, multiplication, and division. It is generally preferable for handicapped students to memorize the combinations of the basic facts after prerequisite concepts have been mastered. Ineffective instruction

Instructional Approaches

and lack of motivation on the part of handicapped students have often caused them to be excused from learning the basic facts. In many cases, these students are capable of mastering this memorization requirement. However, memorization should only occur *after* the student demonstrates an understanding of the basic number concepts described by Piaget as necessary for math proficiency and the concepts integrally associated with the computation of facts and processes (e.g., associative and communicative operations). Emphasis should be placed first on adequate concept development and then on memorization.

The beginning point of instruction in memorizing the basic facts is assessment. If the student is working on addition, the pretest should include all combinations of the basic facts. The pretest can be either written or oral, and the student should be instructed to answer only those problems known immediately. Each student's level of performance should be recorded, since the particular combination of facts mastered and not mastered will vary from student to student.

After the teacher has identified which facts are known and which must be learned, the student's preferred methods of learning the facts should be established. The teacher might consider a variety of methods at the "do," "see," and "say" levels, including counting objects, using the abacus, using the number line, counting on fingers, using card games, playing electronic games, practicing on the calculator, drilling with fact cards, or drilling with records. Some students respond to one particular approach whereas others benefit from a combination. To identify preferred learning styles, the teacher should experiment by assigning the student a specified number of facts to learn and a particular method of practice. Based on the student's performance and expressed preferences, the teacher can document effective strategies.

Several considerations are important in teaching various counting systems. A major factor is that some handicapped students may not ever master rote memorization; therefore, it is important to use a system that will not stigmatize them in upper grades or adult life if they need to continue using it. Seeing a handicapped adult counting on his fingers to compute in a checkbook while standing in line at the bank is evidence of the importance of this consideration related to social acceptability. A method that has demonstrated effectiveness with handicapped students (Kokaska, 1973; Kramer & Krug, 1973) is counting fixed reference points on numerals, as illustrated here.

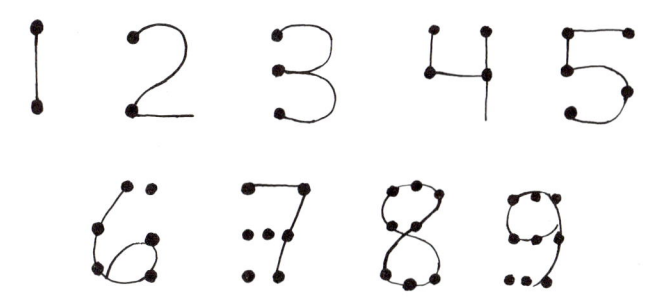

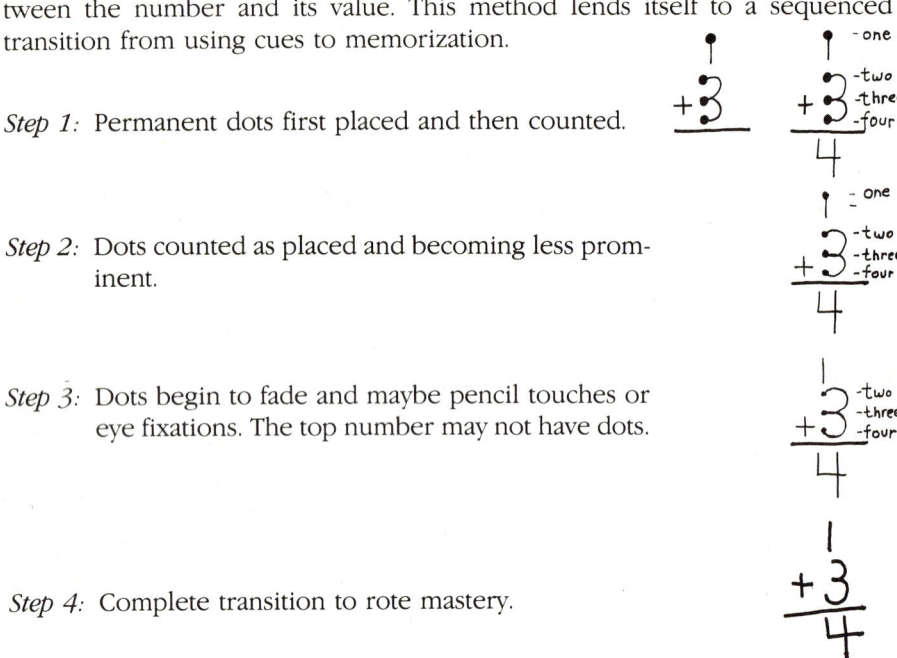

Kramer and Krug (1973) state the advantages of using this system as providing consistency in perception of the numbers and the immediate association between the number and its value. This method lends itself to a sequenced transition from using cues to memorization.

Step 1: Permanent dots first placed and then counted.

Step 2: Dots counted as placed and becoming less prominent.

Step 3: Dots begin to fade and maybe pencil touches or eye fixations. The top number may not have dots.

Step 4: Complete transition to rote mastery.

After the student's method of learning the facts has been identified, the teacher should determine the student's rate of learning facts. Some handicapped students can learn five or six new facts a day; others have a rate of one or two facts per week. To establish learning rate, the teacher can use the following procedure:

1. Make an educated guess in assigning the student a certain number of facts to learn during a daily math lesson.
2. Use practice methods already identified as successful for the student. Remember that some students need more drill than others.
3. Evaluate the student on the assigned facts at the end of the day and at the end of the week. The number of basic facts learned per day, which the student successfully completes on the evaluation at the end of the week, becomes the student's daily learning rate.

When learning rate has been established, the student should be assigned that specified number of facts daily for practice and drill. Facts may have to be adjusted up or down based on the student's performance. The goal is for the handicapped student to master as many facts as possible while working at a success level. If the student consistently misses a number of problems on the weekly mastery test, then the learning rate is too high, the method of instruction is inadequate, or the student is not approaching the task conscientiously. Students can keep records of their progress, graphing the number of problems they learn each week and keeping charts of the particular combinations they learn. In this way, the reinforcement procedure (graphing and charting) for memorizing the basic facts provides an opportunity to learn different math skills.

The probability that handicapped students will learn the basic facts increases greatly when the instruction is geared to the student's level of achievement, preferred learning styles, and rate of learning. The students' awareness of their continuous and consistent progress often provides renewed impetus to master math skills. These same principles of programming memorization of basic facts apply to other aspects of the math curriculum requiring memory skills, such as measurement tables and monetary relationships.

A very successful strategy used with handicapped students is the development of a reference dictionary (Scott, 1968), which is basically a compilation of sheets including examples or referents representing the instructional objectives on which the student is working. The reference dictionary is continually updated as the student progresses from one objective to the next, and it covers approximately twenty days of work at any given point. The sheets can be bound in a notebook or folder. The purpose of the dictionary is to provide a reference model for the student to maximize success on tasks covering the total academic program. In the area of mathematics, the reference dictionary can be a tremendous aid in ameliorating memory deficits of handicapped students. Examples of math skills and corresponding sheets that the teacher or volunteer can develop for the reference dictionary are itemized in Table 7–8.

When handicapped students can refer to an easily accessible guide when they do not remember necessary information to complete a problem or assignment, their independent work habits and overall task success are promoted. The reference dictionary is also an excellent source of review when the student finishes an assignment early or has free time. Essentially, this strategy insures that the students have information they need so that they do not have to rely totally on memory. Some teachers may believe they are being too easy on the student by providing a ready source of reference material and correct answers for the students as they need it, but this viewpoint is pedagogically unsupportable. Programming for success is a characteristic of excellent instruction, not leniency. In addition to reducing the detrimental educational implications of memory problems, the reference dictionary can be a source of reinforcement for the student. As the handicapped learners master the various concepts included in the dictionary representative of instructional objectives, they can underline the concept with a colored magic marker. Generally, students not only enjoy indicating their successes, but they also have "visual proof" of the progress they are making. In the area of basic facts, for example, good feelings on the part of the student and parents are practically assured when the goal of underlining *every* addition or subtraction fact in the dictionary has been

CHAPTER 7 Teaching Mathematics

TABLE 7-8. Examples of Math Skills for Reference Dictionary

SKILLS	REFERENCE DICTIONARY SHEETS
1. Basic facts	1. A sheet with the facts and answers that a student is in the process of mastering.
2. Monetary relationships	2. One nickel = five pennies One dime = ten pennies (Could be written or in pictorial form. Real coins could also be taped to sheet to depict relationships.)
3. Time concepts	2 o'clock
4. Computational processes	4. $\begin{array}{r}2{\mid}6\\+1{\mid}5\\-{\mid}-\end{array}$ Visual prompt for setting up and solving an addition problem.
5. Symbols of metric units	5. mg—milligram g—gram kg—kilogram
6. Word problem clues	6. Clues to knowing when to add: a. What is sum? b. How many all together?

accomplished. Thus, the dictionary can be the basis of on-going record keeping and reinforcement.

A final benefit is that the dictionary can be a vehicle for coordinating the instructional programs of the resource and regular classrooms. The resource teacher might initially set up the dictionary based on the math assessment and give the student assignments requiring the use of the dictionary while in the regular classroom. Again, the dictionary facilitates independent work, since the student has the information needed to complete problems successfully. While nonhandicapped peers are working on other math objectives, the handicapped student can proceed individually. Individualization, in turn, becomes more of a reality in the regular classroom.

Other strategies are effective in increasing the memory of handicapped students. Memory is enhanced when skills and concepts are meaningful to the student. It can be very difficult to memorize information that is not understood or that seems irrelevant. For example, if the objective is for the student to memorize common metric kitchen measures, handicapped students will probably be more successful if they can use those measures in following recipes and can associate favorite foods prepared or measured with the metric units. This type of experiential instruction promotes a clear understanding of concepts as well as long-term retention. Handicapped students often have difficulty remembering because they do not employ active strategies when confronted with a task requiring memory (Ellis, 1970). This point can be illustrated by examining typical ways in which adults remember new information. When you get to the end of this paragraph, look for approximately eight seconds at the following number. After eight seconds, cover the number in the book and write it from memory on a piece of paper. Ready?

$$8\ 1\ 3\ 5\ 9\ 2\ 7\ 0\ 6$$

The important point to consider is not whether you were 100 percent correct, but what you did to try to help you remember. Think about the strategy you used. Some people tend to group a series of numbers into clusters and remember the clusters as one unit, such as 813, 592, 706. Another strategy is to associate the individual numbers or clusters with something that is meaningful. For example, the first two digits, 81, might be associated with the number on someone's football jersey. Other strategies could involve repeating the numbers to oneself (rehearsing) or picturing them in the mind's eye (imagery).

Whatever the particular strategy, the majority of adults actively try to remember when faced with a memory task. A problem of many students who have learning handicaps is that they do not automatically employ strategies when required to use their memory; however, these students can be taught to be more "active" learners. During math instruction, teachers can help handicapped students by teaching them memory strategies, such as clustering, associating, rehearsing, and imagery. An example of each strategy as it relates to mathematics follows:

Strategy	*Example*
1. Clustering	1. Learns social security number by grouping digits into three separate units.
2. Associating	2. Learns the number of days in each month by association with the verse "Thirty Days Has September."

3. Rehearsing	3. Learns to repeat the sequence of solving a problem, such as:
	     16 Work from right to left
	    × 3 Multiply in one's column first
	             Cross-multiply in ten's column
	             Double-check

4. Imagery	4. If a student cannot remember how to form the number 8, she can refer to her reference dictionary and then close her eyes and visualize the 8 and the kinesthetic motions required to form an 8.

In teaching the aspects of the math curriculum that involve memory, the teacher should work toward overlearning with handicapped students (Gearheart, 1976). This often means that a substantial amount of practice and drill is required for students to gain solid proficiency. Once overlearning has occurred, handicapped students are capable of long-term retention. Some teachers have the erroneous impression that teaching handicapped students is a hopeless task, because these students cannot remember information over a long period of time. The teacher may believe, for example, that the students will forget the basic facts learned in one day when a couple of weeks have passed. When this type of forgetting occurs, it means that the students did not attain total proficiency in the first place. If handicapped students are provided with sufficient practice and drill during the memorization process, they are generally capable of long-term retention.

One final consideration is that every handicapped student will not attain proficiency in memorizing math skills and concepts. Some students are at a greater disadvantage relative to memory than others. When students have particular difficulty, it is important to help them compensate for or work around this problem. The notation system—using fixed reference points on numbers—is one strategy applicable to continued use. Another strategy is to use a pocket calculator. In addition to their use for concept development, as previously discussed, they can also be used to compute the basic facts. Other classroom uses are for drill and self-checking. An important consideration for handicapped students is that adult use of a calculator is more socially acceptable than many other counting systems.

Generalization

The generalization of math skills to everyday living experiences is particularly crucial for handicapped students, yet it is often overlooked. The competency testing program implemented in many states, however, is focusing major emphasis on the development of life-role and functional skills (Linde & Olsen, 1980). Because handicapped students need a significant amount of drill to master basic facts and processes, teachers sometimes provide one worksheet after another of isolated computation and fail to help the students make the generalization between the computation and the demands encountered in everyday living. Since some handicapped students are at a disadvantage in making generalizations, the math skills and concepts may not carry over into needed situations.

Teachers can help students to generalize math skills by providing meaningful instruction related to experiences that the student has already encountered or is likely to encounter. Teaching the math content in areas of money, time, and measurement in a relevant context is easy to accomplish. An excellent strategy for teaching the generalization of money skills is to set up a school or classroom store (Schulz, 1973). The students learn skills related to the cost of food and other products, making change, sales tax, special sales, budgeting, record keeping, reading newspaper advertisements, writing checks, and occupational awareness. Thus, students have the immediate opportunity to use math and related skills in a relevant context representing everyday living demands.

Another consideration in teaching for generalization is that the skills learned in one situation must be transferable to another. An unfortunate example highlighting the importance of this consideration happened to Billy, a mentally retarded elementary student:

> *A major objective in Billy's math curriculum was learning to tell time. Billy, his teacher, and his parents all worked very hard providing a great deal of practice for him to learn this important skill. Realizing how hard he was working, his grandparents promised him a new watch when he had accomplished his goal of telling time. Finally, when mastery had been accomplished, Billy received the watch in the mail with great anticipation. He tried to tell his parents the time from his new watch, but he was at a complete loss. The watch had Roman rather than Arabic numerals, and the skills he had worked so hard to accomplish were not immediately transferable.*

This problem illustrates what often happens to handicapped students; yet, it can be significantly minimized as teachers realize the importance of applying newly acquired skills in a variety of ways. Billy's teacher and parents might go back and help him generalize his time-telling skills to clocks with Roman numerals, digital clocks, clocks with no numerals, and clocks representing a variety of shapes, sizes, and types. In this way, generalization can be enhanced.

When handicapped students are learning basic facts and computational processes, it is important for them to use these skills in an experiential context. As each level of increasing skill difficulty is introduced, generalization to everyday situations should be made. Many teachers tend to wait to introduce experiential problems until after a large portion of the facts and processes skills have been learned. This results in the mechanical use of these skills for a long period of time, leading to difficulty when the skills have to be applied in the form of "word problems." Emphasis on generalization should be an integral part of the *introduction* of math skills, as well as a consistent part of practice leading to mastery.

Delayed Language

Students with delayed language development can be at a disadvantage in math as well as in language arts. Regardless of whether the language delay is attributable to mental retardation, a learning disability, or a hearing impairment, teachers can help students minimize this problem. One strategy is for the teacher to use a consistent mathematics vocabulary. Rather than using all the terms, such as *regrouping, renaming,* and *carrying,* to refer to the same concept, the handicapped student's confusion can be reduced by using only one label (Lowenbraun & Affleck, 1976). In the area of telling time, confusion can result from referring to 8:45 as "quarter 'til," "quarter to," "15 minutes before," or "8:45." Consistency in terminology is important.

Teachers should encourage handicapped students to tell them when they do not understand the language used in a classroom discussion or in assignment directions. Students are more likely to let teachers know when they need clarification if teachers respond positively to their requests and not with exasperation. When students do not understand particular vocabulary words or language structures, teachers should systematically teach these language concepts. The fact that handicapped students are deficient in an area is no indication that they cannot significantly improve their skills with sound instruction. Therefore, teachers should not drop the use of language that handicapped students do not understand; rather, they should include language skills related to math as part of the curriculum.

The reference dictionary can be used to minimize language disadvantages. Vocabulary lists related to various math objectives can be kept in the dictionary, with pictures or written definitions, depending on the student's achievement level, to explain the meaning of the word or concept. In the area of time, the vocabulary list might include clock, hour hand, minute hand, o'clock, 30 minutes after, before, second, sixty, A.M., P.M., and many others. When the handicapped students hear the word in class or read it in an assignment and are unsure of the meaning, they can look it up in the dictionary. As vocabulary lists are mastered, more difficult ones can be introduced.

Some handicapped students with language delays benefit more from visual prompts or demonstrations than from lengthy verbal explanations. In teaching the student how to set up a division problem, the teacher might work several examples to provide the student with a model format, such as,

$$8\overline{)66} \quad \quad \square\overline{)37}$$
$$\underline{6\ 4} \qquad\qquad \square\ \square$$
$$2\ R \qquad\qquad \square\ R$$

and/or provide a simply stated procedural outline for solving the problem. The emphasis of math programming might be on the "do" and "see" levels of instruction rather than the "say" for students with language delays.

Fine Motor Problems

Handicapped students with fine motor problems may encounter difficulty in math in making written responses and manipulating objects during instruction.

Students who have significant writing deficiencies are probably going to have difficulty learning to form numerals and engaging in written requirements involved during mathematics instruction in most regular classes. When numerals are initially introduced, it may be helpful for the student to start making large numerals on the chalkboard and on pieces of newsprint and gradually reducing the size of the numerals on notebook paper. Students might trace stencils of numerals and use visual prompts that could gradually be faded:

Some students benefit from physical guidance—actual help in moving their pencil in the desired direction. If writing interferes with the student's ability to demonstrate an understanding of math skills, the teacher could allow opportunities for oral tests, with the student responding directly to the teacher or peer tutor, or using a tape recorder. The use of microcomputers and typewriters for completing assignments are alternatives. Students with fine motor problems may be very slow in completing their work, and writing will probably be more fatiguing for them than for their peers. One easy way to implement adaptation is simply to shorten the length of an assignment.

The other major mathematics consideration for students with fine motor problems is that they may not be able to use some instructional materials involving manipulation adequately (e.g., Cuisenaire rods). If students do not have the necessary coordination to pick up small objects, teachers should use alternate methods of instruction.

Instructional Materials

Only a limited number of math instructional materials have been developed specifically for handicapped students; however, many instructional materials developed primarily for nonhandicapped populations are also useful with handicapped students. In selecting materials, teachers must match the instructional objective and the student's learning characteristics with the particular instructional materials. Since students respond differently to various instructional materials, a major component of individualization is matching the students with their material preferences. No two students, handicapped or nonhandicapped, are exactly alike in their instructional needs. A brief overview of some of the math materials suitable for handicapped students follows. For additional information on materials, readers are referred to Matulis (1981) and Van Etten and Watson (1978).

Stern Structural Arithmetic. *Structural Arithmetic* was designed particularly for handicapped students and covers kindergarten through third-grade levels. It is a sequenced program using concrete materials to teach number relationships and math processes. A teacher's guide and mastery tests are included in the program. Houghton Mifflin Co.

Sullivan Programmed Math. This programmed series of workbooks emphasizes the development of computational skills. It requires minimal reading and has progress tests and a teacher's manual. Webster Division, McGraw-Hill Book Co.

Distar Arithmetic. Distar is a highly structured and sequential program covering kindergarten to third grade. It covers basic math facts, processes, and fractions. The program strongly emphasizes a verbal approach. Science Research Associates, Inc.

The Learning Skills Series. This series of four workbooks was specifically designed for handicapped students at the junior high level. Prevocational skills are emphasized with content on facts and processes, as well as skills related to reading road maps, newspaper ads, recipes, and thermometers. The four workbooks are correlated so that they are appropriate for four different achievement levels. Webster Division, McGraw-Hill Book Co.

Sequential Mathematics. Developed specifically for handicapped students, this individualized program covers skill development in basic facts and processes (addition, subtraction, multiplication, and division). The major components of the program include a diagnostic test, activity segments, mixed practice, and word problems. It is highly sequential, focuses on one skill at a time, and eliminates distracting elements from workbooks. A teacher's guide is available. Harcourt Brace Jovanovich, Inc.

Cuisenaire Rods. Cuisenaire rods are made of wood and vary in length from one to ten centimeters. They are useful in teaching manipulative and conceptual skills from kindergarten through sixth-grade levels. They emphasize a visual and tactile approach to learning. Cuisenaire Company of America, Inc.

Developmental Learning Materials. A wide variety of mathematics aids and games is available, such as clock puzzles, fraction puzzles, money dominoes, sorting box and game, and a multiplication game. The materials are highly motivating, durably constructed, and cover a grade span of kindergarten through upper elementary school. Developmental Learning Materials.

Pacemaker Arithmetic Program. This program, designed for students with learning problems, includes student worksheets on carbon masters covering readiness skills (shape recognition, quantitative concepts, and basic vocabulary) and number concepts through ten. A teacher's manual is included. Fearon Publishers.

The Six Wonderful Records of Facts. These records present addition, subtraction, multiplication, and division facts at presentation rates of both six and four and one-half seconds. The facts are divided into easier and harder sections. John D. Caddy.

I'm OK, You're OK: Let's Go Metric. This workbook includes metric activities covering linear, area, volume, temperature, liquid, and weight skills. Activities are programmed at four reading levels ranging from no skills required to high levels. Midwest Publications Co., Inc.

Clockface with Raised Print and Braille Numbers. This plastic frame clock has both raised numerals and braille numerals on its face as an aid in teaching blind children to tell time. The hands are attached to gears inside the frame so that the hour hand follows the minute hand in proper sequence. American Printing House for the Blind.

Metric-English One-Foot Braille Rulers with Caliper Slides. With the purpose of teaching the relationship between metric and English systems of measurement, raised lines and braille numbers indicate one inch, one-fourth inch, one centimeter, and one-half centimeter intervals. American Printing House for the Blind.

Abacuses. The Crammer abacus is a pocket-sized device that can be used to teach math facts and processes. It has one bead above the bar and four beads below. An enlarged abacus is also available that is easier to manipulate for students who have fine motor problems. Additionally, two instructional books in both braille and large print can be ordered. American Printing House for the Blind.

Calculator Activity Book. A wide selection of activities and games for elementary and junior high students is available in this guidebook. Illustrative of the mathematics operations and concepts included are multiplication, division, square roots, fractions, and decimals. Estimation skills and word problems are also included. Educational Teaching Aids.

Veri Tech Math Lab. Two labs are available at the primary and intermediate levels. A teacher's guide, exercise booklets, and record-keeping charts covering the areas of addition, subtraction, multiplication, division, money, time, measurement, and metrics comprise the labs. Novel self-checking procedures are incorporated. Educational Teaching Aids.

Speak and Math. For grades one through six, this electronic learning aid is programmed with 100,000 mathematical problems in addition, subtraction, multiplication, and division. Word problems and beginning concepts in geometry and algebra are also included. Fast-paced problem solving, praise for correct answers, and encouragement after mistakes are strong features. Earphones for individual practice enable its use in classrooms without disrupting peers. Texas Instruments.

Fundamental Mathematics Drill and Practice Program. This computer software program includes 450 lessons ranging from basic number concepts to prealgebra. It is designed for use with students in grades one through nine. Random House.

The Math Machine. This computer software program provides drill and practice in addition, subtraction, multiplication, and division. A helpful feature is a monitoring system for student progress. Southwest Educational and Psychological Service.

Guidebooks for Teachers

Plus. This book contains dozens of activities, games, and independent work ideas in areas of counting, time, facts, numbers, money, fractions, and others. Educational Service, Inc.

Kids' Stuff Math. This guidebook of ideas covers areas of numeration, sets, fractions, problem solving, and others. Incentive Publications.

Activities Handbook for Teaching the Metric System. Classroom activities in the areas of linear measurement, volume and capacity, area and perimeter, temperature, and mass are included, as well as a basic introduction to the metric system. Allyn and Bacon, Inc.

Math Activities for Children: A Diagnostic and Developmental Approach. Based on the work of Piaget, this book provides sixty-two activities for teachers in the areas of classification, number, space orientation, measurement, knowing versus performing, mathematical memory, and chance and probability. Each activity incorporates an easy-to-follow format with the components of purpose, materials, procedure, levels of performance, and teaching implications. Charles E. Merrill Publishing Co.

Mainstreaming Science and Mathematics: Special Ideas and Activities for the Whole Class. Weekly lesson plans for thirty-six mathematical concepts are included. These concepts include early primary ones (e.g., recognizing and using numerals, learning to count) as well as survival topics appropriate for the junior high level (e.g., understanding banking, forecasting weather). The book is highly practical and presents activities in a succinct fashion. Goodyear Publishing Co., Inc.

The Mathworks: Handbook of Activities for Helping Students Learn Mathematics. This book is written by classroom teachers for other teachers of kindergarten through eighth grade. It includes a description of 223 activities (45 of which are identified as particularly beneficial for handicapped students) in twelve different strands. Examples of strands include spatial relationships, place value, geometry, calculator, and problem solving. Creative Publications.

Guidebook for Parents

Telepac. These programmed workbooks were developed specifically to aid parents in teaching basic math skills to their handicapped child. Two areas included are number symbols and counting. Exceptional Child Center UMC–68.

(Addresses for the publishers of these math materials are included in Appendix B.)

REFERENCES

Algozzine, B., & McGraw, K. Diagnostic testing in mathematics: An extension of the PIAT? *Teaching Exceptional Children,* 1979, *12*(2), 71–77.
Beck, J. J., The microcomputer bandwagon: Is it playing your tune? *The Directive Teacher,* 1982, *4*(1), 12–27.
Burns, P. K., & Bozeman, W. C. Computer-assisted instruction and mathematics achievement: Is there a relationship? *Educational Technology,* 1981, *21*(10), 32–39.
Cawley, J. F., & Vitello, S. J. Model for arithmetic programming for handicapped children. *Exceptional Children,* 1972, *39,* 101–110.
Ellis, N. R. Memory processes in retardates and normals. In N. R. Ellis (Ed.), *International review of research in mental retardation* (Vol. 4). New York: Academic Press, 1970.
Fowler, M. A. Why did he miss that problem? *Academic Therapy,* 1978, *14*(1), 23–33.
Gallagher, J. J. Minimum competency: The setting of educational standards. *Education Evaluation and Policy Analysis,* 1979, *1*(1), 62–67.
Gearheart, B. R. *Teaching the learning disabled.* St. Louis, Mo.: C. V. Mosby Co., 1976.
Goodstein, H. A. The performance of educable mentally retarded children on subtraction word problems. *Education and Training of the Mentally Retarded,* 1973, *8,* 197–202.
Hammill, D. D., & Bartel, N. R. *Teaching children with learning and behavior problems* (2nd ed.). Boston: Allyn and Bacon, 1978.
Howell, K. W., & Kaplan, J. S. *Diagnosing basic skills: A handbook for deciding what to teach.* Columbus, Ohio: Charles E. Merrill Publishing Co., 1980.
Kokaska, S. M. A notation system in arithmetic. *Education and Training of the Mentally Retarded,* 1973, *8,* 211–216.

Kramer, T., & Krug, D. A. A rationale and procedure for teaching addition. *Education and Training of the Mentally Retarded,* 1973, *8,* 140–144.

Lambie, R. A. A systematic approach for changing materials, instruction, and assignment to meet individual needs. *Focus on Exceptional Children,* 1980, 12(1), 1–12.

Linde, J. L., & Olsen, K. R. *Minimum competency testing and handicapped students.* Washington, D.C.: Division of Media Services, Bureau of Education for the Handicapped, 1980.

Lowenbraun, S., & Affleck, J. Q. *Teaching mildly handicapped children in regular classes.* Columbus, Ohio: Charles E. Merrill Publishing Co., 1976.

Matulis, R. S. A bibliography of articles on the teaching of mathematics in special education. *Arithmetic Teacher,* 1981, *28*(71), 53–56.

Piaget, J. *The child's conception of numbers.* London: Routledge and Kegan Paul, 1952.

Reisman, F. *A guide to diagnostic teaching of arithmetic.* Columbus, Ohio: Charles E. Merrill Publishing Co., 1972.

Robin, L. Wild about math. *Media and Methods,* 1982, *18,* 6–7.

Russell, B. E. Calculators in the special education classroom. *The Directive Teacher,* 1982, *4*(1), 6 & 11.

Salvia, J., & Ysseldyke, J. E. *Assessment in special and remedial education.* Boston: Houghton Mifflin Co., 1978.

Schulz, J. B. Simulation for special education. *Education and Training of the Mentally Retarded,* 1973, *8,* 137–140.

Scott, F. Personal communication, 1968.

Smith, J. D., & Jenkins, D. S. Minimum competency testing and handicapped students. *Exceptional Children,* 1980, *46*(6), 440–443.

Smith, R. M. *Clinical teaching: Methods of instruction for the retarded.* New York: McGraw-Hill, 1974.

Turnbull, A. P. (Ed.). *Carolina arithmetic inventory.* Chapel Hill, N.C.: Department of Special Education, University of North Carolina, 1976.

Van Etten, C., & Watson, B. Arithmetic skills: Assessment and instruction. *Journal of Learning Disabilities,* 1978, 7(3), 155–162.

Wieck, C. Computer resources: Will educators accept, reject, or neglect the future. *Education Unlimited,* 1980, *2*(3), 24–27.

8

Teaching Social Studies and Science

A professor in elementary education expressed the opinion that most handicapped students have not experienced failure in science because "most elementary teachers don't teach science." The "back to basics" emphasis on reading skills has resulted in a trend to diminish the amount of time devoted to social studies and science instruction for all children (Gross, Messick, Chapin, & Sutherland, 1978). In fact, the Science Education Databook (1981) shows that students in kindergarten through grade six spend an average of twenty minutes per day on science and twenty-five minutes on social studies.

Teachers of handicapped students, in particular, have emphasized skill development in the language arts and mathematics areas. Although this emphasis is justifiable, examination of the goals for social studies and science reveals strong relevance to the integration of handicapped students in the school and community. There is also evidence that other skills, such as social and work skills, are improved through the social studies and science curricula. A third rationale for teaching these subjects is the opportunity for successful participation by handicapped students. The broad scope of these two fields provides a wide choice of goals, activities, methods, and materials to accommodate all learners.

At the elementary level, social studies and science are usually taught by the classroom teacher and the topics can be interrelated with other curricular studies. At the secondary level, however, these disciplines are specialized and the integration of handicapped students is difficult and frustrating for the content teachers. In an effort to provide practical approaches for teachers at all levels, social studies and science are discussed separately, with a summary presenting problems and techniques common to the two curriculum areas.

SOCIAL STUDIES

Social studies is often associated with history, geography, economics, and civics. More fundamentally, social studies education concerns itself with human beings. It is learning about people: ". . . how they govern themselves and provide for their material and psychological needs, how and why they love and hate each other, how they use and misuse the resources of the planet that is their home . . ." (Jarolimek, 1977, p. 4). Social studies is an important part of the education needed by all children if they are to understand their world and lead productive lives in it.

Assessment

The first step in educational planning for handicapped students who require "specially designed instruction" in order to progress successfully in their classes is the development of the IEP (see chapter 3). The teacher responsible for social studies instruction should develop an IEP for each handicapped student, in cooperation with the special education resource teacher, the student's parents, and any other members of the committee responsible for devising the program.

The foundation of the IEP is assessment, which must be completed to identify the student's level of performance in the content area. Standardized cognitive tests in the social studies are listed in Table 8-1.

In addition to commercial tests, teachers often construct their own assessment tools. One method is to specify the major concepts and skills to be covered throughout the year. Many state- and/or system-adopted curriculum

TABLE 8-1. Social Studies Standardized Tests

TEST	GRADE LEVEL	DESCRIPTION	PUBLISHER
Ralph C. Preston and Robert V. Duffey, Primary Social Studies Test	1–3	Tests social studies understanding in primary levels. Requires no reading or writing on part of children.	Houghton Mifflin Co., One Beacon St., Boston, Mass. 02107
Sequential Tests of Progress, Level 4	4–6	Measures understanding and abilities to read and interpret maps, graphs, the printed word, relationships among facts, concepts, and trends.	Educational Testing Service, Princeton, N.J. 08540
Understanding of Basic Social Concepts from the Iowa Tests of Education Development	3–9	Measures understanding of selected concepts in the social studies.	Science Research Associates, 259 Erie St., Chicago, Ill. 60611
The Progressive Tests in Social and Related Sciences, Parts I and II, Elementary Battery, Form A	4–8	Measures knowledge of American heritage, people of other lands and times, geography, and basic social processes.	Bureau of Educational Research and Service, State University of Iowa, Iowa City, Iowa 52240
Metropolitan Achievement Tests in Social Studies	5–5 7–9	Measures general social studies knowledge and skills. Two levels.	Harcourt Brace Jovanovich, Inc. 757 Third Ave., New York, N.Y. 10017

TABLE 8-1. (Continued)

TEST	GRADE LEVEL	DESCRIPTION	PUBLISHER
Nationwide Current Events Examination	4–8	Measures knowledge of current events.	Educational Stimuli, 2012 Hammond Ave., Superior, Wis. 54880
Emporia Geography Test	4–7	Measures knowledge of place locations and other geographical information.	Bureau of Educational Measurements, Kansas State Teachers College, Emporia, Kans. 66801
Modern Geography	6–10	Measures knowledge of vocabulary, economic and human relations, place geography in the United States and the world, and related information.	Same as above

Source: Adapted from TEACHING ELEMENTARY SCHOOL SOCIAL STUDIES by Pearl M. Oliner, © 1976 by Harcourt Brace Jovanovich, Inc. Reprinted by permission of the publisher.

guides provide a comprehensive analysis of the component skills and concepts in the various topical areas the teacher plans to cover. Teachers might consider collecting curriculum guides in social studies from various sources to help with skill and concept specification. Textbooks are also helpful.

After the teacher has identified the general curriculum, which will serve as the core of the social studies program, a test sampling readiness for the content can be given to handicapped students. These tests can be administered orally by a volunteer or teacher aide. The purpose is not to ask every possible question on every topic, but rather to probe the student's level of knowledge in order to determine whether or not the student is ready to progress according to grade level expectations. For example, in the topical area of geography, a major objective might be map-reading skills. The teacher who plans to use a map of the United States may find that a student with learning problems cannot read a map of the United States and, moreover, has no map-reading skills at all. In such a situation, a teacher clearly learns that instruction must start on a much lower level than might have been anticipated. Planning sound instruction means identifying whether or not a student has the necessary prerequisite skills. If the student does not have these skills, they can be incorporated into the student's IEP.

An important assessment is the documentation of the student's reading level in content texts. Johnson and Vardian (1973) analyzed sixty-eight social studies texts from grades one through six to pinpoint readability levels. A startling finding was that intermediate texts had a readability range from two to twelve years. Generally, their findings suggested that many elementary social studies texts have readability levels above grade level expectations. The assessment implication is that the reading level specified in the student's records might not reflect the student's capability to read social studies texts. For example, a student's reading level might be recorded at the low fourth-grade level; however, the fourth-grade social studies text could have a readability level of sixth grade. Based on the student's reading level, the teacher would expect the student to be able to read the text, unless the teacher was aware of the readability level of the book. To assess the student, the teacher can administer an informal reading inventory, using content from the social studies text (Turner, 1976). The procedure for constructing the inventory is identical to that described in chapter 6. The documentation of the student's reading level correlated to the available texts will guide the teacher in planning appropriate instruction.

The final assessment is to identify the student's preferred learning styles. There are several ways to do this. Questionnaires can be used to gain information on students' preferred learning styles. Another strategy is to talk with the student's former teachers, the student's parents, and the student to find the types of learning situations most conducive to successful achievement. This strategy is particularly important when planning instruction for sensory impaired students. Questions might include: What seating arrangement works best? Does the student need large-print books, magnification, taped texts, or braille? Is the hearing-imapired student able to read lips? How can the student be prepared to understand the technical vocabulary of the content area? What is the student's attention span? Does the student have adequate listening comprehension? Does the student have any problems with handwriting? Will language problems interfere with the student's confidence and ability to participate in class discussions and make oral reports?

Another method of answering these questions is through observation. Teachers can use a combination of all three strategies—questionnaires, interviews, and observation—to identify learning styles accurately in order to plan appropriate social studies instruction for the handicapped student.

Goals and Objectives

Jarolimek (1977) presents three categories of goals for social studies. The first involves understandings; the second includes attitudes, values, ideals, and appreciations; and the third deals with skill development.

Understandings. This goal refers to information and concept acquisition. It includes learning about the world, its people and their cultures; the history and growth of the United States; community life; legal and political systems; career orientation; and basic human institutions and social functions that characterize all societies.

Attitudes, Values, Ideals, and Appreciations. Positive attitudes toward oneself and others are particularly relevant in a class containing handicapped students. The social studies curriculum presents an ideal opportunity to deal with the concept of handicapism, developed later in this chapter. It also provides the setting for handicapped students to understand themselves.

Skills. The third goal deals with the development of skills associated with social studies. Jarolimek (1977) delineates four categories of skills: social skills, study skills and work habits, group work skills, and intellectual skills. Since the responsibility for teaching many of these skills overlaps other curriculum areas, social studies can reinforce such skills and provide essential drill for handicapped students. In addition, the social studies provide practical opportunities to use these skills and show pupils how general skills can be applied to a specific subject area. For example, listening, speaking, reading, and writing skills learned in the language arts curriculum are used and developed through discussion and reporting assignments in the social studies.

Instructional approaches in the three categories of social studies goals are presented in the following section.

Instructional Approaches

In planning social studies curricula to include handicapped students, the following considerations are important:

1. Some handicapped students will be able to handle the same curricular content as the non-handicapped students, with specialized materials/arrangements. For instance, visually handicapped students have access to illumination/magnification devices to read standard texts and texts with enlarged type, as well as the use of tactile devices, such as specially developed relief maps. The auditorily handicapped have available to them amplification of sound devices, or special seating, or hearing aids.
2. Many handicapped students and non-handicapped students will learn the same course content and be more motivated to learn if the content is presented in a manner, or through material, that indicates a more relevant or integrated relationship to standard course content. For example, the development of concepts, as a central core of the social studies curriculum, can be effected with an emphasis on project work of thematic learning centers.
3. A number of handicapped students (mildly mentally handicapped and some learning disabled students) may benefit from a prioritization of the standard social studies content at a particular level that may involve the modification of some course content for some individuals. (Herlihy & Herlihy, 1980, p. 45)

Understandings. Based on the needs and abilities of each handicapped student, the teacher must decide what to teach, what to emphasize, and in what sequence. Herlihy and Herlihy (1980) claim that an emphasis on memorizing information and facts, as opposed to teaching understandings and concepts, is a problem in social studies programs for all students, especially handicapped children and youth. They suggest the use of an essential content checklist so that broad content areas or topics can be broken down into sequential topics or tasks.

In making decisions concerning the amount and kind of content to teach, priorities will be established in developing the student's IEP. Specific objectives are illustrated in Table 8–2.

Attitudes, Values, Ideals, and Appreciations. Even though there seems to be little doubt that values should be taught, there is a great deal of controversy about how they should be taught. One viewpoint, called values clarification, states that the process of valuing rather than the values themselves should be taught. A second opinion holds that students should be encouraged to develop skills necessary to make rational value judgments. A third perspective emphasizes the importance of teaching specific moral education.

The most popular approach is that of values clarification. It is important for teachers to remember that valuing as a process may be new to many handicapped students. For those who operate at a concrete level of cognition, this abstract concept may be difficult. For others, protective parents and environments may have provided extremely structured guidelines for "right and wrong." Teachers need to be alert to ways of eliciting values consistently. An activity suggested in *Life Skills for Health* (1974) is the use of "thought sheets." This method requires students to turn in, once a week, single sheets or four-by-six cards on which they have written some thought of importance to them. Each thought is written after reflection and indicates something of the quality of living or thinking in the preceding week. In reacting to these thoughts and others, teachers should refrain from making judgmental statements, such as "I don't agree," "This is a terrible idea," or "What would your parents think?" Rather, comments should be accepting and thought provoking, such as "This would be a good topic for class discussion," or "If you were President, what would you do about this situation?" Seif (1977) states that children and adults are aware of many conflicting values and that questions about values and value issues have become important tools for organizing learning in the social studies.

Skills. Social skills can be defined as "those behaviors which involve interaction between the child and his peers or adults where the primary intent is the achievement of the child's or adult's goals through positive interactions" (Cartledge and Milburn, 1980). Once social deficiencies are identified, teaching procedures can be structured and implemented. A social skills training program designed to assess children in developing peer relationships has identified nine important areas (Mesibov & LaGreca, 1981). These areas are: smiling, greeting others, joining ongoing peer activities, extending invitations to others, con-

TABLE 8-2. Partial IEP—Social Studies Section—One Semester

CURRENT PERFORMANCE LEVEL	GENERAL STUDENT-CENTERED GOALS	PRIORITY NUMBER	TEACHING APPROACH AND METHODOLOGY MONITORING AND EVALUATION TECHNIQUES SPECIALIZED EQUIPMENT AND MATERIALS
Has completed a ninth-grade Social Studies class with minimal success. Reading is presently measured at the fourth-grade level, and writing skills are marginal.	Will demonstrate a basic understanding of the social characteristics of the American Nation (Sophomore Curriculum).	3	Team Teaching/varied groupings and materials/ adaptations as needed by resource room staff/point system/informal and formal testing/class grade.

GOAL NUMBER	OBJECTIVE NUMBER	SPECIFIC STUDENT-CENTERED OBJECTIVES	QUARTERS DURING WHICH OBJECTIVES WILL BE ADDRESSED 1 2 3 4
3	1	Will identify the six categories of culture (economics, family, religion, education, government, and language/art).	X X
3	2	Will describe contemporary American culture based on six characteristics.	X X
3	3	Will identify the sources of American immigrant groups and Black Americans and Native Americans.	X
3	4	Will identify the reasons for immigration to America.	X
3	5	Will identify immigrant settlement locations.	X
3	6	Will describe the experiences of the immigrant crossing.	X

278

3	7	Will describe the early experiences of the immigrants upon arrival.	X	
3	8	Will identify the impact of America on the immigrants.	X	
3	9	Will identify the impact of the immigrants on America.	X	
3	10	Will compare and contrast recent American immigrants with past groups.		X
3	11	Will identify reasons for existence of racism.		X
3	12	Will actively participate in a small group.	X	X
3	13	Will complete Social Studies readings at a mid-fourth grade level.	X	X
3	14	Will answer test questions utilizing complete sentences.	X	X
3	15	Will answer essay questions by listing major points.	X	X
3	16	Will demonstrate auditory attentive ability by completing guide sheets for listening activities.	X	X
3	17	Will demonstrate ability to organize work by maintaining a student class folder.	X	X
3	18	Will improve note-taking skills by copying outlines from teacher transparencies.	X	X
3	19	Will demonstrate ability to utilize charts and graphs.	X	X
3	20	Will be able to identify continents and oceans and locate 50% of the American states.	X	X

TABLE 8-2. (Continued)

GOAL NUMBER	OBJECTIVE NUMBER	SPECIFIC STUDENT-CENTERED OBJECTIVES	QUARTERS DURING WHICH OBJECTIVES WILL BE ADDRESSED 1 2 3 4
3	21	Will be able to gain meaning and make inferences from Social Studies-related pictures.	X X
3	22	Will be able to construct and draw implications from a time line.	X X
3	23	Will be able to list and describe required Social Studies evidence and data.	X X
3	24	Will draw inferences from 25% of the data and evidence used in class.	X X
3	25	Will identify positive and negative feelings on the social concepts presented.	X X
3	26	Will begin to develop critically a humanistic value system.	X X
3	27	Will demonstrate ability to rationally control her own life and her environment.	X X

Source: J. G. Herlihy & M. T. Herlihy, Eds. *Mainstreaming in the Social Studies.* Washington, D.C.: National Council for the Social Studies, 1980, 26–27. Reprinted with permission of the National Council for the Social Studies.

versing, sharing and cooperating, complimenting others, physical appearance/ grooming, and play skills. The social studies curriculum, with an emphasis on group participation and interaction, provides children with an excellent opportunity to develop such skills.

Another approach to teaching social skills is to develop a course in human relations. Dewey (1978) claims that the study of human relations is almost a "survival course" for special students in helping them find jobs, keep jobs, stay out of trouble with the law, defend themselves against exploitation, and win and keep friends.

Kelly (1979) claims that teachers have an obligation to teach the attitudes and behaviors fundamental to social living. Strategies suggested include the use of appropriate adult models, children's literature reflecting basic social ideals, and simulation games, sociodrama, and role playing.

The development of social skills can take place in a number of curriculum areas: vocational training, home economics, communication, and social studies. In this textbook, additional discussion can be found in the chapters concerned with behavior management and social integration.

Study skills, such as map reading, are a particular component of social studies. Observing, listening, reading, and writing are necessary skills in all subjects. Students can obtain information in a variety of ways: hear it from the teacher, read it, see it happen, or look for it in many sources (Oliner, 1976).

The problem presented by poor readers is discussed later in this chapter, as it is shared in the science curriculum. In the area of social studies, textbooks can be taped by volunteers or peer tutors to circumvent the reading problem. In one fifth-grade classroom where a college student recorded the social studies textbook for children with learning problems, it was found that many of the nonhandicapped students also appreciated a different approach to the textbook assignments.

Some students who do not read well are good conversationalists. Teachers alert to this strength can use it as a teaching evaluative tool and as a means of instructional and social integration.

In teaching conversational skills, children are encouraged to use open-ended questions that require more than a one-word response (Mesibov & LaGreca, 1981). For example, "Do you like to play football after school?" is a closed-ended question, whereas "What do you like to do after school?" stimulates conversation.

Group discussion is one of the most important techniques that social studies teachers at all levels can use. Gross et al. (1978) cite four effective kinds of teacher behaviors that encourage positive student participation in discussions.

> The teacher demonstrates nonjudgmental acceptance of student responses to a question. The more you say, "No," "Someone else?" or "That's wrong," the less likely students are to respond.

An incorrect response can be met by stating the question another way, restating the answer offered to see if you understand, suggesting a connection between the answer and the question, or calling for further ideas on the question.

Probe the students' responses by inviting them or others to give an example of what is meant.

Listen to students; let them finish; show you are listening by eye contact or head nodding. Insist that others listen. Accept silence after you have asked a question; allow time for thinking.

Carefully prepared questions can help students develop thinking and generalizing skills. They also provide opportunities for expression within the group at different ability levels. A sequence of questions starting from a low level of fact and leading to relationships and problem solving can involve slow learners as well as gifted students.

Students' questions are also important to the development of their thinking skills. Good student questions increase total student responses (Gross et al., 1978). In a nonthreatening environment, every child can take part in the discussion.

Kelly (1979) states several ways in which questioning is a valuable tool in the "search for meaning" (p. 133), since it makes that search an aggressive one. Other assets cited are particularly valuable to students with learning problems: questioning is an aid to retention, since it provides an opportunity to apply facts and principles; it offers an opportunity for oral expression; it provides for individual differences; and it is an evaluative tool for teachers and pupils.

Social Studies and Handicapism. A common thread evolves in social studies education concerning its general goals. Gross et al. (1978) state that the basic goals of social studies are to prepare the student for full, responsible citizenship; education and promotion of American values; and development of attitudes crucial to the democratic form of government.

Shaver and Curtis (1981) make a strong point for including a study of handicapism in the social studies curriculum. Social studies teachers, in particular, have realized the need to deal with the denial of some groups to participate fully in the political, economic, and social life of our society.

Because the denial of full opportunity is so crucial in our society, the study of handicapism is as vital as the study of racism and sexism. The negative effects of handicapism are equally important for handicapped and nonhandicapped people. These effects can be viewed in economic, political, and humane terms. A major citizenship goal in including education about handicapped citizens in social studies is "to help students understand the issues raised by handicapism so that they will be better prepared to think about and act on those issues as citizens—not just as adults, but in their daily lives in and out of school" (Shaver & Curtis, 1981, p. 6).

Individualizing Instruction

A number of techniques for meeting the needs of individual students have been employed in the social studies content. Oliner (1976) has identified four types of individualized programs: individually diagnosed learning, self-directed learning, personalized learning, and independent study. Effective use of these methods depends on clearly stated objectives from which the teacher and/or student can choose.

Techniques of individualization described in chapter 4 are particularly relevant to the social studies curriculum. Learning activity packets are effective in concept development and in skill areas, such as writing a research report, interpreting maps, and planning an interview.

Learning centers can be used by individual students to obtain basic information, practice a skill, follow up on something taught to the entire class, or enrich and extend basic information. They can also be used to involve students in small group activities. Jarolimek (1977) claims that "Good social studies programs will not result if pupils constantly work by themselves without the opportunity to interact with others" (p. 26).

Simulation games are popular in social studies programs. Since they provide realistic approaches to life situations, simulations may help slow learners in concept development and generalizations. Particularly at the secondary level, players can develop decision-making strategies and begin to feel that they have some control over the environment. Ellis (1977) cites research indicating that simulations do have positive influence on student activities and are influential in encouraging students to become more actively involved in the learning process.

Microcomputers provide the opportunity for a variety of simulations and games. Using appropriate software, the teacher can, within seconds, present groups of students with simulations and games closely correlated with topics being taught (Saltinski, 1981).

Media, pictures, and charts are used frequently in social studies. Even though they are effective in providing variety, overlearning, and retention, adaptations are necessary for students with visual and hearing handicaps. A number of geographic aids for visually impaired students are available: Braille atlases; relief maps made of molded plastic; dissected and undissected maps of continents and countries; relief globes and mileage scales; and large-type outline maps and land-form models featuring three-dimensional tactile maps (Herlihy & Herlihy, 1980).

> *Manuel's favorite subject is social studies. He listens to the news regularly and is politically aware. Although he is visually impaired, he has acquired excellent geographic concepts through listening, class discussion, and the use of materials from the American Printing House for the Blind. Relief*

284 CHAPTER 8 *Teaching Social Studies and Science*

maps and globes have been of particular value to him in following world events. Manuel's teachers find that other students also benefit from the tactile input of these materials and enjoy having a new dimension to their learning.

Captioned films and filmstrips are available on loan for hearing-impaired

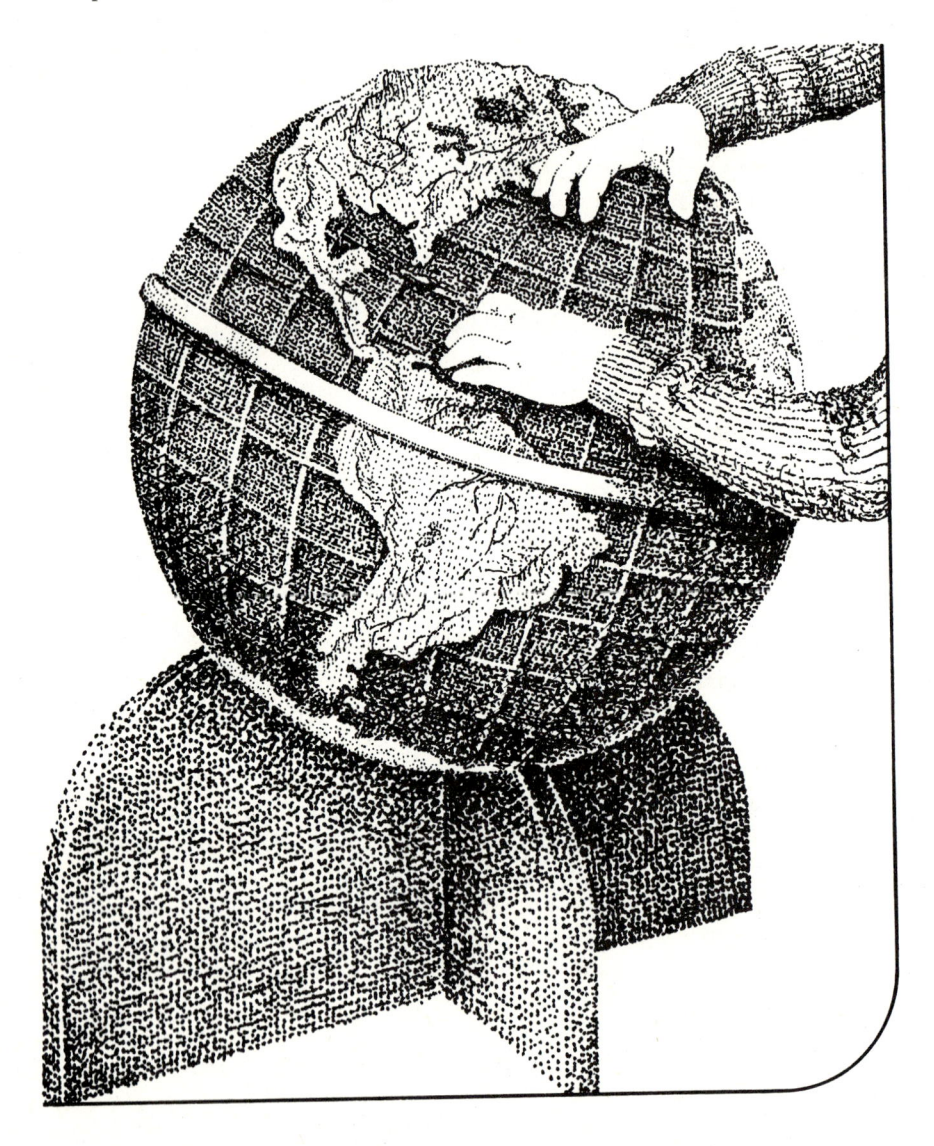

FIGURE 8–1. Tactile Globe

students. Information can be obtained from the Special Office for Materials Distribution at Indiana University.

Activities in social studies should be varied enough to appeal to a broad range of interests and abilities, including those of handicapped students. Jarolimek (1977) claims that such activities as oral and written reports tend to be overused in the social studies. He suggests types of learning activities that should be included:

- *Research:* writing, interviewing, note taking, collecting, using references, reporting, working with maps.
- *Presentation:* telling, announcing, describing, giving directions, reporting, demonstrating, dramatizing, pantomiming, exhibiting, relating events, illustrating.
- *Creative experience:* writing, drawing, sketching, modeling, illustrating, painting, sewing, constructing, soap carving, manipulating, dramatizing, comparing, singing, imagining.
- *Appreciation:* listening, describing, viewing, reading.
- *Observation or listening:* observing, visiting places of interest, viewing pictures of films, listening to recordings.
- *Group cooperation:* discussing, conversing, sharing, asking questions, helping one another, working in a committee.
- *Experimentation:* measuring, collecting, demonstrating, conducting experiments.
- *Organization:* planning, discussing, outlining, summarizing, holding meetings.
- *Evaluation:* summarizing, reviewing, asking questions, criticizing. (p. 27)

The social studies curriculum provides many opportunities for individual and group activities. Because of its relevance to community awareness and living, to the acquisition of skills related to decision making, to values clarification, and to cooperative working, social studies is an important part of every child's learning.

SCIENCE

One of my fondest memories as a parent is that of a science fair in which three of my children participated. Tom, a student in high school, displayed a maze in which he had charted the progress of earthworms. Mary, an elementary school scientist, exhibited a study of the nesting habits of hamsters. Billy, a member of a special education class, showed a chart and description of poisonous plants. Operating on vastly different maturity and ability levels, all three were actively involved in appropriate, relevant, and important scientific investigations.

Victor (1980) states that "a good science program lends itself well to individual learning" (p. 10). Wide ranges of learning activities based on concrete experiences make this discipline particularly adaptable to the mainstreaming process. Yet, investigation shows that only ten to thirty minutes a day are allotted to this major area of learning. Furthermore, generalizations obscure the fact that many classes include no science at all. Even where scheduled, science may not be taught, and science combined with social studies may include little or no science (Hubler, 1974).

If science programs in general are inadequate, science for handicapped students is especially meager. Frequently, students are sent to resource rooms or special service areas during science classes; even if they remain in class they may not participate in science activities. Also, handicapped students may have been deprived of science in their curriculum because it was assumed by most educators that they were not interested in science, that it was too difficult for them, and that they could not manipulate or would break laboratory equipment (Menhusen & Gromme, 1976).

In the past, handicapped children have not been encouraged to consider science as a career. There is a current movement to provide role models and a directory of disabled scientists for children's consideration (Redden, 1979). This effort was reinforced by the United States Postal Service in 1981 with the circulation of a stamp depicting a scientist in a wheelchair (see Figure 8–2).

The American Association for the Advancement of Science (AAAS) Project on the Handicapped in Science concluded from a 1975 survey that most handicapped students, whether in special schools or public schools, receive little science education. The AAAS project is addressing two problems basic to the improvement of science education for handicapped students: (1) the improvement of preservice and inservice teacher training in science to prepare teachers to include the handicapped child in mainstream situations; and (2) the preparation and dissemination of inventories of human and material resources (Redden & Malcolm, 1976).

The National Science Teachers Association has also explored science education for handicapped students. Their stated position is that science should

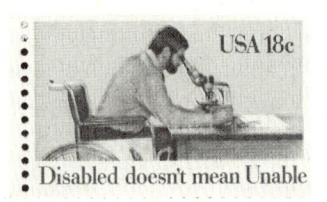

FIGURE 8–2. United States Postage Stamp: "Disabled doesn't mean Unable."

be an integral part of the education of handicapped students from kindergarten through high school (Hofman, 1979).

In a special issue of *Science and Children* devoted to science for the handicapped, Thompson (1976) states that "Science can become an unsuspected ally in the struggle to provide success for handicapped children who seldom enjoy success in school," and that "The time has come to provide for the science education of all handicapped children" (p. 5).

Assessment

Science is a powerful tool for the fulfillment of all children. A child's life is bombarded with stimuli from the environment. For some handicapped children especially, the stimuli are jumbled together. Hadary and Cohen (1978) ask: "How does the child sort these stimuli in a meaningful way? How does he make decisions? How does he gain mastery of his environment? How does he distinguish between fantasy and reality, cause and effect?" (p. 2).

Such questions are the beginning of the continuous evaluation of handicapped students in science programs. Evaluation techniques can be developed based on the type and severity of the handicap, the skill level of the student, and the adopted curriculum of the school system.

Frequently, the scope and sequence of the program will determine the assessment and entry level for the student. In a traditional, discipline-oriented program, students are expected to have acquired specified amounts of basic information prior to entering certain programs of study. In programs based on process skills, performance items are presented. In a program devoted to concept development, the level of understanding can be assessed.

It is essential that science teachers be involved in developing IEPs for their handicapped pupils. For even though the special education teacher and other personnel are familiar with the characteristics of the students, it is the science teachers who know the curriculum, the skills required, and the methods for assessing this information.

Reading is a concern in science as in other curriculum areas. Science teachers need to know which students will have difficulty reading the textbook and other written materials.

In testing for content, a number of standardized science tests are available. Some widely used instruments are listed in Table 8–3.

To diagnose a student's level of understanding, standardized tests, such as the Nelson Biology Test or one of the Cooperative Tests in science, can be used (Simpson & Anderson, 1981). Tests accompanying textbooks are also useful as pretests.

Criterion-referenced tests are probably more valuable in determining the skills of students who have learning problems, since norm-referenced tests

TABLE 8-3. Standardized Science Tests

Coordiniated Scales of Attainment: Science Test. Educational Test Bureau, Minneapolis, Minn.

Every Pupil Test: Elementary Science and Health. Ohio Scholarship Tests, State Department of Education, Columbus, Ohio.

Every Pupil Scholarship Test: Elementary Science. Bureau of Educational Measurements, Kansas State Teachers College, Emporia, Kansas.

Metropolitan Achievement Tests: Intermediate Science Test. Harcourt Brace Jovanovich, Inc., New York, N.Y.

National Achievement Tests: Elementary Science, Forms A and B. Psychometric Affiliates, Chicago, Ill.

Standardized Science Tests: A Descriptive Listing. National Science Teachers Assn., Washington, D.C. (Describes almost all standardized tests available and gives sources for them.)

Sequential Tests of Educational Progress: Science, Forms 4A and 4B. Educational Testing Service, Cooperative Test Division, Princeton, N.J.

SRA Science Achievement Test: Elementary Science. Science Research Associates, Chicago, Ill.

Stanford Achievement Test: Intermediate Science Test. Harcourt Brace Jovanovich, Inc., New York, N.Y.

Source: Reprinted with permission of Macmillan Publishing Company from *Science for the elementary school*, 4th ed., by Edward Victor. Copyright © 1980 by Edward Victor.

tend to accentuate differences in students' abilities. In a given set of instructional objectives, student performance and teacher observation can predict the appropriate entry level for the handicapped student.

There are many assessment methods other than tests. Discussion, when properly conducted, can be useful in appraising the student's knowledge of science content, scientific attitudes, and other behaviors. Observation is another valuable method for evaluating the student's comprehension of science concepts, performance of key operations of science and the scientist, and acquisition of desirable behavioral outcomes (Victor, 1980).

Good teaching and learning call for continuous assessment. Since the objectives of the science program, the content and process being learned, and the methods and materials being used are interrelated and interdependent, teachers should constantly evaluate these aspects (Victor, 1980).

Goals and Objectives

There are two major goals in studying science. One is to become aware of the significant scientific facts on which the major concepts and theories of science are based. The second is to recognize the spirit and appreciate the methods of science. Mead (1978) expresses the overall goal:

When we teach young children to become citizens in our world that depends on science and technology, the problem is to convey to these children something about life, something about what they share with living things, and something about observing non-living things in the environment. (p. 47)

Because of the scientific nature of our society and the individualized needs of its members, each person should be scientifically literate. Scientific literacy, then, is the central goal for teaching science in elementary and secondary schools. The scientifically literate person

- Has knowledge of the major concepts, principles, laws and theories of science and applies these in appropriate ways;
- Uses the processes of science in solving problems, making decisions, and other suitable ways;
- Understands the nature of science and the scientific enterprise;
- Understands the partnership of science and technology and its interaction with society;
- Has developed science-related skills that enable him or her to function effectively in careers, leisure activities, and other roles;
- Possesses attitudes and values that are in harmony with those of science and a free society; and
- Has developed interests that will lead to a richer and more satisfying life and a life that will include science and life-long learning. (Simpson & Anderson, 1981, pp. 6, 7)

Objectives derived from these goals are grouped into three areas: to learn science concepts and conceptual schemes—the content of science; to become familiar with the key operations of science and the scientist—the process of science; and to develop such desirable outcomes as scientific skills, attitudes, appreciations, and interests.

Although the goals and objectives for handicapped students are the same as those for all students, Menhusen and Gromme (1976) see particular benefits for those with learning problems. Science can serve as a vehicle for developing the basic skills of observing, describing, identifying, comparing, associating, inferring, applying, and predicting that lead to problem-solving skills. It can be useful in meeting the physical, psychological, and social needs of handicapped students and can help develop a more positive self-image, identity, and desirable work habits. Development of these skills is discussed in the following section. Finally, there are goals for the teacher.

The teacher must recognize and implement effective ways of utilizing science . . . to achieve the goals of intellectual, conceptual, and cognitive development of the handicapped child. However, above all, the teacher's goal is to develop the ability to accept human beings as human beings, in nonhandicapped children as well as in handicapped ones. (Hadary, 1977, p. 6)

Skills. There is considerable evidence that science is a viable tool in teaching basic and life skills to handicapped students. The nature of science itself demands many modes of learning and thus provides for sensory and physical input. Science also calls for experiences related to life experiences, providing opportunities for concrete learning. Hands-on experiences help to develop abstract thinking, language, and quantitative skills. When activity choices are provided, interest and motivation are likely to be higher.

McConnell (1978) claims that the Human Sciences Program contributes rich resources for skill development. Reading skills include reading for general information, developing and using vocabulary meanings, reading to follow directions, and using verbal reasoning to comprehend and infer. The program also emphasizes listening, speaking, and writing skills. Opportunities are provided to develop quantitative and measurement skills through collecting quantitative observations, organizing data for use, displaying data, interpreting data, and manipulating data.

Research studies cited by the Science Curriculum Improvement Study investigate the contention that there is a positive carryover from innovative science programs to other academic areas. In one study, first-grade students using the SCIS program outperformed the control group in word meaning, listening, matching, alphabet, and numbers. A second study investigated SCIS and achievement in reading, mathematics, and social studies. In using SCIS with fifth graders, improvement was demonstrated in mathematics applications, social studies skills, and paragraph meaning (Renner, Stafford, Weber, Coffia, & Kellog, 1972).

One study specific to handicapped students involved 307 educable mentally handicapped students, aged six to nineteen, who received science instruction (Menhusen & Gromme, 1976). These pupils demonstrated improvement in science skills and a higher level of verbal ability.

Hurd (1970) offers an explanation for the high degree of success and skill development in science programs:

- Laboratory and field experiences get pupils involved; because of the low verbal load, these experiences are less threatening as a means of learning.
- Experiences provided are concrete.
- Experiences and the meaning of observation provide something to talk about.
- Discussions help build verbal mediators to improve the ability to discriminate, classify, label, and generalize.
- Field trips increase the students' ranges of experience and thus their potential for generating desirable science concepts.

Along with the basic skills mentioned, other "survival skills" are necessary for a person to be an effective jobholder, family member, citizen, and consumer (McConnell, 1978). Such skills include the ability to be self-directed in searching for knowledge; the ability to think rationally and to interpose evidence, reason, and judgment between impulse and action; and the ability to interrelate effectively with other humans.

Skills development occurs functionally in an experience-based curriculum. Science study provides the format for handicapped and nonhandicapped students to acquire skills because they are needed and important. Science programs developed specifically for handicapped students focus on skills related to the students' interests and needs.

Instructional Approaches

> The reduction of intellectual zest and curiosity at the junior high school age appears to be more a product of the curriculum and modes of instruction than it is of pupil maturation. (Hurd, 1970, p. 159)

In an adaptation of the Science Curriculum Improvement Study, Linn (1972) demonstrated that by investing a comparatively small amount of time and money, existing curricula can be adapted for special groups of learners. Three underlying themes in science appear to apply to curriculum adaptation and instructional methods: (1) the foundation of all learning in science is firsthand experience with real things; (2) science experiences need not involve unusual, elaborate, or expensive apparatus and materials; and (3) investigating one's environment is an interesting and integral part of an education (Schmidt & Rockcastle, 1968). Science is taught most effectively when it relates directly to the world in which students live.

Many sets of science curriculum modules have been developed around hands-on experiences. A number of science curriculum books and articles are available to help science teachers use materials at hand. Many current projects and products are devoted to developing strategies for teaching science to handicapped students.

The development of Adapting Science Materials for the Blind (ASMB) is a step in giving visually handicapped students hands-on, concrete experiences in science (Schatz, Franks, Thier, & Linn, 1976). An adaptation of SCIS, the program is a sequential, ungraded, physical and life science curriculum consisting of thirteen units for children five to thirteen years old. The following adaptation exemplifies techniques that can be used with any program.

> The SCIS Energy Sources unit (level 5) begins with the children making and flying paper airplanes. Although other mechanical systems such as the stopper popper and rotoplane have been adapted rather successfully for the visually

impaired, there did not seem to be a meaningful way to give a sightless child real experiences with flying paper airplanes. This raised the important question: Why are we flying paper airplanes at this point anyway? Since the answer was to review and reintroduce the specifying and controlling of variables, the project designed an alternate activity using "Hot Wheel" tracks to accomplish the same educational objectives. Visually impaired children explore how far the cars roll on a straight track when one end is raised different amounts. Other variables they can explore and control are type of car, weight of car (adding small weights), surface characteristics of the track (adding cloth, sand, etc.), and multiple humps in the track. (Thier & Hadary, 1973, p. 9)

Science Activities for the Visually Impaired (SAVI) introduces physical and life sciences to visually impaired children in a multisensory way (DeLucchi, Malone, & Thier, 1980). Activities are developed to remediate and stimulate learning; materials are designed for able as well as limited students. The multisensory approach designed for visually impaired students is also appropriate for nonhandicapped students. The activities are compatible with standard science curricula and can be readily incorporated into most science programs.

The Biological Sciences Curriculum Study has developed three programs that have been used successfully with special students. *Me Now*, a program in science and health, was designed for students between the ages of ten and thirteen. *Me and My Environment* is an environmental science program for students from ages thirteen to sixteen. *Me in the Future* deals with careers and decision-making processes relative to the future. The programs are designed for teachers who have limited backgrounds in science and include teacher's guides, slides, posters and pictures, filmloops, worksheets, models, laboratory supplies, and evaluation materials. Six "Principles of Presentation" are used as a guide for developing a curriculum:

1. The tasks should be uncomplicated.
2. The tasks should be brief.
3. The tasks should be presented sequentially.
4. Each learning task should allow for success.
5. Overlearning must be built into the lesson.
6. Learning tasks should be applied to objects, problems, and situations.

The *Me Now* program has also been used successfully in classes for hearing-impaired students with low verbal skills (Egelston & Mercaldo, 1975). This program is particularly attractive for such students because it is (1) a commercially available course that needs very little adaption for use with deaf students, (2) a teacher-directed program that allows control of verbally presented information, and (3) a valid science course feasible for use with deaf children.

Another approach to teaching science to handicapped students is described in the Laboratory Science and Art Curriculum for Blind, Deaf and Emotionally Disturbed Children (Hadary & Cohen, 1978). In a laboratory science, art, and music program, the science curriculum is combined with a program of individualized experiences in which children learn through interacting and by expressing themselves creatively. The program directors feel that science and art stimulate creativity by interaction with natural phenomena. Crafts techniques are adapted for the blind child and lessons are designed to enable special children to use the same techniques as their peers.

This philosophy can be used effectively with students who have various handicaps. In a lesson entitled "Creating the Structure of a Flower," the following science objectives are stated:

- To examine a flower and discover its structure—pistil, stamen, anthers, petals, stem.
- To relate the structures of a flower to the functions.
- To discover the similarities among flowers of different plants. (Hadary & Cohen, 1978, p. 205)

The development of an art project to reinforce the science lesson is presented in Figure 8–3. Such interrelated activities provide tactile stimulation and concrete experience and help students perceive natural form and order.

Individualizing Instruction

Special equipment can be used effectively in science programs. The computer has been used in many ways to individualize instruction for handicapped students (Windbigler, 1979).

The light sensor, produced by the American Printing House for the Blind, affords blind students opportunities for direct observation, experimentation, and discovery. By focusing the light sensor on apparatus used in many basic science experiments, students receive immediate auditory feedback (Franks & Sanford, 1976).

In adapting laboratory equipment used in *Science—A Process Approach* for blind students, the tape recorder was used extensively (Eichenberger, 1974). It was used for laboratory competency quizzes, instructions, and for recording part of the periodic table of the elements. Mathematical problems can be worked with a braille abacus.

Classroom management for the laboratory is suggested by Hadary and Cohen (1978) for successful integration of handicapped students:

- *Laboratory stations* of groups of four are set up in the classroom, with handicapped students intermingled. This provides for individualized instruction, peer teaching, and social interaction.

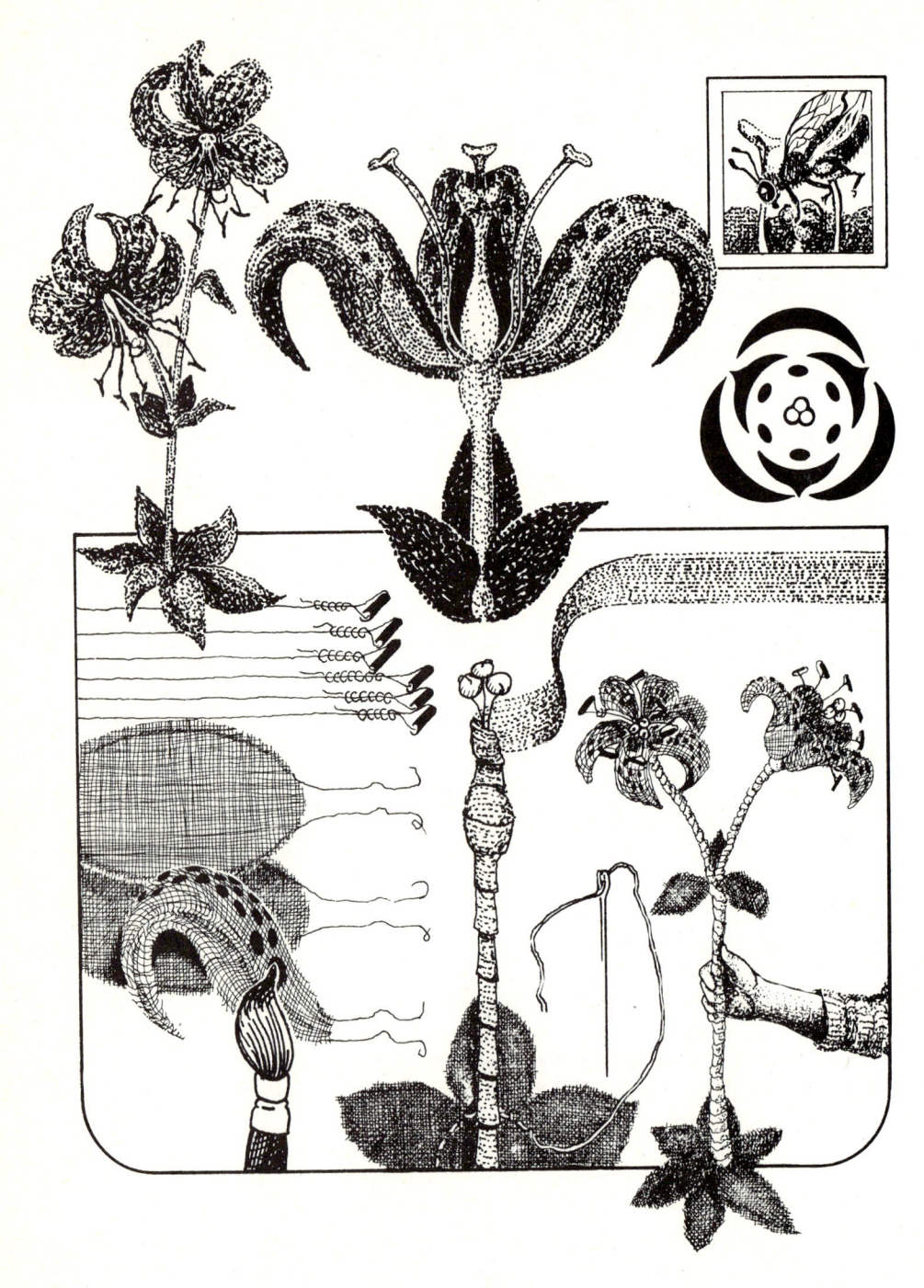

FIGURE 8–3. Science and Art

- *Laboratory materials* for examination and exploration are distributed to each station. Materials are labeled and brailled. Stations and distribution centers remain in the same place all year.
- *Questioning and discussions* should take place in small groups where students can see and hear each other. Demonstrations and introductions to problems are necessary. While the same problem is presented to all students, stations may be engaged in different activities. Example: half of the class (without blind students) is exploring the properties of light with the optics experiments, while the other half (with blind students) is investigating the properties of light with the light sensor.

In the science class referred to above, there are six handicapped children and twenty-four nonhandicapped children. In describing this particular class, Redden (1979) observes that "the handicapped children learn to ask for the help they need, that the other children learn to help but not to help too much, and that there is a great feeling of sharing."

SOCIAL STUDIES AND SCIENCE

Common Problems and Techniques

According to the Science Education Databook (1981), kindergarten through twelfth-grade science teachers perceive problem areas as inadequate facilities, insufficient funds for purchasing equipment and supplies, and lack of materials for individualizing instruction. In the same databook, social studies teachers perceive problem areas as insufficient funds for purchasing supplies and equipment, lack of materials for individualizing instruction, out-of-date teaching materials, lack of student interest in subject, inadequate student reading abilities, and the belief that the subject is less important than other subjects.

Experiences with teaching social studies and science to handicapped students indicate that these problems can be overcome by sensitive and creative teachers. There are, however, several issues that relate to all subject areas, particularly social studies and science. They are content, timing, instructional methods, and reading.

Content. Content is a particularly crucial issue in science and social studies curricula when planning for students whose achievement is significantly below grade and age level expectations. These students typically lack many of the prerequisites necessary to proceed in higher order concept development; however, they are capable of advancing in the hierarchy of concept development when those prerequisites are in place. Sequencing of the content is a major consideration in developing the IEPs for science and social studies. At that time, the sequence of short-term objectives, which will serve as stepping stones to mastery of the annual goals, must be specified. The central concern affecting the sequential introduction of various concepts is that students have the necessary prerequisites to succeed at the new learning task. It is virtually impossible to meet the unique needs of every student in the class during every class period, but teachers have to work on foundation skills with students who are achieving substantially below grade level.

Another content consideration is that some students with learning problems will never catch up entirely with their peers. This means that they may never learn some skills and concepts in the general social studies and science curricula. Therefore, decisions must be made about what is most relevant and most necessary for adult adjustment and community living skills. Sometimes the issue of relevant curriculum decisions regarding adult adjustment and community living is postponed until the senior high years. By that time, some handicapped students have wasted inordinate amounts of time on topics that have no personal value. Science and social studies instruction, even at the early elementary levels, prepares the student for lifelong adjustment. Students handicapped by mental retardation, for example, need the most careful use of instructional time. In almost every case, they are going to learn less than their chronological age peers, and they will probably have lower problem-solving abilities as adults. These factors place a high premium on the value of every instructional hour spent in school.

Relevance to concept development is a central curriculum concern. For every topic the teacher considers including in the science and social studies curricula, these three questions should be asked: Will it help the student be more independent in the community, employment setting, and/or at home? What is the jeopardy of the student's not knowing this information? Will the student be receiving this information from other sources? As the responses to these questions are analyzed, teachers, parents, and students can identify the long-range goals and short-term objectives necessary to develop and implement the IEP effectively.

One strategy for systematically identifying the most relevant content is to have committees of science or social studies teachers in the school system decide jointly on the most essential skills and concepts that should comprise the basic curriculum. This relevant core could be drawn from the state or system-adopted curriculum guide. When the scope and sequence of relevant skills are specified by a systemwide committee, the probability of sequential concept development from grade to grade is increased.

Timing. Handicapped students often require more instructional and practice time before a new skill or concept is mastered. Mentally retarded students typically have a slower learning rate; hearing-impaired students may require more time to learn the technical vocabulary associated with science and social studies content. The problems associated with learning disabilities warrant careful consideration.

Joe has been diagnosed as having a learning disability. Science seems to be his most difficult class. It's the last period of the afternoon, when Joe usually is feeling tired and "hassled." It seems to take him most of the period to settle down and get to work. He wanders around the room, sharpens his pencil over and over, and tries to involve his peers in conversation. That is the reason Joe rarely completes his assignments by the end of class. He is falling farther and farther behind his peers.

The implication of arranging the curriculum so that handicapped students are afforded appropriate amounts of time to master concepts is that often the rest of the class is ready to move ahead whereas the handicapped student needs additional practice. Again, more individualization is required to manage this situation in the classroom. Some portions of the general curriculum can be deleted for students who are achieving substantially below grade level. Leaving out some concepts allows time to concentrate more intensively on more relevant concepts.

Instructional Methods. Language delays, which can interfere with lecture and discussion approaches to instruction, may be directly related to delayed vocabulary development and language problems associated with hearing impairment. The technical language of science and social studies may be difficult for students with delayed vocabularies to understand. In addition, some students who do not understand the technical word itself may not comprehend the words that the teacher uses to explain the technical term. It can be difficult, for example, to explain the terms *photosynthesis* or *electromagnet* to students with significant delays in vocabulary development. It is often helpful to introduce new vocabulary to these students before the vocabulary is used in the context of a lesson. If the students have dictionary skills, they might look up the new words and write the definitions on index cards. Also on the card, they might write the word in a sentence and either draw or find a picture to illustrate the word. All the cards can be kept in a file box. Reviewing the word cards could be done as an assignment or a free-time activity. Students who have not yet mastered dictionary skills will need guidance in initially defining the new vocabulary. This can be done by a teacher, teacher aide, special education resource teacher, volunteer, or peer tutor.

Media (visual and audiovisual), such as pictures, charts, films, filmstrips, maps, and graphs, can be effective instructional materials for many handicapped persons. Students with disadvantages associated with mental retardation and learning disabilities can benefit from experiences and activities that do not penalize them for a lower level of reading achievement. Additionally, these students often associate visual and audiovisual materials with higher motivational appeal.

Teachers must remember that visually impaired students are unable to take advantage of the typical visual media used in social studies and science classes. In addition to adaptations suggested in previous sections, many adaptations enable the blind student to participate in class activities related to visual methods of instruction. When the class is examining and discussing a map of the United States, the blind student can work with the relief map. Thus, "audiotactile" rather than audiovisual instruction is employed.

Many hearing-impaired students are unable to hear the audio portion of films, filmstrips, or videotapes. In some cases, seating close to the machine will help. For students with extremely limited residual hearing, teachers should consider ordering captioned films. These films and filmstrips provide a written statement on each frame or in each sequence that is correlated with the verbal content, thus enabling hearing-impaired students to read what other students are hearing. For information on ordering captioned films, teachers should write to the Special Office for Materials Distribution at Indiana University. Many films are loaned free of charge.

Reading. Karlin (1969) has estimated that 25 percent of the high school population does not possess the reading skills necessary to read the materials and textbooks they are expected to comprehend. The reading problem at the elementary and junior high levels is also very severe. Reading deficiencies can significantly interfere with successful performance in social studies and science unless instructional adaptations are made. Techniques for adapting reading materials are discussed in chapter 6.

Handicapped students, particularly those with learning problems, often have disadvantages associated with reading achievement. Reading problems occur in the areas of word recognition, comprehension, and study skills (reading tables, using the index, scanning, paraphrasing). The following are suggestions for minimizing reading problems while working to improve reading performance.

- Have a peer tutor and a student with a reading problem complete the reading assignment together. Both students might read orally, with the tutor helping to identify words that have not yet been learned. When this strategy is used with blind students, the peer tutor must do all the reading.
- Have students who excel in reading make summaries of chapters for less able readers. The less able reader might participate in the overall development by illustrating the summary with pictures from old textbooks or magazines or by binding several summaries to make booklets. Summaries can be laminated or covered with clear contact paper for repeated use (Turner, 1976).
- The teacher, volunteers, or a peer tutor can underline or highlight the key concepts on each page of the text. Slow readers overwhelmed by the length of the chapter are more likely to read the most important concepts if they are emphasized.

- Volunteers or peer tutors can tape-record the textbook for students who read significantly below grade level. Introductory "organizers" can be included on the tape. For example, a student can be told in advance which points to listen for or the main idea of the selection. Study questions can also be included after paragraphs to check the student's comprehension. This strategy is also helpful for blind students, although the introductory organizers and study questions may be superfluous for blind students who comprehend information easily.
- The language experience approach to reading instruction (see chapter 5) can be used to promote concept development in science and social studies. After information has been presented (through discussion, media, textbook, inquiry experiences), have students summarize the major points in their own words. If they are unable to write or spell adequately, a peer tutor or the teacher can assist them. They can find pictures in magazines or draw pictures that "visually paraphrase" (Turner, 1976) the concepts they are learning. A similar approach is to write stories about the concepts rather than more objective summaries. This method helps students to increase their reading skills while mastering science and social studies concepts. Learning centers with textbooks, reference books, and activities can be developed. Turner (1976) describes a center in which students plan learning activities and experiences for their peers based on a section of a chapter. These experiences can take the form of questions, inquiry activities, an oral report, a group project, or various alternatives. Both the students planning and completing the activities have the opportunity to expand their skills.
- Some partially sighted children need large-print textbooks. Teachers can sometimes borrow these from the State Library for the Blind and Physically Handicapped. If books are not available on loan, magnification equipment might be used or portions of the basic text could be retyped with a primary typewriter. Before retyping material, teachers should make sure that primary type print is large enough for the particular students. If so, perhaps a volunteer could be located to do the typing (the high school typing teacher might know of willing students) or the Lion's Club might be contacted about providing financial help. Another reading alternative to consider is the use of a textbook on a lower grade level for students with severe reading delays. It is also possible to acquire multilevel editions of the same text.
- Finally, text and classroom materials can be rewritten to the reading levels of mainstreamed students. Guidelines for rewriting material are presented in chapter 6.

Even though poor reading skills present a problem, it is possible that more students would develop greater interest in reading if they explored the topics offered by science and social studies. Kelly (1979) states that "Teachers have to recognize, accept and provide for the variability in their students' reading abilities by supplying a plentiful, diverse assortment of reading materials, pictures, films, models and specimens to their classes" (p. 156).

The goals and content of social studies and science are appropriate and essential for handicapped students. The philosophies of the disciplines contribute to the concept of individual differences. With cooperative effort, they can make a positive difference in the education of handicapped students.

REFERENCES

A progress report on the evaluation of Me and My Environment. *BSCS Newsletter,* 1973, *53,* 14–15.

Cartledge, G., & Milburn, J. F. *Teaching social skills to children.* New York: Pergamon Press, 1980.

DeLucchi, L., Malone, L., & Thier, H. D. Science activities for the visually impaired: Developing a model. *Exceptional Children,* 1980, *46*(4), 287–288.

Dewey, M. *Teaching human relations to special students.* Portland, Maine: J. Weston Walch, 1978.

Egelston, J. C., & Mercaldo, D. Science education for the handicapped: Implementation for the hearing-impaired. *Science Education,* 1975, *59*(2), 257–261.

Eichenberger, R. J. Teaching science to the blind student. *The Science Teacher,* 1974, December, 53–54.

Ellis, A. K. *Teaching and learning elementary social studies.* Boston: Allyn and Bacon, 1977.

Franks, F. L., & Sanford, L. Using the light sensor to introduce laboratory science. *Science and Children,* 1976, March, 48–49.

Gross, R. E., Messick, R., Chapin, J. R., & Sutherland, J. *Social studies for our times.* New York: John Wiley and Sons, 1978.

Hadary, D. E. Science and art for visually handicapped children. *Visual Impairment and Blindness,* 1977, *71* May, 203–209.

Hadary, D. E., & Cohen, S. H. *Laboratory and art for blind, deaf, and emotionally disturbed children.* Baltimore: University Park Press, 1978.

Herlihy, J. G., & Herlihy, M. T. Mainstreaming in the social studies. *National Council for the Social Studies,* 1980, Bulletin 62.

Hofman, H. Working conference on science education for handicapped students. In H. Hofman & K. S. Ricker, *Source book: Science education and the physically handicapped.* National Science Teachers Association, 1979, 15–104.

Hubler, H. C. *Science for children.* New York: Random House, 1974.

Hurd, P. D. *New curriculum perspectives for junior high school science.* Belmont, Calif.: Wadsworth Publishing Co., 1970.

Jarolimek, J. *Social studies in elementary education.* New York: Macmillan Publishing Co., 1977.

Johnson, R., and Vardian, E. R. Reading, readability, and the social studies. *The Reading Teacher,* 1973, *26*(5), 483–488.

Karlin, R. What does education research reveal about reading and the high school student? *The English Journal,* 1969, *58,* 386–395.

Kelly, E. J. *Elementary school social studies instruction: A basic approach.* Denver: Love Publishing Co., 1979.

Life skills for health. Division of Health, Safety and Physical Education. North Carolina Department of Public Instruction, 1974.

Linn, M. C. An experiential science curriculum for the visually impaired. *Exceptional Children,* 1972, *39,* September.

McConnell, M. C. Basics . . . and the human sciences program. *The Biological Sciences Curriculum Study Journal,* 1978, April, 10–15.

Mead, M. In C. Charles & B. Samples (Eds.), *Science and society: Knowing, teaching, learning.* National Council for the Social Studies, 1978, Bulletin 57.

Menhusen, B. R., & Gromme, R. O. Science for handicapped children—why? *Science and Children,* 1976, March, 35–38.

Mesibov, G. B., & LaGreca, A. M. A social skills instructional module. *The Directive Teacher,* 1981, 3(1), 6–7.

Oliner, P. M. *Teaching elementary social studies.* New York: Harcourt Brace Jovanovich, 1976.

Redden, M. R. Science education for handicapped children. *Education Unlimited,* 1979, *1*(4), 44–46.

Redden, M. R., & Malcom, S. M. A move toward the mainstream. *Science and Children,* 1976, March, 14.

Renner, J. W., Stafford, D. G., Weber, M. C., Coffia, W. J., & Kellog, D. H. *Research studies of SCIS success in the classroom.* Chicago: Rand McNally and Co., 1972.

Saltinski, R. Microcomputers in social studies: An innovative technology for instruction. *Educational Technology,* 1981, *21*(1), 29–32.

Schatz, D., Franks, F., Thier, H. D., & Linn, M. C. Hands-on science for the blind. *Science and Children,* 1976, March, 21–23.

Schmidt, V. E., & Rockcastle, V. N. *Teaching science with everyday things.* New York: McGraw-Hill, 1968.

Science Education Databook. Washington, D.C.: National Science Foundation, 1981.

Seif, E. *Teaching significant social studies in the elementary school.* Chicago: Rand McNally and Co., 1977.

Shaver, J. K., & Curtis, C. K. *Handicapism and equal opportunity: Teaching about the disabled in social studies.* Reston, Va.: The Foundation for Exceptional Children, 1981.

Simpson, R. D., & Anderson, N. D. *Science, students and schools: A guide for the middle and secondary school teacher.* New York: John Wiley and Sons, 1981.

Thier, H. D., & Hadary, D. E. We can do it too. *Science and Children,* 1973, *II*(4), 7–9.

Thompson, B. E. Science for the handicapped. *Science and Children,* 1976, *13*(6), 5.

Turner, T. N. Making the social studies textbook a more effective tool for less able readers. *Social Education,* 1976, *41,* 38–41.

Victor, E. *Science for the elementary school* (4th ed.). New York: Macmillan Publishing Co., 1980.

Windbigler, J. Computer assistance for physically handicapped students. In H. Hofman & K. S. Ricker (Eds.), *Sourcebook: Science education and the physically handicapped.* Washington, D.C.: National Science Teachers Association, 1979, 179–185.

9

Teaching Physical Education, Music, and Art

Educators frequently are called on to justify programs in physical education, music, and art. When school budgets are cut, these programs are often the first to be proposed for curtailment or elimination (Prescott, 1981). As a state superintendent of public instruction views the problem, "When money is short, then all things are not equal and we find—when forced to make decisions—that some things are more equal than others" (Runkel, 1981). He further suggests some of the questions that school board members may have to ask:

> Can the community, through a community arts program, take over the art program? Can physical education classes be eliminated? Our music programs are fine, but are they absolutely essential to a basic educational program? (p. 38)

The question of what is basic has been responded to by professionals in the three areas. Carlson (1982) claims that the learning domains required for individual development are included in the traditional development objectives in physical education: intellectual, emotional, neuromuscular, and organic.

In referring to the consideration of art as an educational extra, art educators have professed their belief that it belongs in the core and should be in the mainstream of every educational effort at every educational level (Feldman, 1982). A similar philosophy is stated by music educators, who claim that "In every child's life, music can make a difference" (Taylor, 1982, p. 5).

The case for inclusion of the arts (as well as physical education) in the curriculum for all children can be stated as follows:

> . . . the arts offer all people an opportunity to learn, use, and refine specific human resources that are necessary and basic components of human life and hence of education. Strong efforts should be made to underscore the fact that there are areas of experience and expertise in the arts that are vital to the development and understanding of human beings, and that they are central, therefore, to any discussion of what basic education should entail. (Sudano & Sharpham, 1981, p. 48)

Physical education, music, and art have been particularly basic to the education of handicapped students; mainstreaming first took place in these areas. Some students who have not experienced success in academic areas have been

FIGURE 9–1. Basketball Player

successful in physical education and the arts, and success in these areas has contributed to the acceptance and self-esteem of handicapped students. The mother of a student who has had learning disabilities described an exciting experience.

> *Paul tried out for basketball this year. At 6' 1" before his thirteenth birthday, he had height in his favor but not much else. He had never played on a team, and since we live in a rural area he had not had much neighborhood experience either. At the first session I explained this to the coach, and he was very understanding. I could see that he made special efforts to teach Paul the basics of the game.*
>
> *After weeks of practice sessions, it became time to choose ten boys. Paul barely made the team, but he made it! His desire to play and improve and his regular and prompt attendance at practice had made a difference. In addition, the coach was a caring individual who wanted to give Paul a chance.*
>
> *Since this team was community sponsored, there was a provision that each player participate in at least one full quarter of each game. This was a definite benefit for Paul and two other inexperienced players on his team.*
>
> *As the season progressed, Paul played on the starting line-up in most games. Instead of playing just the required one quarter each game, he played two, three, or even four quarters.*
>
> *At the end of the season, the coach said that if he had to choose the most improved player on the team, it would be Paul. He also said that Paul was one of three players on the team who had a future in basketball. He encouraged Paul to play again next year and gave him some tips on improving himself over the summer.*
>
> *Basketball has helped Paul be a part of something he wanted to do. It required self-discipline and hard work. It was a maturing, confidence-building experience for Paul who now has at least one long range goal: improving and participating in basketball next year.*
>
> *I am grateful to both his coach and the community program for giving Paul a chance to play. It is so important to feel part of something worthwhile and to be able to participate, not just sit on the bench and watch the "stars" perform. (Barbara Schulz, letter to the author, 1982. Used by permission)*

Other important factors of physical education, music, and art for handicapped students are the contributions such programs can make as they influence the cognitive, affective, and psychomotor growth of handicapped students. In this chapter, physical education, music, and art are discussed in relation to concept development, mobility, academic progress, and peer relationships.

PHYSICAL EDUCATION

Physical education is the only curricular area specifically mentioned in P.L. 94–142. The law requires that students with handicapping conditions have opportunities comparable to those of nonhandicapped students in extracurricular activities, including interscholastic sports. This special emphasis is warranted for the following reasons, expressed in Congressional testimonies:

> Students with handicapping conditions have the same ranges of interests and needs for active participation in physical activities as classmates without handicapping conditions.
> Individuals with certain handicapping conditions must be in relatively better physical condition than individuals without such conditions to get through the rigors of a vigorous day.
> Active participation in vigorous physical activities provides bases for healthier, happier, more productive, fun-filled lives. (Stein, 1979, p. 6)

Concept Development

Many people associate concept development in physical education strictly with the psychomotor domain; however, physical education incorporates a much broader array of concepts and skills. Sherrill (1976) suggests a model to illustrate the interrelationships of cognitive-perceptual-psychomotor-affective development considered to be an integral part of the physical education program (see Table 9–1).

Many of these behaviors are learned by nonhandicapped students through normal development and in informal physical activities in the neighborhood. Handicapped students, on the other hand, frequently have special needs that require alternative instructional strategies to enhance the probability of their success in learning the underlying concepts and behaviors comprising well-balanced physical development. Many handicapped students can function in regular physical education programs, whereas moderately and severely handicapped students will require adapted programs.

Stein (1979) claims that 90 to 95 percent of those students with handicapping conditions can be successfully integrated into regular physical education programs. He suggests that they can be accommodated by making facilities accessible, by adapting methods and approaches, and by increasing the emphasis on and attention to class organization and class management.

Making Facilities Accessible.   Schools need to modify such facilities as pools, locker rooms, and gyms so that handicapped students have access to them (Aufsesser, 1981). In addition to major accommodations, facilities can be altered or affected by temporary or portable ramps, class schedules, peer tutors, and other common-sense approaches.

TABLE 9-1. Spectrum of Behaviors for Which the Physical Educator Is Responsible

MOTOR DEVELOPMENT	PERCEPTUAL-MOTOR INTEGRATION AND LANGUAGE DEVELOPMENT	PERCEPTUAL-MOTOR-COGNITIVE INTEGRATION	APPLICATION-ANALYSIS-SYNTHESIS-EVALUATION
1. Gross movement patterns requisite to body control and safe locomotion	5. Body image, concept, cathexis	11. Wide variety of play interests	15. Sufficient weekly exercise for optimal health and fitness
2. Fine motor coordinations requisite to self-help skills and daily living activities	6. Fine motor coordinations requisite to academic and/or vocational success	12. Sufficient physical recreational skills, knowledges, and understandings for group acceptance and self-actualization	16. Knowledge and understandings requisite to enjoyment of sports, dance, and aquatics as a spectator, a consumer of television, radio, and other media, and as a participant in discussions
3. Gross motor patterns requisite to play activities	7. Personal attractiveness requisite to social acceptance	13. Relaxation and release of neuromuscular tensions	
	8. Physical fitness	14. Motor skills, knowledges, and understanding requisite to success in one or more physical activities with carryover values	17. Knowledges and understandings requisite to optimal use of community recreation resources and to intelligent decision-making as a voter, citizen, consumer, and parent
4. Perceptual-motor skills related to motor learning and motor performance	9. Positive attitudes toward body, self, others, movement, play, and competition		
	10. Creativity in exploring use of time, space, and energy		

THE INFANT

THE PRESCHOOL CHILD

THE ELEMENTARY SCHOOL CHILD

THE MIDDLE SCHOOL STUDENT

THE SECONDARY SCHOOL PUPIL

Source: From Sherrill, Claudine: ADAPTED PHYSICAL EDUCATION AND RECREATION. (c) 1976 Wm. C. Brown Company Publishers. All Rights Reserved. Reprinted by permission.

The provision of adaptive devices and equipment makes it possible for some handicapped students to participate in regular physical education programs. These include ambulatory devices, such as crutches, walkers, wheelchairs, and scooter boards; leg and arm prostheses; and back braces (Fait, 1978). In addition, there are bowling rails, pushers, and special handle balls; beeper calls and other sound devices that enable visually impaired students to participate in many activities; special wheelchairs for basketball, track events, and marathons; and batting tees and swivel parts on golf carts for paraplegics (Stein, 1979).

Adapting Methods and Approaches. In order to open activities to handicapped students, it may be necessary to adapt methods, approaches, and/or content. Physical education content can be adapted for handicapped students by using differentiated objectives. The decision as to which objectives constitute an appropriate curriculum for a particular student should be based on evaluation of the student's skill level in physical development and motor performance. There are some formal tests, such as the American Alliance for Health, Physical Education, and Recreation (AAHPER) Youth Physical Fitness Test (Hunsicker & Reiff, 1976), which can be used to assess skill levels. The AAHPER Youth Fitness Test includes six test items that provide an overall indication of student fitness in grades five through twelve. National norms are available. Adaptations have been made in several of the test items to tailor this physical fitness test to the special needs of mentally retarded students, in addition to establishing norms for mildly retarded students, ages eight to eighteen (AAHPER, 1976). Most physical education assessment, however, is likely to be informal evaluation using observation to pinpoint strengths and weaknesses.

Mastery learning provides an excellent structure for physical education activities. A model used with handicapped students is based on seven steps:

1. *Physical Demonstration*—the presentation of a psychomotor learning task (by the instructor or teacher aide) in its entirety. The purpose is to provide the students with a visual picture.
2. *Verbal Explanation*—an explanation of a learning task accompanying the physical demonstration which is enthusiastic and animated. (Students often request a repetition of the demonstration and explanation and such requests are granted.)
3. *Manual Manipulation*—actual manipulation of the student through each segment of the psychomotor learning task by the teacher or teacher aide.
4. *Minimal Physical Assistance*—limited physical contact between teacher and student.
5. *Verbal Prompt*—no physical contact between teacher and students. Each student receives verbal instruction and reinforcement as needed.
6. *Upon Request*—implies student mastery of the psychomotor learning task and the ability to perform the task when requested.
7. *Mastery Demonstration*—the incorporation of a variety of psychomotor learn-

ing tasks into a single combination or routine. The mastery demonstration is conducted before an audience composed of other students, teachers, teacher aides, parents. (Chambless, Anderson, & Poole, 1981, p. 21)[1]

A Schedule of Instruction, illustrated in Table 9–2, enables the teacher to identify and evaluate components of each psychomotor task to be learned. The organization of curriculum data in this manner facilitates the preparation and implementation of meaningful IEP's.

Adaptations may include starting at more basic entry points, taking more steps in the teaching process, and using a variety of ways to reach the same goal or objective. Contract techniques (chapter 4) and behavior management strategies (chapter 10) can be used to meet individual needs.

Another consideration is the learning rate of handicapped students. All students differ in the rate at which they learn physical education skills and concepts. Some handicapping conditions impede learning rate more than others; even the same handicapping conditions will impede some persons more than others. Many students with orthopedic handicaps and other health impairments experience muscle weakness and become fatigued fairly quickly in a physical education class. It may also be more difficult for them to develop coordination. Because they can engage only in short periods of exertion, their learning rate may be slower than that of other students. On the other hand, students with learning problems might take longer to master the scoring system of tennis or the rules of football. Consideration of learning rate in the development of physical skills and concepts is essential for successful mainstreaming.

Experienced physical education teachers are aware that many individuals learn and train in unique ways. They also recognize similarities in specific methods that may, on the surface, appear to be different.

Stein (1979) suggests specific adaptations of methods and approaches for handicapped students:

Substitute walking, wheeling, rolling for running, skipping, hopping; use scooter boards, crawling, creeping, or moving in wheelchairs or on leg stumps in place of traditional and conventional means of locomotion; use bounce, roll or underhand toss to replace throwing, catching, batting; use crutches, wheelchair foot rests or prosthetic devices as implements to hit objects such as balls or pucks; substitute sitting, kneeling, lying down for standing; decrease distances as in horseshoes, ring toss, softball; reduce size of playing fields, courts, or areas; restrict players to definite places or positions; substitute lighter, larger, and more easily controlled equipment; add a bell, portable radio, or hand clapping for sound; adjust the number of tries a player is given to hit a ball; use a batting tee or let an individual hit a ball from his/her head; use hands, feet, arms, legs, head, ears, eyes, tongue, and whatever else is unique to the individual. (p. 9)

1. From Jim R. Chambless, Eugene Anderson & Jennifer H. Poole. IEP's and mastery learning applied to psychomotor activities. In Roice, G. R. (Ed.) *Teaching handicapped students physical education.* National Education Association, 1981, p. 21. Reprinted by permission.

TABLE 9-2. Schedule of Instruction

1. MANUAL MANIPULATION	2. MINIMUM PHYSICAL ASSISTANCE	3. VERBAL PROMPT	4. UPON REQUEST
DATE INITIATED	SKILL AND STUNT		DATE MASTERED
1 2 3 4	1. Line Walking according to given directions		1 2 3 4
	The student will be able to:		
	1.1 Stand with the weight evenly distributed on two feet		
	1.2 Step forward and maintain erect body posture while transferring weight from one foot to the other		
	1.3 Transfer his/her weight from heel to toe with arms in opposition to the legs		
	COMMENTS: The instructor should provide verbal cues allowing students to change direction on command. Alternative Method: Many gymnasiums have color-coded boundary lines for various courts which can be used for determining changes in direction.		

Source: From Jim R. Chambless, Eugene Anderson, & Jennifer H. Poole, IEP's and mastery learning applied to psychomotor activities. In G. Robert Roice (ed.), *Teaching handicapped students physical education.* National Education Association, 1981, p. 22. Reprinted by permission.

One appropriate teaching method for all students, regardless of their ability levels, is movement exploration. Sherrill (1976) advocates this approach to physical education instruction, particularly for students with physical handicaps, low fitness, and poor coordination. This approach capitalizes on a process of discovery and inquiry in encouraging students to assume responsibility for identifying problems and developing a plan to solve them. A visually impaired student may discover the most advantageous method of learning to bowl accurately by establishing individual objectives and instructional strategies. In testing out the instructional strategies, students can learn their own strengths and weaknesses and perhaps discover appropriate adaptations that never occurred to the teacher. This type of instruction can help teach the student a problem-solving process that can be used throughout life as physical or motor adaptations must be made.

Movement education is based on a foundation of fundamental patterns and skills. A system of abstract symbols can be used to enable hearing-impaired students to follow directions (Schmidt & Dunn, 1980). When placed on cards, the symbols can be used to reinforce verbal directions for all children.

Class Organization. Class organization and management are crucial to the successful integration of handicapped students into physical education classes. Consideration should be given to one-to-one instruction with a peer tutor or volunteer, small-group instruction, large-group instruction, learning centers, and independent work. To prevent the exclusion of handicapped students, teams should be chosen by the teacher rather than by "choosing sides."

One classroom management model, RAID, is based on these principles:

- R = Rules. Rules in the physical education classroom are established with help from students, thus allowing them to know and to help formulate clear statements of expected behavior. Rules are stated in positive terms (e.g., "Put equipment away" instead of "Don't leave equipment out").
- A = Approval. Approve or reward those students who follow the rules. Approval may be signaled by nonverbal gestures, verbal praise, or special treats such as free time or individual choice of activities.
- I = Ignore. Students who do not follow the rules are ignored. This technique, in order to be most successful, must be paired with the preceding principle of rewarding those who do follow the rules.
- D = Disapprove. Disapproval is shown when student behavior disrupts the learning process for the group. Disapproval is shown by removing rewards or by temporarily removing the student from the activity. (Folio & Norman, 1981, p. 114)

When the teacher and students are concerned with involving everyone, the class emphasis is on playing rather than on winning. In such a class, the physical education teacher asked, "Who won?" The students yelled, "We did!"

Mobility

Mobility training is important for many handicapped students and essential for visually impaired students and those with restrictive orthopedic handicaps. Mobility evaluation must consider the locus of involvements (e.g., legs, arms), the nature of involvement (e.g., paralysis, lack of coordination, loss of limbs), and the rate and stability of motion (e.g., agility, endurance). After evaluating the student's skill level and specifying appropriate objectives, the teacher, with the help of special education resource teachers and a physical therapist (if available), should proceed to adapt or develop physical education activities for the student. A rule of thumb is that games and sports should be changed to the minimum extent necessary to insure the handicapped student's success and safety.

A common misconception is that students with epilepsy should not engage in physical education. On the contrary, physical activity is recommended for many epileptics. The American Medical Association has endorsed the participation of students with epilepsy in physical education programs, except for long periods of underwater swimming, body contact sports that may produce head injuries, and gymnastic and diving activities where heights could be dangerous in the event of a fall (AMA, 1968). Students with cardiac conditions, asthma, and allergies can also benefit from physical education programs. Working with their physicians and parents, the teacher can plan a program alternating short activity periods and rest.

Mobility training for visually impaired students centers around simple map reading and tactile exploration of the environment. Mobility training in the physical education program could involve the following activities:

1. Practice walking a straight line. All sightless persons tend to veer about 1.25 inches per step or walk a spiral-shaped pathway when attempting to traverse a straight line. The ten-year-old, however, should not veer more than ten feet when attempting to walk forward for fifty feet nor more than thirty feet when moving forward 150 feet.

2. Practice facing sounds or following instructions to make quarter, half, three-quarter, and full turns. Blind adults tend to turn too much (100–105 degrees). Full turns are the most difficult with the average person moving only 320–325 degrees.

3. Practice reproducing the exact distance and pathway just taken with a partner.

4. Take a short walk with a partner and practice finding the way back to the starting point alone.

5. Outside, where the rays of the sun can be felt, practice facing north, south, east, west. Relate these to goal cages and the direction of play in various games.

6. Practice determining whether the walking surface is uphill or downhill or tilted to the left or right; relate this to the principles of stability and efficient movement.

7. Practice walking different floor patterns. Originate novel patterns and then try to reproduce the same movement. (Sherrill, 1976, pp. 342–343)

Mobility training also involves instruction in the "long cane" technique by persons trained in the education of blind people and in mobility training specifically (Cratty, 1980).

Mobility considerations must also be examined in light of the special needs of hearing-impaired students. Because the semicircular ear canals are damaged, some deaf students have problems associated with balance and coordination. The multidisciplinary team should assess these students carefully. If a problem exists, balance and coordination exercises, such as dancing and gymnastics, might be added to develop greater skill. Precautions should be taken in climbing activities so that students with balance deficiencies are not placed in dangerous situations.

Some learning-disabled students exhibit inadequate or inappropriate motor behavior and are often referred to as uncoordinated, awkward, or clumsy (Haubenstricker, 1982). Many students with such problems benefit from basic movement experiences involving activities with the balance beam, trampoline, dance, and rhythm.

High activity levels sometimes interfere with success in physical education programs. To help students control their level of activity, teachers might provide a quiet period after periods of intensive stimulation; restricted boundary areas limiting the space in which activity takes place; and reduced choices in activities and schedules. A structured lesson can contribute to a successful experience for these students.

Many students with learning disabilities are extremely sensitive to their low motor performance. Teachers can help to reduce these feelings by teaching less competitive games and sports, for example, swimming, jogging, and bike riding.

The physical development and motor performance of mildly mentally retarded students is generally equal to chronological age expectations. Many of these students compete very successfully in interscholastic athletics. Although there are no unique mobility considerations for this population, it is worth noting that many retarded persons rely more heavily on motor skills than on intellectual skills in adult vocational endeavors. For this reason, the physical education program can be an integral part of their vocational training.

Academic Progress

Many handicapped students experiencing academic difficulty can improve their academic, as well as motor, skills in a well-balanced physical education program. Mathematical skills related to counting, number facts, and processes can be taught by having students learn to keep score in various games and sports. Laying out a volleyball or tennis court offers an excellent opportunity to teach and reinforce measurement skills. Many opportunities exist to work on time concepts, for example, keeping up with the regulation time of a basketball or football game and clocking the time for track events. Some students who do not respond to more traditional approaches might benefit from learning mathematical skills in the meaningful context of physical activities.

Language arts is another curriculum area that can be closely related to physical education. Students might learn to read the rules of games and sports they particularly enjoy and improve their writing skills if given the opportunity to order special material and equipment. Library books, newspapers, and magazines related to sports might motivate students to learn to read.

Every academic subject has possible ties to physical education. When students find their greatest motivation and interest in physical education experiences, teachers should seize the opportunity to improve the students' academic performance as well. This does not require the physical education instructor to teach all subjects; rather, the classroom teacher can plan units of instruction and lesson plans around physical education themes. The coordination of objectives and strategies is essential to maximum student gain.

Peer Relationships

Physical education activities can provide a foundation for facilitating positive peer relationships of handicapped students. The nature of physical activities often involves groups, as in basketball and volleyball teams; interaction can be a natural by-product. Teachers should try to structure opportunities for handicapped students to contribute successfully to group goals.

Physical education programs have been used successfully to increase the social adjustment of mentally retarded students as well as peer relationships with nonretarded students. In addition, it has been noted that students who acquired cooperative behavior in the physical education setting demonstrated a significant increase in overall social interaction (Marlowe, 1979; Santomier & Kopczuk, 1981).

Peer teaching can help the physical education teacher increase the amount of individual attention handicapped students receive. Peer teachers can be used for demonstrating skills, assisting with equipment, keeping records, and working individually with students who have adapted programs (Folio & Norman, 1981).

Peer relationships are improved as positive attitudes develop in all class members. Peer expectations increase as nonhandicapped students broaden their perceptions of the abilities of handicapped students.

MUSIC

Because music is a multisensory experience, it can be a means for handicapped students to develop sensory perception and discrimination, rhythm, tonality, and other skills that contribute to cognitive and affective learning. In addition, music activities can help students develop self-control, concentration, cooperation, and task completion (Smith & Perks, 1978). Music plays an important part in the lives of handicapped children, youth, and adults, contributing to the total growth of the individual.

FIGURE 9–2. Music Group

Concept Development

Music classes are frequently expected to perform in unison, with students beginning and ending the musical selection together, singing each word at the same time, or playing an instrument in a precise rhythm dictated by the music (Beer, Bellows, & Frederick, 1982). Such expectations do not take into account the different learning rates and modalities that handicapped students bring to music classes. Music educators agree, however, that music is just as important to handicapped students as it is to nonhandicapped students. Thompson (1982) suggests that music education can be provided for handicapped learners by clarifying goals, conferring with other teachers, and modifying teaching strategies.

Clarifying Goals. The final report of the Special Projects Committee of the Music Educators National Conference and the National Committee, Arts for the Handicapped, stated:

> . . . the goals for music education for handicapped learners do not differ significantly from the goals for music education for all learners. The process of learning to perform, create, and respond to music makes a significant contribution to the development of that part of every being which is uniquely human. Although various handicapping conditions may limit the means through which individuals can make music and respond to music, the potential for enhancing the human experiences through musical learning does not change. (Thompson, 1982, p. 26)

In addition to the development of aesthetic responsiveness, there is considerable emphasis by music and classroom teachers on the development of motor skills, perceptual skills, social skills, and other nonmusical behaviors.

Conferring with Other Teachers. The special education teacher, the classroom teacher, and the music teacher need to share information and ideas. Communication can be facilitated by participating in the IEP meeting, observing students in various situations, and discussing the strengths and weaknesses of individual students as they relate to music.

Modifying Teaching Strategies. There are music curriculum considerations that can help students progress in concept development. The teacher should use music that is meaningful to and valued by students. When concepts are introduced, the selected music should clearly illustrate the concept. The lesson plan should move gradually toward using many different music examples, requiring finer degrees of discrimination and understanding, so that mastery is possible. Some students learn more efficiently through one sensory channel than another, or from responding to music through one form or another. Generally, it is educationally sound to provide practice on music concepts in various ways, using diverse materials. Welsbacher (1972) advocates the multisensory approach when teaching upward movement of melody by having students *move* their hands up as the music portrays upward movement; *sing* sequences that move upward; *play* instruments, such as the xylophone, to depict upward movement; and *look* at pictures illustrating upward movement. By approaching concept development through different experiences and providing sufficient practice for mastery, teachers can help handicapped students to progress in the quality and rate of their concept formation.

For some handicapped students, only minor musical adaptations will be necessary. Students with emotional problems will probably need adaptations only in the area of behavior management. Students with learning disabilities may lack the gross and fine motor coordination appropriate for their age or may have perceptual problems that result in impaired visual or aural reception of music (White, 1982). Orthopedically handicapped students encounter problems with the physical manipulation of instruments and with classroom organization for maximum mobility. It is necessary, therefore, to pinpoint the sensory, physical, and behavioral problems to be considered.

Hearing-impaired students require adapted instructional approaches in music to develop musical concepts. As discussed in chapter 1, hearing impairment must be considered according to each student's hearing pattern as related to frequency (pitch) and intensity (loudness). Hearing-impaired students vary in the pitch range of their handicap. Thus, some of these students might be less handicapped in learning musical concepts when examples are used at a high rather than low pitch level, or vice versa. Also, some students benefit from amplification more than others in minimizing intensity disadvantages. Developing residual hearing through auditory awareness and auditory discrimination activities is of special benefit to the hearing-impaired student, as well as to the blind student who must rely on acute hearing for safety and space orientation.

Even students with severe hearing impairments can successfully develop musical concepts. Deaf students can experience music through touch and vision and learn concepts through those sensory channels. These students can associate the sounds of instruments through feeling the vibrations. Fahey and Birkenshaw (1972) suggest that large drums or the timpani, bass xylophones, and base metallophones have been found most helpful in training deaf students to distinguish the vibrations of musical instruments from other environmental sounds. Students can also feel the vibrations of the piano and rhythm band instruments. By having students feel the instrument and indicating when the music starts and stops, teachers can reinforce the tactile perception of sound. Rhythmic visual clues can be provided to deaf students by using a metronome so that they can "see" fast and slow tempos. They can observe another student dance to a musical selection and then go through the steps of the dance themselves. For readers who would like more information, Fahey and Birkenshaw (1972) outline a multitude of specific instructional strategies for teaching musical concepts to deaf students.

Often teachers have assumed that the ear is the most essential factor in successful musical experiences. It must be remembered that all handicaps can be minimized with adapted instructional approaches. Epley (1972) describes her personal experience of playing the bass drum and cymbals in the university band following an accident that resulted in her becoming deaf. She stated that "alert eyes, strict counting, and self-confidence" enabled her to play successfully and find enjoyment with the rest of the band.

> Why did I ask to join the band and risk the work of the other band members and the director? Why did I decide to make participation in music an aspect of my whole life? Aaron Copland once said that to stop the flow of music would be like the stopping of time itself, incredible and inconceivable. In my opinion he is absolutely correct. Music can provide a feeling of achievement, give a personal pleasure as well as pleasure to other people, and in general, furnish an individual with a way to express himself. For these reasons, I want to continue taking part in soundless musical activities. This can only be possible, however, if musicians will open up their world to me and the thousands of other handicapped persons and let us join in their music-making. (p. 39)

Steps developed to teach music to deaf students can be used with students who have varying degrees of hearing loss. Perkins (1979) suggests starting with the young student sitting on the piano while the teacher plays. The student hears the music through a hearing aid, sees the teacher striking the keys, and feels the music through vibrations of the piano. As students focus on music, they begin to respond to it, to discriminate between sounds, and to substitute visual and auditory stimulation for the tactile stimulation.

In integrating the visually impaired student with sighted students, the usual visual approach must be modified. Auditory and tactile stimuli can be used for all students. Lam and Wang (1982) suggest the introduction of braille and conventional printed symbols to the visually impaired student. Since it is impossible to provide raised printed music scores, a knowledge of printed music symbols and braille music symbols helps the student understand the teacher in a mainstreamed situation. Some students may have the opportunity to use an optacon, an electronic device that converts the image of printed letters or symbols into a tactile form.

Very little adjustment is needed for visually impaired students in activities based on auditory input, such as clapping or rhythmic pattern recognition. In teaching notational skills, raised symbols can be constructed from pipe cleaners or felt, or by drawing with a crayon on a piece of window screen mounted on cardboard (Lam & Wang, 1982).

Students might also learn concepts through verbal instruction and physical guidance. For example, a blind student learning to play a guitar might be given a verbal explanation of finger positioning for a particular chord and then guided into the particular position by the teacher's placing the student's fingers correctly. Since blind students typically develop keen auditory abilities, they might learn to play instruments or sing musical selections by "ear." To capitalize on this approach, the teacher can tape selections for them to listen to or model over and over. The American Printing House for the Blind and the Division of the Blind and Physically Handicapped of the Library of Congress (see Appendix B) have a wealth of resources that are available to music teachers. Some of these include slow taping of instrumental music, large-print and braille music, books explaining the braille music code, and records and tapes of music periodicals (Mooney, 1972). In addition, help is available from the National Braille Association Reader-Transcriber Registry and the Lexington Educational Aids Workshop.

Mobility

Portions of the music curriculum, such as singing, dancing, rhythmic development, and instrumental instruction, require movement of one type or another. Each music curriculum subcomponent incorporates different types of mobility requirements focused on various body parts, including the oral cavity, lower trunk, arms, hands, and fingers. Some music experiences, such as playing a flute, require fine motor control, whereas clapping to keep time with rhythm is a gross motor activity. Mobility rate and stability are also important factors to consider as related to music. The rhythm of group music activities typically sets the rate at which students should perform or participate in the activity. Students who have slow rates of mobility may have a difficult time keeping up with a fast tempo, whether singing, playing instruments, or engaging in any other type of music experience. Finally, stability of motion is an important consideration when activities require physical endurance because of extended lengths of movement. These activities include participation in the marching band, frequent and extended practice and performance sessions of the school orchestra, and dancing classes. Mobility adaptations can be made in the music curriculum to minimize the disadvantages of blindness, deafness, and orthopedic handicaps.

On the whole, visual impairment is less of a handicap in music than in some other areas of learning. However, one subcomponent of the music curriculum that warrants special consideration is rhythmic movement, particularly when a visually impaired child is young and just learning skills related to orientation and mobility. Some visually impaired students may not be as secure or coordinated in rhythmic movement as their peers, due possibly to previous limited opportunities to explore the endless variations of movement. Rhythmic activities can aid the development of mobility skills. Visually impaired students may begin with large free movements, with gradual emphasis on the refinement of the movements. In helping to structure rhythmic activities for the visually impaired student, the teacher can use verbal directions and physical guidance, which involves helping to move the student's limbs or body in the desired manner.

Rhythmic movements can be valuable in teaching the visually impaired student concepts related to motion, such as a wheel rolling, trees swaying in the wind, and an elephant walking. Special emphasis might also be given to teaching visually impaired students popular dance steps to enhance their social acceptance, participation, and self-confidence at school social functions.

Deaf children can use movement to learn rhythms they cannot hear. They can observe a particular rhythmic sequence done in different meters and then reproduce the pattern by clapping or playing rhythm instruments. This kinesthetic approach to teaching rhythm can be a valuable teaching strategy (Fahey & Birkenshaw, 1972). Movement exercises combined with music can improve all students' agility, posture, and physical fitness.

Adaptations in the music program should be considered for orthopedically handicapped students. Students unable to walk might crawl, roll over, clap their hands, or engage in some other response when rhythmic experiences are being shared by the class. Students with physical handicaps might learn rhythm by observing dance or gymnastics activities or by combining rhythmic activities with their physical therapy sessions. Playing instruments is another music experience that can be adapted for students with mobility disadvantages. Teachers should analyze the various degrees of coordination and types of movement required to play different instruments.

Academic Progress

Although music educators disclaim the central purpose of music education as a catalyst or reinforcer for other areas of study, this is an important purpose in music for handicapped students (Reichard & Blackburn, 1973). In the language arts curriculum, music is an appropriate tool in teaching many skills, including listening and reading. In developing oral communication skills, music is invaluable.

Music activities provide excellent opportunities for helping students with communication handicaps. Many students who have stuttering problems are more fluent when singing than when talking. Singing provides a structured rhythm that can be an excellent therapeutic tool. Instructional strategies need to be carefully coordinated among the music teacher, classroom teacher, and speech therapist to maximize the overall benefit of music experiences for students with communication handicaps. The speech therapist can suggest ways to help students who stutter minimize this handicap through music, which might generalize to other communication experiences. Additionally, if music poses no problems for these students, they should have the opportunity to sing in the school chorus or to join in similar experiences to gain recognition for their strengths in this area.

Articulation problems lend themselves to possible remediation activities in music. Teachers and students can make up songs that incorporate the particular sounds the student is working on in speech therapy. Such an example using the M sound is:

> Miles away there is a man
> Who makes the children happy.
> Miles away this merry man
> Sings songs to make them happy.
> (Flowers, 1963, p. 104)

While the student is being provided practice in speech, instruction on music concepts, such as melody, harmony, and rhythm, can be built into the experiences with song writing. Another opportunity for improving articulation is to provide vocal warm-up drills to exercise the lips, tongue, and larynx. Students can also be taught particular positioning of the parts of their oral cavity. This can help students learn to produce sounds correctly and can carry over to lipreading training for hearing-impaired students.

Music is an excellent vehicle for helping students disadvantaged by voice problems related to pitch, intensity, quality, and flexibility (chapter 1 includes an explanation of these communication handicaps). For example, students can be taught rhythm, which is necessary for appropriate flexibility in speaking, by clapping the accents of words or phrases, walking the rhythmic sequence, or illustrating it by playing percussion instruments (Fahey & Birkenshaw, 1972). Practice should be structured to insure generalization to speech patterns. Activities can also be provided to help students identify various instrumental pitch levels and experiment with matching their speech with the range in levels. Students with speech problems associated with pitch will be helped best if music teachers coordinate their program with that of the speech therapist. In order to provide appropriate practice for students with voice problems and to promote generalization of communication skills learned through music to other speech and language experiences, teachers should pick songs and experiences that emphasize natural rhythmic accents, tonal inflections, and pitch.

Students who are disadvantaged by very low reading levels might learn concepts through music that they fail to master from reading their textbooks. One reading program, Hits (ModuLearn, Inc.), uses popular hit songs to teach phonetics, structural analysis, vocabulary, and comprehension skills. Skills in arithmetic, social studies, physical education, socialization, and all other curriculum areas can be reinforced through music experiences.

The development of perceptual skills can be facilitated by the use of motor skills (laterality, directionality, and regular pulse response); sequential memory (songs, chants, and movement); intellectual organization (study of form); and listening (following directions, mood sensitivity, and similarities and differences in sound). Science lessons could include a study of acoustics, and social studies could use songs that chronicle historical events. The social aspects of music are reinforced in folk dancing, games, and ensemble work (McCoy, 1982).

Peer Relationships

Music activities can provide opportunities for handicapped students to share experiences with their nonhandicapped peers, develop hobbies that promote peer relationships outside of school, and receive positive recognition accentuating their strengths, which could result in heightened classroom status. The group nature of many music activities provides an excellent setting for student interaction, and teachers should try to insure that handicapped students have the skills to make positive contributions to the group. For example, if several students are writing a song together and the handicapped member has severe language delays and poor penmanship, this student probably will not be able to participate effectively in this assignment. Positive peer relationships involve both giving and receiving. Teachers should structure situations in which the handicapped student can contribute to and draw from the group resources. The student with language and writing problems may be very successful in a group activity aimed at devising a folk dance. Handicapped students should be considered for the school chorus, orchestra, and other music activities on the same basis as other students. They should not be automatically ruled out simply because they are handicapped.

Hobbies related to music can be enjoyable leisure activities throughout one's life. Hobbies can also be socializing catalysts in neighborhoods and the community. Students who have special difficulty forming friendships might be aided by developing hobbies that provide natural ties with other persons. In music, these hobbies might include playing in a rock or folk band, participating in choral groups, collecting records, attending concerts, singing in the church choir, or joining a dancing group. If handicapped students are so inclined, teachers should encourage the development of such hobbies and provide an opportunity for the hobby to be shared with the class. Sharing hobbies within class can help build the bridge to sharing outside the school.

Some musically talented handicapped students may achieve more in this curriculum area than in any other. Being at a significant disadvantage in some subjects makes it particularly important to "shine" in others. If music is the student's strength, teachers should capitalize on this successful experience to help the handicapped student receive the respect of peers. The student might be asked to conduct the class's singing, write a class song, demonstrate how to play an instrument, play the lead in a musical performed by the class, participate in school-sponsored and community-based special events in music, or act as a peer tutor on music activities. This should not be viewed as favoritism to the handicapped student, and certainly similar opportunities should be extended to nonhandicapped students talented in music.

Music can be a strong social reinforcer. A group of music makers, working together, can develop a sense of belonging, unity, and acceptance (Smith & Perks, 1978).

ART

Goodlad and Morrison (1980) claim that education is incomplete when it fails to include art. Therefore, a school curriculum including little or no time for art is inadequate, whatever the level of the students' achievement in reading, mathematics, or science.

Concept Development

Art activities allow students to develop and participate at individual rates and ability levels and to study and adapt to their environments. Since basic skills and subjects can be taught through art, it has proven to be valuable in remedial instruction (List, 1982).

Art enables handicapped students to initiate their own ideas and materials, rather than to assume passive roles (Smith & Perks, 1978). As with music, the full benefits of art for handicapped students can be derived through clarifying goals and modifying curriculum and teaching strategies.

Clarifying Goals. Art instruction, like music and other creative art forms, has many purposes. As part of the general curriculum, art should promote social, personal, and perceptual/conceptual development. As a discipline, art should help students understand and appreciate the feelings, ideas, and values that major traditions of art communicate (Clark & Zimmerman, 1981).

The following are general goals for art programs:

- The arts develop creativity in children.
- Art experiences assist in the development of intelligent consumers and producers.
- Cooperative endeavors and social adjustments result from participation in group art activities.
- The visual experience promotes the growth and development of the child.
- Art activities and experiences provide for the release of emotion and feelings. (List, 1982, p. 5)

For handicapped students, art has many benefits. It provides a medium of communication for students with limited speech and writing abilities; it helps expand the student's frame of reference by providing new experiences; it is useful in developing manual dexterity; it provides opportunities to work cooperatively with others; it can be coordinated with other classroom learning experiences to help develop various concepts; and it can help in preparing for work situations (Krone, 1978).

Modifying Curriculum and Strategies. As in other disciplines, the content of art instruction must be ordered in developmental sequences that meet the individual needs of learners (Clark & Zimmerman, 1981). Lowenfeld and Brittain (1964) have provided a developmental sequence of artisitic abilities (see Table 9–3). This model outlines a hierarchy of skills and concepts that can be used in assessing a student's developmental level and in planning appropriate art activities.

After initial assessment has been accomplished and teachers have an idea of a particular student's strengths and weaknesses, adaptations in the art curriculum may be needed to accommodate the student's unique needs. Adaptations may have to be made in what is to be taught (content), how the content is to be taught (methods/materials), and when the content is to be taught (timing/sequence).

Many characteristics associated with handicapping conditions necessitate content modifications of the art curriculum. Learning-disabled or mentally retarded students may have short attention spans or difficulty in remembering directions. These characteristics often require curriculum adaptation in timing and sequence. Additionally, lowered functioning in some academic subjects may create problems in art. For example, if the students are expected to read a poem and illustrate it with a painting, students with learning problems may

TABLE 9-3. Summary of Developmental Stages

SUMMARY: PRESCHEMATIC STAGE—FOUR TO SEVEN YEARS

CHARACTER-ISTICS	HUMAN FIGURE	SPACE	COLOR	DESIGN	MOTIVATION TOPICS	MATERIALS
Discovery of *relationship* between drawing, thinking, and environment. Change of form symbols because of constant search for definite concept.	Circular motion for head, longitudinal for legs and arms. Head-feet representations develop to more complex form concept. Symbols depending on active knowledge during the act of drawing.	Self as center, with no orderly arrangement of objects in space: "There is a table, there is a door, there is a chair." Also emotional relationships: "This is *my* doll."	No relationship to nature. Color according to emotional appeal.	No conscious approach.	Activating of passive knowledge related mainly to self (body parts).	Crayons, clay, tempera paints (thick), large bristle brushes, large sheets of paper (absorbent).

326

SUMMARY: SCHEMATIC STAGE—SEVEN TO NINE YEARS

CHARACTER-ISTICS	HUMAN FIGURE	SPACE	COLOR	DESIGN	MOTIVATION TOPICS	MATERIALS
Formulation of a definite concept of man and environment. Self-assurance through repetition of form symbols, schemata. In pure schema no intentional experience is expressed, only the thing itself: "the man," "the tree," etc. Experiences are expressed by deviations from schema. Use of geometric lines.	Definite concept of figure depending on active knowledge and personality, through repetition: schema. Deviations expressing experiences can be seen in— (1) Exaggeration of important parts. (2) Neglect or omission of unimportant parts. (3) Change of symbols.	First definite space concept: base line. Discovery of being a part of environment: important for cooperation and reading. Base line expresses— (1) Base (2) Terrain Deviations from base line express experiences. Subjective space: (1) Folding over (egocentric). (2) Mixed forms of plan and elevation. (3) X-ray pictures. (4) Space-time representations.	Discovery of relationship between color and object; through repetition: color schema. Same color for same object. Deviation of color schema shows emotional experience.	No conscious design approach.	Best motivation concentrates on action, characterized by *we, action, where*. Topics referring to—(1) Time sequences (journeys, traveling stories). (2) X-ray pictures (inside and outside are emphasized), factory, school, home, etc.	Colored crayons. Colored chalks. Tempera, poster paint. Large paper. Bristle and hair brushes. Clay: (1) Synthetic (2) Analytic

SUMMARY: STAGE OF DAWNING REALISM—NINE TO ELEVEN YEARS

CHARACTER-ISTICS	HUMAN FIGURE	SPACE	COLOR	DESIGN	MOTIVATION TOPICS	MATERIALS
Gang age. Removal from geometric lines (schema). Lack of cooperation with adults. Greater awareness of the self and of sex differences.	Attention to clothes (dresses, uniforms), emphasizing difference between girls and boys. Greater stiffness as result of egocentric attitude, and the emphasis on details (clothes, hair, and so forth). Tendency toward realistic lines. Removal from schema.	Removal from base-line expression. Overlapping. Sky comes down to base line. Discovery of plane. Filling in space between base lines. Difficulties in spatial correlations as result of egocentric attitude and lack of cooperation.	Removal from objective stage of color. Emphasis on emotional approach to color. Subjective stage of color. Color is used according to subjective experience.	First conscious approach toward decoration. Acquaintance with materials and their function.	Self-awareness stimulated by characterization of different dresses and suits (professions). Cooperation and overlapping through group work. Subjective cooperation through type of topic: "We are building a house." Objective cooperation through team work.	Paper cutting. Crayons. Poster paint. Flat, colored chalk. Clay. Papier-mâché. Wood. Collage materials. Metal. Prints.

Source: Reprinted with permission of Macmillan Publishing Company from CREATIVE AND MENTAL GROWTH, 4th Edition by Viktor Lowenfeld and W. Lambert Brittain. Copyright © 1964 by Macmillan Publishing Company.

be unable to read the poem. The use of a peer tutor or a tape presentation can eliminate this particular problem. Some students with learning problems have difficulty with spatial orientation, which is an important prerequisite to higher level artistic functioning. These students may be unable to draw a human figure without gross body distortions. The spatial problems of some students can be remediated through sound instruction and practice; other students will always have significant spatial problems.

Teachers should help students compensate for their deficiencies by developing interests and talents in other artistic endeavors that they can perform successfully. Many students with learning problems have strong talents in art. In these cases, teachers should use the artistic channel to teach other academic skills and to improve self-concepts.

Blind and partially sighted students, as well as orthopedically handicapped students with hand and arm involvement, often require adaptations in all areas of the art curriculum—content, methods/materials, and timing/sequence. Because of limitations imposed by the handicap, students may be below the developmental level in art predicted on the basis of chronological age (Table 9–3). Teachers have to determine student performance levels and provide instruction at those levels in order to establish a strong foundation of artistic skills and concepts. The teaching/learning style options described in the earlier section on physical education also apply to art education. These include visual guidance, verbal guidance, multisensory instruction, and the movement exploration approach.

As for multisensory instruction, blind students typically learn best through a combination of auditory, tactile, and kinesthetic experiences. When teaching blind students macramé, the teacher might provide verbal instruction in how to make a particular knot, have the student feel the texture of the knot (loose, tight, smooth, pointed), and guide the student's hands and fingers through the sequence of steps involved in making the knot. Other art activities that have been mastered and enjoyed by blind students include experiences with clay, sculpture, printmaking, collages, finger painting, papier mâché, and ceramics. A variety of textures should be used and explored to familiarize blind students with their environment and to refine the tactile skills necessary for learning braille. Art media are plentiful, including paper (regular, sandpaper, tracing paper, wax paper), wood, textiles, wet sand, string, yarn, pipe cleaners, wires, rubber, plastic, and glass.

The adaptation that is usually necessary for concept development to proceed is in the sequencing of art activities.

The sixth-grade class was making crayon collages by coloring a sheet of paper with different colors. After the coloring was completed, they outlined each different color section by gluing string around its border. David, a blind student, participated in the activity by reversing the procedure: first, he glued string in various patterns on the sheet and then he colored

FIGURE 9–3. Collage by Visually Impaired Student

the inside of each section. His collage, depicted in Figure 9–3, was one of the best in the class.

The range of individual differences in approach and ability is tremendous in art productions. Examples of the range are shown in Figure 9–4, drawn by a seven-year-old nonhandicapped student, and Figure 9–5, drawn by an eleven-year-old mentally retarded student.

Even though drawings are not used to make judgments about students, they can be used to plan activities appropriate for them. Using Lowenfeld and Brittain's developmental stages (Table 9–3), students can be grouped into levels of instruction based on their art samples. Art lessons can be developed that meet individual student needs within a class and still provide common experiences.

Mobility

Art experiences and activities frequently require movement. Some are gross movements, such as finger painting; others require very fine control, such as sketching or carving very small figures. Orthopedically handicapped students, particularly those who have limited mobility in their arms, hands, and fingers, may require adaptations in the art curriculum. For some students who cannot hold a pencil, crayon, or paint brush in the typical fashion, a ball of clay or foam rubber sponge attached to the tool provides a better grip. Students who have jerky or uncoordinated movements frequently have papers slip off their desks, spill paint, or knock crayons to the floor. Teachers can use masking tape to position the paper on the student's desk or table. Students who have uncontrolled movements or who are particularly clumsy can work at a special

FIGURE 9–4.
Drawing by a Seven-Year-Old Student

table away from the major material storage areas in the classroom. Limits can be placed on how many materials they may have on their table at one time, and a special area of the table can be set aside for materials and supplies. Reserving one area of the table for materials encourages students to be particularly careful with haphazard movements in that direction. A sturdy rack with holes for paint jars also prevents spillage.

Some students with physical limitations may also have extreme difficulty manipulating small objects. Rather than making a collage or junk sculpture with small pieces of material, they may have to use larger materials that are easier to handle. Other students with more severe limitations will require more substantial adaptations.

Art activities involve a tremendous range of mobility requirements. Because of the variety of possible activities, teachers can be tremendously flexible when making needed adaptations for handicapped students.

332   CHAPTER 9   *Teaching Physical Education, Music and Art*

FIGURE 9–5. Drawing by an Eleven-Year-Old Student

Academic Progress

Art provides student-centered experiences that are adaptable to every aspect of the school curriculum and to all skill areas. It is particularly relevant to the language arts, science, mathematics, and social studies.

The Language Arts.   Art is a method of expression. Through art, students can become more sensitive to their own ideas and feelings and communicate these with peers and adults. Art is an important form of communication for all students, but it may have especially important implications for students with language handicaps who are impaired in some channels of communication.

The language experience method of teaching reading (see chapter 5) has traditionally been a vehicle for incorporating art. Students describe their experiences; the teacher or a peer writes down the words of the student; and the student illustrates the words through art projects and learns to recognize and comprehend the words in written form. Art can be a very important component of the language experience approach to reading instruction.

Science. Art can be used to teach science as it relates to concepts of texture, color, pattern, space, shape, and form. Specific topics can be interrelated through science and art. As described in chapter 8, science and art activities have been particularly valuable in programs for visually impaired students.

Mathematics. Through art, concepts of form and shape can be developed. Art can also be used to teach counting, numbers, graphs, measurement, symbols, fractions, proportions, and time (List, 1982).

Social Studies. In the social studies curriculum, art can play a major role. For example, many students unable to read the textbook can learn concepts about foreign customs by analyzing pictures and other visual media; they can demonstrate their knowledge of these customs by constructing collages, shoebox stories, murals, and props for a play. This instructional strategy should not be used in a singular fashion, but rather combined with other strategies into a multisensory approach.

Peer Relationships

Art education provides many opportunities for students to work together and to share their expertise. When handicapped students have special talents in art, they should have the opportunity to receive peer recognition and classroom status.

Art instruction can be planned to encourage small-group interaction. For example, group murals can be vehicles for learning artistic and academic skills and concepts and for increasing positive peer interaction. Teachers must try to insure that handicapped students make positive contributions to the group and are regarded as assets rather than liabilities.

Art hobbies that stem from school experiences can carry over into neighborhood and community experiences. These hobbies can initiate lifelong leisure interests. As community experiences and leisure interests develop, handicapped persons increase their opportunities for interacting with peers. Art can serve as a bridge between people of similar interests.

The arts (music, art, dance, and drama) can enhance the cognitive, social, and emotional development of handicapped students and adults. The National Committee, Arts for the Handicapped, was created in 1975 for the purpose of coordinating the development of a nationwide program of all arts for all handicapped students. The organization is committed to the belief that "the arts can provide unique ways of acquiring skills and knowledge as well as bringing opportunities for beautiful experiences, and that handicapped people have a right to a full measure of both" (Appell, 1979).

SUMMARY

Physical education, music, and art are essential elements of education for all children and youth, including those who are handicapped. These three areas of experience offer avenues of expression, approaches to learning, and development of skills for leisure activities. In addition, there are components in each of the disciplines that are relevant to the acquisition of vocational skills. Perhaps the most important benefit lies in the development of positive self-concept. Through experiences provided in physical education, music, and art, many handicapped students are successful in personal and shared experiences.

REFERENCES

AAHPER. *Special fitness test manual for mildly retarded persons.* Washington, D.C.: AAHPER Publications, 1976.

AMA. The epileptic child and competitive school athletics. *Pediatrics,* 1968, *42,* 700.

Apell, L. S. Enhancing learning and enriching lives: Arts in the education of handicapped children. *Teaching Exceptional Children,* 1979, *11*(2), 74–76.

Aufsesser, P. M. Adapted physical education. *Journal of Physical Education, Recreation and Dance,* 1981, *52*(6), 28–31.

Beer, A. S., Bellows, N. L., & Frederick, A. M. D. Providing for different rates of music learning. *Music Educators Journal,* 1982, *68*(8), 40–43.

Carlson, G. P. Physical education is basic. *Journal of Physical Education, Recreation and Dance,* 1982, *53*(1), 67–69.

Chambless, J. R., Anderson, E., & Poole, J. H. IEP's and mastery learning applied to psychomotor activities. In G. R. Roice (Ed.), *Teaching handicapped students physical education.* National Education Association, 1981, 20–22.

Clark, G., & Zimmerman, E. Toward a discipline of art education. *Phi Delta Kappan,* 1981, *63*(1), 53–56.

Cratty, B. J. *Adapted physical education for handicapped children and youth.* Denver: Love Publishing Co., 1980.

Epley, C. In a soundless world of musical enjoyment. In Malcolm E. Bessom (Ed.), *Music in special education.* Washington, D.C.: Music Educators National Conference, 1972.

Fahey, J. D., & Birkenshaw, L. Bypassing the ear: The perception of music by feeling and touch. In Malcolm E. Bessom (Ed.), *Music in special education.* Washington, D.C.: Music Educators National Conference, 1972.

Fait, H. F. *Special physical education.* Philadelphia: W. B. Saunders Co., 1978.

Feldman, E. B. Art in the mainstream: A statement of value and commitment. *Art Education,* 1982, 35(2), 4–5.

Folio, M. R., & Norman, A. Toward more success in mainstreaming: A peer teacher approach to physical education. *Teaching Exceptional Children,* 1981, 13(3), 110–113.

Flowers, A. M. *The big book of sounds.* Danville, Ill.: Interstate, 1963.

Goodlad, J. I., & Morrison, J. The arts and education. In J. J. Hausman (Ed.), *Arts and the schools.* New York: McGraw-Hill, 1980, 1–21.

Haubenstricker, J. L. Motor development in children with learning disabilities. *Journal of Physical Education, Recreation and Dance,* 1982, *53*(5), 41–43.

Hunsicker, P., & Reiff, G. G. *Youth fitness test manual.* Washington, D.C.: AAHPER Publications, 1976.

Krone, A. *Art instruction for handicapped children.* Denver: Love Publishing Co., 1978.

Lam, R. C., & Wang, C. Integrating blind and sighted through music. *Music Educators Journal,* 1982, *68*(8), 44–45.

List, L. K. *Music, art and drama experiences for the elementary curriculum.* New York: Teachers College Press, 1982.

Lowenfeld, V., & Brittain, W. L. *Creative and mental growth* (4th ed.). New York: Macmillan Publishing Co., 1964.

Marlowe, M. The games analysis intervention: A procedure to increase the peer acceptance and social adjustment of a retarded child. *Education and Training of the Mentally Retarded,* 1979, *14*(4), 262–268.

McCoy, M. In the mainstream. *Music Educators Journal,* 1982, *68*(8), 51.

Mooney, M. K. Blind children need training, not sympathy. In M. E. Bessom (Ed.), *Music in special education.* Washington, D.C.: Music Educators National Conference, 1972.

Perkins, C. E. Music to their ears. *Instructor,* 1979, *89*(4), 134–136.

Prescott, M. P. The crisis in music education. *Music Educators Journal,* 1981, *68*(3), 35–38.

Reichard, C. L., & Blackburn, D. B. *Music based instruction for the exceptional child.* Denver: Love Publishing Co., 1973.

Runkel, P. E. When funds are low, what gets cut? *Music Educators Journal,* 1981, *68*(4), 38, 57.

Santomier, J., & Kopczuk, W. Facilitation of interactions between retarded and nonretarded students in a physical education setting. *Education and Training of the Mentally Retarded,* 1981, *16*(1), 20–23.

Schmidt, S., & Dunn, J. M. Physical education for the hearing impaired. *Educating Exceptional Children,* 1980, *12*(3), 99–102.

Sherrill, C. *Adapted physical education and recreation.* Dubuque, Iowa: William C. Brown Co., 1976.

Smith, J., & Perks, W. *Humanism and the arts in special education.* Albuquerque, N.M.: University of New Mexico, 1978.

Stein, J. U. The mission and the mandate: Special education, the not so sleeping giant. *Education Unlimited,* 1979, *1*(2), 6–11.

Sudano, G. R., & Sharpham, J. Back to basics: Justifying the arts in general education. *Music Educators Journal,* 1981, *68*(3), 48–50.

Taylor, R. G. Overtones. *Music Educators Journal,* 1982, *68*(8), 5.

Thompson, K. Education of handicapped learners. *Music Educators Journal,* 1982, *68*(8), 25–29.

Welsbacher, B. T. More than a package of bizarre behavior. In M. E. Bessom (Ed.), *Music in special education.* Washington, D.C.: Music Educators National Conference, 1972.

White, L. D. How to adapt for special students. *Music Educators Journal,* 1982, *68*(8), 49–50, 63–67.

10

Managing Classroom Behavior

Managing the behavior of handicapped students is one of the primary factors in determining successful mainstreamed placements. Two facets of behavior have to be considered. First is the curtailment of inappropriate behavior:

David never enters a room; he falls into it. He stalks about the room, breaking things, creating confusion, and being the class clown. The other children laugh at him, and he destroys all my well-laid plans.

Second is the increase of appropriate behavior:

I have twenty-five fourth graders and Tony. Tony rarely completes his assignments. How can I help him complete his work and still meet the needs of the other students?

Handicapped children and youth can acquire immature or antisocial behavior for many reasons. They may be overprotected at home, where temper tantrums, interruptions, or overbearing attitudes are permitted. They may have been enrolled in special schools or special classes, where behavior standards were not as high as in other situations. They may function at a level where most persons do not expect normal behavior from them. They may have experienced chronic failure in school that has resulted in rebellious behavior. They may have special problems, such as hyperactivity or serious emotional disturbances, that contribute to their behavior problems. Regardless of the reason, inappropriate behavior can be replaced by acceptable behavior. This change alone can make a tremendous difference in the degree to which students are accepted by teachers and peers.

After talking with David about his behavior, we listed things that needed to be changed. We made a chart, with space for check marks each time he entered the room quietly, put his books away promptly, etc. With each five checks, David can spend thirty minutes working on his string art, which he loves to do. We also set up a check system for the other students, giving them checks for not laughing at David, and removing checks when they do laugh. I feel that David is gradually assuming responsibility for his own behavior.

DEFINING TEACHER EXPECTATIONS

Behavior problems occur when there is a discrepancy between what the teacher expects and what students do (Regan, 1979). Teachers might expect attention in class—but some students want to sleep; teachers might expect class members to get along with each other—but some students fight; teachers might expect work to be handed in on time—but some students are chronically late. Thus, the two important dimensions that need to be examined are teacher expectations and student behavior. This section focuses on teacher expectations; it is followed by strategies for recognizing and defining student behavior.

A necessary first step to increasing the appropriate behavior of all students is for the teacher to define behavioral expectations. Such expectations evolve from the teacher's values and beliefs about how students should behave in the classroom. Remember that the same behavior is seen *differently* in *different* situations and by *different* people (Barnes, Eyman, & Engolz, 1974). One teacher stated her values and beliefs as follows:

> *I believe that teachers should operate in a highly authoritarian manner. Students should be told what is expected of them, and any infraction of the rules should bring an automatic detention period. Without exception, rules and sanctions should be consistently applied.*

Another teacher stated an alternative philosophy:

> *Classroom discipline is an area where I usually don't have too many problems. Part of the reason for that is that I am a very relaxed teacher and many things don't bother me. I am not a reactor. At the beginning of each year, we jointly discuss what is acceptable behavior and what is not. They help set the rules and if I can't live with something, I tell them so and we compromise, and vice-versa.*

Obviously, the basic beliefs of these teachers will influence the actual rules they devise and their methods for applying contingencies to both appropriate and inappropriate behavior. There is no set of "correct" beliefs and values; rather, teachers need to delineate a philosophy that is consistent with their personality and instructional style.

The clarification of beliefs and values is a foundation for specifying actual classroom rules. Clear rule setting is helpful for all students with a history of behavior problems. Such students benefit from expectations that are explicit, fair, and within their range of achievement. An elementary teacher reported rules that he and his students developed:

1. Stay on task and follow directions
2. Have school supplies ready and assignments completed

3. Raise your hand to receive permission to talk
4. Walk to and from classes in line with no talking.

Once rules are developed, they should be put in writing and posted in class. Particularly at the beginning of the year, students may need reminders and clarifications of the rules. A secondary social studies teacher described the procedures she uses:

> *I believe the first week of class is very important and can set the tone for the year. During that week I spend 90 percent of my time deciding with the students what the ground rules will be, how routines will be handled, and what the operational mechanics of the classroom will be. Future problems can be avoided by putting the rules down in writing. By taking care of these things during the first week, we can spend the rest of the year more beneficially learning about government.*

Once rules have been established, it can be helpful to review those rules with the class on a periodic basis to discuss any needed changes. Students can also be encouraged to identify areas in which they have made progress and areas that need more improvement.

DEFINING STUDENT BEHAVIOR

In recalling our definition of behavior problems—a discrepancy between what teachers expect and what students do—it is necessary for teachers to recognize and define student behavior that deviates from their expectations. Educators frequently use ambiguous terms in describing student behavior. For example, the phrase "short attention span" could refer to an inability to sit still for five minutes, inability to listen for half an hour, inclination to roam about the room, or any number of behaviors. Behavior should be defined in observable, countable, and repeatable terms.

Once the behavior is defined, it is helpful for teachers to explore factors that are contributing to the problem. Questions that teachers should consider in identifying factors include (Regan, 1979):

1. Does the student have the prerequisite skills to complete the expected tasks? Assessment of the student's current level of performance may reveal skill deficiencies requiring instructional changes. When instruction is delivered at the appropriate level, behavior problems may dissapear.
2. Are there personal, family, classroom, or environmental factors contributing to the student's behavior problems? Such factors include the student's health, whether the student is hungry, the existence of competing responsibilities limiting sleep and attention to school work (e.g., outside employment), and

whether the classroom arrangement is conducive to the student's learning style.

3. Does the student have motivational problems? In such cases, the student may not have the initiative or desire to conform to teacher expectations as set forth in classroom rules.

Analyzing student problems according to these three questions can assist teachers in planning intervention strategies. In the first case, the problem is primarily an instructional one that will likely require instructional strategies tailored to individual needs. In the second case, the problem is created by "barriers" and the most effective intervention is the removal of those barriers.

Sandra, a sixth-grade student from a low income background, kept her head on her desk for most of the school day. She did not pay attention to class discussions and would not complete assignments. Her withdrawn and passive behavior greatly interfered with her performance. Her teacher was quite concerned, even irritated with her. One afternoon when she was reprimanding Sandra, the teacher noticed that Sandra's gums were bleeding. Upon inspection, she realized that Sandra had permanent teeth growing under permanent teeth. The teeth were cutting through the tops of her gums. Sandra then told the teacher, "All I think about is how much I hurt." The school nurse worked with Sandra, her family, and a local dentist in arranging for the dental surgery needed to correct this problem. Once Sandra returned to school, her attention increased dramatically.

In the third case, the problem is primarily a motivational one requiring intervention strategies to increase the student's interest and initiative. It is important to recognize that student problems rarely fall neatly into one of these categories. Students frequently have combinations of problems; thus, a comprehensive approach to ameliorating problems is often needed.

GENERAL MANAGEMENT STRATEGIES

A teacher's selection of management strategies is influenced by many considerations. As previously discussed, the teacher's behavioral expectations—including both values and classroom rules—are critical determinants of how problem behaviors are actually managed. Other important considerations are the definition of the student's problematic behavior and the factors contributing to that behavior. This section focuses on general management strategies that are effective in preventing behavioral concerns from becoming major problems. These general management strategies include teacher preparation, individualized instruction, communication, room arrangement, assigned responsibility, signals to students, and parental involvement. The next section focuses on strategies based on behavioral principles.

Sufficient Teacher Preparation

Sufficient preparation is a key to successful classroom management. If all a teacher has prepared for a fifty-minute class period is twenty minutes of work, it is very likely that behavioral problems are going to occur. Students should be busy and interested. Typically, the busier the students, the fewer the behavior problems. Although thorough preparation is a time-consuming task for teachers, it can save time in the long run by preventing teachers from spending inordinate amounts of time dealing with problems. It is basically a question of whether time is spent preventing problems or dealing with problems after they occur. A teacher described her support of this strategy as follows:

> *My best defense has always been an aggressive offense. I try to keep the students so busy that they do not have time to make trouble. There are many activities available to suit each child's learning level and interests. This takes much advance preparation to be sure, but I am convinced that it is worth it. I rarely have behavior problems and that makes classroom time much more productive.*

As with all strategies discussed in this chapter, no approach is successful with all students. In some cases, thorough teacher preparation still does not curtail behavioral problems, as in the case of a student who is highly aggressive.

Individualized Instruction

Closely related to the issue of teacher preparation is the need to individualize instruction as a strategy for improving behavior. It is impossible to separate totally instructional and management interventions. As discussed earlier, a major factor contributing to some students' behavior problems or lack of learning is that instruction is not tailored to their performance level and to the input/output modes most effective for their learning (see chapter 4). Students engaged in productive, challenging, and interesting tasks that have successful outcomes are far more likely to behave appropriately. Frequently, task requirements need to be adapted for students with behavioral problems. One strategy for individualization follows:

> *Teaching in a junior high learning center was a new experience for me. The junior high student has that "constant bouncing energy"—particularly one of the students in my English class. Joe is short on attention*

span, giving ten minutes at most to his work and then wandering about the room. I tried to channel his interests to other activities and then have him return to the initial task until it was completed. If Joe began to "wander," I would have him take his turn on the computer if it was not in use. He loved to work with it. He was also a good speller. I would then have him pronounce words for another student. After perhaps 15 to 20 minutes of the period had elapsed, he could be steered back to the original English assignment for another ten minutes. For the remainder of the time, I would let him choose a book from the reading area, if his tasks had been completed. Reading was his second love, after the computer. Joe was able to do special assignments if his attention could be focused long enough. He also enjoyed teaching other students how to use the computer.

Such task variation can be done for one student or for the entire class. Not every student can or needs to read *Canterbury Tales*. Some behavior problems are the result of frustration with material that is too difficult or too easy for the particular student. Activities can be varied: class discussions; completing short written assignments, locating reference materials in the library; writing review questions; engaging in small-group work; taking a short quiz; and grading papers. Such variation helps students keep active and directed. A substitute teacher made the following observation:

The biggest behavioral problem I have encountered is students talking while I was lecturing. I noticed that they paid attention when I started writing notes using the overhead projector.

It is helpful for teachers to ask when behavior problems arise: Can I change the way I teach or approach this subject to meet the individual needs of the students?

Communication

The nature of communication between the teacher and students can substantially influence whether behavior problems increase or decrease. When frustration arises because of the discrepancy between teacher expectations and student behavior, communication can become difficult. Teachers should consider these four guidelines when communicating with students in conflict situations:

1. Focus communication on the student's behavior without judging or attacking. A helpful strategy is to use "I" rather than "you" messages (e.g.,

"I'm concerned about the number of times you interrupt the conversations of others," rather than "You are rude and annoying").

2. Be firm and consistent in applying rules and assigning consequences. It can be helpful to remind students that they have the choice to abide by the rules or accept the consequences of breaking them (e.g., "Connie, I know you don't want to be on Bill's team because you feel most of your friends are on another team. Perhaps next time you can get on the team you want, but for now you have the choice to play on Bill's team or sit out this game"). Once the choice is stated, the teacher should not respond to the student's protests or complaints.

3. Angry feelings are natural, particularly when the student has engaged in behavior that is dangerous to others. Strive to express angry feelings in a rational and clear fashion without escalating the intensity of your feelings or those of the student. The old adage "to proceed like the ticking of a clock in a thunderstorm" is a good strategy for handling situations charged with emotion. A teacher who is able to exercise self-control and moderate reaction is much better equipped to deal with students who have emotional problems and still need to learn these skills.

4. Teacher confrontations should never occur in front of an entire class. When that happens, the student can gain sympathy and support from other class members. Also, the teacher is placed in the position of proving control. Often, the amount of time it takes to walk out of the classroom can diffuse anger enough so that the teacher can calmly explain how the behavior was inappropriate and what consequences will be necessary. Without an audience, the student may no longer feel it necessary to demonstrate a lack of fear. The student should not be given the opportunity to "swagger" back into the classroom. As an alternative, the student can spend the rest of the class period in the hall doing assignments and make up an appropriate amount of time in detention sessions.

Conflict situations rarely call for just one of these guidelines. Frequently, they must be used concurrently.

Ongoing communication can also be used to prevent conflict. As will be discussed in the next section on behavioral techniques, praise is a powerful contributor to promoting positive behavior. Frequently, communication with students focuses on correction or criticism. Communication should also hinge on "catching students being good." A physical education teacher reported that positive communication is an effective strategy in her class:

I usually walk up and down my squads when I take attendance and make comments to my students. I often comment on general rules that had been neglected in the past but are now being followed. "Thanks for taking off your jewelry." "Gee, you remembered your gym clothes on a

Monday." "You got an A on the test for the first time—I'm proud of you!" It is amazing how often the students remind me that they remembered. They like the positive attention.

Another strategy for maintaining ongoing communication with students is to have classroom meetings. As described by Glasser (1969), this approach involves providing specific opportunities for students to discuss relevant issues, build trusting relationships with peers, and increase their sense of cohesiveness in the classroom. Zeeman and Martucci (1976) reported the successful use of classroom meetings in a special education class with learning-disabled students. The classroom meeting strategy is discussed further in the next chapter regarding its use in enhancing the social integration of handicapped and non-handicapped students.

Room Arrangement

The arrangement of the room can influence the degree to which students meet the behavioral expectations of the teacher. For students with short attention spans, it is particularly helpful to have a portion of the room set up for change of pace activities. One possible arrangement is illustrated in Figure 10–1. Such an arrangement enables students to work on center and reinforcement activities without disrupting the concentration of their peers. Another alternative is to arrange separate areas for students who are distracted by the movement and noise of peers. These areas should be used as aids to concentration rather than as punishment for disruptions.

Another environmental feature that can minimize behavioral disruptions is adequate storage for personal belongings. When students have a specified and private place to keep their belongings, conflicts over lost materials or disputes over ownership can be minimized.

Assigned Responsibility

Some students engage in inappropriate behavior as a way of seeking attention. An effective strategy for dealing with such students is to provide extra attention by assigning them classroom responsibilities. A secondary history teacher used this approach with success:

> I had been warned to "watch out for Robert" long before he entered my class. He had created chaos in one class after another, year after year. I decided to give him extra attention and responsibility starting on the first day he walked into my class.
> The duties delegated to Robert were running audio-visual equipment

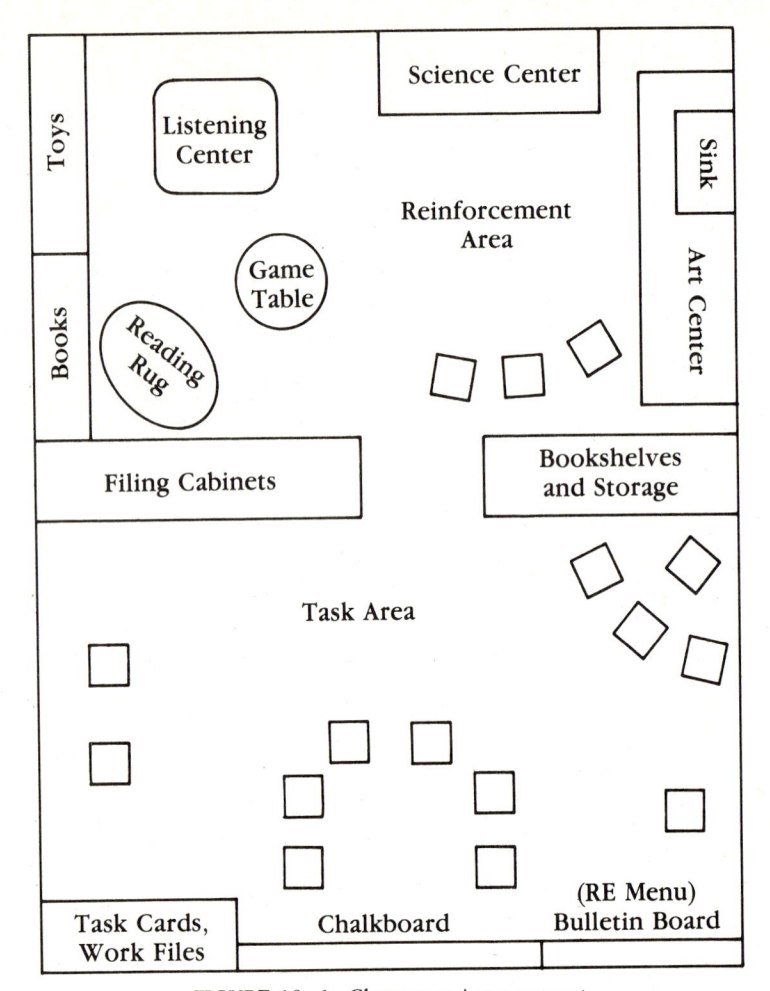

FIGURE 10-1. Classroom Arrangement

and collecting and filing student papers. He liked to work with audio-visual equipment and also seemed to like the "leadership" role of collecting papers given to him by other students. I found that he was anxious to please and to have someone place trust in him. I never had any real problems with him but did remind him on a couple of occasions, when I sensed he was slipping a little, that he had certain responsibilities and would need to show that he deserved to keep them.

Other special duties that can be assigned to students needing extra attention include taking attendance, being on the school safety patrol, caring for plants, fixing bulletin boards, writing the daily schedule on the blackboard, keeping a class calendar, running errands, and straightening the room. Handicapped students often get overlooked in the assignment of special responsibilities, yet these duties can have many positive benefits. In addition to providing extra attention, other outcomes can include heightened status among peers (discussed in the next chapter) and a recognition that the teacher trusts them and values their contribution to the class.

Signals to Students

Some students can be reminded to redirect their attention to the task at hand by verbal and nonverbal signals from teachers. Direct verbal signals are simply requests to students to behave appropriately. Indirect verbal signals are also effective.

> *Eileen is an excessive talker. She not only fails to get her work done on time, but she also disrupts her classmates. Her teacher sometimes uses Eileen's name in a sentence that has to do with what he is presenting. Consistently, Eileen stops talking when she hears her name.*

Other nonverbal signals include gestures, facial expressions, and turning lights on and off.

Often the teacher's immediate presence is a signal to students to behave appropriately. An effective technique is for the teacher to move about the classroom while students are working on assignments. Physical proximity allows for individual assistance and also enables teachers to deal with behavior problems in a discreet manner.

Parental Involvement

The involvement of parents in decision making about intervention strategies and in actually delivering consequences for school behavior can be very effective for some students. The IEP conference provides an opportunity to discuss intervention strategies and to determine parental willingness to work cooperatively with the teacher. At this time, the teacher can explain classroom rules for appropriate behavior and the consequences for misbehavior.

Parent conferences can be held when behavior problems arise to discuss the problem and obtain suggestions from parents on management strategies that have been effective in the past. After such a conference is held, continued communication with the parents regarding the student's progress will help the student realize that both teachers and parents are serious about the need for behavior change. Such communication can include notes, phone calls, or periodic conferences. An important point to remember is that parents need to be told about good behavior as well as about problems. Also, many parents of handicapped students have repeatedly witnessed instances in which their child was rejected or isolated. Thus, it is particularly important for teachers to convey to these parents that their handicapped child is accepted and respected.

BEHAVIOR MANAGEMENT PRINCIPLES AND STRATEGIES

The following techniques for changing specific student behaviors are based on the work of B. F. Skinner and his associates (Skinner, 1953). They involve the systematic application of behavioral principles and procedures.

The effectiveness of behavior management with handicapped students has been documented (Gresham, 1981; MacMillan & Forness, 1970) with reference to all categories of handicapping conditions. Behavior management strategies have been used with the full range of classroom problems including reducing disruptive behavior, increasing peer interactions, and improving performance in academic subjects. There has been some criticism that behavior management is a tool for manipulating people. With the understanding that this technique is primarily a positive approach, embodying strategies long used by parents and teachers, such criticism may dissolve.

When presented with the principles of behavior, many teachers exclaim, "Why, I've been doing that for years!" They have been rewarding good behavior and ignoring or punishing bad behavior. Certainly, behavior management is not new. The new aspect is the *systematic* approach to using the principles of behavior. In other words, the techniques formerly used at random are now being employed in an organized, scientific way. Because behavior is predictable, the systematic use of behavior management is effective.

Once understood, the principles of behavior can be explained to peers, paraprofessionals, and volunteer helpers in the classroom. Because the objectives are specific, communication between the teacher and other assistants is increased. Teachers can give procedural directions for behavioral programs that others can implement.

Principles of Behavior

A young mother took her three-year-old daughter to an egg hunt. Because there were older children participating and the competition was keen, Mary found no eggs. Her mother was surprised, therefore, to see that she had one of the prizes. Asked how she got the prize, Mary replied, "I cried for it."

Children learn at a very early age that their behavior produces consequences. In contemplating behavior change, therefore, the teacher seeks to arrange the consequences to promote the desired behavior.

Two kinds of behavior are delineated: *respondent* and *operant*. Respondent (reflex) behavior refers to those reponses that are elicited by special stimulus changes in the environment (Keller, 1969). It is usually associated with involuntary muscular movements, such as the contraction or dilation of the pupils of the eyes, response to touching a hot stove, and watering of the mouth at the taste of some particular food.

Operant (voluntary) behavior, on the other hand, is the conscious response to one's environment, maintained through reinforcement. Thus, operant behaviors are of major concern to teachers who wish to change a student's behaviors. Whether or not operant behaviors are changed depends on what happens following each operant behavior (Reinert, 1976). The general rule in behavior management is that desirable behavior should be rewarded (reinforced) and that undesirable behavior should not be rewarded. Behavior that is reinforced tends to be repeated; behavior that is not reinforced tends not to be repeated (Thompson & Grabowski, 1972).

Increasing Behavior

One way to increase the likelihood of a behavior recurring is to follow that behavior with a positive or favorable event. This is called positive reinforcement.

In the school cafeteria, Henry picked up Miss Lassiter's lunch tray and carried it to the table for her. Miss Lassiter smiled and said, "Thank you, Henry. That was very thoughtful."

It must be remembered that one can increase the likelihood of undesirable behavior as well as desirable behavior by positive reinforcement.

Jamie pulled at Mr. Owen's jacket, "Mr. Owen, let me have the ball." Mr. Owen ignored Jamie; Jamie continued to pull at his jacket. Mr. Owen said, "Oh all right, Jamie, you can have the ball, but stop pulling my jacket!"

It also must be noted that sometimes teachers inadvertently *punish* desirable behavior rather than reward it.

"Teacher, I've finished all my math problems." "Fine. Here are ten more for you to do."

Two conditions are required to make positive reinforcement work:

1. Make the positive event come *after* the desired behavior.
2. Be sure the consequence is favorable (Mager, 1972).

Another way to increase the likelihood of a behavior recurring is to follow the behavior by taking away an unpleasant event. This is called *negative reinforcement*.

Tom was very annoyed by Cindy, who chattered constantly. When he did not do his work, Cindy was instructed to sit next to Tom. When Tom was working well, Cindy was moved to the other side of the room.

In many cases, a desired behavior must be broken into small steps. This is done for two reasons: first, the student may not be able to perform the entire behavior and therefore cannot be reinforced for it; second, teaching a task through a series of small steps minimizes the number of errors made by the student. In behavior management there are several techniques for breaking tasks into small steps.

Shaping. Shaping is the process of reinforcing a student for closer approximations to the desired reponse. The first step is to state the desired (or target) response. The first response (approximation) that occurs, which roughly resembles the target behavior, should be reinforced. When the student has been reinforced for this response repeatedly, a closer approximation is required before reinforcement occurs again.

"Susan, sit on the chair." The first approximation is for Susan to look in the direction of the chair. She is reinforced. When Susan has been reinforced for this response several times and is looking at the chair often, more is required. The next approximation is for her to take a step toward the chair in order to be reinforced. The sequencing of events continues until sitting in the chair is all that is reinforced.

It is important to raise the standards for reinforcement so the student will go on to the next step. However, standards should not be raised so rapidly that the student cannot receive reinforcement.

Chaining. For most learning tasks, one response does not complete the criteria for learning the entire behavior. Chaining techniques are used to teach behaviors that occur in a sequence. The complex behavior is broken into simple components to be learned one at a time and chained together to obtain the complete behavior. The distinguishing characteristic of chaining is that reinforcement is delivered after the last step. Frequently referred to as *backward* *chaining,* this technique requires completion of the task before reinforcement and is a powerful teaching device.

> *A picture puzzle is assembled except for the last piece, which is placed adjacent to its proper place. Only a small effort is required for the student to complete the task and see the final product. Reinforcement is delivered for finishing the task. Later, two pieces are omitted from the puzzle and reinforcement is delivered for completion. Finally, the child completes the entire task and is reinforced.*

There are several conditions to chaining. First, the student must know how to perform each unit; second, the student must perform each unit in the proper sequence; third, the units must be performed in rapid succession to be sure they are linked together; fourth, the chain must be repeated until the learning has taken place; fifth, reinforcement must be present in the learning of chains and the reinforcement must be immediate.

To set up a chain of events, the teacher must acquire the skills of task analysis, pertinent to any target behavior. Task analysis was defined and described in chapter 4.

Fading. In using fading, the stimuli are varied until a response made in one situation is made in another. Changes are made in the condition under which the behavior occurs rather than in the nature of the task itself. An example cited by Thompson and Grabowski (1972) is teaching children to color inside a heavy raised outline (cardboard template or yarn); later the height of the outline is reduced and still later replaced by a heavy drawn outline. Ultimately the outline is the usual printed one. A similar technique is illustrated in Figure 10–2.

Decreasing Behavior

Behavior is weakened or suppressed by *punishment* or *extinction.* When a behavior is followed by punishment, the likelihood of the behavior recurring decreases. The use of an aversive event (such as spanking) is the form generally used. A second type of punishment (response cost) is used when positive reinforcement is withdrawn. A third type of punishment (time-out) involves isolating the student from reinforcement for a stated time.

To be effective, punishment must be intense and last long enough to be viewed as aversive, and must be administered every time and immediately following the undesirable behavior (Blackham & Silberman, 1975).

The effects of punishment are less predictable than those of reinforcement. Some of the undesirable side effects may include avoidance of the punisher;

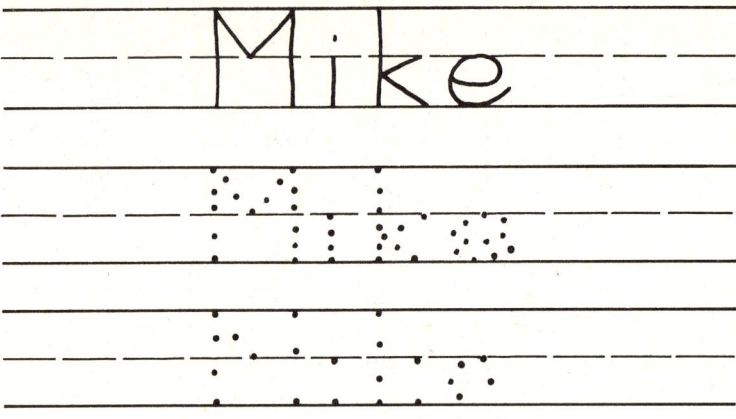

FIGURE 10-2. Example of Fading

model for aggression provided by the teacher; and increase of fear, withdrawal, and tenseness.

Blackham and Silberman (1975) present guidelines to avoid such side effects from punishment:

> Use punishment infrequently and never as the only method for controlling or eliminating undesirable behavior.
> Specify clearly the acceptable and unacceptable behavior and the consequences for each. When a child is punished, he or she should know the reasons for the punishment.
> Punish the undesirable behavior as soon as it appears; do not wait until the behavior has run its course.
> Provide desirable behavioral alternatives for the child.
> While punishing the undesirable behavior, reinforce the behavior you wish to promote.
> Be consistent in punishing behavior you wish to eliminate. Inconsistent punishment may make the undesirable behavior more durable (p. 71).

A second way to reduce the likelihood of a behavior's occurring is *extinction*. Since behavior is maintained by positive or negative reinforcements, withdrawal of the reinforcement weakens the behavior.

> Jamie pulled on Mr. Owen's jacket, "Mr. Owen, let me have the ball." Mr. Owen ignored the pulling. Jamie continued to pull his jacket, but when she didn't get the ball, she stopped.

Ignored behavior usually increases at first; this is part of the extinction process. Many teachers do not continue to ignore the behavior long enough; it is difficult to do. However, it does help eliminate nonproductive and disruptive responses since these behaviors are often attention-getters.

There are certain potentially dangerous behaviors that cannot be ignored. Physical attacks, horseplay with scissors, and self-injurious behavior cannot always be handled by removal of reinforcement. In such cases, various forms of punishment should be considered. The choice of aversives may progress from those for students functioning at very low levels to those that apply to mature persons: electric shock; spanking; withdrawal of love, affection, or approval; denial of privileges or removal from a rewarding setting; scolding or social disapproval; and self-disappointment. The punishment should be selected in terms of the functional maturity of students and should be perceived by them as aversive. When punishment is used, it is important to use it consciously and systematically (MacMillan, Forness, & Trumbull, 1973).

BASIC PROCEDURES

Observing and Recording

Once the principles of behavior are understood, there are basic procedures to follow to insure maximum success from the method. The first procedure is to *define and describe operationally the behavior to be changed*. As discussed earlier in the chapter, behavior should be defined in observable terms. The test for *observable* behavior is: Can other persons (who agree on the definition of the behavior) see the same behavior at the same time? Do they all agree as to when the behavior did or did not occur? Do they agree on how many times it occurred and the force or intensity with which it occurred? If such agreement can be reached, the behavior is observable.

When the behavior has been pinpointed, a target must be set in observable terms. Thus, the goal "to decrease John's aggressiveness" would be inappropriate. The target "to decrease John's kicking" would be observable, countable, and therefore subject to change. In addition to the previous questions, a very simple test of observable behavior is: Can you count it?

Neisworth and Smith (1973) suggest that the teacher avoid the use of expressions such as "ability to," "potential for," "capacity for," and so forth. The teacher is not interested in Sue's ability to add two-digit numbers but in her *doing* it.

When the target behavior has been identified and stated in operational terms, the teacher should *observe and record* that behavior. Sometimes viewed as a chore and a time-consuming effort, this process is a timesaver and an essential element in successful behavior management strategies. Many trial-and-error methods that have been used traditionally in the classroom are not discarded because there is no proof that they do or do not work. If good records are maintained, the teacher can easily keep or reject a particular intervention, depending on the recorded results. Another important advantage is that such records are reinforcing to the teacher, to the parent, and to the student.

In observing and charting behavior, the teacher often realizes that the behavior does not occur at the originally perceived frequency. On consideration, the behavior may be seen as annoying to the teacher only and not of sufficient frequency or duration to need altering.

There are two types of observation of concern in the classroom. The *frequency count* is a measurement of the number of times a behavior occurs. A frequency count could be taken of the number of times Ann cries during a stated observation period. The *time interval* observation is a measurement of the length of time a behavior is exhibited. The length of time Ann cries may be more pertinent than the number of times she cries.

An accurate measurement of behavior before intervention is referred to as the *baseline*. Since the purpose is to record an average of the behavior, the recording may be done for a short length of time each day over a five-day period. It is desirable that the behavior be recorded in the setting where change is desired. Data obtained during the baseline period are usually plotted on a graph (see Figure 10–4). The line and bar graphs are most frequently used.

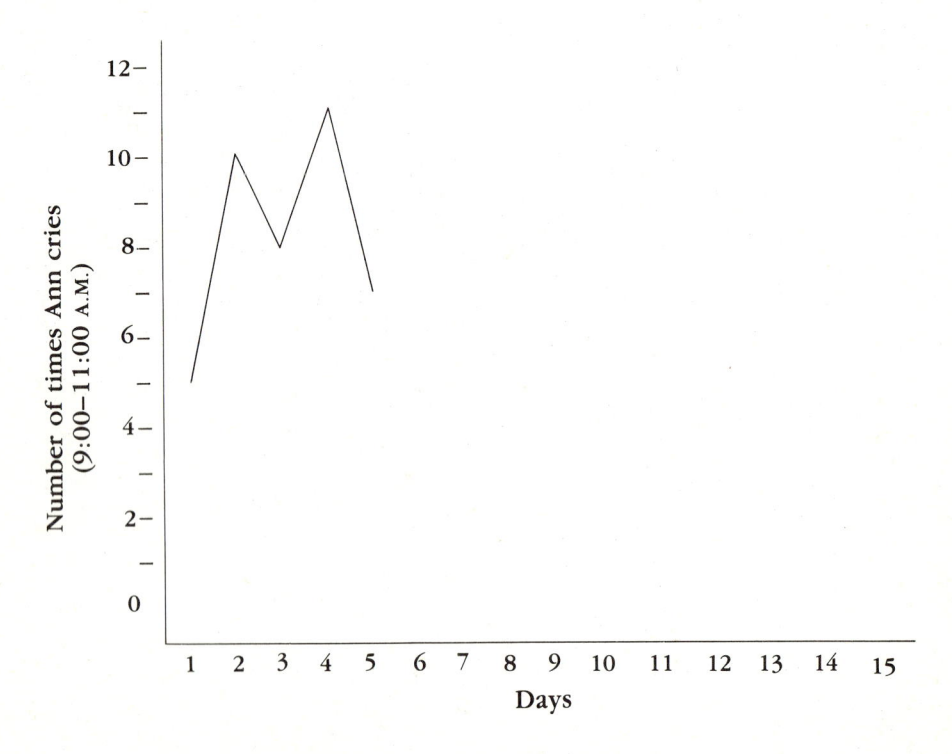

FIGURE 10–3. Record of Baseline Data

The horizontal axis in both graphs usually identifies the time period, while the vertical axis denotes the criteria used to evaluate intervention effects.

Frequency can be counted by recording a mark on a sheet of paper each time the behavior occurs (see Figure 10–5) or by using a mechanical counter or stop watch. Kubany and Sloggett (1974) describe an effective method. The teacher sets a timer to correspond with the target intervals indicated on the chart; when the timer bell rings, the teacher glances at the student and identifies what he is doing at that instant. After recording the behavior, the teacher immediately resets the timer and proceeds with instruction.

Teachers who feel they cannot manage recording while teaching can use other methods. If paraprofessionals, volunteer aides, or parents are available, they can be classroom recorders. Students themselves can record certain behaviors. Moving the recording task from the teacher to the students in sequenced steps increases the students' potential for self-direction. For example, if the teacher is recording class behaviors, such as in seat on time, on a daily chart, students can assume this responsibility. Individual behaviors can be recorded on a piece of masking tape on a child's desk. After observing the teacher's method, students can record their own behavior (Sarason, Glaser, & Fargo, 1972). Heady and Niewoehner (1979) describe a system of self-charting in which a student recorded on a piece of paper taped to her desk the number of times she interrupted during a target period. A positive outcome of self-recording is that it frequently decreases the student's disruptive behavior (Heward, 1979). This decrease is probably attributable to the fact that the student becomes more aware of the problem behavior.

Number of times Ann cries
(9:00–11:00 A.M.)

Day	1	2	3	4	5	Weekly Total	Average
	||||‾	||||‾	||||‾	||||‾	||||‾		
	||||‾	|||	||||‾	||		41	8.2
	6	7	8	9	10		
	||||‾	||||‾	||||‾	||||‾	||||		
	||||‾	||||‾	||||‾	||||‾		46	9.2
	11	12	13	14	15		
						7	1.4

FIGURE 10–4. Form of Recording Frequency

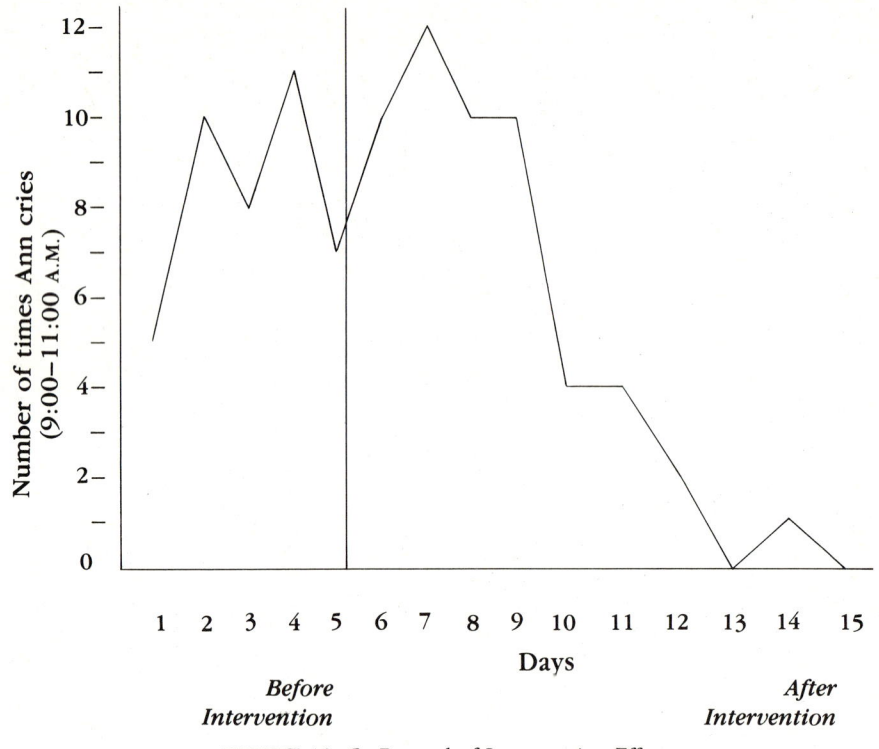

FIGURE 10–5. Record of Intervention Effect

Recording is continued after the intervention is introduced (see Figure 10–5) to determine the effectiveness of the plan. Although day-to-day fluctuations will occur, a well-planned program usually produces the desired effects. If the teacher is uncertain about what produced the desired effect, or suspects that other variables have contributed, the intervention can be stopped and the recording continued. The results will indicate whether or not the intervention is effective. However, most teachers are reluctant to withdraw a plan that is working!

Recording behavior change is useful even if the particular intervention does not appear to be effective. For example, Bill is sent from the room every time he kicks a classmate. The kicking behavior is recorded and does not decrease with the intervention. Rather than being discouraged, the teacher may discard this intervention and seek another one. At the least, one technique has been tried and proved ineffective. This is certainly more productive than continuing a poor strategy.

Once the baseline data have been charted, the teacher can decide whether or not to proceed with an intervention. The successful arrangement of consequences requires specific attention to behaviors and how they are affected by reinforcement. Arranging consequences requires the teacher to decide which reinforcers to use, how much reinforcement is necessary, and the schedule of reinforcement to employ.

Reinforcers

Since reinforcement is contingent on the student's response, it can be used to increase appropriate behavior or to decrease inappropriate behavior. The *selection of the reinforcer* demands sensitivity from the teacher. Care must be exercised that the chosen event is rewarding to the student.

> *Tommy made an outstanding score on his achievement tests. As a reward, the teacher suggested that he go home an hour early. Tommy walked home, miserable and lonely, and waited for his friends to join him.*

Since a reinforcer is defined by its effect on behavior, it is a highly individual event; it is the teacher's task to find reinforcing events for specific students. This can be done by observing what the student does with free time, asking what the student would work for, or systematically arranging a consequence and observing its effect on the student's behavior (Wallace & Kauffman, 1973).

Neisworth and Smith (1973) present a hierarchy of reinforcer categories:

1. Self-generated reinforcers (satisfaction with a job well done, etc.)
2. Self-management of tangible reinforcers (allowing yourself to watch television only after you've completed an unpleasant chore)
3. Social approval, attention
4. Management of tangible reinforcers (tokens, trinkets, food, water) by others (p. 87).

It is suggested that one should use reinforcers as high in the hierarchy as possible and revert to basic reinforcers only if the higher ones are unsuccessful.

Interventions

The final step in the behavior management process is *to choose and implement a particular strategy*. The choice will depend on the behavioral level of the students, the resources available, and the preference of the teachers. There are advantages and disadvantages to each of the systems presented. The teacher is encouraged to experiment with each and to discover techniques appropriate for particular situations and students. Reinforcement systems used in schools may be classified as primary, social, modeling, token, and contingency management.

Primary Reinforcement. Primary (tangible) reinforcers are particularly effective with students who exhibit immature or bizarre behavior. When paired with praise and approval, they can be starting points toward nontangible reinforcers. Most students respond to edibles, such as cookies, ice cream, or candy.

Although the use of primary reinforcement is usually considered most appropriate for younger children, older students sometimes need to begin a reinforcement program at this level. Additionally, primary reinforcement can be used as an occasional treat for students at middle and secondary levels. An eleventh-grade teacher described how she used food as a reinforcer.

The students in my study hall were always quiet and well behaved. The rules I set for them were always followed. I routinely used praise as a reinforcement technique. One day I brought them each a cupcake and told them how much I appreciated their cooperation. They appreciated the special reward of cupcakes.

There are several precautions to take when using primary reinforcers. The reinforcers need to be changed frequently so the student doesn't become satiated and therefore not reinforced. The strength of edible reinforcers may be increased if used prior to meal time. If the student is obese or has diet problems, special consideration must be given to the choice of edibles. Diet colas, crackers, raisins, or cereal may be used instead of the usual cookies and candy.

The cost of primary reinforcers must be taken into consideration. Some schools allow instructional material funds to be used for purchasing reinforcers; some reinforcers may be obtained from the school cafeteria. A team of fourth-grade teachers devised an ingenious method. Rather than asking several parents to furnish refreshments for a school party, they asked every student to bring something. The leftover cookies, potato chips, and candy were put into canisters to be used for primary reinforcers. Many teachers purchase reinforcers out of personal funds. Since this can be expensive, teachers are advised to use the resources available to them.

Because reinforcement systems are chosen to suit the students, there may be just a few children who receive edible reinforcers. It is important for the class members to understand that rewards may differ. This difference will not present a problem if each student knows that appropriate behavior will be rewarded in some way.

Social Reinforcement. Social interaction or attention is another powerful reinforcer. The strength of social reinforcement is demonstrated in a study reported by Dmitriev and Hawkins (1974). A child had refused to speak for two years and had been placed in a remedial class. After many trial and error patterns of treatment, a behavior management specialist suggested that teacher attention be withdrawn. The child was prompted to speak selected words and when she did not speak, all teacher attention was withdrawn. Within twenty-two days of this treatment, the child was speaking more than four hundred words a day and was reinstated in a regular classroom. She had been receiving teacher attention (social reinforcement) for *not* speaking.

Approval from the teacher and from peers promotes desirable behavior in most students. Smiles, pats, and verbal approval have worked well for teachers for many years. Easy to administer, inexpensive, and adaptable to any age group, social reinforcers are ideal. However, depending on the teacher's interaction with the student, the student's previous experience with teachers, and the severity of the student's behavior problem, social reinforcement may not be totally effective. In this event, it can be paired with a primary or token reinforcer. As appropriate behavior increases, the tangible reinforcer can be faded out. One teacher, who wished to establish good behavior in his classroom, gave a Fruit Loop (cereal) for attention, academic performance, and so on. Inappropriate behavior was ignored. With the Fruit Loop, he always said something like "I like a good worker." He later discontinued the cereal, relying on the praise as a social reinforcement.

A classic study of the effects of teachers' behavior on students' behavior (Thomas, Becker, & Armstrong, 1968) indicates that teachers who use approval for good behavior will find that frequency and duration of appropriate behavior will increase. It further suggests that teachers who try pleasantly to get students to stop inappropriate behavior, and who talk to them in an attempt to get them to understand what they're doing wrong, will find an increase in inappropriate behavior. The authors conclude that "unless an effort is made to support desirable classroom behaviors with appropriate consequences, the children's behavior will be controlled by others in ways likely to interfere with the teacher's objectives" (p. 45).

The rule that seems to work is to give praise and attention to behaviors that facilitate learning. Tell the students what they did to deserve the praise. Try to reinforce behaviors incompatible with those you wish to decrease. Inappropriate behavior may be strengthened by paying attention to it even though you think you are punishing (Madsen, Becker, & Thomas, 1968).

Modeling. Modeling refers to implementing systematic strategies to teach students to imitate appropriate peer behaviors. Many proponents of mainstreaming suggest that a major benefit of such placements is that handicapped students will emulate the behavior of their nonhandicapped classmates. Such emulation does not automatically occur (Gresham, 1981); however, teachers can structure opportunities for students having problems to recognize precisely the more appropriate behavior of their classmates.

A veteran teacher, convinced of the power of modeling, described techniques she uses:

When I see William not holding his pencil correctly, I praise Virginia for what a good job she is doing and ask her to show us how she is doing it. William is not feeling bad because he was not correct; he has learned what is correct and will try hard to do what Virginia is doing. When I want the group's attention, I announce that table three really wants to learn about (anything) and is ready to listen. Other students then have an example of the behavior I expect from them.

For modeling to be effective, students must attend to the appropriate behavior of peers, retain the information they learned, practice the behavior on their own, and receive some incentive for their efforts (Bandura, 1977). In providing incentives to students, teachers can use social reinforcement or tokens (discussed in the next section).

Peer tutoring and cooperative learning activities described in chapter 4 are excellent formats for using modeling as an intervention strategy. An important consideration for teachers is to choose carefully the tutors and group members who will provide positive examples of behavior based on the particular needs of a handicapped student.

Token Economy. The token system of reinforcement is usually implemented in classrooms when social reinforcers such as praise have been ineffective in controlling a student's behavior. Skinner (1953) defines the token as a generalized reinforcer distinguished by its physical specifications. He cites money as the most common example, since it can be exchanged for primary reinforcers of great variety. This system involves the presentation of a token (checkmark, poker chip, star, school money, points) following specified behaviors. When students have accumulated a sufficient number of tokens, they can exchange them for "back-up" reinforcers, such as candy, toys, school supplies, or desirable activities.

The tokens initially function as neutral stimuli, acquiring reinforcing properties by being exchangeable for back-up reinforcers. Teacher praise and approval will increase in effectiveness as reinforcers when paired with the tokens. A general goal of token systems is to transfer control of responding from the token systems to other conditioned reinforcers, such as teacher praise and grades (Kuypers, Becker, & O'Leary, 1968).

Token systems have been used effectively with handicapped students in many situations. Their success has been demonstrated with retarded students (Birnbrauer, Wolf, Kidder, & Tague, 1965), with emotionally disturbed students (Hewett, 1967), with cerebral palsied students (Stone, 1970), with learning-disabled students (McKenzie, Clark, Wolf, Kothera, & Benson, 1968), and with nonhandicapped students (O'Leary & Drabman, 1971). The system is highly individualized. It also overcomes many of the objections to a primary reinforcement system, such as one student asking, "How come Johnny gets candy for sitting still and I don't?" Tokens are available to all class members and can be earned by achieving individual goals.

Several organizational patterns to token economies have been suggested. Hewett (1967) refers to his highly structured situation as an engineered classroom, in which the emphasis is on alerting students to the work efficiency orientation of the classroom. As students enter the class in the morning, they pick up a work record card ruled into squares. As they move through the day, the teacher and aide recognize their accomplishments by checking off squares on each student's card. The students save their completed work cards and exchange them weekly for candy, small toys, or trinkets. An exchange board in the room displays tangible rewards available for one, two, or three cards filled with checkmarks. The philosophy of the program says to students, "We want you to succeed at all costs. If you will meet us half way and function reasonably well as a student, we will give you tasks you can do, need to do, and will enjoy doing, and we will reward you generously for your efforts" (p. 466).

Another token system utilizes a point system (O'Leary & Becker, 1967). On the first day of the token period, instructions are written on the chalkboard: In Seat, Face Front, Raise Hand, Working, Pay Attention, Desk Clear. The procedure is explained to the students; the tokens are ratings placed in booklets on each desk. Ratings from one to ten are given, reflecting the extent to which the students follow instructions. The points can be exchanged for back-up reinforcers. The frequency with which ratings are given is gradually decreased, and the number of points required to obtain a prize is gradually increased. Group points are also given for total class behavior, to be exchanged for popsicles at the end of the week. Since teacher time may be a factor, it is interesting to note that in this particular program the ratings took only three minutes.

In a program for orthopedically handicapped students who exhibited deviant behavior, the class day was divided into five learning periods. A behavior chart was supplied for each period. At the end of each period, the students were given one penny if they had carried out all the behaviors and lessons on the chart. At the end of class, the students who had earned five pennies could buy a toy from the teacher (Stone, 1970).

The choice of tokens can be as varied as the choice of reinforcers. One teacher used S & H green stamps as tokens, with a field trip to the redemption store scheduled twice a year (Lankford, 1974).

One of the greatest advantages of the token system is that tokens can be dispensed immediately following the desired behavior, providing an ideal situation for building new behaviors. They can be dispensed by the teacher or the aide, and should be accompanied by a comment such as "Good work, Sue!"

To help the student learn to delay reinforcement and thus deal with society's reward systems, the time for exchange of tokens is gradually extended. In the beginning, tokens may be exchanged at the end of each day; later, at the end of each week. The exchange period is reinforcing in itself and may follow a less desired activity. Tokens should be easy to dispense, easy to carry to the area of exchange, and their value should be understood by all the students. They may be given for approximations of the desired behavior and for progress in any specified activity.

An efficient token system should gradually withdraw material reinforcers (e.g., candy, toys) and rely on reinforcing activities. If this is the goal, the teacher should consider advancing to a contingency management program.

Contingency Management. The term *contingent* implies a relationship between what one does and what happens afterward. Salaries are contingent on job performance; teaching positions are contingent on certification. The contingencies of our environment control our behavior. Therefore, a teacher can control (change) a student's behavior by arranging contingencies (Haring & Phillips, 1972). A contractual agreement between the teacher and the student, contingency management helps the student to assume responsibility for motivating personal behavior, and facilitates the shift from external control to self-management (Homme, Csanyi, Gonzales, & Rechs, 1970).

> *In a preschool class for mentally retarded youngsters, a little girl was observed to go to her teacher for a task (a lacing board), go to her desk and complete the task, return the board to her teacher, and go to the sand table to play.*

Contingency management is based on the Premack Principle (Premack, 1959), which states that a low-probability behavior (such as working math problems) can be increased in frequency when its performance is followed by the opportunity to engage in a high-probability behavior (such as listening to a favorite record). This system, like the token system, is particularly suitable for use with handicapped students in a regular classroom, since it can be individualized. It has been used successfully with handicapped as well as with nonhandicapped students.

Langstaff and Volkmor (1975) outline the procedures in planning a contingency management program:

> *Setting up a reinforcement (RE) menu.* A list of reward activities (high-probability behaviors) from which students may choose. RE activities are available to the student only upon completion of a specified task (low-probability behavior) [see Figure 10–6].

> *Arranging the classroom.* In the beginning, it is helpful to divide the room into two areas—a task area where students can work quietly and an RE area where they may spend their free time (see Figure 10–1). Arrangements may be flexible to accommodate a self-contained classroom, a resource room, or an open situation.

RE MENU

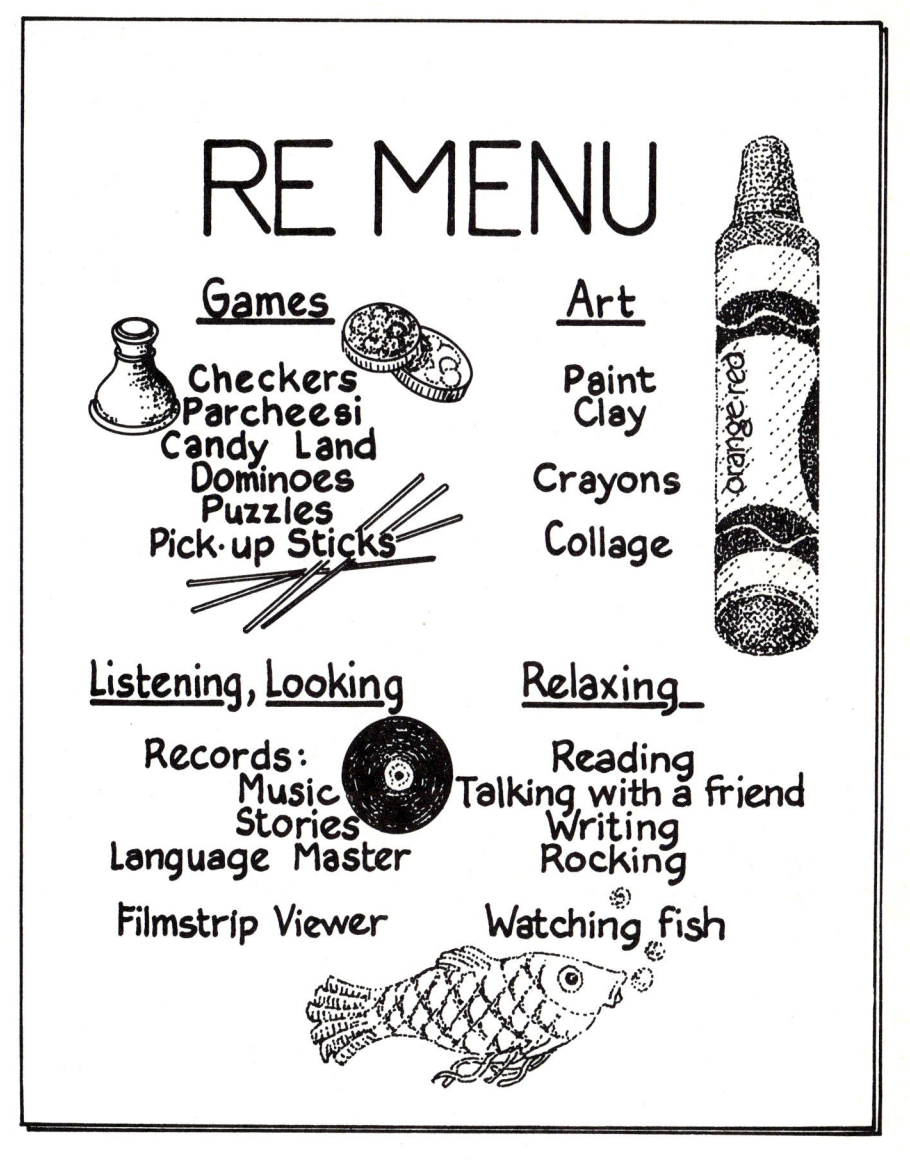

Games
- Checkers
- Parcheesi
- Candy Land
- Dominoes
- Puzzles
- Pick-up Sticks

Art
- Paint
- Clay
- Crayons
- Collage

Listening, Looking
- Records: Music, Stories
- Language Master
- Filmstrip Viewer

Relaxing
- Reading
- Talking with a friend
- Writing
- Rocking
- Watching fish

FIGURE 10–6. RE Menu

Scheduling task and RE time. At first, the schedule should be designed so that all students start tasks at the same time, finishing within two to three minutes of each other. When the child finishes, he signals for the teacher to come and check his work and he is immediately excused to the RE area. The RE time should be kept to five- to eight-minute periods.

A desk signal is used by the student to indicate task completion. A teacher signal is used to call the students back to the task area from the RE area.

Preparing tasks for students. Initial tasks should be slightly below competency level to insure success when the program begins. Directions should be clear; task cards or individual folders should be presented. Students should be observed as they work and helped if they are confused. Group work may be conducted while individual students are working on assignments.

Explaining the system to the students. A chart may be posted explaining the system:

Do some work . . .
Have some free time . . .
Do some more work . . .
Have some more free time . . .
Work is whatever is assigned,
Free time is whatever you want to do
                IF
1. Your work is finished correctly.
2. You respect the right of others.
3. You remember safety rules.
4. You remember school rules. (Langstaff & Volkmor, 1975, p. 63)

One teacher evaluated her program in a learning disabilities resource room:

> My recent experience with contingency management had produced a much more effective and successful learning atmosphere. The implementation of the program involved a great deal of organization and preparation. I explained the program to the children and made it possible for them to offer suggestions in regard to their potential reinforcers.
>
> The reward area consisted of an art center, listening center, game area, and relaxation area. It is crucial to remove activities which have little or no reinforcement value from the reward area.
>
> The task area was structured to provide easy access for teacher-student interaction and emphasized individualized instruction. A horseshoe-type seating arrangement permitted me to sit in the center, easily accessible for each child.
>
> The students became involved by having the opportunity to make a nonverbal sign that was used for signifying they were working, needed help, or had finished their assignment. A timer was used to indicate a return to the task area from the reward area, or to return to their regular classes.
>
> An individual folder was prepared for each student to contain the work for that day. Folders were given to the students each day and assignments explained.
>
> I was pleased with the results I saw; the children enjoyed the program and expressed a desire to continue with it.

Besides promoting desirable behavior, contingency management has other advantages. Because the RE items are not consumable, there is little expense involved. There is little opposition from parents or school critics because the reward is an activity. Most important, this system involves the student in the decision-making process and leads toward self-direction.

Toward Self-Management. It is hoped that the value of tokens, tangible items, and reinforcing events will give way to the satisfaction of succeeding in school and receiving recognition as a student from one's peers, teachers, and parents. Teachers are interested, therefore, in building study behavior. In order to do so, teachers must first teach students how to learn and how to behave appropriately in the classroom.

If students are to learn to manage their own behavior, they should be involved in changing it.

> *Tommy, who was considered incorrigible, was asked by his teacher to list things about himself that he would like to change. Without hesitation, he stated that he would like to "quit talking so much and learn to ignore troublemakers."*

Teachers can help students achieve this self-management goal by encouraging them to make behavioral choices systematically by:

1. considering all their alternatives for a given decision,
2. identifying consequences for each alternative,
3. considering how each alternative would make them feel,
4. choosing the most appropriate alternative, and
5. evaluating their choice after they have acted on their decision (Silverman, 1980).

Many students who respond to reinforcement systems with enthusiasm decide at a later time that they don't need them. This is the ultimate goal of behavior management: to help students realize that their actions produce consequences and that they, themselves, can change their actions and thus achieve goals that they set.

REFERENCES

Bandura, A. *Social learning theory.* Englewood Cliffs, N.J.: Prentice-Hall, 1977.
Barnes, E., Eyman, B., & Engolz, M. D. *Teach and reach: An alternative guide to resources for the classroom.* Syracuse, N.Y.: Human Policy Press, 1974.
Birnbrauer, J. S., Wolf, M. M., Kidder, J. D., & Tague, C. Classroom behavior of retarded pupils with token reinforcement. *Journal of Experimental Child Psychology,* 1965, *2,* 219–235.
Blackham, G. J., & Silberman, A. *Modification of child and adolescent behavior.* Belmont, Calif.: Wadsworth Publishing Co., 1975.
Dmitriev, V., & Hawkins, J. Susie never used to say a word. *Teaching Exceptional Children,* 1974, *6,* 68–76.
Glasser, W. *Schools without failure.* New York: Harper and Row, 1969.
Gresham, F. M. Social skills training with handicapped children: A review. *Review of Educational Research,* 1981, *51*(1), 139–176.

Haring, N. G., & Phillips, E. L. *Analysis and modification of classroom behavior.* Englewood Cliffs, N.J.: Prentice-Hall, 1972.

Heady, J., & Niewoehner, M. Academic and behavior management techniques that work. *Teaching Exceptional Children,* 1979, *12*(1), 37–39.

Heward, W. L. Teaching students to control their own behavior: A critical skill. *Exceptional Teacher,* 1979, *1*(4), 3–5/11.

Hewett, F. M. Educational engineering with emotionally disturbed children. *Exceptional Children,* 1967, *33,* 459–467.

Homme, L., Csanyi, A. P., Gonzales, M. A., & Rechs, J. R. *How to use contingency contracting in the classroom.* Champaign, Ill.: Research Press, 1970.

Keller, F. S. *Learning: reinforcement theory.* New York: Random House, 1969.

Kubany, E. S., & Sloggett, B. B. Coding procedures for teachers. In E. J. Thomas (Ed.), *Behavior modification procedure: A sourcebook.* Chicago: Aldine, 1974.

Kuypers, D. S., Becker, W. C., & O'Leary, D. K. How to make a token system fail. *Exceptional Children,* 1968, *35,* 101–109.

Langstaff, A. L., & Volkmor, C. B. *Contingency management.* Columbus, Ohio: Charles E. Merrill Publishing Co., 1975.

Lankford, M. Friday is payday. *Teaching Exceptional Children,* 1974, *6*(2), 147–148.

MacMillan, D. L., & Forness, S. R. Behavior modification: Limitations and liabilities. *Exceptional Children,* 1970, *37,* 291–297.

MacMillan, D. L., Forness, S. R., & Trumbull, B. M. The role of punishment in the classroom. *Exceptional Children,* 1973, *40,* 85–96.

Madsen, C. H., Jr., Becker, W. C., & Thomas, D. R. Rules, praise, and ignoring: Elements of elementary classroom control. *Journal of Applied Behavior Analysis,* 1968, *1,* 139–150.

Mager, R. F. *Who did what to whom?* Champaign, Ill.: Research Press, 1972.

McKenzie, H. S., Clark, M., Wolf, M. M., Kothera, R., & Benson, C. Behavior modification of children with learning disabilities using grades as tokens and allowances as back up reinforcers. *Exceptional Children,* 1968, *34,* 745–752.

Neisworth, J. T., & Smith, R. M. *Modifying retarded behavior.* Boston: Houghton Mifflin Co., 1973.

O'Leary, D. K., & Becker, W. C. Behavior modification of an adjustment class: A token reinforcement program. *Exceptional Children,* 1967, *33,* 637–642.

O'Leary, D. K., & Drabman, R. Token reinforcement programs in the classroom: A review. *Psychological Bulletin,* 1971, *75*(6), 379–398.

Premack, D. Toward empirical behavior laws: I. Positive reinforcement. *Psychological Review,* 1959, *66,* 219–233.

Reinert, H. R. *Children in conflict.* St. Louis: C. V. Mosby Co., 1976.

Sarason, I. G., Glaser, E. M., & Fargo, G. A. *Reinforcing productive classroom behavior.* New York: Behavioral Publications, 1972.

Silverman, M. *How to handle problem behavior in school.* Lawrence, Kans.: H & H Enterprises, Inc., 1980.

Skinner, F. B. *Science and human behavior.* New York: Macmillan Publishing Co., 1953.

Stone, M. C. Behavior shaping in a classroom for children with cerebral palsy. *Exceptional Children,* 1970, *36,* 674–677.

Thomas, D. R., Becker, W. C., & Armstrong, M. Production and elimination of disruptive classroom behavior by systematically varying teacher's behavior. *Journal of Applied Behavior Analysis,* 1968, *1,* 35–45.

Thompson, T., & Grabowski, J. (Eds.). *Behavior modification of the mentally retarded.* New York: Oxford University Press, 1972.

Wallace, G., & Kauffman, J. M. *Teaching children with learning problems.* Columbus, Ohio: Charles E. Merrill Publishing Co., 1973.

Zeeman, R., & Martucci, I. The application of classroom meetings to special education. *Exceptional Children,* 1976, *42*(8), 461–462.

11

Enhancing Social Integration

As defined in chapter 2, mainstreaming is the instruction *and* social integration of handicapped and nonhandicapped students in a regular education class. The primary emphasis in preceding chapters has been on instructional integration; this chapter focuses on the equally important component of social integration.

Social integration refers to the teacher and peer interaction in the classroom. Such interaction has at least three components: affective, cognitive, and behavioral. The affective component of social integration focuses on feelings toward or perceptions of handicapped students. A perception that is essential for successful mainstreaming is the acceptance of and respect for human differences. The second component, characterized as cognitive, includes the knowledge and understanding that students have of individual differences, in general, and handicapping conditions, in particular. Finally, the behavioral component focuses on students' actions—verbal, nonverbal, and physical—toward classroom peers. The affective, cognitive, and behavioral components interact to determine the degree to which social integration of handicapped and nonhandicapped students is actually achieved in mainstreamed classrooms and schools.

There are many benefits to the achievement of social integration for handicapped and nonhandicapped students, as well as for teachers. All persons involved in mainstreaming have the opportunity to recognize and value the uniqueness of all people, to increase their knowledge about the body and its functioning, to expand their friendships, and to enhance their own self-confidence and self-esteem in learning to handle new situations with success. It is very important to be aware of the reciprocity of the beneficial outcomes of social integration. Nonhandicapped people have a great deal to gain from handicapped friends, just as handicapped individuals can learn from their nonhandicapped peers.

This chapter addresses the issue of social integration according to the following dimensions:

1. need for social integration intervention,
2. teacher variables associated with social integration,
3. student variables associated with social integration, and
4. resource materials.

NEED FOR SOCIAL INTEGRATION INTERVENTION

A consistent theme in the literature is that handicapped students are frequently rejected and alienated in regular class settings. The bulk of the research on the degree of social integration has been conducted with mentally retarded and learning-disabled populations. The rejection of mentally retarded students by nonhandicapped classmates has been documented in a sizable number of research studies (Bruininks, Rynders, & Gross, 1974; Goodman, Gottlieb, & Harrison, 1972; Gottlieb & Budoff, 1973; Iano, Ayers, Heller, McGettigan, & Walker, 1974; Reese-Dukes & Stokes, 1978). In synthesizing the findings from a number of these studies, Gottlieb (1975) concluded that mildly retarded students are accepted less frequently and reacted to more negatively than their nonhandicapped peers.

Similar trends of rejection have also been documented with the learning-disabled population. From a series of research studies on sociometric status and social behavior, Bryan (1978) reported that a substantial number of learning-disabled students have a difficult time establishing friendships with peers. Specific findings indicated that, as compared to nonhandicapped peers, learning-disabled children received significantly more votes on social rejection and significantly fewer votes on social attraction, were less accurate in comprehending nonverbal communication, and made significantly more competitive statements. A related finding was that teachers, as well as peers, make negative evaluations of these children. Bruininks (1978) found that learning-disabled children had the same needs for inclusion and affection as nonhandicapped peers; however, they had a higher need to express control. She also found learning-disabled students to be less popular and to have poorer self-concepts.

Social integration problems have also been identified in children with other types of handicaps. Force (1956) reported that elementary students preferred nonhandicapped class members over physically handicapped ones for friends, playmates, and workmates. Emotionally handicapped students have also been reported to be more socially isolated than nonhandicapped classmates (Vacc, 1972).

The age at which nonhandicapped students are aware of differences associated with handicaps is an important consideration in documenting the need for intervention. The research of Richardson (1970) revealed that first graders consistently favored nonhandicapped over handicapped children. In studying the attitudes of even younger children, Jones and Sisk (1967) found that four-year-olds were aware of limitations caused by handicaps and that evidence of rejecting attitudes existed in some five-year-olds. Thus, it appears that rejecting attitudes on the part of nonhandicapped children develop early and that these attitudes tend to be consistently predisposed across handicapping conditions.

A major void of information exists on the social acceptance of handicapped students by similarly handicapped students and by those with different types of handicaps. It can be speculated, however, that handicapped children and youth are likely to have stronger preferences for interacting with some individuals and not others. To the extent they might reject peers with some types of handicaps, the need for social integration is just as important for them as it is for nonhandicapped classmates.

Another reason for such intervention with handicapped children and youth is that frequently they need assistance in understanding the nature of their own handicap and in developing an acceptance and respect for their individuality, including the strengths and weaknesses associated with their handicap. This need is poignantly expressed by Bill Hartford, who has a stuttering handicap:[1]

> There is a certain self we present to people, and we use the words beautiful and ugly to describe the self. Stuttering is an aberration of the self, an aberration of vocal expression. Stuttering is ugly and I have always thought myself ugly. One of the things that was ugly about me was stuttering. I was ugly, period.
>
> Because this most expressive part of me—the vocal musculature—is not reliable, I can't depend on it. It is likely to fail me. My whole body image goes to hell with that. It's affected the way I look at myself. From body image to whole self-concept, and it starts with the fact that this most important and expressive part of my body, my speech, is unreliable.
>
> I was the only one in my grammar school who stuttered, until the eighth grade, when another person came in who stuttered. She was a beautiful girl. It sounds juvenile, but I learned that I really couldn't blame stuttering for my ugliness any more. I knew that this girl stuttered, and that she was a beautiful girl.
>
> I was kind of a shy kid and I didn't talk to girls often. I certainly would never talk to this girl about her speech. That is common among us stutterers; we never talk about our stuttering even to another stutterer. I've changed a lot since then—I now talk about my stuttering with anyone.

This statement reflects a major need to assist handicapped students in developing an understanding of their handicap and a positive self-image.

In summary, it is obvious that positive social integration of nonhandicapped and handicapped children and youth is unlikely to occur spontaneously in mainstreamed classrooms. Social integration, similar to academic areas of the curriculum, warrants a systematic approach to intervention. The encouraging aspect of such intervention is that it has been quite successful in ameliorating patterns of rejection and alienation.

It is difficult to isolate and identify the precise reasons for the occurrence of social integration problems. A complex set of variables interact leading to negative attitudes. These variables can be classified into two major groups: teacher and student variables. A description of variables and intervention strategies for each of these groups follows.

1. From VOICES: INTERVIEWS WITH HANDICAPPED PEOPLE by M. D. Orlansky and W. L. Heward. Columbus, Ohio: Charles E. Merrill Publishing Company, 1981, p. 27. Reprinted by permission of the publisher.

TEACHER VARIABLES

Teacher variables that can influence the degree of social integration include teachers' attitudes toward handicapped students and their level of competency in teaching handicapped students.

Teacher Attitude

It has been documented repeatedly that teachers' views of students are a strong force in determining the nature of the interaction between teachers and students and, in turn, the students' achievement (Rosenthal & Jacobson, 1968; Good, 1970; Brophy & Good, 1974; Purkey, 1970). Teachers constantly communicate important attitudinal messages to students about individual differences. It becomes obvious to all students whether or not teachers favor high-achieving students; feel respect, pity, or disgust for students who have special problems; believe that every person has inherent value; or are prejudiced against those who are different. Teachers generally are far more transparent than they care to believe.

Based on a comprehensive literature review on teacher attitudes toward handicapped students, Clark (1980) concluded that teachers typically are uncomfortable with handicapped students and have negative attitudes about their placement in regular classes. Further, teacher attitudes have been identified as crucial to the success of any mainstreaming program (MacMillan, Jones, & Meyers, 1976). Teacher attitudes not only set the tone for the relationship between teachers and handicapped students, but also substantially influence the attitudes of nonhandicapped classmates.

> *Kate, a third grader, has been classified as educable mentally retarded on the basis of formal diagnostic tests. Kate goes to the resource room for one and one-half hours every day. Her classroom teacher tends to exclude her from almost all activities on the basis that "no child with her limited development can effectively participate in the regular classroom." When other students in the class fail to achieve according to the teacher's expectations, the threat voiced by the teacher is, "If you cannot do your assignments, you will have to go with Kate to work with the other EMR's in the resource room." Both Kate and her peers get the message.*

Although this is an extreme example, it is a true story. A teacher's views and behavior can be extremely influential in defining respect for differences within the classroom.

When considering attitudes toward handicapped students, the most basic question teachers should ask themselves is: Does less able mean less worthy?

Teachers might analyze their response to this question by documenting whether they genuinely believe that handicapped students should be entitled to consideration for placement in a regular class and whether they deserve the same rights, privileges, and responsibilities as their nonhandicapped peers. If teachers can honestly affirm that "less able does not mean less worthy," they must make a commitment to implement the intervention strategies that will be subsequently discussed. Additionally, teachers should check themselves constantly, because people sometimes tend to avoid handicapped persons without realizing it. If students who stutter take longer to say something, teachers may avoid the fact that they want to communicate rather than allow them to stammer throughout their response. Similar situations occur with students representing the range of handicapping conditions. It often requires more time and effort for the teacher to make curriculum adaptations and to arrange situations that promote social integration for handicapped students who need this help than for students who are automatically accepted by their peers. If teachers believe that handicapped students are just as worthy as other students, the extra investment of time and effort does not create negative barriers between teachers and handicapped students.

Many teachers may believe that "less able does mean less worthy." This does not necessarily mean that these teachers are cold and insensitive people who have no place in the teaching profession. It may mean that these teachers have had extremely limited contact with handicapped persons. Because separate classes, schools, and residential centers for handicapped students were favored in the past over educational settings that brought together handicapped and nonhandicapped persons, many practicing and prospective teachers have had limited contact with handicapped persons. Given this lack of exposure, many people tend to imagine more differences than really exist. Sometimes negative stereotypes based on imagination or myths can cloud a person's perception of other human beings. This is an understandable phenomenon, but it does not have to become a lifelong attitude. People's attitudes toward handicapped individuals can be changed through accurate information and positive encounters.

Theresa had just graduated from college and was considering the possibility of entering graduate school in the field of education. Her roommate, who was a member of the local Association for Retarded Citizens (ARC), convinced Theresa to come along on an ARC recreational function that involved taking approximately forty-five handicapped children (mentally retarded, severely emotionally disturbed, and multiply handicapped) on a hayride and picnic. Theresa was hesitant about going along for several reasons. Although she had never been around handicapped persons to any significant degree, she had the idea that it might be dangerous to be with them. She wondered if they would bite her, make inappropriate sexual advances, or start a fire in the hay. On the one hand, Theresa told herself that she was being ridiculous, but on the other hand, she had strong

> *reservations. Theresa's roommate insisted that she come along, and Theresa hesitantly decided to go. As the trucks were loaded with children, Theresa began to relax a little as she began to join in with the children's singing. She looked closely at the children. Some were attractive, and some were unattractive. Some were talkative, and some were shy. There seemed to be a great variety of shapes, colors, sizes, and personalities. When they arrived in the country at the setting for the picnic, the children started running through the meadows, playing games, eating hotdogs, laughing, fighting, joking, and generally doing the things that children do. Toward the end of the picnic, Theresa wandered over to her roommate and whispered, "Where are the handicapped children?" Not understanding Theresa's question, the roommate gave her a puzzled look. Theresa repeated, "Where are the handicapped children? These are just children."*

The fact that teachers have had limited opportunities to develop positive attitudes toward handicapped persons does not mean that they cannot begin to develop them.

An important strategy for teachers is to get to know handicapped people as *people*. The fear of the unknown can be overcome by finding out handicapped persons' likes and dislikes, strengths and weaknesses, hobbies, interests, and future plans. Sometimes teachers only get to know handicapped children and youth as students. They know a student's level of performance, particular disability, curriculum needs, and learning styles; but that is not enough. It is also important to know the student as an individual and, furthermore, to find joy and naturalness in the relationship.

When teachers and nonhandicapped students encounter handicapped children and youth for the first time, perhaps before they are entirely comfortable with their new relationships, they might follow some helpful guidelines. People should behave naturally in the presence of handicapped persons. Being tense, oversolicitous, or sympathetic toward handicapped persons can be offensive. Carry on a normal conversation; attitudes of pity or charity are unproductive. Ideally, attitudes of equality and respect should form the foundation of associations with handicapped individuals.

The disadvantages associated with people's handicaps may be inconvenient for them, but these handicaps may not prevent them from full participation in regular class activities. Debora Ann Butler, a teacher of visually impaired children, expressed this point of view:[1]

> I've been blind since birth, so I don't feel I'm really missing anything by not seeing. I don't feel handicapped; to me it is more an inconvenience than a handicap. The only things I can't do are drive a car and just pick up a printed

---

1. From VOICES: INTERVIEWS WITH HANDICAPPED PEOPLE by M. D. Orlansky and W. L. Heward. Columbus, Ohio: Charles E. Merrill Publishing Company, 1981, p. 77. Reprinted by permission of the publisher.

book and read it. It bothers me when people say, "Oh, you're handicapped." I feel I can do the same things a sighted person does, even though I might do some things differently.

Handicaps are often in the eye of the beholder. Teachers and peers need to guard against negative attitudes and perceptions that might impose a greater handicap on the person than really exists.

Overprotectiveness represents an unfavorable attitude toward handicapped persons. Encouraging independent behavior in handicapped students is often more difficult than with their nonhandicapped peers. Sometimes, there is a natural tendency to want to protect or to prevent failure; however, it is important for teachers to strike the proper balance between needed support and encouragement of independence. This balance may have a slightly different definition in each individual situation.

Teacher Competency

A second teacher variable influencing the degree of social integration is competency, which refers to the teacher's knowledge and skill in teaching handicapped students. Teacher competency influences social integration in a variety of ways.

First, a relationship has been documented between a teacher's knowledge about handicapping conditions and the existence of positive attitudes (Shaw & Gillung, 1975; Yates, 1973). It is obvious that people are more enthusiastic about engaging in experiences in which they feel confident and competent rather than in experiences in which they feel threatened and apt to fail. Second, the competence of the teacher can determine whether handicapped students achieve academic success in the classroom and thus receive the status and respect that are outcomes of such success. A third important factor in teacher competency is the teacher's skill in systematically implementing the student-oriented social interventions discussed later in the chapter.

The effects of increasing teacher competency regarding social integration interventions were documented by Leyser and Gottlieb (1980). They provided a two-hour workshop to teachers, a training manual, and periodic consultation on implementing strategies, such as classroom discussions, peer tutoring, and simulations, to improve the social status of handicapped students. An analysis of pre- and posttest sociometric data, focusing on the four most socially rejected students in the classroom of each of the teachers receiving training, revealed a significant improvement in social acceptance at the end of a ten-week period. Thus, a short-term training program aimed at increasing teachers' skills resulted in substantial gains for the students.

STUDENT VARIABLES

Most of the research, general literature, and training guides developed on the subject of social integration among handicapped and nonhandicapped students is aimed strictly at improving the attitudes of nonhandicapped children and youth toward handicapped peers. As indicated previously in this chapter, handicapped students may have negative perceptions of handicapped and nonhandicapped classmates. Also, students in both groups may have negative perceptions of themselves that interfere with their ability to interact with peers. Thus, a broad intervention program is required that focuses on improving the interaction skills and self-esteem of *all* students.

Student variables that can influence the degree of social integration in mainstreamed classrooms include knowledge about handicapping conditions, structure of peer interactions, and degree of classroom status achieved by the students.

Knowledge

All students need information about the nature of handicapping conditions, in general, and the specific effects that these conditions have on their classmates or on themselves. It is natural for children and youth to be curious about differences.

> *Joe is hearing-impaired. His second-grade classmates wonder why he wears "the funny wires that go in his ears." At the beginning of the year, they frequently asked Joe and Mr. Parks, their teacher. Mr. Parks quickly told them to "mind their own business" and "not be so cruel." They finally stopped asking, but they still wondered. The main thing they figured out from Mr. Parks's response was that it must be something shameful. Joe was also confused by Mr. Parks's reaction. He decided that Mr. Parks must not like hearing aids. That meant, in his way of thinking, that Mr. Parks must not like him either.*

Such curiosity should not be interpreted as cruel, but rather as genuine interest in learning about differences.

Students frequently have misconceptions about handicapped people. In a survey of 400 high school students (*IRUC Briefings,* 1977), many misconceptions were documented, such as:

- people with muscular dystrophy are also retarded (47%),
- epilepsy is related to emotional illness (47%),
- blind people are unable to attend college or work (59%), and

- speech deficits are usually related to mental retardation (55%) and/or emotional problems (53%).

More than half of the respondents indicated a desire to broaden their knowledge about handicaps by hearing handicapped speakers, seeing films, and visiting facilities.

In planning instructional activities to increase student knowledge, consideration should be given to the "similarity-attraction" model as discussed by Asher (1973). This model postulates that attraction to an individual increases as the perceived similarity of that individual to one's self increases. As applied to classroom interventions, the similarity-attraction model suggests that as knowledge about handicapping conditions is presented and discussed, the emphasis should be on similarities between handicapped and nonhandicapped persons. This model, however, should not be interpreted to mean that differences should be masked or denied.

Several different strategies can be used to increase student knowledge. Three such strategies include instructional programs, classroom discussions, and simulations of handicaps.

Instructional Programs. Units of instruction can be taught on many different topics. Social studies is an obvious curriculum area in which such topics as handicapping conditions, architectural accessibility, the handicapped activist movement, and media stereotypes of handicapped persons can be developed into meaningful and comprehensive instructional units.

Instructional units can also be developed in other curriculum areas, including:

1. civics—federal and state legislation pertaining to rights for handicapped people,
2. health—individual differences,
3. science—the mechanics of hearing aids and auditory trainers,
4. music—contributions of blind composers and musicians,
5. biology—genetic screening and amniocentesis, and
6. home economics—adapting the home environment for physically handicapped persons.

Learning centers can be developed to teach students about handicaps. An example is a learning center on communication skills that was presented in chapter 4 (Schulz, 1981). In this center, students learned about new forms of communciation—sign language, Braille, semaphore. Similar to instructional units, a wide range of topics can be addressed through learning centers.

An increasing amount of literature on the topic of handicaps is available for children and adolescents. It can be excellent resource material for instructional units, learning centers, or independent reading. A comprehensive annotated bibliography of current books appropriate for children from kindergarten through high school has been prepared by Ms. Patricia Bishopp, the librarian at Meeting Street School, 667 Waterman Avenue, East Providence, R.I. Copies of this bibliography can be obtained by writing to her (Robinson, 1979).

When choosing books for classroom use, teachers should be aware that media portayals of handicapped persons through books (Biklen & Bogdan, 1977; Mullins, 1979; Schwartz, 1977) and television (Donaldson, 1981) have frequently presented a negative sterotypic image. Persons evaluating resource material should avoid the following stereotypic views:

- presenting disabled persons in a sensational manner;
- one-dimensional characterizations of disabled persons;
- having disabled persons as targets of ridicule;
- reference to superhuman attributes; and
- reference as objects of pity (Biklen & Bogdan, 1977).

If the goal of intervention is to enhance the student's knowledge, then the teacher should judiciously choose materials to avoid these stereotypic perspectives.

An excellent instructional activity for a secondary English composition class would be to evaluate critically a range of literature with handicapped characters. Examples of books to include are *Treasure Island, Of Human Bondage, Moby Dick,* and *Of Mice and Men.*

In addition to printed material, an increasing number of television programs, movies, and films are focusing on issues associated with handicapping conditions. These media resources can also be used as a basis for classroom instruction. Again, nonstereotypic criteria should be used when reviewing media materials to determine their potential classroom value.

Classroom Discussions. It is likely that the use of instructional units, learning centers, books, and media will result in the need for classroom discussions on particular areas of student interest. Caution should be taken to insure that the discussions are based on accurate information, avoiding the possibility that uninformed biases would form the core of the exchanges (Siperstein, Bak, & Gottlieb, 1977). An excellent strategy for classroom discussions is to invite handicapped adults to meet with the class and discuss the nature of their disabilities and the feelings associated with them. This strategy has several major advantages including the opportunity for students to get first-hand information about the day-to-day reality of handicaps, the placement of a handicapped person in the "status" position of teacher, and the identification of a role model for handicapped students.

Ron, a handsome and muscular adult, talked with a kindergarten class about his physical disability. He explained how he plays basketball in his wheelchair and even demonstrated some "crack" shooting. He got a big laugh from the students when he described his softball technique of sliding into first base on his back wheels and handlebars. Many questions were asked during the discussion, such as: "Can you drive a car?" "Will you ever be able to walk?" "Do you wish you could walk?" As the open and lively discussion drew to a close, one of the children commented to Ron, "I have been looking at your wheelchair the whole time. But next time I see you, Ron, I will be able to look you in the eyes."

When handicapped adults were used as speakers to college classes, Donaldson and Martinson (1977) reported a significant increase in positive student attitudes. Their research also indicated that video-taped discussions of handicapped adults resulted in similar positive attitudinal changes. In implementing such a strategy, they pointed out the importance of selecting handicapped individuals who present nonstereotypic images and who are not overly sensitive or self-pitying about their handicaps.

In addition to having handicapped adults discuss the nature of their handicaps, meaningful learning experiences can be provided by having these adults share their interests, talents, and career responsibilities. These topics help students identify common characteristics and interests; this identification is consistent with the previously discussed similarity-attraction model. A blind poet might read his poems; an adult paralyzed from the waist down might demonstrate methods of increasing upper body strength; and a deaf person might give a pottery lesson. Such situations provide opportunities to accentuate similarities rather than differences.

Discussions can provide opportunities for handicapped students in the classroom to share information about their own disabilities or to answer questions about them. The teachers might talk with the handicapped students, parents, and the school counselor when planning a method of providing information to nonhandicapped classmates at the beginning of the school year. Many handicapped children and youth can explain the nature of their handicaps succinctly to their peers. This ability to provide a self-explanation is very important, since handicapped students are frequently quizzed about "what's wrong" when the teacher is not around.

Sherry has a physical disability referred to as cerebral palsy. She uses a walker to get around her third-grade class. When her peers ask her about why she uses the walker, she immediately tells them that the walker's name is Hi-O Silver and that Hi-O can help her get anywhere she wants to go. She goes on to tell them that she has cerebral palsy, which means that her muscles have not developed in the same way as most other people's. Sherry's parents helped her learn to respond to questions in this fashion. Her teacher established the type of classroom atmosphere in which questions and responses could be discussed in an honest and open fashion.

Some students may prefer to have the teacher provide classmates with information about their individual handicaps. Such information can be provided before a student enters the class or during a classroom discussion. When the student is present, it is preferable for the student to participate in some way in the discussion—demonstrating special equipment, such as a wheelchair, large-print books, or a hearing aid; sharing a description of physical therapy sessions; or describing what it is like to be in a hospital and to have surgery. Such communications should be characterized by openness, respect for differences, and identification of similarities among all students.

Parents can be excellent resources for classroom discussion. A third-grade teacher described a way she capitalized on the expertise and willingness of a parent to expand the knowledge of her students:

Janie had a severe hearing impairment. She attended a special class next door to ours. The biggest problem was communication with Janie during recess and at school functions. How could my third graders feel comfortable communicating with her? They were afraid to talk to her.

Janie's mother came to my class and taught the children sign language. The whole class loved it! They learned very fast. They started going to Janie everyday asking for her help in learning more signs. This gave them a common ground. The children were no longer hesitant in approaching her.

Like all children, they always think of more than one way to "skin a cat." How could they talk to their friends in the lunchroom when they were supposed to be silent? Sign language—it was great for everyone!!

Although many parents are interested in such participation, other parents feel uncomfortable explaining their child's handicap to others. One parent stated such a perspective.

I get so tired of always being asked to explain Larry's handicap. It seems like every time Larry enters a new situation—school, church, scouts, community recreation—I am always asked to come in and explain mental retardation. I often want to say, "Can't someone else do it?" I almost feel like it puts me in the position of asking or begging other people to be nice to him. As a parent, that feeling makes me sad.

Several cautions apply to classroom discussions. First, insure that handicapped students and their parents are comfortable being the focus of classroom discussions. Teachers should adhere to their preferences and recognize that some people prefer to maintain a lower profile. Second, respect for the student should be maintained at all times. The mother of an orthopedically handicapped student provided an illustration of an unintended insult:[1]

In high school, a teacher didn't mean harm but upset Sara's friends, who later came to her very indignant. Sara came to us in tears. This was the first time my husband and I went to see the principal; and once again the teacher had done what she thought was a kind thing. But neither the children, nor Sara, nor we saw it as that: After Sara's first day in class, she told subsequent classes about Sara, and said they should all be thankful they were not like Sara. Sara's friends did not see her as such a deformed person, and they resented the implication.

We thought it very bad taste to single out a person—handicapped— to make others feel fortunate. The teacher apologized but not to Sara, nor did she mention it to the children.

Thus, such discussions should in no way portray the handicapped person as pitiful or pathetic. Rather, the discussion should focus on ability as well as on disability, on feelings, and on coping.

Teachers are encouraged to deal with issues and concerns directly related to the handicap, rather than avoid them. When classroom peers ask specific questions about the handicap, these questions should be viewed as natural and worthy of honest answers. When peers are provided with adequate understanding, they in turn can provide explanations to other students when questions arise. Thus, the handicapped individual does not always have to provide the explanations. Once classmates clearly understand handicaps and develop a sensitivity to differences, questions of "what's wrong" with a particular student become practically nonexistent.

Simulation. A third strategy that can be used to increase student knowledge is the actual simulation of handicaps. Simulation requires nonhandicapped students to act as if they have a handicap through the use of special equipment and according to specified instructions.

Resource materials included at the end of the chapter include a variety of simulation activities for use with students. With younger age groups, puppetry can also be used as a mode for simulation. Puppets with handicaps can be made by the students or community volunteers. Puppets can also be purchased commercially (see *The Kids on the Block* in the resource list at the end of the chapter).

The effects of simulation on the modification of attitudes was studied by Clore and Jeffrey (1972). They had one group of students use a wheelchair to travel a specified route; another group followed along at a distance of twenty

---

1. From UNDERSTANDING AND WORKING WITH PARENTS OF CHILDREN WITH SPECIAL NEEDS edited by James L. Paul. Copyright © 1981 by Holt, Rinehart and Winston. Reprinted by permission of Holt, Rinehart and Winston, CBS College Publishing.

feet and observed the person simulating the orthopedic handicap. Using several attitudinal assessments, they found a significant increase in positive attitudes for the students who participated. This difference was evident immediately and was maintained over a four-month period. The authors attributed this positive change to the development of empathy.

Several guidelines should be considered when using simulation. Wright (1979) cautions that simulations can result in negative emotions, such as fear, loneliness, and helplessness, as students experience difficulty with coping. Such negative emotions could be projected on the handicapped population as a whole. The immediate simulation of a handicap without the prior development of coping skills is not at all the same situation as that of a classsmate who has had a particular handicap for a period of time and has learned to compensate for it. Thus, when simulation is used as a teaching strategy, nonhandicapped students need to experience successful coping responses rather than just frustration and awkwardness. Successful coping responses can be accomplished by such activities as requesting the installation of a paper cup dispenser when the student cannot reach the water fountain (Wright, 1979) or learning to ask for assistance in a nondefensive manner when maneuvering a wheelchair onto an elevator. The important point is that students conclude simulation experiences with a greater insight about the nature of handicaps and about possibilities for adaptation. An excellent concluding activity, after students have participated in simulations, is to have a handicapped speaker discuss the types of adaptations he or she has learned to make. Students are likely to have a far greater appreciation of such adaptations after they have participated in simulations.

Structured Peer Interactions

Based on the research cited earlier in the chapter by Gottlieb (1975) and Bryan (1978), interaction among handicapped and nonhandicapped students usually does not occur spontaneously in mainstreamed classrooms. Furthermore, unstructured contact does not lead directly to more positive attitudes on the part of nonhandicapped persons (Donaldson, 1980). An effective type of intervention, however, is to structure experiences systematically to provide opportunities for students to work or enjoy leisure activities together. Structured interactions can be planned using a variety of strategies. This section discusses four strategies: planned activities to increase communication, peer tutoring, cooperative instruction, and teaching friendship skills.

Planned Activities to Increase Communication. A variety of activities can be planned by teachers to increase communication among students. A frequently used technique is to have regularly scheduled sharing times throughout the school year to enable students to share their experiences, special activities, feelings, and ideas. Sharing time can be structured to accomplish various purposes. A teacher described a strategy for structuring as follows:

> *Sometimes we get a ball of yarn and throw it from one person to another. The person who catches the yarn has to say something good about the person who threw it. Another time we used the yarn, the persons catching it had to say something nice about themselves. I have seen some really good results in class morale and closeness.*

Another strategy for structuring communication through planned activities is to use a communication wheel (see Figure 11–1). This wheel can be used at the beginning of school to increase peer interaction. All students should be provided with a copy of the wheel and should be encouraged to seek help from each other.

Peer Tutoring. Peer tutoring, discussed in chapter 4, is a familiar concept. As related to social integration, it represents an effective strategy for bringing handicapped and nonhandicapped students together to accomplish a defined goal. It is very important that handicapped students have the opportunity to provide tutoring as well as to receive it.

> *Jazmina is an active, energetic second grader. She has boundless energy for everything except reading. She stumbles over words and is still reading at a primer level at the end of second grade. Her peers tease her sometimes and it makes her afraid she will be laughed at in her reading group. She gets very tense during reading period. Jazmina excels in gymnastics. Her teacher planned a unit on tumbling in the physical education class and asked Jazmina to help some of her classmates learn to do headstands, handstands, and cartwheels. Jazmina was delighted to serve as a peer tutor, and the students who had been teasing her quickly learned a side of Jazmina they had never known.*

"Helping" relationships often turn into friendships. The nonhandicapped student may be amazed at the adaptations and compensations that a handicapped peer is able to make. As students become aware of each other's strengths and weaknesses, respect for individual differences and spontaneous interactions can be natural by-products.

Opportunities for both nonhandicapped and handicapped students in regular classes to provide peer tutoring to moderately and severely handicapped students in special classes can also be arranged. Poorman (1980) has outlined a detailed program to prepare regular class students for these tutoring experiences.

Cooperative Instruction. Cooperative instruction refers to the structuring

383 Student Variables

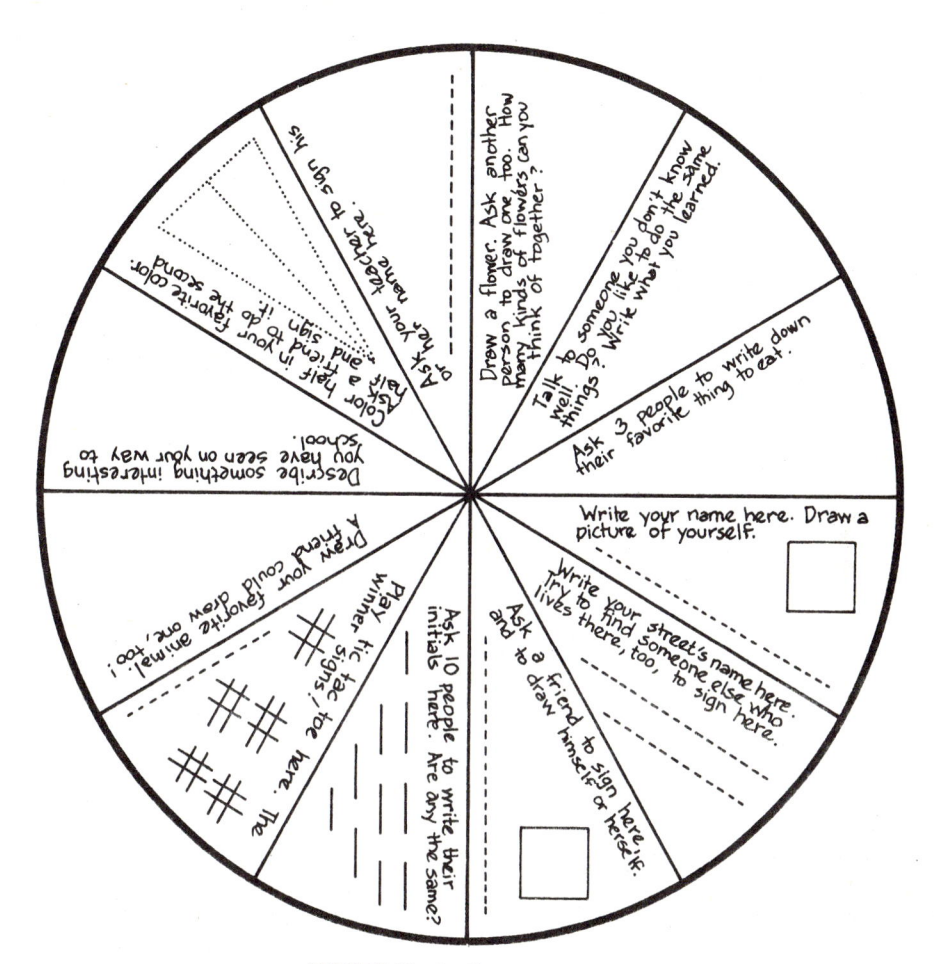

FIGURE 11-1. Communication Wheel

of learning situations so that students work together to achieve common goals. In contrast, individualistic instruction results in independent student achievement, for example, a goal accomplished by one student is not tied to that of other students. Cooperative instruction was discussed in chapter 4. Documentation exists on the value of cooperative instruction in enhancing peer interactions of handicapped and nonhandicapped students. Johnson and Johnson (1981) compared the outcomes of cooperative and individualistic learning experiences for handicapped and nonhandicapped third graders. The instruction consisted of a daily, twenty-five-minute math lesson for sixteen days. In the cooperative condition, students were divided into five small groups; four of the groups included one handicapped student. The students were instructed to work together to complete assignment sheets. All students were expected to contribute ideas, and the teacher rewarded the group as a whole. The individualistic condition had students working alone and the teacher rewarding students on an individual basis. The results for each variable investigated in the study are summarized here:

Variables	Results
1. Interaction between handicapped and nonhandicapped students during instruction	1. In cooperative condition, nonhandicapped students asked handicapped peers more questions, offered more suggestions, and provided more help
2. Amount of off-task behavior	2. No significant differences between the two conditions
3. Interaction between handicapped and nonhandicapped students during free-time after instructional sessions	3. More cross-handicap interactions occurred in the cooperative condition
4. Nomination of friends	4. Trend for more nominations of friends among handicapped and nonhandicapped students in the cooperative group

A major finding of this study for social integration intervention is that the interaction occurring during the structured activities generalized to unstructured situations in which students could choose classmates with whom to interact.

These findings suggest that group activities, such as sociodrama, art projects, science projects and games, can be used to structure successful interaction among handicapped and nonhandicapped students. Rather than providing singular or isolated instruction to handicapped students, attempts should be made to meet their individual needs within small working groups.

Teaching Friendship Skills. Friendship skills involve a range of behaviors including sharing, cooperation, communication, verbal complimenting, non-aggressiveness, and participation. Because of previous rejection and alienation, handicapped students may have had limited opportunities to develop these skills. There is a paucity of research on the level of friendship skills of handicapped students; however, one study at the junior high level indicated that mentally retarded students were more limited in interpersonal skills than their nonhandicapped classmates (Kingsley, Viggiano, & Tout, 1981).

Behavior management techniques discussed in chapter 10 apply to teaching friendship skills. Gresham (1981) provides a comprehensive review of research on the application of these techniques to social skills training.

Setting clear behavioral standards has particular relevance for students with learning and behavior problems. Often, these students are not attuned to some of the subtle nonverbal cues that reflect peer approval or disapproval of their behavior. Thus, they may behave inappropriately because the rules and standards of behavior are not clear to them.

When Cindy started her menstrual period, she did not understand what was happening or why she had physical cramps. It was a source of great anxiety to her. Anytime a teacher or classmate asked her how she was, she always responded in terms of whether it was just before, during, or after her menstrual period. Her reactions became a class joke, and classmates increased the frequency of asking only to laugh when she responded in her stereotypic manner. Her teachers felt sorry for her, because she did not have any friends and lived at an institution for mentally retarded persons in the community. They did not want to embarrass her by telling her that her frequent comments about menstruation were socially inappropriate. When the school counselor heard some of Cindy's classmates laughing about her conversation, she set up an appointment with Cindy and explained the bodily changes associated with menstruation and guidelines for appropriate conversation. They brainstormed about other responses Cindy could make when she was asked how she was feeling. The counselor also talked with Cindy's teachers and peers and encouraged them to praise Cindy for appropriate conversation. Cindy kept a diary of her conversations and reviewed it with the counselor on a weekly basis. After her initial meeting with the counselor, Cindy never made any more inappropriate comments about menstruation.

Nonhandicapped students also frequently need assistance with friendship skills as they relate to handicapped peers. One problem that can arise in mainstreamed classrooms is name-calling, such as "retardo," "crip," and "four-eyes." Such negative interactions can be handled in a variety of ways in teaching more appropriate social behavior. Salend and Schobel (1981) described an instructional unit they taught to a fourth-grade class on the function of names. The major topics within the unit were acquisition and meaning of names, how names are different, and positive or negative effects of nicknames. On the last topic, one of the activities was a discussion of the negative effects of nicknames and of the importance of considering another person's reaction to the nickname.

Just as it is important for all students to develop sensitivity to the feelings of their classmates, it is also important for handicapped people to develop strategies for dealing with name-calling. Mothers of young handicapped children identified the greatest benefit of mainstreaming for their children to be preparation for the "real world" (Turnbull & Winton, in press). One mother stated this perspective as follows:

Some of the other kids would pick on him or beat him up or something, and he'd just let them pick on him. They'd call him some real names . . . really surprised me . . . 'retarded,' 'cripple,' or stuff like that . . . really bad names . . . But as far as I know, they've quit doing that. He's finally learned to stand up for himself.

Schulz (1979) discussed the importance of "facing the label" in preparing her mentally retarded son for successful employment as an adult.

The strongest example I can present is the experience of my son, who is mentally retarded. Although aware of his retardation, he was raised and educated in protective environments; he was never called "stupid," "fat," "dumb." When he went to work he failed, not because he lacked the necessary skills, but because he had not learned to deal with the threats and jeers of his co-workers. (p. 51)

Teachers need to be comfortable in helping handicapped students deal with name-calling as they simultaneously work with them in developing friendships.

Nellie, a student in Ms. Wilson's third-grade class, goes to the resource room for instruction thirty minutes each day. The resource room is referred to as the EMR class around the school. Some of Nellie's peers teased her about going to the resource program and started calling her "EMR" and "retardo." Nellie came to Ms. Wilson and asked "What does it mean to be an EMR?" Ms. Wilson's heart dropped. How should she respond? She did not want to hurt Nellie's feelings; yet she valued honest communication with her students. She responded to Nellie by indicating that EMR stands for educable mentally retarded. She went on to explain that the term educable mentally retarded is sometimes used to refer to students who have more difficulty learning school subjects than some of their classmates.

She asked Nellie if sometimes her reading and arithmetic lessons were hard for her to understand. Nellie affirmed that they were. Ms. Wilson reassured Nellie that educable mentally retarded does not mean that Nellie cannot learn at all nor that she has difficulty learning everything. Nellie's performance in art projects was pointed out as an area where she had less difficulty than many of her classmates. Ms. Wilson reminded Nellie that all people have difficulty learning some things. The point that individual people have different strengths, weaknesses, interests, and learning rates was strongly stressed. Ms. Wilson told Nellie that she could understand how she did not like being called EMR. Ms. Wilson encouraged Nellie to remember the progress she was making from going to the resource program and to ignore students who have not yet learned that name-calling is unkind.

After this initial conference, Ms. Wilson and Nellie jointly chose some representative work assignments that Nellie had done in the resource room. These were shared with the class during a "show and tell" period, along with a description of the types of work done in the resource room. Ms. Wilson also worked with the class during language arts in writing scripts and producing puppet shows on sensitivity to feelings. Some of the students who had been doing the name-calling had puppets cast in roles of needing special help in order to understand their school work. Through the simulated experience with the puppets, these students began to get the message of what it is like when the shoe is on the other foot. Ms. Wilson realized that name-calling would not be eliminated immediately, but that systematic steps could be taken to teach respect for differences. She knew that merely punishing the students who were teasing Nellie might only teach them to call others names when they knew the teacher would not find out. Replacing the negative attitudes and behavior with positive attitudes and behavior was Ms. Wilson's goal.

Degree of Classroom Status

Classroom status refers to the prestige or recognition that students have among their peers. Students who have status in the classroom are likely to have fewer problems with social integration. In a sociometric study of learning-disabled students (Siperstein, Bopp, & Bak, 1978), it was found that this group was less popular than their nonhandicapped classmates. An interesting trend detected, however, was that of the six best-liked, learning-disabled children in the study, five received nominations for best athlete in the class. Thus, it was speculated that the status gained through athletics helped to compensate for some of the students' other areas of deficit.

To help develop status, teachers first need to insure that students have an opportunity to achieve success. Success is important for all students, but it can be of special significance to handicapped students. Some handicapped students, unfortunately, experience overwhelming amounts of failure in their school careers. Sometimes the failure is more teacher-based than student-based, as when teachers routinely set expectations for handicapped students on a much higher academic level than their achievement level warrants. Inaccurate or insufficient assessment can lead directly to failure. Teachers can eliminate a large number of failure experiences by planning appropriate instruction. The IEP can be the focal point of successful instruction.

Purkey (1970) suggests questions that teachers might consider in developing a classroom atmosphere characterized by success. These questions include:

- Do I permit my students some opportunity to make mistakes without penalty?
- Do I make generally positive comments on written work?

- Do I give extra support and encouragement to slower students?
- Do I recognize the successes of students in terms of what they did earlier?
- Do I take special opportunities to praise students for their successes?
- Do I manufacture honest experiences of success for my students?
- Do I set tasks which are, and which appear to the student to be, within his abilities? (p. 56)

As handicapped students experience success, they can become more confident about their strengths and more positive in their self-concept. Likewise, their nonhandicapped peers have the opportunity to recognize their strengths. All of these factors can contribute to the enhanced, social integration of handicapped and nonhandicapped students.

The status of handicapped students can be increased by insuring their successful inclusion in extracurricular activities and prestige positions in the school. In many situations, handicapped students are not chosen to be captains of the ball teams, stars in the class play, or editors of the school newspaper. These positions, however, typically have status in most elementary and secondary schools. Teachers cannot always arrange peer relationships or determine which students are chosen by their classmates for special honors, but the teacher's influence and guidance can serve as a strong model. It is important for teachers to be sensitive to classroom and school opportunities that might capitalize on the strengths and interests of handicapped students. These opportunities should also be generally associated with status and prestige.

Charles is in his last year of elementary school. He is mentally retarded and has low academic achievement in all areas. He also has some emotional problems. At the beginning of the year, his teacher was acutely aware of his inferior class position. When basketball season started, Charles was very disappointed because he knew he was not skilled enough to go out for the team. He loved basketball and spent every afternoon practicing. His teacher had a great idea. Would the coach allow Charles to be the basketball manager? The teacher carefully described the situation to the coach and stated reasons why he thought Charles would do a very good job as team manager. The coach agreed to give Charles a chance to prove himself. When the teacher told Charles of this opportunity, he was overwhelmed with excitement. He could hardly wait until the first day of practice. Faithfully and diligently, Charles worked at his job and performed in an outstanding manner. The coach and team grew to respect him as their manager and friend. Charles had the opportunity to travel with the team to all out-of-town games and was awarded a plaque at the sports banquet. The opportunity to be basketball manager was the beginning of new peer perceptions toward Charles. No longer was he the "kid with problems" or the "EMR student." Charles was the basketball manager. This position carried status.

In addition to being managers, some handicapped students successfully participate in interscholastic athletics.

Kathy and Frances are upper elementary students with significant learning problems. They were first-string players on the school's volleyball team. Their classmates came to games to cheer them on. The school letter each received is their most prized possession.

Handicapped students can be members of the school chorus, members of an honor club, active in drama productions, members of the safety patrol, members of the school newspaper staff, or peer tutors of other students.

James Oates is not your typical sixth grader. He serves on the Safety Patrol in the cafeteria before school starts each day. He relies on his ears to help him maintain order, since he is totally blind. James has a full day splitting time among his sixth-grade class, his vision resource teacher, and the gifted and talented program. In addition to his studies, James is serving his second term as the student council president. (Lauber, 1980, p. 38)

Whatever the nature of involvement, the important point is that handicapped students have opportunities to excel in areas valued by others. The end result is usually increased peer and self-respect.

Achieving Social Integration

Social integration will be enhanced when careful attention is given to developing positive attitudes toward handicapped students and to establishing a classroom environment characterized by open and honest communication, success, and respect.

> Mark has a long history of school failure. He has been ostracized frequently by his peers. When Mark reached the fourth grade, his teacher made a commitment to try to create for him an environment more conducive to learning. She first referred him for special education services. Mark was tested, and it was found that he qualified for services from the learning disabilities resource program. A committee comprised of Mark's classroom teacher, resource teacher, coordinator of special education services, and parents was established to develop an IEP for him. The committee worked very hard to pinpoint Mark's level of achievement and to plan the next steps.
> When the IEP was completed, Mark's teacher, Ms. Turner, felt that she had a good idea of where to start. With the help of the resource teacher, she gathered some instructional materials on Mark's level. As the years progressed, Mark systematically moved toward higher levels of mastery. He was proud of what he learned and appeared to be a happier and more outgoing child overall.

Ms. Turner arranged for Mark to lead storytime in a first-grade class one day a week. Because of the work he had done and knowledge he had obtained at home in his parent's garden, he became "Chief Advisor" for the classroom window garden. He took excellent care of the plants and always seemed to know what to do when one began to droop. Mark's peers admired him for his gardening skills.

Ms. Turner observed that classroom peers gradually began to include Mark in more and more activities as "one of the guys." This pleased her very much, and one day she expressed her pleasure to a nonhandicapped peer who invariably included Mark in informal classroom groups. The peer was puzzled that Ms. Turner would make such a statement. The peer's reply was, "What's the big deal about including Mark? He's neat."

Perhaps the ultimate goal is for social integration for handicapped and nonhandicapped students to be so natural that it is not a "big deal."

RESOURCE MATERIALS

Only in recent years have commercial materials been developed on the topic of enhancing social integration. Representative samples of these resources are included in this section (to order, see Appendix B). Readers are also urged to contact the professional and volunteer organizations listed in Appendix A. Many of these organizations have resource lists of materials aimed at the special needs of the handicapped people whom they represent. These organizations also offer pamphlets that can be extremely useful in planning social integration activities. One strategy for collecting this information would be to have students write these organizations for information as an activity in a language arts lesson.

Mainstreaming: What Every Child Needs to Know about Disabilities. Units of instruction designed for grades one through four are provided in the areas of blindness, deafness, physical disabilities, and mental retardation. Instructional activities include using classroom discussions; simulations; exposure to aids and appliances; guest speakers; and books, movies, slides, and videotapes. Excellent resource lists are also included. The Exceptional Parent Press.

Kids Come in Special Flavors: Classroom Experience Collection. This collection of social integration materials includes a teacher's guide book of detailed activities and resource lists, storybooks, cassette tapes for acquainting students with hearing impairments, paper and pencil tasks for simulating problems of the mentally retarded and learning-disabled students, and equipment related to the special needs of visually impaired and orthopedically handicapped students. It is aimed at the elementary level. Kids Come in Special Flavors.

Everybody Counts! A Workshop Manual to Increase Awareness of Handicapped People. A collection of simulation activities covering the full range of handicapping conditions is included in this guidebook. Detailed instructions and graphic illustrations enable the reader to implement the activities with success. The activities are geared to the secondary level. Council for Exceptional Children.

Put On a Handicap. A teacher's manual and a record provide a range of instructional activities including simulations, discussions, and examining prosthetic aids and appliances. The record contains songs that are educational and fun. Kimbo Educational Materials.

I Am, I Can, I Will. This series featuring Mr. Rogers includes fifteen titles aimed at helping handicapped children understand their feelings. The titles are available in several media formats including films, videotapes, audio cassettes, and books. Teacher guides are also available with suggestions for follow-up activities to encourage the expression of feelings. Hubbard Scientific.

The Kids on the Block. Six handcrafted and engaging puppets representing a range of handicaps are available in this program. A teacher's guide is also available that includes ten scripts, numerous ideas for follow-up activities, and an extensive bibliography of children's literature related to handicaps. The Kids on the Block.

Special People Behind the Eight-Ball. This book is a compilation of an extensive annotated bibliography of literature categorized according to handicapping conditions. Books appropriate for both elementary and secondary levels are included. The Exceptional Parent Bookstore.

People You'd Like to Know. Ten films focusing on handicapped youth, ages eleven to fourteen, are included in this series. The films focus on the similarities of these young people to the nonhandicapped population. Encyclopedia Britannica Education Corporation.

Different From You and Like You Too. This filmstrip explores the concept of individual differences and encourages children to ask questions of their handicapped peers. It is suitable for an elementary audience. Lawren Productions, Inc.

REFERENCES

Asher, N. W. Manipulating attraction toward the disabled: An application of the similarity-attraction model. *Rehabilitation Psychology,* 1973, *20,* 156–164.

Biklen, D., & Bogdan, R. Media portrayals of disabled people: A study in stereotypes. *Bulletin,* 1977, *8*(6,7), 4–9.

Brophy, J., & Good, T. *Teacher-student relationships—Causes and consequences.* New York: Holt, Rinehart and Winston, 1974.

Bruininks, R. H., Rynders, J. E., & Gross, T. C. Social acceptance of mildly retarded pupils in resource rooms and regular classes. *American Journal of Mental Deficiency,* 1974, *78,* 377–383.

Bruininks, V. L. Peer status and personality characteristics of learning disabled and nondisabled students. *Journal of Learning Disabilities,* 1978, *11*(8), 29–34.

Bryan, T. H. Social relationships and verbal interactions of learning disabled children. *Journal of Learning Disabilities,* 1978, *11*(2), 58–66.

Clark, F. L. The development of instrumentation to measure regular classroom teachers' attitudes toward mildly handicapped students. Doctoral Dissertation, University of Kansas, 1980.

Clore, G. L., & Jeffrey, K. M. Emotional role playing, attitude change and attraction toward a disabled person. *Journal of Personality and Social Psychology,* 1972, 23, 105–111.

Donaldson, J. Changing attitudes toward handicapped persons: A review and analysis of research. *Exceptional Children,* 1980, *46*(7), 504–513.

Donaldson, J. The visibility and image of handicapped people on television. *Exceptional Children,* 1981, *47*(6), 413–416.

Donaldson, J., & Martinson, M. C. Modifying attitudes toward physically disabled persons. *Exceptional Children,* 1977, *43*(6), 337–341.

Force, D. G. Social status of physically handicapped children. *Exceptional Children,* 1956, *23,* 104–107.

Good, T. Which pupils do teachers call on? *Elementary School Journal,* 1970, *70,* 190–198.

Goodman, H., Gottlieb, J., & Harrison, R. H. Social acceptance of EMR's integrated into a nongraded elementary school. *American Journal of Mental Deficiency,* 1972, *26,* 412–417.

Gottlieb, J. Public, peer, and professional attitudes toward mentally retarded persons. In M. J. Begab & S. A. Richardson (Eds.), *The mentally retarded and society: A social science perspective.* Baltimore: Univesity Park Press, 1975.

Gottlieb, J., & Budoff, M. Social acceptibility of retarded children in nongraded schools differing in architecture. *American Journal of Mental Deficiency,* 1973, *78,* 15–19.

Gresham, F. M. Social skills training with handicapped children: A review. *Review of Educational Research,* 1981, *51*(1), 139–176.

Iano, R. P., Ayers, D., Heller, H. B., McGettigan, J. F., & Walker, V. S. Sociometric status of retarded children in an integrative program. *Exceptional Children,* 1974, *40,* 267–271.

IRUC Briefings. Washington, D.C.: Information and Research Utilization Center, Physical Education and Recreation for the Handicapped, American Alliance for Health, Physical Education and Recreation, 1977.

Johnson, R. T., & Johnson, D. W. Building friendships between handicapped and nonhandicapped students: Effects of cooperative and individualistic instruction. *American Education Research Journal,* 1981, *18*(4), 415–423.

Jones, R. L., & Sisk, D. A. Early perceptions of orthopedic disability. *Exceptional Children,* 1967, *9,* 42–43.

Kingsley, R. F., Viggiano, R. A., & Tout, L. Social perception of friendship, leadership and game playing among EMR special and regular class boys. *Education and Training of the Mentally Retarded,* 1981, *16*(3), 201–206.

Lauber, A. James Oates. *Education Unlimited,* 1980, *2*(4), 38–39.

Leyser, Y., & Gottlieb, J. Improving the social status of rejected pupils. *Exceptional Children,* 1980, *46*(6), 459–461.

MacMillan, D. L., Jones, R. L., & Meyers, C. E. Mainstreaming the mildly retarded: Some questions, cautions and guidelines. *Mental Retardation,* 1976, *14,* 3–10.

Mullins, J. B. Making language work to eliminate handicapism. *Education Unlimited,* 1979, *2,* 20–24.

Orlansky, M. D., & Heward, W. L. *Voices: Interviews with handicapped people.* Columbus, Ohio: Charles E. Merrill Publishing Co., 1981.

Paul, J. L., & Beckman-Bell, P. Parent perspectives. In J. L. Paul (Ed.), *Understanding and working with parents of children with special needs.* New York: Holt, Rinehart and Winston, 1981.

Poorman, C. Mainstreaming in reverse with a special friend. *Teaching Exceptional Children,* 1980, *12*(4), 136–142.

Purkey, W. W. *Self concept and school achievement.* Englewood Cliffs, N.J.: Prentice-Hall, 1970.

Reese-Dukes, J. L., & Stokes, E. H. Social acceptance of elementary educable mentally retarded pupils in the regular classroom. *Education and Training of the Mentally Retarded,* 1978, *13*(4), 356–361.

Richardson, S. A. Age and sex differences in values toward physical handicaps. *Journal of Health and Social Behavior,* 1970, *11,* 207–214.

Robinson, M. G. Awareness program helps children understand needs. *Education Unlimited,* (1979), *1*(2), 25–27.

Rosenthal, R., & Jacobson, L. *Pygmalion in the classroom: Teacher expectation and pupils intellectual development.* New York: Holt, Rinehart and Winston, 1968.

Salend, S. J., & Schobel, J. Coping with namecalling in the mainstreamed setting. *Education Unlimited,* 1981, *3*(2), 36–38.

Schulz, J. B. Facing the label. *Education Unlimited,* 1979, *1*(4), 50–53.

Schulz, J. B. Communication station—a learning center for mainstreaming. *Teaching Exceptional Children,* 1981, *13*(2), 81–82.

Schwartz, A. V. Disability in children's books: Is visibility enough? *Bulletin,* 1977, *8*(6,7), 10–15.

Shaw, S. F., & Gillung, T. B. Efficacy of a college course for regular class teachers of the mildly handicapped. *Mental Retardation,* 1975, *13*(4), 3–6.

Siperstein, G. N., Bak, J. J., & Gottlieb, J. Effects of group discussion on children's attitudes toward handicapped peers. *Journal of Educational Research,* 1977, *7,* 131–134.

Siperstein, G. N., Bopp, M. J., & Bak, J. J. Social status of learning disabled children. *Journal of Learning Disabilities,* 1978, *11*(2), 49–53.

Turnbull, A. P., & Winton, P. J. Comparison of mothers' perceptions toward mainstreamed and specialized placements. *Journal of Pediatric Psychology,* in press.

Vacc, N. A. Long-term effects of special class intervention for emotionally disturbed children. *Exceptional Children,* 1972, *39,* 15–22.

Wright, B. A. The coping framework and attitude change: A guide to constructive roleplaying. Paper presented at the American Psychological Association Annual Conference, New York, 1979.

Yates, J. R. Model for preparing regular classroom teachers for "mainstreaming." *Exceptional Children,* 1973, *39,* 471–472.

APPENDIX

A

Professional and Consumer Organizations

For more information on handicapped students, contact the following organizations:

Alexander Graham Bell Association for the Deaf, Inc.
3417 Volta Place, N.W.
Washington, DC 20007

American Association on Mental Deficiency
5101 Wisconsin Avenue
Washington, DC 20016

American Foundation for the Blind, Inc.
15 West Sixteenth Street
New York, NY 10011

American Printing House for the Blind
1839 Frankfort Avenue
P.O. Box 6085
Louisville, KY 40206

American Psychological Association
1200 Seventeenth Street, N.W.
Washington, DC 20036

American Speech and Hearing Association
10801 Rockville Pike
Rockville, MD 20852

Association for Children with Learning Disabilities
4156 Library Road
Pittsburgh, PA 15236

Captioned Films for the Deaf
Special Office for Materials Distribution
Indiana University
Audio-Visual Center
Bloomington, IN 47401

Closer Look
Box 1492
Washington, DC 20013

Council for Exceptional Children
1920 Association Drive
Reston, VA 22091

Cystic Fibrosis Foundation
3379 Peachtree Road, N.E.
Atlanta, GA 30326

Epilepsy Foundation of America
1828 L Street, N.W.
Washington, DC 20036

The Library of Congress
Division for the Blind and Physically
  Handicapped
Washington, DC 20542

National Association for Retarded
  Citizens
2709 Avenue E East
Arlington, TX 76011

National Association of State Directors of
  Special Education, Inc.
1201 Sixteenth Street, N.W.
Washington, DC 20036

National Association for the Visually
  Handicapped
305 East 24th Street
New York, NY 10010

National Association of the Deaf
814 Thayer Avenue
Silver Spring, MD 20910

National Easter Seal Society for Crippled
  Children and Adults
2023 West Ogden Avenue
Chicago, IL 60612

National Epilepsy League
6 North Michigan Avenue
Chicago, IL 60602

National Federation of the Blind
Suite 212, 1346 Connecticut Avenue,
  N.W.
Washington, DC 20036

National Society for the Prevention of
  Blindness, Inc.
79 Madison Avenue
New York, NY 10016

National Foundation
March of Dimes
1275 Mamaroneck Avenue
White Plains, NY 10605

APPENDIX

B

Addresses of Publishers

Allyn and Bacon, Inc.
7 Wells Avenue
Newton, MA 02159

American Association on Mental
 Deficiency
5210 Connecticut Avenue, N.W.
Washington, DC 20015

American College Testing Program
P.O. Box 168
Iowa City, IA 52240

American Guidance Service, Inc.
Publishers' Building
Circle Pines, MN 55014

American Newspaper Publishers
 Association Foundation
The Newspaper Center
Box 17407
Dulles International Airport
Washington, DC 20041

American Printing House for the Blind
1839 Frankfort Avenue
P.O. Box 6085
Louisville, KY 40206

Bell Telephone System
American Telephone and Telegraph
 Company
195 Broadway
New York, NY 10007

Benefic Press
10300 West Roosevelt Road
Westchester, IL 60153

Bennett Publishing Co.
809 West Detweiller Drive
Peoria, IL 61615

Butterick Publishing
Division of American Can Co.
708 Third Avenue
New York, NY 10017

John D. Caddy
Box 251
Canoga Park, CA 91305

Center for Applied Research in
 Education, Inc.
521 Fifth Avenue
New York, NY 10017

APPENDIX B *Addresses of Publishers*

Children's Book Centre
140 Kensington Church Street
London W 8, England

Council for Exceptional Children
1920 Association Drive
Reston, VA 22091

Creative Publications
P.O. Box 10328
Palo Alto, CA 94303

Creative Teaching Press
Monterey Park, CA 91754

Cuisenaire Company of America, Inc.
12 Church Street
New Rochelle, NY 10805

Developmental Learning Materials
7440 Natchez Avenue
Niles, IL 60648

Edmark Associates
655 South Orcas Street
Seattle, WA 98108

Educational Design Associates
P.O. Box 915
East Lansing, MI 48823

Educational Insights
150 West Carob
Compton, CA 90220

Educational Service, Inc.
P.O. Box 219
Stevensville, MI 49127

Educational Teaching Aids
657 Oak Grove Plaza
Menlo Park, CA 94025 (Veri Tech Math Lab)

Educational Teaching
159 West Kinzie
Chicago, IL 60610 (calculator)

Encyclopedia Britannica Education Corporation
425 North Michigan Avenue
Chicago, IL 60611

Exceptional Child Center
UMC–68
Utah State University
Logan, UT 84322

The Exceptional Parent Bookstore
296 Boylston Street
Boston, MA 02116

The Exceptional Parent Press
Room 700, Statler Office Building
Boston, MA 02116

Fearon Publishers
6 Davis Drive
Belmont, CA 94002

Field Education Publications
609 Mission Street
San Francisco, CA 94105

Follett Publishing Co.
Customer Service Center
Box 5705
Chicago, IL 60680

Garrard Publishing Co.
1607 N. Market Street
Champaign, IL 61820

Globe Book Co., Inc.
175 Fifth Avenue
New York, NY 10010

The Goodheart-Willcox Co., Inc.
123 West Taft Drive
South Holland, IL 60473

Goodyear Publishing Co.
Santa Monica, CA 90401

Harcourt Brace Jovanovich, Inc.
757 Third Avenue
New York, NY 10017

Harper and Row Publishers, Inc.
10 East 53rd Street
New York, NY 10022

Houghton Mifflin Co.
53 West 43rd Street
New York, NY 10036

APPENDIX B *Addresses of Publishers*

Hubbard Scientific
PO Box 104
Northbrook, IL 60062

Incentive Publications, Inc.
Box 12522
Nashville, TN 37212

Janus Book Publishers
3541 Investment Blvd.
Suite 5
Hayward, CA 94545

Jastak Associates, Inc.
1526 Gilpin Avenue
Wilmington, DE 19806

Junior League of Spartanburg, Inc.
Spartanburg, SC 29301

Kids Come in Special Flavors
Box 562
Forest Station
Dayton, OH 45405

Kids on the Block
c/o Barbara Aiello
Suite 1040
Washington Building
Washington, DC 20005

Kimbo Educational Materials
Box 477
Long Branch, NJ 07740

Lawren Productions, Inc.
PO Box 666
Mendocino, CA 95460

Learning Concepts, Inc.
2501 North Lamar
Austin, TX 78705

Lectro-Stik Corporation
3721 North Broadway
Chicago, IL 60613

Lexington Educational Aids Workshop
3413 Montavesta Road
Lexington, KY 40502

Little Brown Bear Learning Associates, Inc.
PO Box 561167
Miami, FL 33156

Love Publishing Co.
6635 East Villanova Place
Denver, CO 80222

McGraw-Hill Book Co. and McGraw-Hill Films
330 West 42nd Street
New York, NY 10036

Charles E. Merrill Publishing Co.
1300 Alum Creek Drive
Columbus, OH 43216

Midwest Publications Co., Inc.
P.O. Box 129
Troy, MI 48084

ModuLearn, Inc.
San Juan Capistrano, CA 02675

National Braille Association
Reader-Transcriber Registry
5300 Hamilton Ave., Apt. 1404
Cincinnati, OH 45224

The National Committee,
Arts for the Handicapped
1701 K. Street, N.W.
Washington, DC 20006

New Readers Press
Division of Laubach Literacy, Inc.
Box 131
Syracuse, NY 13210

Northwestern University Press
1735 Benson Avenue
Evanston, IL 60201

Olympus Publishing Co.
1670 East 13th South
Salt Lake City, UT 84105

Perry-Neal Publishers, Inc.
P.O. Box 2721
West Durham Station
Durham, NC 27705

APPENDIX B *Addresses of Publishers*

Prentice-Hall, Inc.
Box 500
Englewood Cliffs, NJ 07632

Pruett Publishing Co.
2928 Pearl Street
Boulder, CO 80301

Psychological Corporation
304 East 45th Street
New York, NY 10017

Random House, Inc.
Microcomputer Software
201 East 50th Street
New York, NY 10022

Reading Joy
Naperville, IL 60540

Frank E. Richards Publishing Co., Inc.
324 First Street
Liverpool, NY 13088

William H. Sadlier, Inc.
11 Park Place
New York, NY 10007

Scholastic Book Services
906 Sylvan Avenue
Englewood Cliffs, NJ 07632

Science Research Associates, Inc.
259 East Erie Street
Chicago, IL 60611

Southwest Educational and
 Psychological Service
P.O. Box 1870
Phoenix, AZ 85001

Teaching Resources Corp.
100 Boylston Street
Boston, MA 02116

Texas Instruments
P.O. Box 53
Lubbock, TX 79408

United Graphics, Inc.
1401 Broadway
Seattle, WA 98100

J. Weston Walch, Publisher
Box 658
Portland, ME 04104

Webster Division
McGraw-Hill Book Co.
30th Floor
1221 Avenue of the Americas
New York, NY 10020

Western Psychological Services
12031 Wilshire Blvd.
Los Angeles, CA 90025

Word Making Productions, Inc.
60 West 400 South
Salt Lake City, UT 84101

Index

Abeson, A., 67
Absenteeism, 16
Affleck, J. Q., 232, 264
Agard, J. A., 49
Albert, B., 172, 176
Allen, J. B., 101, 104
Allen, R. V., 180
Aloia, G. F., 57
Alpha-Line cards, 163
Anderson, E., 309–310, 311
Anderson, N. D., 289
Apple, L. E., 29
Architectural barriers, 10, 307, 308
Armstrong, M., 359
Art, 324–334
    academic progress, 332–333
    concept development, 324–330
    importance of, 304, 324, 334
    mobility, 330–331
    peer relationships, 333–334
Asher, N. W., 376
Ashton-Warner, S., 211, 217, 220
Attention span, 5, 20
    aided by format changes, 105–106
    behavior management and, 340, 345
    mathematics and, 246–248
Auding, 140
Audiovisual materials, 146, 171, 212, 213
Auditory Perception Training, 145
Autism, 13, 121
Aversive event, 351

Bailey, D. B., 103
Baker, E. L., 102, 103
Ballard, J., 67
Barnes, E., 339
Bartel, N. R., 149, 248
Basic Reading Skills List, 192
Beck, J. J., 123, 256
Becker, W. C., 359, 360, 361
Beckman-Bell, P., 48
Behavior:
    adaptive, 3–4
    aggressive, 41
    dangerous, 353
    inappropriate, 41, 338, 345, 359, 385
    operant, 349

    passive, 21, 41
    respondent, 349
Behavior management, 338–365
    basic procedures, 353–365
        contingency management, 362–364
        defining expectations, 339–341
        observing and recording, 353–357
        reinforcement, 357, 358–359
    general strategies, 341–348
        assigned responsibility, 345–347
        communication, 343–345
        parent involvement, 347–348
        room arrangement, 345, 346
        teacher preparation, 342
    specific techniques, 348–353
        decreasing behavior, 351–353
        increasing behavior, 349–351
Bentley, G., 108
Bigge, J. L., 163
Biklen, D., 377
Birch, J. W., 32, 33, 34, 56
Birkenshaw, L., 318, 321, 322
Blacher-Dixon, J., 49
Blackburn, J. E., 117
Blackham, G. J., 351, 352
Blind, 27; (*see also* Visually handicapped)
Bloom, L., 148, 153
Bogdan, R., 377
Bower, E. M., 39–40
Boyd, G. A., 169–170
Braille, 27
    alphabet, 198
    defined, 197
    equipment, 267, 283
    in learning centers, 114
Braithwaite, J., 116
Branching activity, 119
Brantley, J. C., 67, 80, 83, 86, 91, 92, 95
Bricker, W. A., 147, 148
Brigance, A. H., 173
Brittain, W. L., 325, 326–328
Brown v. *Board of Education*, 58
"Buddy" system, 36, 152–153
Budoff, M., 56

Cady, J. L., 175–176
Calculator, 255–256, 262

Caption Cards, 156
Cartledge, G., 277
Cerebral palsy, 9, 10, 128, 151
Chambless, J. R., 309–310, 311
Chaney, C. M., 145
Chapin, J. R., 281–282
Children's books:
   Charlotte's Web, 175
   high interest books, 223
   Story of My Life (The), 114, 175
Clanfield, M., 169
Clark, F., 101, 104
Classroom meetings:
   behavior management and, 345
   social integration and, 377–380
Clay, J. E., 118
Cognitive levels, 102–103
Cohen, D. A., 110, 113
Cohen, S. A., 223–224
Cohen, S. B., 138, 142, 143, 150, 168–169
Cohen, S. H., 287, 293, 295
Communication:
   hearing handicapped and, 33–34
   language experience approach, 221–222
   social integration and, 362–364
   with service provider, 125–126
Communication skills (*see* Language arts)
Communication wheel, 382, 383
Community volunteers, 71
   in tutorial programs, 113
   large-print typing, 299
   learning activity packets, 119
   textbook taping, 281
Computer-assisted instruction, 121–124
   in mathematics, 256, 268
   in reading, 226–227
   LOGO and PLATO, 121–122
Computer banks, 87, 122
Conflict situation guidelines, 343–344
Contingency management, 362–364
Contracts, 116–117
Cook, M. B., 113–114, 116
Cooper, T. T., 209
Corman, L., 57
Counselors, 69
Craig, L. C., 224
Cross-grade matching, 225
Cruikshank, W., 53, 73
Cuisenaire rods, 8, 252, 265
Curry, L., 90, 91
Curtis, C. K., 282

Dahlberg, H., 123
Dale, D. M. C., 201
Deaf, 32; (*see also* Hearing handicapped)
Dechant, E. V., 202, 208–209
Developmental lag, 18–19
Developmental Syntax Program, 156

Diana v. *State Board of Education,* 58–59
Dictionary skills, 297
Diem, R. A., 123
Distar program, 222
Distractibility, 20, 105–106, 160
Dolch Word List, 210, 224
Donaldson, J., 378, 381
Drug therapy, 20–21
Dunn, J. M., 312
Dunn, L. M., 57
Dyslexia, 18–19

Edmark Reading Program, 222
Education for All Handicapped Children Act (*see*
   Public Law 94-142)
Edwards, T. J., 196
Elementary and Secondary Education Act, 187
Ellis, N. R., 5, 261
Engolz, M. D., 339
Environment:
   factors affecting language, 154
   factors affecting learning, 7
   "least restrictive," 65–66, 88
   sensory knowledge of, 138–139
   writing skills and, 176–177
Epilepsy, 13–17, 313
Epley, C., 319
Error analysis, 238–240
Evaluation process, 78–85, 126–129
Eyman, B., 339

Faas, L. A., 149
Fader, D. N., 224
Fahey, J. D., 318, 321, 322
Federal Register (*see* Public Law 94-142)
Filmstrips, 179, 284, 297
Fine motor skills, 18, 264–265
Finger spelling, 33–34, 114
Flowers, A. M., 322
Folio, M. R., 312, 315
Forness, S. R., 39, 348, 353
Fowler, M. A., 238, 240
Frostig, M., 160, 163, 213

Gallagher, J. J., 27, 234
Gallagher, P., 101, 104
Games:
   electronic, 123, 248
   in mathematics, 247–248, 266
   orthopedic handicaps and, 9
   in reading, 227
Gearheart, B. R., 27, 235–236, 262
Gentry, J. R., 169
Getman, G. N., 200
Gillespie, E. B., 92
Gillespie, P. H., 192, 206
Gillespie-Silver, P., 193, 194, 222
Glick, H. M., 53
Goldstein, S., 90, 91

Gottlieb, J., 49, 56, 57, 369, 374, 377
Grabowski, J., 349, 351
Grading, 126, 129–133
Grimes, L., 122
Gresham, F. M., 348, 359, 384
Grimes L., 122
Gromme, R. O., 286, 289, 290
Grosenick, J. K., 56
Gross, R. E., 272, 281–282
Grossman, H. J., 3, 4
Guskin, S., 57

Hadary, D. E., 287, 289–290, 292, 293, 295
Hall, M. A., 204
Hammill, D. D., 18, 149, 248
Handicapped:
  defined, 2
  educational characteristics, 2–43
  legislation for, 59–67
  parents' rights, 67
  placement alternatives, 49–52
  right to an education, 58–59
  social integration, 53, 368–391
Hannaford, A., 122
Hannan, C., 169
Hanson, B. A., 222
Hart, B. O., 201, 202, 204–205
Health impairments, 13–17
Hearing aid, 34, 153
Hearing handicapped, 32–38
  auditory training, 146
  "buddy" system, 36
  classroom procedures, 35
  defined, 32
  finger spelling, 34, 114
  language problems 151–153
  lipreading, 33, 36
  mathematics and, 253
  music and, 318–319, 321
  physical education and, 314
  reading and, 201–204
  science and, 292–293, 296, 298
  social studies and, 284–285, 296, 298
  special equipment, 34–35, 38, 156
Herlihy, J. G., 276, 277, 278–280
Herlihy, M. T., 276, 277, 278–280
Heward, W. L., 355, 361
Hobbies, 323, 333
Hobson v. Hansen, 58–59
Hofmeister, A. M., 158, 165
Howell, K. W., 234, 238
Hresko, W. P., 154, 166, 169
Hughes, K., 123
Human Sciences Program, 290, 291
Hurd, P. D., 290, 291
Hurwitz, T. A., 36
Hyperactivity, 20–21
Hypoactivity, 21, 105

Individualized education program:
  defined, 64, 85, 98
  developing the program, 78–95
    coordinating committee, 78, 80–83
    evaluation and referral, 78–85
    IEP document, 64–65, 78, 85–89
    IEP meeting, 65, 89–95, 124–127
  implementing the program, 98–133
    computer-assisted instruction, 121–124
    contracts, 116–117
    curriculum adaptation, 98–107
    input/output modes, 107–110
    learning activity packets, 117–121
    learning centers, 113–116
    tutorial programs, 110–113
  legal requirements, 64–65
  parent involvement, 65, 79, 83, 91
  program coordination, 124–126
  student involvement, 91–92
  task analysis, 87, 99–102
Informal reading inventory, 193, 195, 275
Instructional materials (*see also* Mathematics):
  filmstrips, 179, 284, 297
  for language skills, 156–157
  for listening skills, 145
  primary typewriter, 156, 225, 299
  for reading skills, 207, 212–213, 215
  tape recorder, 177, 179, 204, 225–226, 293
  writing kit, 174
Intelligence testing, 3, 4, 57–58, 205
In This Sign, 114
Itinerant teachers, 51, 197

Jarolimek, J., 272, 275, 276, 283, 285
Jenkins, J. R., 112
Jensen, M. A., 222
Johnson, D. W., 112, 383
Johnson, L. E., 192, 206
Johnson, R. B., 99
Johnson, S., 99
Jones, R. L., 57, 369, 371

Kandaswamy, S., 110, 113
Kaplan, J. S., 234, 238
Kauffman, J. M., 199, 200, 203, 206
Kaufman, M. J., 49
Kean, J. M., 162, 170
Keller, Helen, 114, 147
Kelly, E. J., 281, 282, 300
Keogh, B. K., 49
Kephart, N. C., 145
Kirk, S. A., 27
Kohl, H., 176, 207, 213–214
Kolstoe, O. P., 210–211
Kramer, T., 257–258
Krug, D. A., 257–258
Kucera-Francis List, 210
Kukic, M. B., 49

INDEX

LaGreca, A. M., 277, 281
Lambie, R. A., 248
Langstaff, A. L., 362–364
Language, 43; (see also Speaking; Speech)
   delayed, 25, 263–264, 297
   development, 147–149
   stimulation for reading, 204–205
Language arts, 138–181; (see also Reading)
   art and, 332–333
   coordinating elements of, 138–139
   listening, 139–146
   physical education and, 315
   speaking, 147–157
   writing, 157–181
Language barrier, 7, 154
Language Big Box, 156
Language Development Pak, 156–157
Language experience approach, 179–181
   art and, 332–333
   in reading, 202, 205, 221–222
   in science and social studies, 299
Language Making Action Cards and Stickers, 157
Language Master, 171, 212, 213
Latta, R., 172
Laubach, Dr. Frank C., 222
Lauber, A. James Oates, 289
Lavor, M. L., 67
Learning activity packets, 117–121, 171, 283
Learning centers, 113–116
   communication station, 114–115
   discovery center, 114
   laboratory station, 293, 295
   language center, 155
   listening station, 114, 145, 226
   for reading, 221
   for social studies, 283, 299
Learning disabilities, 17–22
   academic difficulty, 19–20
   activity level, 20–21
   defined, 17–18
   physical education and, 306, 310, 314
   reading and, 200
   science and, 297
   social integration and, 369
   using computer technology, 121–122
Learn to Listen, 145
Learning rate, 6–7, 122, 310
Lee, D. M., 180
Lehr, D. H., 49, 53
Leonard, J. A., 103
Lerner, J. W., 140–141, 163, 166, 169
Levitt, M. C., 49
Linde, J. L., 234, 262
Lions Club, 72, 299
Lipreading, 33, 36
List, L. K., 324, 325, 333
Listening, 139–146
   assessment, 141–144

   improving skills, 144–146
   as total process, 140–141
Lowenbraun, S., 232, 264
Lowenfeld, V., 325, 326–328
Lynch, E., 91

McConnell, F., 33, 154
McConnell, M. C., 290, 291
McLean, J., 151
MacMillan, D. L., 4, 57, 348, 353, 371
Mager, R. F., 349–350
Mainstreaming, 48–73
   coordinating services, 61–63, 124–126
   defined, 49
   evaluation of students, 63–64
   history, 56–59
   inservice training, 55–56, 63
   legal guidelines, 52, 54, 59–67
   placement alternatives, 49–52
   purposes, 48–56
   science and, 286
   shared responsibility, 54–55, 68–73
Management systems, 192–193
Maslow, P., 160, 163, 213
Mason, G. E., 226
Mass, L. N., 196, 204
Mathematics, 232–269
   assessment, 232–240
   components, 234, 241–245
   experiential learning, 260, 262–263
   goals and objectives, 240–245
   instructional adaptation, 242, 246–265
   instructional materials:
      calculators, 255–256, 262
      computers, 256
      games, 247–248
      programs, 265–268
      reference dictionary, 259–260, 264
      teachers' guidebooks, 268–269
   levels, 249–253, 257
   peer tutoring, 246, 254–255
   physical education and, 314–315
May, F. B., 194, 210
Mayhall, W. F., 112
Me and My Environment, 292
Me in the Future, 292
Me Now science program, 292
Mead, M., 288–289
Memory, 5, 105–106, 206
Menhusen, B. R., 286, 289, 290
Mental retardation:
   defined, 3
   developmental period, 4
   environmental factors, 7
   intellectual functioning, 3–6
      attention span, 5, 8
      IQ ranges, 41
   learning rate, 6–7

INDEX

physical education and, 314, 315
   reading and, 205–207, 212
   social studies and, 276
Mesibov, G. B., 277, 281
Messick, R., 272, 281–282
Meyen, E. L., 49, 53
Meyers, C. E., 57
Milburn, J. F., 277
Miller, J. F., 147, 153
Mills v. D.C. Board of Education, 58
Mobility:
   art and, 330–331
   music and, 320
   orthopedic handicaps, 9–11
   physical education and, 313–314
   visual handicaps, 28–29
Mooney, F. F., 205, 213, 215
Morgan, D. P., 87, 90, 91, 95
Moursund, D., 122
Muenchow, S., 53
Multisensory approach, 28, 292, 318
Murray, C., 69
Muscular dystrophy, 11
Musgrave, G. R., 133
Music teaching, 316–324
   academic progress, 321–323
   concept development, 317–320
   importance of, 304, 323, 334
   mobility, 320–321
   peer relationships, 323–324

Name calling, 385–387
Neisworth, J. R., 353, 357
New Streamlined English Series (The), 222–223
Norman, A., 312, 315

O'Leary, D. K., 360, 361
Oliner, P. M., 274, 281, 283
Olsen, K. R., 234, 262
Orthopedic handicaps, 8–13
   art and, 330–331
   handwriting, 160, 163
   mathematics and, 232, 253, 264–265
   music and, 321
   physical education and, 309, 310, 313
   speech problems, 151
   using computer technology, 121
Otto, W., 187, 195–196, 216
Overlearning, 262, 283

Paraprofessionals, 70
   in behavior management, 355
   learning activity packets, 119
   in tutorial programs, 113
Parents, 71
   in behavior management, 347–348
   legal rights, 66–67
   role in IEP, 65, 67, 79, 83, 91
   in tutorial programs, 113

Pasamanick, J., 155, 160
Paul, J. L., 48, 53, 73
Peabody Language Development Kit, 157
Peer relationships, 40–41, 277, 281
   art and, 333–334
   grading and, 132
   music and, 323, 324
   physical education and, 315
Peer tutoring, 110–113, 225, 246
   in reading, 298, 299
   for social integration, 382
Perceptual handicaps, 17–19
Perks, W., 316, 324
Personke, C., 162, 170
Phonemes, 148, 203
Phonics, 168–169, 202, 204, 213–214
Physical education, 304–315
   academic progress, 314–315
   concept development, 307–312
      classroom management model, 312
      mastery learning model, 309, 310
   importance of, 304, 306, 334
   mobility training, 313–314
   peer relationships, 315
Piaget, J., 248, 249
Pickering, C. T., 223
Pickett, A. L., 113
Piechowiak, A. B., 113–114, 116
Plaskon, S. P., 138, 142, 143, 150, 168–169
Poole, J. H., 309–310, 311
Popham, W. J., 102, 103
Positioning, 10, 34, 152
Powell, W. C., 117
Premack Principle, 362
Psychological processes, 17–18
Public Law 94-142, 2–3, 8–9, 13, 17–18, 22, 27, 32, 38, 54, 59–65, 81–82, 88, 307
Purkey, W. W., 387–388

Raiser, L., 39
Reading, 186–227
   assessment and goals, 186–193, 196
      inventories, 193, 195, 275
   comprehension, 215–218
   functional, 218–219
   importance of, 186, 208
   instructional materials, 212–213, 219–223
   instructional techniques, 196–219, 223–227
      computer-assisted, 226–227
      language experience approach, 221–222
      peer teaching, 225
   prerequisites to, 196–209
   word recognition, 209–215
Reading organizer, 216, 217, 299
Reading readiness, 196, 209
Redden, M. R., 286, 295
Regan, M. K., 128, 339, 340–341
Reid, D. K., 154, 166, 169

Reinforcement (*see* Behavior management)
Reisman, F., 238, 240
Resource room, 51, 101, 124, 126, 364
Resource teacher, 68, 101–102, 110, 188
   braille reading, 197
   learning activity packets, 119
   mathematics, 260
   scheduling services with, 124–126
   spelling group, 166–167
   writing skills, 166–167, 174
Reynolds, M. C., 56
Ruder, K. F., 147, 148, 150
Runkel, P. E., 304
Russell, B. E., 255

Salvia, J., 188, 192, 234
Savage, J. F., 205, 213, 215
Schiefelbusch, R. L., 147, 148
Schiff, P. M., 176
Schmidt, T., 192
Schubert, M. A., 53
Schulz, J. B., 114, 115, 118, 263, 386
Science, 285–300
   art and, 293, 294
   assessment and goals, 287–291
     literacy, 289
     teacher's goals, 289–290
   importance of, 286, 287, 289, 290
   instructional approaches, 291–295
Science—A Process Approach, 293
Science Curriculum Improvement Study, 290, 291
Scofield, F., 101, 104
Seizures, 14–17
Semmel, M. I., 110, 113
Serious emotional disturbance, 38–43
   behavior problems, 39, 41
   learning problems, 39–40
   peer relationships, 40–41
   reading and, 207–208
   science and, 293
Sharpham, J., 304
Shaver, J. K., 282
Sherrill, C., 307, 310, 313–314
Short work periods, 20, 106
Sign language, 33–34
Signature guide, 163–164
Silverman, M., 351, 352, 365
Similarity-attraction model, 376, 378
Simpson, R. D., 289
Skinner, B. F., 348, 360
Sloane, E., 122
Smith, J., 316, 324
Smith, P. B., 108
Smith, R. J., 187, 195–196, 216
Smith, R. M., 249, 353, 357
Social integration, 53, 368–392
   components of, 368

   peer interaction, 381–387
     classroom status, 387–389
     cooperative instruction, 382–384
     friendship skills, 384–387
   resource materials, 391–392
   student knowledge, 375–381
     classroom discussions, 377–380
     instructional programs, 376–377
     simulation, 380–381
   teacher attitude, 371–374
Social Studies, 272–285, 295–300
   assessment and goals, 273–276
   handicapism and, 282
   importance of, 272, 285
   instructional approaches, 276–285
     social skills training, 277, 281
     values clarification, 277
Spache, E. B., 199, 203
Speaking, 147–157; (*see also* Language; Speech)
   assessment, 149–150
   instructional techniques, 154–157
   music and, 321–322
   special problems, 151–154
   speech impairments, 22–26
Special education (*see also* Mainstreaming):
   classroom program and, 124–126
   defined, 60
   planning process, 78–93
   related services, 61–63
   self-contained special class, 49, 51–52
   teachers, 51–52, 55, 68, 69; (*see also* Resource teacher)
Special equipment, 11
   for hearing handicapped, 34, 35, 38
   for visually handicapped, 30, 267, 283, 284, 293
Special services committee, 78, 80–83
Speckels, J., 209, 213
Speech:
   delayed, 263–264
   impairments, 22–26
   music and, 321–322
   reading and, 204–205
   stuttering, 23, 26, 370
Spelling (*see* Writing)
Spelling Reference Book (The), 175
Sports (*see* Physical education)
Stein, J. U., 307, 309, 310
Stein, R., 91
Stevens, D. J., 123
Stewart, F., 118
Stone, M. C., 360, 361
Strauss, A. A., 163, 200
Strickland, B., 67, 80, 83, 86, 90, 91, 92, 95
Stuttering, 23, 26, 370
Sudano, G. R., 304
"Survival" skills, 281, 291
"Survival" words, 172, 212
Sutherland, J., 281–282

INDEX

Tachistoscope, 213, 247
Talbert, E. G., 169–170
Tape recorder, 177, 179, 204, 225–226, 293
Task analysis, 87, 99–101
   in learning activity packets, 119
   in mathematics, 242
Taylor, R. G., 304
Taylor, S. E., 140
Teacher aides (see Paraprofessionals)
Teachers, 342
   adaptive equipment and, 11
   attitude, 43, 371–374
   inservice training, 55–56, 63
   legislation for handicapped and, 61, 63
   role in IEP:
      communication, 10, 13, 41
      coordinating services, 124–126
      evaluation, 81–85
      referral, 78–81
      setting goals, 86–87
   shared responsibility, 54–55, 68–73
Tests, 127–129, 141, 149, 158–159, 167, 173, 187–193, 200, 204, 233–238, 273–274, 287–288, 309
Therapists, 70, 152
Thier, H. D., 292
Thomas, D. R., 359
Thompson, B. E., 287
Thompson, K., 317
Thompson, T., 349, 351
"Thought sheets," 277
Tiedt, I. M., 141, 169
Tiedt, S. W., 141, 169
Tjossem, T. D., 6
Tracking, 59
Turnbull, A. P., 5, 49, 53, 59, 66, 67, 80, 83, 86, 90, 91, 92, 95, 242, 243–245
Turnbull, H. R., 67
Turner, T. N., 298, 299
Tutorial programs, 16, 110–113

Values clarification, 277, 339
Van Nagel, C. V., 39
Van Riper, C., 23
Vardian, E. R., 274–275
Venezky, R. L., 187, 188, 192, 193
Victor, E., 286, 288
Visual defects, 199
Visually handicapped, 27–31
   art and, 329
   capabilities of, 27

   classroom procedures, 30
   cognitive functioning, 28
   handwriting, 163–165
   language problems, 151–153
   listening skills, 141
   mathematics and, 253
   multisensory approach, 28, 292, 318
   music and, 319–321
   orientation and mobility, 28–29
   physical education and, 309, 313
   reading and, 197–201, 205
   science and, 291–292, 293, 297–299
   services for, 51
   special equipment, 30, 203, 267, 283, 284, 293
Vocabulary, 154, 212
Volkmor, C. B., 362–364

Wallace, G., 199, 200, 203, 206
Warning signals:
   of hearing impairment, 33
   of visual impairment, 27
Watt, D., 121–122
Weighting system, 132–133
Weintraub, F. J., 67
Weir, S., 121–122
Weishahn, M. W., 27, 33, 34
Wheeler, T. C., 172
Wieck, C., 122, 123–124, 256
Wilson, R. M., 188, 189–191, 205, 215
Word attack skills, 215, 216, 227
Writing, 157–181
   assessment, 158–159, 167–169, 173
   handwriting, 158–166
      instructional techniques, 160–162
      left-handed students, 161–162
      manuscript and cursive, 162–163
      special problems, 10, 163–166
   spelling, 166–172
      instructional technqiues, 169–172
   written expression, 172–181
      creative writing, 175–176
      functional writing, 173–175
      instructional techniques, 169–172

Yard, G. J., 38, 39
Yoder, D. E., 147, 153
Yoshida, R. K., 57
Ysseldyke, J. E., 188, 192, 234

Zero reject, 60
Zigler, E., 6, 53